Coincidence and Counterfactuality

Frontiers of Narrative

Series Editor
David Herman, Ohio State University

Coincidence and Counterfactuality

Plotting Time and Space in Narrative Fiction

HILARY P. DANNENBERG

University of Nebraska Press
Lincoln and London

Acknowledgment for previously published material appears on p. 233, which constitutes an extension of the copyright page.

© 2008 by the Board of Regents of the University of Nebraska

All rights reserved

Manufactured in the United States of America

∞

Library of Congress Cataloging-in-Publication Data

Dannenberg, Hilary P.
Coincidence and counterfactuality: plotting time and space in narrative fiction / Hilary P. Dannenberg.
　p. cm. — (Frontiers of narrative)
Includes bibliographical references and index.
ISBN 978-0-8032-1093-6 (cloth: alk. paper)
1. Space and time in literature.
2. Coincidence in literature. 3. Fiction—Technique. 4. Fantasy fiction, English—History and criticism. I. Title.
PN3383.S67D36 2008
809.3'9384—dc22
2008001129

Set in Minion.
Designed by R. W. Boeche.

For Richard and for Eva,
who were my golden links to life while I was writing this book

That was a memorable day to me, for it made great changes in me. But, it is the same with any life. Imagine one selected day struck out of it, and think how different its course would have been. Pause you who read this, and think for a moment of the long chain of iron or gold, of thorns or flowers, that would never have bound you, but for the formation of the first link on one memorable day.

Charles Dickens, *Great Expectations*

Contents

List of Figures	x
Preface	xi
Introduction	1

Part 1: Theorizing Time and Space in Narrative Fiction

1. Cognitive Plotting *Crossing Narrative Boundaries and Connecting Worlds*	19
2. Ontological Plotting *Narrative as a Multiplicity of Temporal Dimensions*	45
3. Spatial Plotting *Paths, Links, and Portals*	65

Part 2: Theorizing Coincidence and Counterfactuality

4. The Coincidence Plot	89
5. Counterfactuals and Other Alternate Narrative Worlds	109

Part 3: Coincidence and Counterfactuality in the History of Narrative Fiction

6. The Metamorphoses of the Coincidence Plot	141
7. The Narrative Evolution of Counterfactuals	181
Conclusion	225
Source Acknowledgments	233
Notes	235
Glossary of Key Terms	249
Works Cited	255
Index	283

Figures

1. A Traditional Model of Narrative Communication	22
2. The Reading Experience as Immersive Journey	24
3. The Essential Structure of the Coincidental Encounter within the Traditional Coincidence Plot	68
4. Actual and Counterfactual Paths of Time in Austen's *Mansfield Park*	69
5. Multiple Actual Worlds and the Transworld Journey of the Protagonist in De Camp's "The Wheels of If"	70
6. Coincidental Relationships and Double Identity in Austen's *Persuasion*	97

Preface

This book has a long history, the essentials of which can be narrated in terms of fortunate convergences and counterfactuals. The story begins at the University of Mainz in 1992 in a conversation about possible topics for a postdoctoral thesis (the German *Habilitation*) with Wolfgang G. Müller. If, in this conversation, Professor Müller had not animated my thoughts with the suggestion that coincidence in literature would be an interesting subject to work on, then a substantial part of this book would certainly never have come into existence. I am deeply grateful to Wolfgang G. Müller for steering my thoughts in the direction of coincidence and for his subsequent encouragement of my project.

Following these beginnings, if Professor Helmut Bonheim had not given me the opportunity to join the English Department at the University of Cologne, thereby providing me with a firm basis from which to pursue an academic career in the field of English literature, then I would certainly never have had the opportunity to interact with a lively community of narrative theorists in Cologne, in particular Richard Aczel, Andrea Gutenberg, Barbara Korte, Ansgar Nünning, Manfred Jahn, Claudia Sternberg, and Natascha Würzbach. Without Helmut's kind and constructive support, I would have missed a key chance to become involved in the field of narrative studies.

I am also deeply indebted to Monika Fludernik, who subsequently gave me the opportunity to work at the Department of English at the University of Freiburg and in doing so provided the framework for me to complete my *Habilitation* and also, in parallel, to begin work in the field of postcolonial anglophone studies. In Freiburg I also began working on a separate project exploring counterfactuals and alternate worlds in narrative fiction, and it was then that I decided to merge the two projects into a single diachronic study of parallel plot developments. I am deeply grateful to Professor Fludernik for encouraging me to extend the focus of the project back as far as Renaissance fiction. This was an ambitious idea that I would not have developed on my own, but it gave the project an extended comparative focus without which the observation of key developments in the evolution of narrative fiction would not have been possible. In addition, Monika Fludernik encouraged me to establish contacts with the Society for the Study of Narrative Literature (SSNL), as a result of which I attended the annual International Narrative Conference several times and had the chance to present parts of my project on coincidence and counterfactuality.

In particular I wish to thank Margaret Freeman, David Herman, Brian McHale, Irene Kacandes, Uri Margolin, Jim Phelan, Gerry Prince, Peter Rabinowitz, Brian Richardson, Marie-Laure Ryan, Claudia Sternberg, Meir Sternberg, Mark Turner, and Tamar Yacobi for their academic dialogue, help, encouragement, and suggestions during the development of this project. I owe a great debt to Eva Nussbaum, Greta Olson, and Elizabeth Shipley for proofreading the first, longer version of this book, which was submitted as a postdoctoral dissertation at the University of Freiburg. The preparation of the final book manuscript would not have been possible without invaluable support and assistance from Marie Endres, Astrid Feldbrügge, Antje Friedrich, Katharina Grabs, Franziska Harprecht, Anna Linetsky, Kerstin Müller, Marion Soßna, and Sandra Steinert at the Universities of Leipzig and Bayreuth.

My deep thanks go in particular to David Herman, the editor of the Frontiers of Narrative series, for his energetic commitment to this book project and his positive, constructive, and indefatigable capacity for help and support in its final stages. My very warm thanks also go to Ladette Randolph at the University of Nebraska Press for her professionalism and commitment to the publication of this project.

Coincidence and Counterfactuality

Introduction

> And as for coincidences in books—there's something cheap and sentimental about the device . . . the sudden but convenient Dickensian benefactors; the neat shipwreck on a foreign shore which reunites siblings and lovers. . . . I'd ban coincidences, if I were a dictator of fiction.
>
> When the writer provides two different endings to his novel (why two? why not a hundred?), does the reader seriously imagine . . . that the work is reflecting life's variable outcomes? . . . The novel with two endings doesn't reproduce . . . reality; it merely takes us down two diverging paths.
>
> Julian Barnes, Flaubert's Parrot (1984, 67, 89)

Convergent and Divergent Plots and Character Trajectories

Geoffrey Braithwaite, the self-opinionated narrator of *Flaubert's Parrot*, clearly has a serious problem appreciating plot in narrative fiction. Braithwaite's metanarrative comments are nevertheless notable because they refer to examples of the two major plot patterns investigated in this study. Contrary, however, to Braithwaite's opinion, these two plots are not the vagaries of particular genres or periods but phenomena that can be traced in a variety of forms through the developmental history of narrative fiction. They constitute key examples of how narrative fiction plots character trajectories across the space and time of fictional worlds and endows them with the cognitive and emotional power that makes them compelling narratives. Indeed, these plots are so widespread that studying their historical development provides us with a map of the evolution of the modern novel.

As many studies have shown (e.g., Harvey 1965; Phelan 1989; Forster 1990), plot and character are inextricably intertwined. The plots of coincidence and counterfactuality are configurations of characters' life journeys across narrative worlds. The major form of the coincidence plot narrates the initially divergent but ultimately convergent paths of individual family members and culminates in recognition and reunion. All key forms of the counterfactual involve the remapping of the life trajectories of characters to create altered outcomes and often dramatically transformed life stories. It is this central character focus that gives both these plots their narrative or, rather, human interest and accounts for their perennial success in works of fiction. The present study proposes a new cognitive, reader-oriented theoretical model in order to analyze the sources of their narrative power and their historical evolution as key plots in narrative fiction.

Formulated as spatial metaphors, the plots of coincidence and counterfactuality can be mapped as the opposing patterns created when vectors in time and space move together or move apart, tracing pathways that either converge or diverge. Convergence involves the intersection of narrative paths and the interconnection of characters within the narrative world, closing and unifying it as an artistic structure. Divergence, conversely, concerns the bifurcation or branching of narrative paths and thereby creates an open pattern of diversification and multiplicity. Convergence is a form of narrative unification most typically represented by the type of closed ending that provides a clear "sense of an ending" (Kermode 1967)—a form that was most prevalent in pre-twentieth-century fiction (Korte 1985a) and was typically constituted in the nineteenth century by the frequent use of marriage in closure (Reed 1975, 120–25). Coincidence in narrative fiction is a plot pattern with fundamentally convergent tendencies because it creates relationships that interlink characters across the space and time of the narrative world. Divergence, in the general form of the open ending (i.e., where the characters' life plots are not knotted together but left to fan out into an unwritten future), has been seen as a particular phenomenon of the twentieth century (Korte 1985a), a period in which women authors write "beyond the ending" (DuPlessis 1985) of the euphorically convergent tying of the marriage knot. It has also been claimed that only with the watershed of modernism did plot lose its linearity (Hughes and Lund 1991). However, as this study shows, plot divergence—in the form of counterfactuals and other forms of alternate-world construction—is not a specifically twentieth-century phenomenon at all but can be traced from much earlier beginnings.[1] Indeed, the history of narrative fiction traced in this study shows how key texts are the product of a dialectic between convergent and divergent tendencies. George Eliot's *Daniel Deronda* (1876) and Jeanette Winterson's *The Passion* (1987) are notable works of fiction because, seen in the light of the development of coincidence and counterfactuality, they represent the intersection of conflicting plot conventions and cultural pressures.

The traditional and most powerful form of the coincidence plot has existed since at least the Oedipus story. It achieves its power through its central component of kinship reunion. The most crucial component of the coincidence plot in its complex form of representation is a cognitive one and concerns *recognition*—what Aristotle called *anagnorisis* (Poetics 52a30–52b6, 1996, 18–19). It is in the management and presentation of recognition—above all in terms of suspense management, the representation of character consciousness, and the spatial depiction of the recognition scene—that the narrative power of the coincidence plot can be measured. The other key feature of the coincidence plot that lends itself to extensive analysis is the narrative explanation of the coincidence of characters' paths in the narrative world: what system of justification, if any, does a novel's discourse provide for implausibilities of plot?

The timing of the recognition scene is crucial in determining whether coincidence is part of a negative or a positive plot. The type of relationship between the coinciding characters and the timing of recognition, that is, whether it is instantaneous or deferred, can make the difference between euphoric and tragic versions. Delayed recognition between close relatives can result in unintentional incest or lead to other serious misunderstandings and family tragedies. Variants of this essentially Oedipal form produce a catalog of family disasters and near misses from Sir Philip Sidney's *Old Arcadia* (ca. 1580) to Paul Auster's *Moon Palace* (1989). Family reunion can, however, involve a euphoric element, and this form was milked in particular by Victorian novelists; by contrast, modernism's antipathy to previous literary conventions is reflected in its avoidance of coincidence involving kinship. The euphoric family reunion plot was then reinstituted, both realistically and parodistically, in postmodernist fiction. Indeed, postmodernism's postrealist attitude to plot meant that narrative no longer had any compunctions about the improbabilities of temporal and spatial manipulation involved in the coincidence plot, leading to a widespread resurgence of the coincidence plot.

While the traditional coincidence plot has survived right down to the contemporary novel, new forms have also emerged. In the modernist period a different type of coincidence emerges that is based not on the literal kinship of blood links or on the connections of friendship between characters but on a connecting principle of *analogous relationships*. Subsequently, in the postmodernist genre of historiographic metafiction, networks of analogical coincidences are used to link multiple temporal levels.

The modern novel, therefore, continually reveals new and interesting (and indeed for this reason "novel") configurations of the coincidence plot right up to the present. However, the fact that the coincidence plot occurs in texts designated both as "romances" and as "novels" undermines the claims of genre theorists who have polarized the novel and the romance (Reeve 1930; Watt 1987; Congreve 1991, 474). In fact, far from being the novel's generic other, elements from the romance have frequently been re-infused with the novel and thus have regenerated novelistic realism to produce new forms.

Counterfactual thought experiments about what might have been constitute a key form of human consciousness (Roese and Olson 1995c). Speculations by characters in novels about how their life might have developed differently therefore constitute a highly realistic technique of character depiction that simulates human cognitive activity. While the rhetorical use of counterfactuals is already evident in a Renaissance romance like Sidney's *Old Arcadia*, it is in the subsequently developing genre of the fictional autobiography that counterfactual life plots become a key feature. In Daniel Defoe's *Moll Flanders* (1722), for example, Moll speculates in two counterfactual sketches of her first liaison about what would have happened if she had not sacrificed her "virtue" to her first lover: "Had I acted as became me, and resisted as virtue and honour required, this gentleman had either desisted his attacks, finding no room to expect the accomplishment of his design, or had made fair and honourable proposals of marriage" (Defoe 1978, 48).

While the eighteenth century is the spawning ground of such autobiographical thought experiments in narrative fiction, the nineteenth century is the site of a more widespread proliferation of alternate worlds. The novels of Jane Austen, Charlotte Brontë, George Eliot, and Thomas Hardy, for example, all contain counterfactual plots of biographical development. These alternate plots can be seen as attempts to break out of both the intertextual and cultural pressure of the convergent marriage plot and other unrealistically euphoric forms of closure. While they do not actually write "beyond the ending" in the manner of twentieth-century women novelists (DuPlessis 1985), these authors certainly write "around" the ending by embedding alternate versions in the novel's discourse. Moreover, the fact that Austen, Brontë, Eliot, and Hardy also use forms of the coincidence plot reveals an underlying tension between the literary pressure of romance-oriented convergence and a countermovement toward plot divergence in this phase of the novel's development. Counterfactuals in nineteenth-century narrative fiction thus also highlight another aspect of the ongoing historical tension between realism and romance.

The key role of the nineteenth century as the site of the emergence of advanced forms of counterfactuality is also confirmed by the beginnings of the genre of alternate history in this period. In the twentieth century a plethora of different fictional systems of multiple alternate worlds subsequently emerge. In science fiction meddling time travelers become capable of creating different or multiple versions of history with differing ontological hierarchies. Notably, transworld journeys between factual and counterfactual worlds, as in L. Sprague de Camp's "The Wheels of If" (1940), create a story with multiple versions of the same character. Later in the twentieth century, as the work of Brian McHale (1987, 1992) has extensively shown, the multiple-world tendency grows apace in postmodernist fiction. Experimental postmodernist narrative creates multiple story versions, as in the double ending of John Fowles's *The French Lieutenant's Woman* (1969). Historiographic metafiction blends alternate history with postmodernism and combines biographical and historical counterfactuals. In this genre, history is no longer under threat of attack by time-traveling saboteurs, as in science fiction, but its overall status and claim to be authoritative fact are under question.

The historical ubiquity of plots of coincidence and counterfactuality therefore provides extensive material for the study of the technical development of the novel over the centuries. An analysis of the development of these plots reveals what distinguishes earlier forms of narrative fiction from their more recent progeny by identifying new techniques and strategies that evolved in the representation of coincidence and counterfactuality. Among other things, these strategies concern the processes by which coincidence is domesticated and subsumed into the ostensibly "possible" worlds of the novel as opposed to the more fabulous and distant worlds of the romance. By investigating the history of coincidence and counterfactuality in narrative fiction, we can therefore observe in detail the evolution in the modern novel of the narrative techniques that create a state of immersion in the reader. As Marie-Laure Ryan (2001) suggests in her comprehensive study of immersion and interactivity across literature and media, "immersion" is a more useful concept than "realism" to describe the narrative phenomena that accompanied the rise of the modern novel.

Immersion is also linked to another key concept in narrative theory—that of *narrativity* used in the sense of a qualitative aspect of narrative. This involves identifying the kind of narratives that Gerald Prince refers to as those that are "more narrative than others, [and] as it were . . . 'tell a better story'" (1982, 141). (This comparative and qualitative sense of narrativity has also been designated as *tellability* by William Labov [1972] and Ryan [1991], but the latter term is not as satisfactory for application to novelistic discourse because of its primary contextualization in Labov's study of oral narrative.) The plots of coincidence and counterfactuality are excellent narrative phenomena with which to perform a transhistorical study of how the novel develops qualitative narrativity. Thus, this study shows how the coincidence plot of romance develops greater narrativity when it is transformed by more sophisticated forms of suspense and character-cognitive depiction in the narrative discourse of the modern novel. It also shows how counterfactuals develop increasing narrativity in the evolution of the novel when authors, from Defoe in the eighteenth century to Philip K. Dick in the twentieth century, tap into and explore the human psyche's fascination with events that might have been.

The ultimate aim of this study is therefore a historically wide-ranging but closely targeted investigation of two major but hitherto uncharted plot patterns. The primary step in the achievement of this goal is the formulation of a new model for the analysis of the narrative plotting of time and space. This model, which is presented in the first three chapters of this study, is mainly illustrated with material from the plots of coincidence and counterfactuality. However, its major parameters—the key cognitive operations that plots stimulate, the ontological structuring of narrative time, and the cognitive simulation of the bodily experience of space—are applicable to the study of time and space in narrative fiction as a whole. This model does not aim to reduce the concept of "plot" to a synchronic typology but to register diachronic variation and to highlight patterns of diversity and development in narrative fiction. This sensitivity to diversity is produced by a cross-fertilization of narrative theory with cognitive and psychological research.

Now that section 1 has introduced the major textual phenomena to be examined, section 2 of this introduction will briefly chart the major areas of previous research that flow into this study. Section 3 then outlines the study's own theoretical contribution and structure.

A Brief History of Approaches to Plot and Related Theories

"Narrativity" also has a different, more normative, and less qualitative sense when it is used to refer to the intrinsic properties of all narratives as opposed to other forms of discourse. Prince (1999, 44) usefully distinguishes this generic sense of narrativity as "narrativeness." As part of the ongoing quest to capture the elusive spirit of narrativity, twentieth-century criticism has provided a plethora of plot definitions.[2] Despite its apparent simplicity of reference, *plot* is one of the most elusive termini in narrative theory. The repeated attempts to redefine the parameters of the term are symptomatic of the extreme complexity of the temporal dimension of narrative and indicate that "plot" itself is too complex to be satisfactorily enclosed (or "plotted") by one definition. The history of plot theory has been documented by a number of critical surveys, each of which—like the summary below—undertakes its own individual journey across an extensive and varied theoretical terrain.[3]

Narrative, Plot, and Story: A Glimpse into the Terminological Thicket

If many theories of plot have one thing in common, it is that they see plot as something more complex than story, which is a simpler and more consensually constant term referring to the basic chronology of events out of which something more complex, plot, is constructed.[4] The constructedness of plot in comparison to story is already evident in the fact that, while one can speak of "telling a story," one cannot in the same way talk of "telling a plot," because the plot *is* the telling. Theories of plot can thus be compared with each other in terms of how far and in what way they see plot as being different from story.[5] In classical literary theory, Aristotle's concept of *mythos* formulates plot as the conversion of the bare bones of story into a tightly structured aesthetic unit with a beginning, a middle, and an end. In early-twentieth-century criticism, E. M. Forster (1990, 87) saw plot as consisting in the creation (and also the suspenseful suppression) of causal connections between the individual events that constitute the chronology of the story. Contemporaneous to Forster, the Russian formalists Boris Tomashevsky (1965, 66–67) and Viktor Shklovsky (1990, 170) focused on the plot's (*sjuzhet*'s) rearrangement of the linear chronology of story (*fabula*) and the resulting subversion of the causal-linear structures of the story. Other models did not focus on plot's transmutation of story but sought to uncover the grammar, or *langue*, of plot by uncovering recurrent patterns in the stories of a larger corpus of narratives (see Dundes 1964; Greimas 1966; Propp 1968; Bremond 1970; Füger 1972; Prince 1973; Todorov 1977). A different form of the story-condensification method was practiced by the anthropologist Claude Lévi-Strauss (1963, 206–31) in his reconfiguration of the Oedipus myth in terms of binary oppositions. Notably, Claude Bremond (1980) addressed plot from a different perspective, seeing it as including virtual events that may be desired or strived for by characters but that never actually occur in the narrative world.

Other studies produced a variety of generically oriented plot models based on both story and more complex understandings of "plot." The American New Critic R. S. Crane (1952, 620) distinguished between different types of subject matter, which he named plots of action, character, and thought. Northrop Frye (1971) identified four "generic plots" in his "theory of myths": comedy, romance, tragedy, and irony/satire (see also Scholes and Kellogg 1966, 207–39). Mikhail Bakhtin's (1981, 84–258) concept of the *chronotope* proposed a combined analysis of the parameters of time, space, and perspective in particular epochs to define generic categories such as "adventure time" and "biographical time." Distinctions in the plot formulae of high and popular genres of narrative were focused on by Tzvetan Todorov (1977) and Umberto Eco (1981).

Ruth E. Page observes that "no single plot typology has yet been able to account for" the complexities of "gender . . . across and within cultures" (2006, 52); this indicates the necessity of a flexible approach in feminist narrative theory. Such flexibility can take the form, as in Page's study, of "synthesising aspects of analysis derived from different paradigms" (2006, 52) in order, for example, to analyze the representation of real-world female characters in contemporary media narratives (2006, 116–43). A productive flexibility can also be derived from a focused but diachronic approach to narrative. Thus, the feminist analysis of narrative has isolated different plot types arising out of the stereotypical allocation and limitation of roles due to a protagonist's gender. Nancy K. Miller (1980) distinguishes between euphoric and dysphoric plots of female development. Rachel Blau DuPlessis (1985) differentiates between the female protagonist as "hero," in which she is an independent agent in her own "quest plot," and as "heroine," in which she is constrained within a love plot; Andrea Gutenberg (2000) undertakes a comprehensive survey of female plots charting variations of the romance, quest, and family plot (see also Russ 1973; Abel 1983; Miller 1985; Hirsch 1989); Lois E. Bueler (2001) investigates the development of the *tested woman plot*, a deeply patriarchal plot pattern, across several genres and periods of literary history. While the present study does not have an exclusively feminist agenda, its diachronic focus pinpoints key developments in the representation of female characters within love plots, showing how the plots of coincidence and counterfactuality reflect and respond to key changes in the cultural and social position of women.

The story-discourse distinction (itself based on the Russian formalists' *fabula/sjuzhet* model) has also been a key field for the formulation of plot theory. Seymour Chatman's definition of "plot" as "story-as-discoursed" (1978, 43) represents one solution: here "plot" becomes a fundamental bridge concept between the abstract level of story and its textual realization. By contrast, Meir Sternberg (1978, 13) differentiates between the four terms *story, fabula, sjuzhet,* and *plot*; in marginalizing the latter as being "dispensable" in contrast to the other three terms, he firmly privileges sjuzhet over plot. Gérard Genette's (1980) influential theory of order (itself greatly indebted to Lämmert [1991] and widely adopted by other narrative theorists), explores forms of anachrony—a discourse's deviation from story order through movements into the past (analepsis) and the future (prolepsis) of the story. Building on a distinction made by Günther Müller (1968), Genette distinguishes between the time of "narrative and story" (1980, 94); this concept—now more commonly formulated as discourse time versus story time—foregrounds the fundamental ontological divide between the time elapsing in the fictional world (and "experienced" by characters) and time elapsing for the reader as she reads the text.[6] This ontological divide, however, as chapter 1 of this study shows, is completely suppressed by narrative strategies that draw the reader into the text, creating a state of immersion.

In the new intellectual climate of poststructuralist reorientation, many of the existing models were subjected to critique and revision, and this indicated the ultimate inadequacy of the story-discourse distinction to comprehend the complexities of narrative temporality (see, e.g., Herman 2002, 214–20; Richardson 2002a). These criticisms reflected the feeling that plot, and indeed the spirit of narrativity, had managed to evade the systematic net that structuralism had set up.[7] Peter Brooks (1992) and Paul Ricoeur (1984, 1985, 1988) are both critical of structuralist models for their static naming of parts and "their failure to engage the movement and dynamic of narrative" (Brooks 1992, 20): "The plot is a movement.... [T]o know all the roles—*is not yet to know any plot whatsoever*" (Ricoeur 1985, 43). Ricoeur himself distinguishes the sense-making activity brought to plots by using the related term *emplotment* to distinguish "the dynamic character of the configurating operation" (1984, 65).[8] For Brooks "plot" is not localizable as a single definition but can be comprehended in terms of "narrative desire" or "textual erotics" so that "the reading of plot [is] a form of desire that carries us forward, onward, through the text" (1992, 37).[9]

Extending the Narrative Dimensions of Plot

In *The Sense of an Ending* Frank Kermode underlines the importance of a narrative's creation of subterfuge regarding the final outcome of events: "The story that proceeded very simply to its obviously predestined end would be nearer myth than novel or drama.... [T]he interest of having our expectations falsified is obviously related to our wish to reach the discovery or recognition by an unexpected and instructive route" (1967, 18). Hayden White approaches the question of plot and closure from a different avenue—the analysis of historiography:

> Common opinion has it that the plot of a narrative imposes a meaning on the events that comprise its story level by revealing at the end a structure that was immanent in the events *all along* . . . Does the world really present itself to perception in the form of well-made stories, with central subjects, proper beginnings, middles and ends, and a coherence that permits us to see "the end" in every beginning? (1980, 19, 23)

White's comments highlight how closure imposes one meaning and significance on a series of events by crystallizing it into a rigid structure. Conversely, White implies, if we perceive narrative from the preclosure position, it constitutes something much more ontologically open and pluralistic, as yet devoid of a final organizing pattern. White therefore understands "plot" as the final postclosure state of a narrative in which teleological patterns have been imposed on a sequence of events.

By contrast, other theoreticians—from Bremond's (1980) conception of plot as a "network of possibilities," through Brooks's (1992) idea of "narrative desire" and James Phelan's (1989) concept of "narrative progression," to Ryan's (1991) "principle of diversification"—have defined "plot" as an ontologically or interpretatively unstable dimension that exists *before* the narrative text comes to an end. While it is important to distinguish between them, it is not necessary to choose between these two conceptions of plot; they can be seen as two key aspects that create the narrative dynamics of plot. Phelan's concept of narrative progression is founded particularly on this dual aspect: narratives are "developing wholes" (1989, 15) moving toward closure. Studying a narrative's progression involves investigating "how authors generate, sustain, develop, and resolve readers' interests in narrative" (Phelan 1989, 15) and how a narrative's design, particularly its ending, is determined by its beginning and middle. The role of causality in the dynamics of plot has also received more substantial attention in recent key works by Brian Richardson (1997) and Emma Kafalenos (2006).

The study of the ontological dynamics of narrative has also been stimulated by the application of possible-worlds theory to the study of narrative fiction. A philosophical concept adopted by various disciplines (Allén 1989), possible-worlds theory's basic premise is that any world (the real world or, equally, a fictional one) can best be understood not as a single world but by applying the thesis that "the world we are part of is but one of a plurality of worlds" (Lewis 1986, vii). Dependent on the given perspective, different worlds can form the perspectival center of a system of multiple worlds in a flexible, recenterable conceptual system (Ryan 1995b) in which each world is actual from the perspective of an inhabitant of that world (Lewis 1979, 184). The work of Lubomír Doležel (1976a, 1976b, 1988, 1998) has been central to the literary application of possible-worlds theory, while the work of Thomas G. Pavel (1985) and Ryan (1991) has represented the most imaginative applications to drama and narrative fiction, respectively.[10] Ryan (1991) sees plot in narrative as an interaction of virtual and actual worlds: the "private" worlds of characters constituted by their wishes, knowledge, intentions, and obligations can deviate from or conflict with the "reality" of the actual world of the text, thereby generating conflict and tellability—the stuff of interesting narrative. Ryan's (2001) study *Narrative as Virtual Reality* extended the concept of virtuality in connection with that of immersion and interactive electronic texts. David Lewis (1973, 1986) and Nicholas Rescher (1975) established important premises within possible-worlds philosophy for the study of counterfactuals and transworld identity that have been taken up in the study of literature by Uri Margolin (1996) and represent key points of departure for the ontological consideration of plot and character in the present study.

The overall tendency toward the diachronic application of narrative theory (see, e.g., Fludernik 1996a, 2003) has also been reflected in the studies of plot that undertake a combined focus on the *formal-developmental* and *cultural* dynamics of specific plot patterns across an extensive historical period.[11] As Bueler observes: "Watching a single plot move between genres is a superb way to study generic forces at work. Linked to the story of genre is the history of cultural attitudes and changes" (2001, vii). Bueler's rigorous definition of the narrative coordinates of the tested woman plot enables her to chart this literary embodiment of patriarchal culture across the centuries. Similarly, Gutenberg's (2000) harnessing of possible-worlds theory and feminist concepts allows her to pinpoint key developmental patterns in the female plots of romance, quest, and the family from the eighteenth to the twentieth century.

The Worlds of the Reader and the Cognitive Turn

The consideration of the reader's processing of narrative plots and related questions has long constituted a key field in the enrichment of plot definition and analysis. Plot and the reader's response were crucial in Todorov's (1977, 42–52) typology of detective fiction, which differentiated between the whodunit, which aroused retrospective-looking curiosity, and the thriller, which aroused anticipatory suspense. Sternberg (1978) studied in depth the effect on the reader of narrative plot structures using differing constructions of expositional information (see also Perry 1979; Kafalenos 1999). In attempting to postulate the nature of the mental world constructed by the reader of narrative fiction, research has focused on the reader's pleasurable or imaginative response to fiction (Nell 1988; Walton 1990; Gerrig 1993; Ryan 2001; Warhol 2003) and on the assumptions the reader brings to the text before the act of reading takes place (Rabinowitz 1987).

In its contemporary state, narrative theory has now achieved substantial enrichment and invigoration through extensive cognitive reorientation (see, e.g., Fludernik 1996a; Jahn 1997, 1999; Abbott 2000; Herman 2003). David Herman's work constitutes a comprehensive intersection of narrative theory and cognitive approaches, including considerations of narrative temporality and spatialization, and investigates "the process by which interpreters reconstruct the storyworlds encoded in narratives" (2002, 5). Herman reconceptualizes and expands the scope of Genette's *anachrony* in the concept of *polychrony*: "Polychronic narration can be described as a specialized cognitive instrument" that "cues interpreters to rethink the scope and limits of narrative itself" (2002, 220). Other recent groundbreaking work in narrative theory (Palmer 2004; Zunshine 2006) has also used cognitive theory in particular to focus on the representation of character consciousness and the reading of fiction.

These cross-fertilizations of narrative theory with cognitive approaches have, however, not yet produced substantial results in the study of plot. As well as drawing its input from the research mentioned in the sections above, the current study profits substantially from the specific areas of research outlined below in order to formulate new parameters for the analysis of plot, time, and space in narrative fiction.

One major focus of cognitive research has been on the mind's figurative use of particular schemata in language and reasoning as a whole: "Image-schematic structures [are] metaphorically projected to structure our abstract reasoning in ongoing problematic situations of life, art, or science" (Johnson 1987, xxxviii). Research has, for example, focused on sense-making activities in human language, literature, and culture in the field of categorization (Lakoff 1987), conceptual metaphor and abstract reasoning (Lakoff and Johnson 1980; Turner 1987; Johnson 1987), and the conceptual blending of mental input spaces (Fauconnier and Turner 2003). Precisely because the cognitive research explores the overall sense-making patterns that the human mind within the human body uses to negotiate its way through the spatial and temporal environments of life, it can be used to study plot by investigating how narrative fiction simulates both the experience and conceptualization of time and space. Mark Turner's (1987) work on patterns of causation, kinship, and similarity offers important parameters for this study's exploration of basic schemata that are used to structure and connect time, characters, and events in the fictional world. Mark Johnson's (1987) work on the role of key schemata in the bodily negotiation of space provides the cornerstones for the analysis of the fictional simulation of characters' movement in space using the key schemata of the path, the container, and the portal.

A further, as yet underexploited source of fuel for narrative theory and the study of specific narrative plots is offered by research into nonliterary forms of narrative. The substantial body of recent research into counterfactuals across the fields of cognitive science (Turner 1996; Fauconnier and Turner 1998a, 1998b, 2003), psychology (Kahneman and Miller 1986; Roese and Olson 1995c), and political studies (Tetlock and Belkin 1996a) is used extensively in the present study. The cognitive study of counterfactuals—above all the mental process of "conceptual integration" or "blending" (Fauconnier and Turner 1998a, 2003) of input spaces that occurs when a counterfactual world is constructed—provides invaluable new insights for a reader-oriented analysis of counterfactuality that moves beyond the more philosophical preoccupations of possible-worlds theory. Indeed, current research into counterfactuals across the disciplines reflects the realization that, far from being abstract philosophical speculations, "counterfactuals are everywhere": "Our species has an extraordinary ability to operate mentally on the unreal, and this ability depends on our capacity for advanced conceptual integration" (Fauconnier and Turner 2003, 238, 217). Likewise, the psychological research into social and emotional patterns of counterfactualizing in everyday human experience reflects the fact that "counterfactual thinking is an essential feature of consciousness" (Roese and Olson 1995a, 46)—as this study shows, this mode of thinking has also substantially shaped the modern novel across the centuries. The human fascination with the quirks of coincidence in real life has also given rise to a large body of popular and some academic literature. Accordingly, this study also integrates research into coincidence as a real-life phenomenon (notably, Johnson 1899; Kammerer 1919; Jung 1967) to facilitate a clearer definition of the fictional plots of coincidence.

A Guide to This Study and Its Research Contribution

The plurality of plot theories and definitions outlined above reveals the sheer impossibility of isolating the essential nature of plot. This stems less from imprecision in the theoretical definitions than from the sheer plurality of aspects involved in narrativity (in the sense of Prince's [1999] "narrativeness"). Plot and the larger mental operation of *plotting* in its most extensive sense can be understood as any attempt to make sense of a larger, unorganized entity by constructing some kind of reductive and selective system. This act of construction has *cognitive*, *temporal*, and *spatial* aspects. On one level, narrative fiction itself, in the finite form of a book, represents the attempt to create a miniature map or "plot" of time and space with a beginning and an end. This sense of *plot* as an organizing and delimiting system also underlies the other major semantic variants of plot outside narrative. Defining a plot of land involves the erection of borders on a map, while a conspiratorial plot involves the attempt of a group of individuals to impose a particular event structure on the larger flow of time in order to achieve a particular end. This view of plot as a mapping operation is also stressed by Brooks (1992, 11–12).

All models (or plots) of plot in narrative involve a cognitive operation and an act of construction: an act of *plotting* (Ricoeur's "emplotment"). Moreover, the reading of narrative is fuelled by two different aspects of plot. First, there is the intranarrative configuration of events and characters, which is an ontologically unstable matrix of possibilities created by plot in its still unresolved aspect. This in turn fuels the reader's *cognitive desire* to be in possession of the second aspect of plot—the final configuration achieved at narrative closure when (the reader hopes) a coherent and definitive constellation of events will have been achieved.

Because of this complexity and dynamism, plot can never be arrested in one clear and stable definition. The present study greets the intrinsic complexity and mutability of plot in theory and narrative practice as both inevitable and exciting. It takes this multifariousness by the horns and develops a more pluralistic strategy that does not consist in reducing "plot" to a typological series of moves or stages. Instead, it identifies two widespread plot patterns in the history of narrative fiction (coincidence and counterfactuality) and uses these as an experimental field in which to apply a cognitive model for the analysis of plot that analyzes the representation of fictional time and space as manifested in narrative discourse within three interlocking conceptual frameworks. This produces an analytical model that can register change and variation and is thus capable of mapping the development of plots of narrative fiction over several centuries. The application of this method in the diachronic study of the novel in part 3 of this study results in key findings in a variety of fields: it monitors the evolution of plot in the history of novelistic discourse; it sheds light on the role of key authors (such as Daniel Defoe, Jane Austen, and George Eliot) in the development of qualitative narrativity; it contributes to feminist narrative theory by highlighting key developments in the cultural evolution and interaction of male and female representations of the love plot; it pinpoints the cultural dynamics of the cognitive plotting of narrative events by highlighting key shifts in the narrative explanation of fictional events over the centuries.

In the three chapters that form part 1 of this study, therefore, the plotting of time and space in narrative fiction is investigated from three different perspectives—cognitive, ontological, and spatial. All three chapters share a cognitive dominant, so that cognitive theory also shapes the chapters on ontological and spatial aspects of plot. These chapters formulate a theoretical model that can be applied to the plots of narrative fiction as a whole. They are, however, within the historical context of this study, extensively illustrated by examples of the plots of coincidence and counterfactuality. Part 2 then contains two further theoretical chapters that fully introduce and define the fictional plots of coincidence and counterfactuality, also incorporating important nonliterary research into the study of these phenomena. The two chapters of part 3 then present a historical map of the development of coincidence and counterfactuality in narrative fiction from the Renaissance to the present day.

Chapter 1 proposes a cognitively oriented mapping of narrative genre that focuses on the processes of readerly immersion and its opposite—expulsion. The chapter explores two key strategies for creating narrative immersion: the first concerns the major sense-making operations or plotting principles of causation, kinship, and similarity, which are used in particular by realist texts to represent a narrative world as an autonomous system; the second concerns narrative suspense, in which the reader liminally plots the alternate possible futures of the story. Chapter 2 shows how realist texts produce alternate possible worlds by a process referred to as temporal orchestration. It then analyzes the structure of a particular type of alternate possible world—the counterfactual—from a readerly perspective and in doing so reformulates the possible-worlds concept of transworld identity within a cognitive framework, showing how the reader blends various mental input spaces in a dual process of identification and differentiation. Finally, the concept of ontological hierarchy is introduced as a means of mapping the history of the world structures from realist to postmodernist fiction. Chapter 3 explores the human mind's use of spatial schemata to make sense of both time and the physical environment. It shows how narrative theory itself has frequently used spatialized representations of time and goes on to examine the spatial metaphors of time used in fictional texts, in particular the conceptualization of time as a pathway. The chapter then explores how the experience of space is simulated in narrative fiction through the use of the schemata of the path, the container, and the portal.

Chapter 4 undertakes the first cross-disciplinary survey of the highly fragmented research on the topic of coincidence, including the substantial body of research on the real-life phenomenon (Johnson 1899; Kammerer 1919; Jung 1967), in order to propose a clear and comprehensive definition of what coincidence in narrative fiction is. The chapter's analysis of the configuration of the coincidence plot focuses in particular on the representation of the recognition scene, which utilizes strategies of narrative suspense, temporal orchestration, and spatial representation, and on the narrative explanation of coincidence itself. Chapter 5 integrates the spectrum of research into counterfactuals and related phenomena across the disciplines in order to propose a model for the analysis of counterfactuals in narrative fiction. In addition to the concept of transworld identity explored in chapter 2, terms from the analysis of counterfactuals in the psychological sciences (Roese and Olson 1995c)—particularly the concepts of counterfactual emotions and downward versus upward counterfactuals—as well as approaches to causality in the political sciences (Tetlock and Belkin 1996a) prove fruitful.

Chapters 6 and 7 map key developments in the history of coincidence and counterfactuality in narrative fiction. The chapters thus contain a developmental "narrative of progress" for each plot pattern but also examine key texts in which the narrative forces of convergence and divergence intersect. Chapter 6 shows how the narrative strategies of key Renaissance authors mark them out as significant innovators in the early history of the novel; it then goes on to show how key texts of the early modern novel considerably deepened the cognitive dimensions and immersive capabilities of the coincidence plot before it firmly established itself as a central novelistic plot pattern subject to a plethora of different manifestations in novels of the later eighteenth and nineteenth centuries. In mapping the twentieth century, the chapter first shows how modernist novelists remodeled coincidence in accordance with the new aesthetic and then demonstrates how the playful plurality fuelling postmodernism led to a renaissance of the coincidence plot in both old and new forms. Chapter 7 charts how, from a limited rhetorical use in Renaissance fiction, counterfactuals feature in significant new forms in the rising novel. Nineteenth-century fiction is shown to be a key ground for a multiplication of forms of counterfactual narrative both in realist texts and in the emerging genre of alternate history. Finally, the chapter shows how the narrative impulse of the counterfactual spawned a complex array of narrative forms and subgenres in the twentieth century: complex counterfactual speculations on the edge of fantasy and realism, multiple alternate histories and transworld journeys in the rapidly expanding genre of science fiction, self-destructing contradictory story versions in experimental metafiction, and the blending of historical counterfactuals with postmodernist relativity in historiographic metafiction.

Read in conjunction, chapters 6 and 7 show how, in the interactive history of coincidence and counterfactuality, the nineteenth century is the site of a struggle between forces of narrative convergence and divergence. There is an underlying sense that the convergent pressures on plot to depict harmonious conclusions and happy marriages are inimical to social realism and a realistic depiction of the position of women, since they follow the plot agendas of comedy and romance. Novels such as Charlotte Brontë's *Villette* (1853), George Eliot's *Daniel Deronda*, and Thomas Hardy's *Tess of the d'Urbervilles* (1891) all use forms of the counterfactual to stress the discordant and nonconvergent life plots of their heroines. In the latter part of the twentieth century, the vectors of coincidence and counterfactuality meet again in the genre of historiographic metafiction. Historiographic metafiction capitalizes on the implausibility of the coincidence plot by employing it in antirealistic narrative constructions in which the author leaves his or her fingerprints on the text in the form of unlikely similarities and correspondences. This postmodern form of self-reflexive convergence is sometimes combined with the counterfactual, manifested in an array of diverging representations and interpretations of historical figures and events that deconstruct the narrative authority of history. Historiographic metafiction is thus, at present, the closing point of a long and fascinating developmental interaction of the convergent and divergent impulses of narrative, represented in the interplay of the plots of coincidence and counterfactuality.

Theorizing Time and Space in Narrative Fiction

1

1. Cognitive Plotting
Crossing Narrative Boundaries and Connecting Worlds

Each individual reader with her or his own personal cultural background interacts with a text to create a unique virtual dimension (Iser 1972). The reader's historical-temporal location, identity within global and regional culture, and of course gender are key factors influencing the individual shape of the virtual world the reader creates. Nevertheless, despite this potential for individual readings of narrative texts, this study works on the assumption that "audiences share many things—conceptual systems, social practices, commonplace knowledge, discourse genres" (Turner 1987, 4)—so that "one can study narrative structure not only in terms of concrete textual features but also in terms of the shared interpretative strategies by which readers make sense of them" (Rabinowitz 1987, 1). Such an approach presupposes a broad consensual area of readerly reaction to the plots of narrative fiction—a discourse form that over the past centuries has evolved into the dominant literary genre and can thus be seen as a major system of human communication. Indeed, only because reader responses do fall within a consensual field is it possible to classify narrative texts in terms of subgenres and speak of "metafiction" or "realism." Equally, the repeated use of particular textual strategies by authors is a sign that a large body of readers are capable of responding cognitively toward a text in the way envisaged by the author generating the text (Eco 1981, 7). After discussing the phenomenon of readerly immersion and its opposite, expulsion, this chapter proposes a framework to analyze the reader's mental responses to narrative plots in terms of her varying ability to generate a cognitive environment that allows the reader to mentally cross the boundary between her own and the fictional world and sustain belief in the reality of the fictional world. The focus is on narrative texts' generation of key sense-making activities (*plotting principles*)—notably, causation, kinship, and similarity—and on narrative suspense.

Liberation and Belief in Narrative Fiction

In introducing his study of Renaissance culture, Stephen Greenblatt states that "the effectiveness of [literature] depends upon the ability to delight"; "pleasure is an important part of my sense of literature—that is, part both of my own response . . . and of what I most wish to understand" (1990, 9). From Aristotle's catharsis to Brooks's (1992) "textual erotics," the power of literature to move, motivate, or delight has received widespread critical attention. Recent contributions to the aesthetics of readerly enjoyment and emotional engagement with the text include Nell (1988), Gerrig (1993), Keitel (1996), Hogan (2003), and Warhol (2003). However, one of many aspects that remain to be explored is the historical development of narrative fiction in terms of its evolution of strategies of pleasure and enjoyment. By what means has narrative fiction evolved to become the major literary genre of human culture in the course of the last three centuries, during which time writers have responded to a massive cultural demand by generating a corpus of narrative fiction that has reached an unequalled state of generic diversity? In proposing a cognitive model that is applied to a broad range of genres, the present study highlights aspects of this evolutionary process.

Even in the age of virtual reality, it is still impossible to gain admission to a live performance of the reading experience. As Ryan observes: "We can no more observe the stages of our own immersion than we can watch ourselves falling asleep" (2001, 170). Cognitive and metaphorical models nevertheless allow us to gain theoretical access to the reader's mind and her experience of narrative texts and thus explore the power narrative has on readers. The application of cognitive theory (Turner 1987; Johnson 1987; Fauconnier and Turner 2003) to analyze the conceptual systems the mind uses to understand time and space can help us to see how particular plot strategies in fiction tap into deep sources of meaning in the human mind. In tandem with this, we can construct metaphorical models of the reading experience in order to describe its deeper power and attraction for the reader. Thus, Victor Nell speaks of being "lost in a book" and explores the phenomenon of the state of being "transported": the reader's "absorption" and "entrancement" create "a pleasure . . . as rousing, colorful and transfiguring as anything out there in the real world" (1988, 1). Richard J. Gerrig (1993) likewise uses the metaphor of "being transported." The concept of readerly immersion, explored in detail by Ryan (2001), is particularly useful. Conceptually, it keeps a foot in both the real and the narrative world, comprehending both the simulatory and the imaginative or "escapist" aspects of the reading experience by creating an image of the reader mentally sinking into the narrative world and thus capturing her mental, boundary-crossing journey into that world while she nevertheless simultaneously occupies an ontological and a corporeal habitat in the real world.

The pleasure of the reading experience can therefore be grasped by conceiving of it as a journey of exploration into a new world—a journey whose very attraction resides in the exhilaration of jumping across and transgressing ontological boundaries and mentally relocating oneself far away from one's true spatiotemporal or ontological level. In this vein, another metaphor—that of liberation—illuminates the power of narrative. In critiquing Freud's "assertion that artists' work is motivated by the desire 'to achieve honour, power, riches, fame and the love of women,'" Ursula K. Le Guin counters Freud's materialism with a boundary-crossing model of escape that sees a very different impulse motivating both artists and readers: "The pursuit of art, then, by artist or audience, is the pursuit of liberty. If you accept that, you see at once why truly serious people reject and mistrust the arts, labelling them as 'escapism'" (1979, 150).

Le Guin's equation of art with liberty helps us to understand how, in immersive texts, the reader's belief in the narrative world, escape, and liberation are all interdependent aspects. Belief is central to many of the "plots" and narratives generated by human culture. Other major cultural phenomena—religion and politics are two key examples—also involve the construction of distant or different worlds into which ultimately, it is hoped, liberation (eschatological in the case of religion, social or ideological in the case of politics) will take place. Only through a belief in the existence or feasibility of these other worlds can serious religious worship or political activity take place. Likewise, only through a belief in the narrative world can the process of narrative liberation and immersion take place.

Seen this way, the reading experience is not so much a "willing suspension of disbelief" (Coleridge 1975, 169) as a *willing construction of belief* by the reader—the temporary refugee from the real world. A narrative world is thus a mental construction that provides a place of escape and liberty for the human mind to move to beyond the framework of its true ontological spatiotemporal boundaries. The reading of fiction can thus be described as the *cognitive simulation of ontological liberation*.

In her poetics of immersion, Ryan (2001) assesses a variety of textual strategies, from free indirect discourse to narrative suspense, that promote different types of temporal, spatial, and emotional immersion in the reader. Ryan, moreover, locates immersion within a historical framework, rejecting the proposal that narrative realism is simply one of many conventions: "The literary effect that was pioneered by Richardson, Fielding, and Smollett, and perfected in the next century by the likes of Balzac, Dickens and Gogol . . . is not the art of revealing 'how things are,' nor the art of imitating real-world speech acts, but the art of getting the reader involved in the narrated events" (2001, 161). This approach differs from approaches to novelistic realism that center on the text's creation of seemingly quotidian surface detail (Barthes 1968; Watt 1987). In the historical development of fiction, therefore, successful texts have capitalized on the reader's desire for narrative liberation by evolving key strategies to stimulate immersion.

The Reader in the Narrative World: Immersion and Expulsion

Over the past three centuries immersive fiction has formed the main body of novels that readers have read and enjoyed. However, nonimmersive counter-strategies have long been present in narrative fiction (Wolf 1993), and the marked increase of metafictional strategies within postmodern culture indicates some form of paradigm change (as in the celebrated example that occurs in chapter 13 of Fowles's *The French Lieutenant's Woman*). On the overall reading market, however, anti-illusionist fictions have never succeeded in displacing immersive fictions; experimental postmodernist texts have provided more excitement for narrative theorists than for the general reader, who can, though, appreciate the thrill of a little "soft metafiction" (Wolf 1993; Fludernik 1996a).

1. A Traditional Model of Narrative Communication

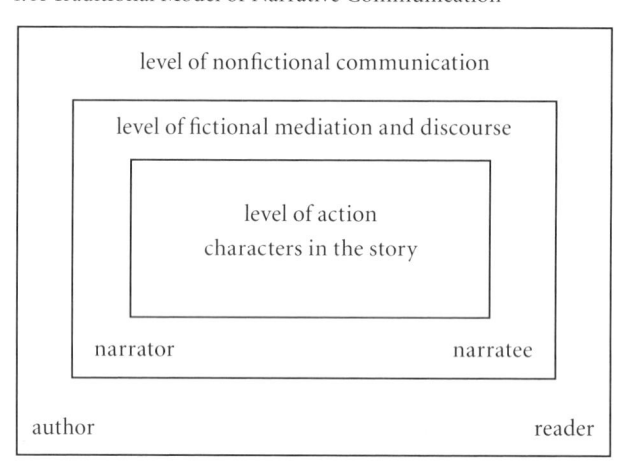

```
┌─────────────────────────────────────────────────────────┐
│          level of nonfictional communication            │
│  ┌───────────────────────────────────────────────────┐  │
│  │      level of fictional mediation and discourse   │  │
│  │  ┌─────────────────────────────────────────────┐  │  │
│  │  │              level of action                │  │  │
│  │  │           characters in the story           │  │  │
│  │  │                                             │  │  │
│  │  └─────────────────────────────────────────────┘  │  │
│  │                                                   │  │
│  │   narrator                              narratee  │  │
│  └───────────────────────────────────────────────────┘  │
│                                                         │
│   author                                        reader  │
└─────────────────────────────────────────────────────────┘
```

The effect created by metafiction can be comprehended in terms of the radical reversal of the immersion process: metafiction gives the reader a cognitive shock by expelling him from his imaginative sojourn in the narrative world.[1] While immersion involves the mental crossing of boundaries between the real and the fictional world, metafiction firmly reestablishes the boundaries between the reader and the world of the story. These two different readerly experiences can be illustrated by comparing two models of narrative communication. The diagram in figure 1, which is based on Manfred Jahn and Ansgar Nünning (1994, 285), illustrates an approach to narrative that stresses the ontological boundaries between the reader and the fictional world.[2] In this model the author and reader occupy one hermetically sealed realm. Beyond this, the narrator and his fictional addressee, the narratee, are located in the transitional realm of mediation. Inside the center box, far away from the level of the reader, lies the narrative world itself. While this figure is enlightening for the analysis of the constituent parts of narrative fiction, it in fact provides an antidiagram of what happens when someone picks up an immersive work of fiction and starts reading precisely because the act of immersive reading involves the reader's overriding of her true ontological level and her mental relocation into the narrative world. This traditional model constructs hierarchical levels in which communication is only postulated between ontological peer groups. This segregation is technically correct, since I, the real-world reader on the outer level, cannot actually have a two-way conversation with, say, Moll Flanders—but if I had lived in the eighteenth century I might have had a conversation with Daniel Defoe. However, the model contains no hint of the boundary-transcending power of the reading experience, in which the reader is mentally absorbed by the narrative world, its setting, characters, and plot.

This traditional model, however, describes precisely what happens in metafiction. The shock tactics of metafiction bring about *expulsion*, and the reader is forcefully ejected from her mental sojourn within the narrative world and jolted back to her own ontological level. The boundaries that ontologically separate her from the narrative world are reestablished and sealed; sustained belief in the narrative world is no longer possible.

Expulsive effects can, however, also occur without involving a calculated metafictional strategy. For example, if the text's justification of the implausibilities of the coincidence plot is sloppy, the effect is similar to metafiction but without the thrill. Both metafiction and mismanaged realism can thus lead to the expulsion of the reader from her imaginary position in the narrative world.

By contrast, the immersed reader's experience can be comprehended in terms of the diagram in figure 2 (p. 24). The reader sinks down into the narrative world and becomes oblivious to her own ontological level. The reader's immersive interaction with the text is a mental journey across boundaries, and as long as the narrator does not draw attention to his own separate level, he also recedes to a less conscious level even though the information he

2. The Reading Experience as Immersive Journey

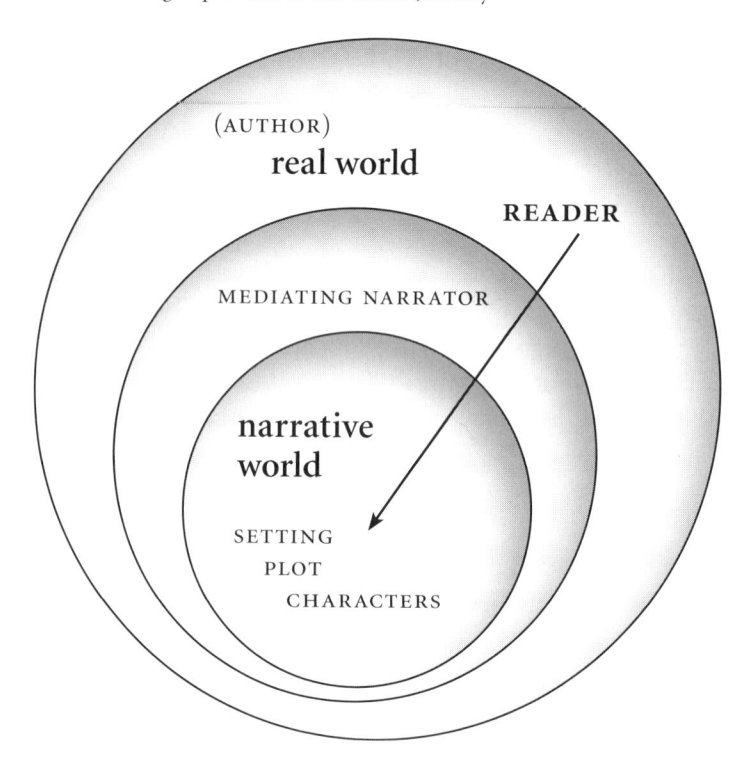

```
                    (AUTHOR)
                    real world
                                    READER
            MEDIATING NARRATOR

              narrative
              world

                SETTING
                PLOT
                CHARACTERS
```

provides allows the reader to simultaneously construct and explore the narrative world in her mind.

The popular narrative genres of fantasy and science fiction can be located between the extremes of immersion and expulsion: their narrative environments are sustained by realist cognitive strategies, even though their fantastic plots are potentially expulsive due to their departure from real-world rules and norms. This illustrates the key point that realism and immersion are not automatically equatable. Immersion occurs in various forms and combinations across the narrative genres. Importantly, immersion also involves narrative's cognitive power to *override* the reader's consciousness of a text's antirealistic signals. This process can be observed in examples of the coincidence plot and some fantastic forms of counterfactual that combine stories that are unlikely or even preposterous with cognitive strategies that persuade the reader to believe in the autonomy of the fictional world, thereby allowing her to remain immersed and ignore signals that are potentially expulsive.

World Construction: The Plotting Principle

Narrative fiction uses a repertoire of sense-making operations to establish (or, in antirealist texts, sometimes to undermine) the autonomy of the narrative world and thus create an environment for immersion. Put most simply, realist texts (and semirealist texts, such as the genre of science fiction) attempt to camouflage the ultimate, extradiegetic causal level of the author (who actually writes the text and thus causally manipulates all events within it) by constructing a narrative world with its own intradiegetic connective systems. If these are convincing, the reader is encouraged to believe in the internal logic and autonomy of the narrative world and thus that it is a "re-creation" as opposed to a fictional "creation" (Sternberg 1985, 99). These connective systems are created by the text's suggestion to the reader that she should understand the narrative world's configuration of events and characters using the same basic cognitive operations that she uses to make sense of the real world.

Causation has long been singled out as a fundamental principle in the construction of narrative plots. Aristotle emphasized the enhanced effect of plots involving causal connections as opposed to purely random events upon the audience: "Fear and pity ... occur above all when things come about contrary to expectation but because of one another" (*Poetics* 52a2–11, 1996, 17). Forster defined plot, in contradistinction to story, as "a narrative of events, the emphasis falling on causality" (1990, 87). Structuralist plot analysis generally backgrounded the question of higher sense-making structures created by plot, but more recent work has stressed its key role in configuring narrative (see, e.g., Culler 1981; Fludernik 1994; Adams 1996, 129–41; Richardson 1997; Palmer 2004; Kafalenos 2006).[3] Richardson proposes an agent-based typology of causality in fictional worlds, differentiating between "four major systems of causation: supernatural, naturalistic, chance, and metafictional" (1997, 62). Kafalenos (2006) explores in particular the question of narrative agency in the representation and interpretation of characters' actions within the plot.

The construction of causal relationships is a key operation of the human mind (Piaget 1974), but it also interacts and indeed overlaps with other forms of *connection* (Turner 1987; see also Fauconnier and Turner 2003, 75–87). For example, a cognitively directed analysis of the representation of the coincidence plot reveals how fiction constructs connective systems of character relations, notably using the schema of *kinship*. Kinship plots activate the reader's sense of *lineage*, tapping into a *progenerative* (Turner 1987) model of causation that is part of the reader's own experiential model of family relationships. The activation of the lineage schema therefore disposes the reader to process the text as a realistic one representing the types of connections (human relationships) familiar from her own life. The connections of kinship and personal relationships can be held to be such an important personal cognitive parameter for the reader that kinship plots within coincidence can produce highly immersive states that override the reader's consciousness of the ultimate causal level of the author as manipulator of plot, thereby sustaining immersion.

I therefore use the term *plotting principle* to refer collectively to key sense-making operations suggested by the text. A plotting principle is a specific textual strategy generally used to forge meaningful connections for the reader between events and characters within the narrative world, thereby creating immersion. Plotting principles can, however, also be short-circuited, leading to readerly expulsion from the narrative world. The connecting force of causation together with patterns of kinship and similarity are fundamental plotting principles in narrative fiction.

Causation

Turner (1987, 139–83) shows how, contrary to other attempts to define it as a unified concept, causation is a cluster of different cognitive operations that do not all apply in the same contexts.[4] On the basis of the reasoning used in the coincidence plot and counterfactuals, the following variations are dominant forms of explanation used in the causal justification or construction of narrative events:

1. "*Causation as progeneration* . . . express[es] paths by which things in the world, the mind, and behaviour can spring from one another."
2. "*Causation as action (direct manipulation, applied force)*" involves "someone directly manipulating some preexisting objects."
3. "*Causation as necessary and sufficient conditions*" conceives of "the cause of an effect as all the conditions necessary for that effect to happen." (Turner 1987, 141–43, my numbering)

I will refer to these three types of causation as *causal-progenerative, causal-manipulative,* and *causal-sufficient* forms of explanation. Type 1, causation as progeneration, is a cognitive pattern used to comprehend a randomly initiated but causally linked sequence of events in time. (The biological concept of progeneration as *lineage* is a way of expressing the conception of time [and plot] as something causal and linear.) By contrast, type 2, causation as action, involves the intentional manipulation of events by an agent. The following examples illustrate the historical transition away from a construction of events in which a providential god—implicitly located in a *metaworld* that is part of the narrative world—is deemed to be causally manipulating events toward more pluralistic forms of causal justification.

Causation in the Coincidence Plot

In the traditional form of the coincidence plot, characters with a previous connection (of kinship, friendship, or even enmity) are brought together under remarkable and apparently random circumstances. In order to sustain immersion, the ultimate causal-manipulative level of the author is camouflaged by the assertion of intradiegetic causal processes. Tobias Smollett's *Roderick Random* (1748) provides a rudimentary form of this type of explanatory strategy. In picaresquely opportune fashion, Roderick has just happened to be in the right place at the right time to save his beloved Narcissa from the unpleasant molestations of Sir Timothy: "But heaven would not suffer so much goodness to be violated; and sent me, who passing by accident near the place, was alarmed with her cries, to her succour.—What were the emotions of my soul, when I beheld Narcissa, almost sinking beneath the brutal force of this satyr! I flew like lightening [*sic*] to her rescue" (Smollett 1981, 229).

This narrative explanation substitutes a different causal agent—God ("heaven")—for the real one—the author—but retains the basic causation type—manipulation. The explanation is not particularly convincing (certainly not for a modern reader), since it is offered in a trite nutshell by Roderick simultaneously with the narration of the event itself.

More sophisticated narratives use subtler explanatory strategies. In Charlotte Brontë's *Jane Eyre* (1847) the major coincidence plot has the heroine wander aimlessly across North England after her flight from Rochester, only to faint on the doorstep of a family who turn out to be her own cousins. The intradiegetic causal explanation of this event, however, is hidden much earlier in the narrative and only acquires retrospective significance: "Sympathies, I believe, exist (for instance, between far-distant, long-absent, wholly estranged relatives asserting, notwithstanding their alienation, the unity of the source to which each traces his origin) whose workings baffle mortal comprehension. And signs, for aught we know, may be but the sympathies of Nature with man" (Brontë 1966, 249). In keeping with the Romantic tradition in Brontë's writing, human beings are here placed in an interactive network with "Nature." If "sympathies" to other human beings are sufficient (i.e., if the individuals concerned are good Romantics), they will be subject to the attraction of "the unity of the source" (i.e., kinship and lineage). Brontë's intradiegetic explanation is therefore a complex variant of type 3, causation as necessary and sufficient conditions, combined with type 1, causation as progeneration, which is here expressed in reverse order through the idea of tracing a line back to origins. While *Jane Eyre* is not without its own providential component, in comparison with *Roderick Random*, God is no longer allowed the position of single causal manipulator in the more romantically pluralistic world of Brontë's novel.[5]

In E. M. Forster's *A Room with a View* (1908) a coincidental encounter in England between former acquaintances from a holiday in Italy gives rise to a conversation between the clergyman Mr. Beebe and George Emerson, who offer two different explanations of this event:

> "And what a coincidence that you should meet Mr Vyse!... Though, as a matter of fact, coincidences are much rarer than we suppose. For example, it isn't pure coincidentality that you are here now, when one comes to reflect."
>
> To [Mr. Beebe's] relief, George began to talk.
>
> "It is. I have reflected. It is Fate. Everything is Fate. We are flung together by Fate, drawn apart by Fate." (Forster 1978, 147)

George Emerson's understanding of fate invokes inexorable causal-manipulative forces operating outside his control or comprehension. Mr. Beebe, on the other hand, tells George off for believing in fate and speaks in favor of his ability to causally affect or manipulate his environment:

> "You have not reflected at all," rapped the clergyman. "Let me give you a useful tip, Emerson: attribute nothing to Fate. Don't say, 'I didn't do this,' for you did it, ten to one. Now I'll cross-question you. Where did you first meet Miss Honeychurch and myself?"
>
> "Italy."
>
> "And where did you meet Mr Vyse, who is going to marry Miss Honeychurch?"
>
> "National Gallery."
>
> "Looking at Italian art." (Forster 1978, 147)

Mr. Beebe uses an argument that invokes aspects of causation types 1 and 3: a mutual interest in Italy has set up necessary and sufficient conditions for the characters to come together again; or, as Mr. Beebe subsequently puts it, Italy is the causal-progenerative *source* of their meetings. As in the passage from *Jane Eyre*, the use of causal-progenerative reasoning involves the tracing of links backward in time:

> "There you are, and yet you talk of coincidence and Fate! You naturally seek out things Italian, and so do we and our friends. This narrows the field immeasurably, and we meet again in it."
>
> "It is Fate that I am here," persisted George. "But you can call it Italy if it makes you less unhappy." (Forster 1978, 147)

This passage, which both foregrounds and relativizes different explanatory systems, is symptomatic of a major shift in the presentation of explicational strategies within the transition from nineteenth-century realism to modernism.

While the idea of fate creates a deterministic matrix in which particular events are held to be unavoidable, the concepts of chance, chaos, and randomness can be understood as mental attempts to break out of the cognitive need to construct order through causal explanations.[6] In literary texts, simulated chance can function in a similar fashion to simulated causation—it distracts the reader from the ultimate causal-manipulative level of the author by implying that nothing at all influences events in the narrative world. For example, in Robert Greene's *Pandosto* (1588), the two key events used to construct the coincidence plot are represented as the product of changeable weather at sea (Greene 1987, 173, 194–95). In both these passage, however, the text stresses the principle of randomness through the personification of fortune as a coquettish and unpredictable woman: "Fortune, minding to be wanton[,] ... thought after so many sour looks to lend a feigned smile" (Greene 1987, 173). The example well illustrates the cognitive struggle to organize disorder. The personification of fortune as a capricious manipulator implies causation type 2 even while it evokes randomness.

Causation in Counterfactuals

Causation is a key component of the what-might-have-been narratives framed by counterfactuals and has been focused on in nonliterary research (Roese and Olson 1995c; Tetlock and Belkin 1996a). However, Turner's (1987) distinction between causal-manipulative and causal-progenerative systems of explanation allows a finer differentiation of the reasoning that underlies the causal link evoked between a counterfactual's antecedent and its consequent (i.e., between the hypothetical alteration and the new outcome it creates).

In Daniel Defoe's *Robinson Crusoe* (1719), Crusoe constructs a counterfactual version of his shipwreck: "Another reflection was of great use to me ... and this was, to compare my present condition with what I at first expected it should be; nay, with what it would certainly have been, if the good providence of God had not wonderfully ordered the ship to be cast up nearer to the shore, where I not only could come at her, but could bring what I got out of her to the shore" (Defoe 1965, 141).

Two different levels of causation are involved in this passage. The counterfactual argument is constructed using the causal-progenerative reasoning that is typical of the linear link generally constructed between antecedent and consequent in counterfactuals: in the real world the ship was cast aground near the shore, and the causal-progenerative result of this event was that Crusoe was able to salvage many useful things from it. In the counterfactual world he constructs, the ship is not wrecked near the shore, leading to a less favorable consequent. The second level of causal reasoning is the conclusion Crusoe draws by contrasting the actual scenario with the counterfactual one: the actual course of events is proof that a providential God exists who "wonderfully orders" everything and is therefore the ultimate causal manipulator of events in Crusoe's world. This argument has the key rhetorical effect of reinforcing both the reality and desirability of the narrative world; it instates the world Crusoe inhabits as part of a complete and autonomous universe, one that extends to a larger metaphysical framework in which a *metaworld*, complete with an orchestrating deity, is implied to exist over and above the physical world of characters.

In Henry Fielding's *History of Tom Jones* (1749), counterfactuals articulated by the heterodiegetic narrator assert the reality of the narrative world in a different way. For example, in narrating the novel's central chaotic sequence of multiple encounters at the inn at Upton, Fielding's narrator observes that if "Squire Western . . . who was come hither in pursuit of his daughter . . . had . . . fortunately been two hours earlier, he had not only found her, but his niece into the bargain" (Fielding 1966, 490). Here the narrator conceals the ultimate causal-manipulative level of the author by suggesting that the narrative world is subject to a random interplay of phenomena within its own autonomous system of time and space. In contrast to the example from *Robinson Crusoe*, the causal-manipulative level of Providence is absent and has been replaced by a more pluralistic worldview that suggests multiple possible causal-progenerative sequences (Squire Western does/does not meet his daughter) that are produced according to the random interplay of events and not as part of any grand divine scheme. Fielding's use of counterfactuals thus points to the waning power of an omnipotent causal-manipulative deity in the eighteenth-century narrative worldview.

Even in the form of a brief insert, as in the example from *Tom Jones* above, counterfactual narratives play a key contributory role to realist fiction's simulation of a credible environment that in turn sustains the immersed reader's belief in the narrative world. The reality-enhancing cognitive power of such causal connections is twofold. First, the inbuilt causal reasoning of counterfactuals acts to reinforce the impression of the reality of the fictional world by activating the same causal patterns that the reader uses to make sense of real life, allowing her to equate the fictional world with the real one. Second, the causal framework of the specific counterfactual asserts a network of causal relationships across the narrative world, creating a seemingly substantial autonomous environment, be it one with an orchestrating deity (Defoe) or one with a more mundane sense of the random interplay of entities (Fielding). In view of their realism-enhancing potential, it is not surprising, as further examples in this study will show, that counterfactuals are a recurrent and increasing feature in novels designated as realist in the eighteenth and nineteenth centuries.

Counterfactual scenarios in semirealist texts such as science fiction still operate very closely on causal lines, even if the patterns of causation are generated by fantastic plots such as the fictional science of time travel. Thus, in texts like Isaac Asimov's *The End of Eternity* (1955) and John Brunner's *Times without Number* (1962), time travelers interfere with the causal-progenerative sequences of history, causally manipulating strategic events in order to create a counterfactual version of history. Causal links can also be constructed across alternate worlds to bind them together into a unified system. Thus, in John Wyndham's short story "Random Quest" (1961), a misfired scientific experiment causes the hero, Colin Trafford, to be displaced into a historically counterfactual world. Within its fantastic scenario, such a story therefore still conforms to the key plotting principle of realism—causation. This is one reason why science fiction texts also have immersive power. Both the integrated system of mundane world and providential metaworld of *Robinson Crusoe* and the multiple worlds of a science fiction narrative are represented as coherent, autonomous systems through the connecting principle of causation.

Kinship

As Turner (1987) shows, models of kinship learned from the experience of family relationships lie at the heart of human sense-making operations. Systems of kinship are constructed both by the idea of *lineage*—the linear, causal-progenerative paths of genealogy—and by the idea of *similarity*—the genetic correspondences between siblings or between parents and children. Among the ten "metaphoric inference patterns" that Turner (1987, 25–29) identifies, the most relevant concepts of kinship for the analysis of fictional plots are *similarity, causation as progeneration*, and *lineage*.

The coincidence plot centers in particular on representations of the discovery of identity within systems of biological kinship. I suggest that both the narrative power of this plot and its successful recurrent use across fiction despite its obviousness as a literary device are due to the deep cognitive power that representations of biological kinship activate within the mind of the reader. Due to the basic and quite literally "familiar" (i.e., familial) level of cognitive response it can elicit in the mind of the reader, the kinship plot makes the narrative world a "real" one for the reader. Above all, the pivotal position within the coincidence plot of the *recognition scene* (in which estranged family members discover their true identity) can be attributed to the deep cognitive imprint and consequent emotional power that kinship recognition has in real life. As Johnson and Morton (1991) show, a child's ability to identify its parents in contrast to other faces constitutes one of the most basic and comforting human experiences from early childhood onward. The crucial emotional-cognitive power that the experience of child-parent bonding and identification has within the formation of identity in childhood is indicated by the extent to which child-parent identification (more so than romantic reunion within a love plot) is the most frequently and emotively used form of reunion occurrence of the coincidence plot. I suggest that the kinship recognition scenario is so basic in human experience that, when activated in narrative fiction, it has the power to override the potentially reality-destroying signals of implausibility in the coincidence plot. The recognition phase of the coincidence plot thus presents a quintessentially "meaningful" experience for the human subject (the reader) precisely because it enacts long-established, reassuring, interconnecting patterns crucial to a human being's sense of identity and security. The tracing of kinship connections involves both the networking of characters by mapping progenerative lines back to previous generations as well as analogical links involving the perception of genetic similarities.

Kinship in the Coincidence Plot

Jane Eyre is a prime example of how narrative uses the cognitive plot of kinship. The submerged causal explanation of the novel's central coincidence (as discussed above) expresses a sense of "sympathies . . . between far-distant, long-absent, wholly estranged relatives asserting . . . the unity of the source to which each traces his origin" (Brontë 1966, 249) and in doing so constructs a powerful map of kinship that evokes ideas of group, similarity, and lineage. This is then consolidated in the recognition scene in which Jane discovers that Mary, Diana, and St. John Rivers are her cousins:

> Circumstances knit themselves, fitted themselves, shot into order: the chain that had been lying hitherto a formless lump of links was drawn out straight—every ring was perfect, the connexion complete. I knew, by instinct, how the matter stood, before St John had said another word . . .
> "Your mother was my father's sister?"
> "Yes."
> "My aunt, consequently?"
> He bowed.
> "My uncle John was your uncle John? You, Diana, and Mary are his sister's children, as I am his brother's child?"

"Undeniably."

"You three, then, are my cousins; half our blood on each side flows from the same source?"

"We are cousins; yes."

... Glorious discovery to a lonely wretch! (Brontë 1966, 410–11)

The first part of the passage is a metaphorical description of the cognitive process of kinship construction taking place in Jane's mind as she herself "plots" the family relationships involved. Here the text actually highlights the fact that (re)cognition is a mental process in which order, form, and connections are created out of random phenomena: "order" and "the chain" emerge from a "formless lump." The conversation between Jane and St. John then fills in the details of lineage, and the renewed reference to "source" reiterates the sense of kinship as both group and lineage. The reader, in turn, becomes immersed in the mental and emotional experience of kinship recognition, and this suppresses his consciousness of the artifice of the coincidence plot at the key point of its revelation.

Similarity

Just as kinship interlocks cognitively with causation in the progenerative-linear model, so do some aspects of similarity overlap into the field of kinship. This is because the perception of similarity involves the recognition of "family resemblances" (Wittgenstein 1977; Turner 1987), which, in terms of biological kinship, involves the identification of genetic inheritance and thus of the connecting structures of lineage and genealogy.

Similarity in the Coincidence Plot within a Causal-Progenerative Framework

A recognition scene from Paul Auster's *Moon Palace* (1989) describes the narrator's perception of genetic resemblance between generations when he realizes that an apparent stranger is his father: "I found myself studying the contours of his eyelids, concentrating on the space between the brows and the lashes, and all of a sudden I realized that I was looking at myself. Barber had the same eyes I did.... We looked like each other, and the similarity was unmistakable.... I was Barber's son, and I knew it now beyond a shadow of a doubt" (Auster 1990, 296). Here kinship, causation (father-son procreation), and similarity (genetic resemblance) are all bound up in the depiction of the moment of recognition. This passage is particularly identifiable as a twentieth-century rendering of the kinship recognition scene because of its detailed mapping of facial characteristics and the emphasis on genetic similarity.

Similarity within a framework of kinship creates a multidirectional matrix of biological links, mapping relationships through the model taken from real-life experience. Corresponding genetic features are perceived both laterally (similarities between siblings) and linearly (similarities between parents and offspring, as in those perceived by the narrator in *Moon Palace*): "In our mental models of kinship, we blend the vertical, the lateral, and the hierarchical. Lateral can always suggest vertical (brothers share a parent)" (Turner 1987, 29). The component of biological progeneration within the family structure lends it an essential causal-linear structure that is cognitively associated with real-world experience.

Similarity in the Coincidence Plot without a Causal-Progenerative Framework

By contrast, similarity instated *outside* the field of biological kinship loses the causal-linear element. This absence thwarts the application of real-world cognitive patterns in the mind of the reader. It creates what Jean Baudrillard calls the "hyperreal"—"the generation by models of a real without origin or reality" (1988, 166). This occurs in the plots of many works of postmodernist fiction that subvert causal-linear structures and progenerative patterns by constructing predominantly analogous systems of correspondence based on similarity. This, figuratively speaking, produces the kind of challenge to the human conception of the real that would be invoked by pointing out a similarity between two sons and at the same time stating that they have no biological parent. The human mind cannot process this kind of constellation in terms of the progenerative-causal model and thus has problems ordering it into a realistic context.

A prime example of this is the postmodernist form of the coincidence plot used in historiographic metafiction. Thus, in Ruth Prawer Jhabvala's *Heat and Dust* (1975) there are, on two separate time levels, uncanny similarities and correspondences between events in the lives of two women: a nameless narrator who travels to India in the 1970s and her step-grandmother Olivia, whose life in India in the year 1923 the narrator researches and in turn narrates in her journal. Both women are involved in a triangular relationship with one Englishman and one Indian; both become pregnant by their Indian lovers at the very same location in scenes with repeated motifs and verbatim repetitions of words and phrases; both contemplate abortion. The novel, however, never gives the reader any criteria with which to sort these events into a linear hierarchy involving causation as progeneration. It thus remains unclear whether the similarities are generated by the narrator constructing an anachronistic, fictionalized narrative of Olivia's life on the later time level or whether the similarities are part of a temporally linear sequence in which the narrator is imitating Olivia's behavior, which she has read about in her letters. The result is a causal paradox with no solution, precisely because no progenerative beginning, "source," or "original" can be pinpointed. Behind these enigmatic similarities, of course, glimmers the ultimate causal-manipulative figure of the author weaving an insoluble conundrum.

The above example underlines how, in its variety of forms, the coincidence plot is a plot par excellence. It utilizes a whole range of cognitive connecting patterns. In the traditional form of the coincidence plot this involves a reality-simulating combination of biological kinship, similarity, and causation, whereas in the postmodern form similarity dominates without kinship or lineage and thus suppresses causation.

Kinship and Similarity in Counterfactual Plots

Counterfactuals in fiction reveal a similar range of variations. The multiple counterfactual worlds generated in science fiction display analogical relationships of similarity, but they retain sufficient interconnective causation to create a coherent narrative world. For example, in Wyndham's "Random Quest" the narrator, Colin Trafford, who is transferred to a historically counterfactual world, finds himself inhabiting the body of a different, counterfactual version of himself who (he infers from the way people treat him) has developed a less pleasant personality due to the altered counterfactual conditions of his environment. The two different versions of Colin Trafford thus constitute a science fiction form of lateral (sibling) kinship. However, these two figures are still located within a causal-progenerative framework that links the two worlds of the text into a cohesive universe. This becomes clear at the moment when Trafford contemplates the point of divergence where the other Colin Trafford began to develop differently in the counterfactual world that resulted from an altered historical antecedent in the mid-1920s: "[This] Colin Trafford looked like me—right down to the left thumb which had got mixed up in an electric fan and never quite matched the other side—indeed, up to a point, that point somewhere in 1926–7 he *was* me. . . . We had the same parents, the same genes, the same beginning. . . . But later on, things on our different planes must have run differently for us" (Wyndham 1965, 160–61). The two versions of Colin Trafford are instated within parallel causal-progenerative sequences in which their shared lineage is mapped. Despite the science fiction plot, causation and similarity balance each other according to real-world cognitive expectations.

Conversely, the multiple story versions of metafictional alternate worlds practice a more radical and exclusive form of similarity. For example, Robert Coover's

"The Babysitter" (1970) is potentially the stuff of realist fiction: Mr. and Mrs. Tucker go to a party, leaving the babysitter in charge of their children. These characters are actants in multiple fragmented versions of the evening's events. In contrast to "Random Quest" there is no causal framework *within* the narrative world to link the analogous sections of the story together. The only conceivable causal-progenerative framework that the reader can apply to such a text is that of the author himself creating different story variants.

In both traditional realist texts and the semirealist texts of science fiction, the interacting cognitive plotting principles of kinship, similarity, and causation thus function holistically to convince the reader that the fictional world is an autonomous one. Within the flow of reading the reader is given no cause to perceive an ontological dichotomy between the narrative world and his own that could prevent him from believing in that world and destroying his state of immersion. In nonrealist metafictionally inclined texts, this balance is not upheld: the reader cannot mentally construct the narrative world as one functioning according to the balance of cognitive principles he applies to the real world.

As seen above, transitions in the use of the plotting principle indicate major conceptual shifts in human culture and pave the way for the formation of new genres. At the same time, particularly powerful cognitive parameters, such as the recognition of kinship in the coincidence plot, have proven so successful that they have become intertextual paradigms and set off their own causal-progenerative patterns of lineage in narrative history. Seen this way, a progenerative line stretches all the way from *Oedipus the King*, through *Pandosto* and *Jane Eyre*, right down to *Moon Palace*.

Narrative Suspense and Liminal Plotting

The ability of texts to create immersive states in the reader is closely bound up with the text's ability to draw the reader into a complex mental engagement with the narrative world by suggesting a variety of possible versions of events. Key aspects of this process of *ontological plotting* and *temporal orchestration* will be discussed in chapter 2. The present section focuses on key cognitive aspects in the creation of narrative suspense, which stimulates the reader to imagine multiple versions of the story's future.

In his study of Alfred Hitchcock, François Truffaut observes how in his films Hitchcock "hinge[s] the plot around a striking coincidence, which provides him with the master situation. His treatment from then on consists in feeding a maximum of tension and plausibility into the drama, pulling the strings ever tighter as he builds up toward a paroxysm" (1967, 10). The example of Hitchcock indicates how pivotal a role coincidence can play in the generation of suspense in cinematic as well as in print narrative. The following section reviews and expands key aspects of suspense theory and then applies it to the coincidence plot in narrative fiction.

Todorov (1977, 42–52) distinguishes between two key responses: *curiosity* about gaps of information in the past world of the text and *suspense* about what will happen in the future. However, as Alfred Hitchcock observes, suspense tends to provoke a more urgent and emotional response in the recipient: "The whodunit generates the kind of curiosity that is void of emotion, and emotion is an essential ingredient of suspense" (Truffaut 1967, 51). Sternberg illustrates in detail how Homer's *Odyssey* intricately harnesses the dynamics of both curiosity and suspense. He pinpoints three essential features: the emotional dynamics of the suspense experience, in which the reader experiences alternate states of *hope* and *fear* regarding a positive or negative outcome (Sternberg 1978, 56–89); the text's stimulation in the reader's mind of "hypotheses . . . about the outcome" (1978, 65); and the distinction between "what" and "how" hypotheses in the structuring of suspense (1978, 89), that is, the difference between suspense centering on alternating hope and fear and suspense involving an interest in how the outcome is to be reached. More recently, in examining suspense as a form of temporal immersion, Ryan (2001, 141–48) conflated these distinctions by proposing a broader definition of suspense that comprises both the anticipation of the story's future and readerly curiosity about gaps in the past. Ryan also proposes the concept of "metasuspense"—a less immersive strategy that is focused on the discourse because it arouses the reader's curiosity about how the author will resolve the literary work's artistic design.

Richard Gerrig characterizes suspense as lying in uncertainty, but this "can take its toll only if readers allow themselves to consider a range of possibilities" (1993, 77). Contradictory opinions exist on the number of future possibilities inherent in suspense. Noël Carroll limits suspense to a binary either/or scenario: "With suspense, the question we are prompted to ask does not have an indefinite number of possible answers, but only two. Will the heroine be sawed in half or not? . . . [W]ith suspense, we are 'suspended' between no more than two answers" (1996, 75–76). By contrast, Victor Nell cites a "cliffhanger" from *A Thousand and One Nights* in which the story breaks off with the reader asking: "Will the merchant slaughter the calf or discover in time that it is his bewitched son?" (1988, 57). Nell observes that "we do not await the second night's tale in order to discover if the calf was slaughtered because we know the storyteller must spare its life. The listener's need is to know how this is achieved rather than whether it will happen" (1988, 57). From this it becomes clear that the *what* form of suspense characterized as essentially binary by Carroll is based on the invocation of a less pluralistic future-world scenario than the *how* form of suspense discussed by Nell, which, similar to mystery and detection narratives concerning lacunae in the past narrative world, engenders multiple alternate possibilities.

Both these types of suspense, the binary *what (either/or)* and the more multifaceted *how*, can occur in conjunction. A classic example is a scene in which characters sit around a table unaware that there is a bomb under it, as described by Hitchcock: "The bomb is underneath the table and the public *knows* it, probably because they have seen an anarchist place it there. The public *is aware* that the bomb is going to explode at one o'clock and there is a clock in the décor. The public can see that it is a quarter to one" (Truffaut 1967, 52; see also the discussion in Brewer 1996, 114). The power of this scene lies in the audience's superior knowledge and its inability to intervene in a precarious situation. As Hitchcock comments: "The audience is longing to warn the characters on the screen: 'You shouldn't be talking about such trivial matters. There's a bomb beneath you and it's about to explode!'" (Truffaut 1967, 52). This scene grips the audience in a rich suspense structure. Will the bomb go off (binary *what [either/or]* suspense)? *How* might the people sitting at the table notice the bomb (someone might kick it accidentally/notice a ticking noise/glance under the table while pulling his socks up, etc.)? If they do discover the bomb, *how* might they react to the threat (run away/defuse it/throw it out of the window)?

Such future-oriented suspense functions as a highly immersive narrative technique because it preoccupies the reader's mind so fully with events and possibilities in the narrative world that it suppresses his awareness of his true ontological location. I would like to designate the mental constructions that the reader makes during such suspenseful sequences as *liminal plotting*. This term refers to the reader's semiconscious mental images of possible future events that are logical extrapolations of the action, although they are not depicted in the text itself. In the case of the bomb under the table scene the strongest liminal image would be that of the flare and noise of a bomb exploding, but at the same time the reader's mind would be constructing some of the other *how* possibilities sketched above. These images can be called *liminal* precisely because they are half-formed responses that are evoked in the recipient's mind at the same moment as he processes the scene taking place in the actional present of the narrative. Suspense therefore has the power to create what can be called *double immersion*. The recipient's attention is spliced between two temporal realms within the narrative world: he is caught by the actual narrative scene with the bomb under the table, but, even while he is gripped by this scene, the liminal images in his mind concerning future events flicker on the edge of his consciousness. This process of double immersion has the power to create a strong state of obliviousness to the recipient's real-world environment.

One of the questions that has preoccupied recent suspense research is why readers are capable of experiencing suspense in narratives whose outcome they already know. Gerrig (1993, 1996) calls this the "resiliency" of suspense, Carroll (1996) the "paradox" of suspense (see also the discussion in Ryan 2001, 145–48). The processes of liminal plotting and double immersion can be used to explain this phenomenon: they work to suppress the recipient's conscious knowledge of the actual outcome of events precisely because they create two overriding levels of mental activity centering on events in the fictional world. First, the precarious situation in the narrative here and now (the characters sitting while there is a bomb under the table) draws the recipient into the narrative world so effectively that he experiences the fictional time relations as if they were his own. As Truffaut comments: "The art of creating suspense is also the art of involving the audience, so that the viewer is actually a participant in the film" (1967, 11). Naturally, then, the reader cannot "believe" in the future events given to him by his previous knowledge of the text if *experientially* he is participating in events in a section of time before those events happen. Second, the liminal images of the multiple possible futures created in the recipient's mind by the suspenseful situation function as an additional suppresser of the actual future outcome, which the reader really knows. This is because, seen from the actional present of the precarious situation, these multiple future scenarios do not yet have an *ontological hierarchy* in which one version is more actual than another. The immersed reader therefore views the future as a zone of multiple unactualized possibilities and is cognitively incapable of privileging the known outcome over the other possible versions.

Suspense and the Coincidence Plot

The coincidence plot has, figuratively speaking, its own bomb under the table. This is the moment of *recognition*—the point at which the coinciding characters discover each other's identity. The recognition process is potentially very explosive when the coincidental encounter involves estranged relatives who are unaware of each other's true identity. In order, however, for a suspense situation analogous to the bomb-under-the-table scenario to exist, the reader must be aware of the characters' true identity prior to the characters themselves. In this case, the possible future moment of recognition becomes the focus of his anticipation, and he may plot multiple future possibilities involving *whether* recognition will occur, *how* it will come about, and, additionally, *how* the characters will respond to the revelation. This character-cognitive element gives suspense in the coincidence plot heightened power, since the anticipatory focus is not purely event oriented but also psychologically fascinating. Suspense is not exclusively produced by zero knowledge on the character level; it can also be created if there is unilateral recognition and one of the coinciding characters is already aware of the relationship. In such situations of *staggered recognition* the reader's sense of anticipation may even be intensified if he vicariously shares the cognizant character's own speculations about possible future recognition scenarios.

These different possible combinations of knowledge imbalance on the part of characters and the reader can be designated as *cognitive stratification*. The phenomenon is similar to dramatic irony, in which "ironic contradictions" arise from the contrast between the superior knowledge of the recipient and the inferior knowledge of a character on stage (Pfister 2000, 88). Cognitive stratification, however, concerns not only imbalances in character-reader knowledge but also those between characters within the fictional world in situations of staggered recognition.

A comparison of three novels' suspense strategies—Greene's *Pandosto*, Defoe's *Moll Flanders,* and Auster's *Moon Palace*—illustrates the variable parameters of the coincidence plot's handling of anticipatory suspense and provides a diachronic sketch of narrative fiction's evolving capacity to create immersion by using suspense. In Greene's *Pandosto*, delayed recognition means that father-daughter incest is only just averted. In the denouemental section of the narrative, King Pandosto of Bohemia desires to make the newly arrived stranger, Fawnia, his concubine, unaware that she is his long-lost daughter. While the characters are not aware of their true relationship, the reader is, since the prior text has narrated Pandosto's earlier cruel casting out of the baby Fawnia to sea and her subsequent rescue on the Sicilian coast by a shepherd. The reader's suspense about whether recognition will take place is further increased when its likelihood is reduced by the discourse's suggestions of two negative future scenarios. Pandosto, it is suggested, may force himself on Fawnia, thus committing incest and rape at the same time: "My power is such that I may compel by force" (Greene 1987, 200). Alternatively, it is suggested that he may simply have Fawnia put to death if she does not comply: "Assure thyself thou shalt die" (Greene 1987, 202). Either of these outcomes seems most probable until at the last minute Fawnia's shepherd stepfather reveals her true identity. Greene's plotting of coincidence thus provides a suspenseful narrative through the implication of *multiple possible alternatives*. *Pandosto*'s tripartite set of future possibilities (rape, death, or recognition) indicates that Carroll's (1996) positing of a basic binary structure of narrative possibilities in *what* suspense is not borne out in narrative practice even as early as the Renaissance.

Pandosto is, however, much weaker on the character-cognitive level of suspense enhancement: there is, for example, little focalization of Fawnia's response to Pandosto's treatment of her, which would additionally fuel the reader's anticipation. By contrast, Defoe's *Moll Flanders* provides an innovative example of suspense creation by exploiting the potential of staggered recognition. From the unwitting revelations of her mother-in-law, Moll discovers that she has coincidentally encountered and married her own half-brother (Defoe 1978, 101). Moll's narration of this discovery is followed by weeks of story time and many pages of discourse time, in which she, and with her the reader, anticipates the possible form and consequences of full cognizance on the part of her own mother and half-brother. The reader's liminal plotting of a catastrophic recognition scene between Moll and her brother is intensified by a passage in which Moll describes her brother's reaction when she only hints that he is not her lawful husband:

> He turned pale as death, and stood mute as one thunderstruck, and once or twice I thought he would have fainted; in short, it put him in a fit something like an apoplex; he trembled, a sweat or dew ran off his face, and yet he was cold as a clod, so that I was forced to run and fetch something for him to keep life in him. When he recovered of that, he grew sick and vomited, and in a little after was put to bed, and the next morning was, as he had been indeed all night, in a violent fever. (Defoe 1978, 106)

This scene seems to prefigure a subsequent recognition scene, thereby inflating the reader's anticipation of negative future events; in fact, it remains a virtual future world, since Moll's diplomatic management of the actual revelation ensures that her brother receives the knowledge with relative calm.

Through an intricate time structure, the recognition process in Auster's *Moon Palace* is subject to even more complex stretching and manipulation. The narrator, Marco Fogg, discovers that a complete stranger, a man called Barber, is his own father. Fogg reveals this information proleptically, so that the reader knows a recognition scene between Fogg and Barber is coming—the text does not even bother with the more basic *what* suspense. However, Fogg combines these anticipations with an unspecified reference to a disastrous future accident: "Ten months later, when Barber lay dying in a Chicago hospital with a broken back, he told me that he had begun to suspect the truth as early as that first conversation in the hotel lobby" (Auster 1990, 237). Like *Moll Flanders*, therefore, the text provides fragmentary images that enable the reader to liminally plot a future catastrophic recognition scene. However, just when the reader has learned that recognition *is* coming somewhere ahead in the future and in some calamitous form, the narrative moves in the opposite direction, departing on a lengthy retrospective that leaves the reader, these future fragments installed in his mind, to wait for over fifty pages for the narration of the disastrous recognition scene between Fogg and his father.

The narrative realization of the coincidence plot therefore shows us in detail how suspense is intensified when the reader is stimulated to liminally plot future possibilities. This process is only one example of a larger narrative phenomenon that is referred to in this study as *temporal orchestration*—a multifaceted narrative strategy that works to capture the reader's attention by suggesting multiple versions of events. Other forms of temporal orchestration will be considered in the exploration of *ontological plotting* in chapter 2.

Conclusion: Possible and Impossible Worlds

The questions addressed in this chapter regarding narrative genre and cognitive response can be encapsulated by juxtaposing the concepts of the possible versus the impossible world. This distinction is not a new one to narrative theory and literary semantics and has been applied differently by various theoreticians (Heintz 1979; Eco 1989; Doležel 1988; Walton 1990; Ashline 1995). My use of these terms aims to express the crucial difference between the cognitive strategies of texts in a larger realist framework (from traditional realism to science fiction) and those texts that severely disrupt the immersive experience and expel the reader from cognitive integration in the narrative world. A possible world in this sense refers to a text's basic ability to facilitate a sustained world-constructing capacity in the reader, something that metafictions undermine but that semirealistic genres like science fiction inculcate through their use of plausible, world-cohesive causation patterns. For the strict logician (e.g., Eco 1989; Walton 1990, 64), the premises of some science fiction texts may be found to be faulty on close inspection. However, the use of real-world explicative patterns, in particular causation, in conventional science fiction texts masks this illogicality for the immersively inclined reader. The normal consumer of such texts will be able to continue his sustained imaginative presence in the narrative world as long as the interconnecting principle of causation constructs a "solid" environment.

Therefore, even if the narrative world is exotic or ontologically far removed from the real world of the reader (as in science fiction) or involves other unlikely contortions of time and space (as in the coincidence plot), the plotting principles of the real world can be used to create possible worlds out of potentially incredible scenarios. Such strategies facilitate the reader's sustained imagination of an autonomous and coherent narrative universe. Conversely, hard or soft metafictional techniques either fully undermine or temporarily interrupt the reader's immersive experience, expelling him back to his own ontological level.

Suspense also sustains the reader's mental construction of a possible world, since it firmly binds the reader's mental activity onto the ontological level of that narrative world, doubly suspending his attention between the actional present and possible future worlds. This cognitive entrapment on the level of ongoing narrative events has the effect of allowing the reader to view that world as one nascent with future possibilities—and thus truly a possible world.

2. Ontological Plotting
Narrative as a Multiplicity of Temporal Dimensions

Plot as the Sum of Alternate Possible Worlds

Ontological plotting refers to the analysis of narrative fiction's coordination of the alternate possible worlds that give it depth and interest. In Charles Dickens's *Great Expectations* (1861) Pip eventually discovers the identity of his secret benefactor. However, the completely different alternate set of relationships that are implied to exist before this discovery actually give the novel its narrative force. Similarly, in Jane Austen's *Sense and Sensibility* (1811) the prospect of the development of a love plot between Elinor Dashwood and Edward Ferrars disintegrates when Elinor hears of his marriage to Lucy Steele—but this version of events subsequently turns out to be an ephemeral construct. In George Eliot's *Daniel Deronda* (1876) the heroine, Gwendolen Harleth (tellingly depicted at the outset of the novel at a roulette table with its many alternate possible outcomes), frequently mentally reviews her different possible futures in life; later, when she has placed her bet on marriage with Grandcourt, the unexpectedly cruel reality of that marriage gives her cause to wistfully contemplate counterfactual versions of her life in which she did not marry Grandcourt. These three examples show how alternate possible worlds, which might at first sound like something out of fantastic fiction or a feature of the ontological dominant of postmodernism (McHale 1987), in fact play a major role in the realist tradition.

The reader devours a narrative with the desire of being able to trace a causal-linear sequence of events through fictional time; she wants more than story, she wants *plot* in the sense of Forster's (1990, 87) definition. Sophisticated narratives, however, use the *temporal orchestration* of alternate possible worlds to frustrate this desire; indeed, they intensify the reader's desire for causal-linear clarity by suggesting more than one possible version of events. In chapter 1 we already saw how suspense involves a form of temporal orchestration that evokes multiple future versions of events. Two archetypal narratives illustrate the way in which both past and future fictional time can be involved in this process. The detective story hinges on the retrospective revelation of the details of the crime from the past narrative world (as Todorov [1977, 42–52] shows, distinguishing it from the thriller). However, the final revelation that "X murdered Z" only achieves value because it emerges as "*the* story" from a variety of alternate possibilities such as "Y murdered Z," "Z killed himself," or "Z faked his own death and is in fact still alive." In the love story, if boy does finally get girl, this ending only becomes interesting because the alternative ending (boy loses girl) is presented to the reader as a substantial virtual prospect in the future narrative world until very late in the discourse. Complex novels, which move beyond these more formulaic plot configurations, involve the interweaving of possible versions of both past and future worlds. In its intranarrative state, plot is therefore the dynamic interaction of competing possible worlds. While the reader is immersed in the ongoing narrative, the story has not yet crystallized but is still in a state of ontological flux in which the authoritative version is one of many competing possibilities. Thus, as Phelan observes, viewing plot from a preclosure perspective involves considering how "we experience the ending as determined by the beginning and the middle" (1989, 111).

A sensitivity to ontological plurality allows us to view all fiction and its reading as the interaction of worlds. By contrast, in approaches that instate only one world version as the analytical yardstick, "the vast, open, and inviting fictional universe is shrunk to the model of one single world" (Doležel 1998, x). The same limitations also apply to methods of plot analysis that reduce their attention to the single-world version conceived of as *story*. This is because narrative does not simply tell one chronological story but, as already seen in the examples above, weaves a rich, ontologically multidimensional fabric of alternate possibilities.

In formulating the concept of the "disnarrated," Prince (1988, 1992) showed how "events that do not happen" but "are . . . referred to . . . by the narrative text" (1992, 30) constitute an integral part of narrative. Similarly, in proposing the "principle of diversification," Ryan (1991) showed how the success or tellability of individual narratives can be attributed to the generation of complex systems of alternate possible worlds. This study builds on Prince's and Ryan's work by showing how the ability to construct, coordinate, and juggle different alternate possible worlds is a key feature in the developmental history of narrative fiction. An analysis of the historical development of plot shows how, with the rise of the novel, more sophisticated plots develop involving the temporal orchestration of alternate world versions: more than one version of the past or future is suggested as a possibility by the text. Read in conjunction with the historical account in chapter 7, this chapter shows how the fictional plotting of alternate worlds has branched out into increasingly diverse subgenres, particularly since the mid-nineteenth century. The key distinction here is that while fictional genres across the board, whether realist, semirealist (fantasy and science fiction), or antirealist (metafictional), all use alternate possible worlds, they use them with differing forms of ontological hierarchy. Realist texts are ultimately single-world texts: they conform to the ontological expectations of the real world. The sophisticated realist plot involving mystery or suspense may stage a refined juggling of the virtual and the actual, but ultimately only one actual world is allowed to exist at closure. However, in nonrealist texts the strict ontological hierarchy of realism is subverted, leading to all manner of multiple-world narratives.

Narrative fiction's evolving capacity to generate multiple-world versions can also be seen in a larger anthropological-cognitive context, that of humankind's advanced skills in "the construction of the unreal": "People pretend, imitate, lie, fantasize, deceive, delude, consider alternatives, simulate, make models, and propose hypotheses. Our species has an extraordinary ability to operate mentally on the unreal, and this ability depends on our capacity for advanced conceptual integration" (Fauconnier and Turner 2003, 217). This chapter considers two different kinds of "unreal" world in narrative fiction: the multiple past and future worlds created by temporal orchestration and the alternate world versions created by counterfactuals. In doing so it will review key concepts from possible-worlds theory and narrative theory and, particularly in the case of counterfactuals, will combine them with cognitive theory.

Possible-worlds theory, with its a priori postulation of a "plurality of worlds" (Lewis 1986), has provided the conceptual framework for an analysis of plot as the dynamic network of alternate possible worlds.[1] At the center of possible-worlds theory is the notion of the relativity of the idea of a single world, or "*the* world," and its replacement by the conceptualization of a system of possible worlds in which the ontological center is relocatable. Every possible world is real from the perspective of its inhabitants (Lewis 1979, 184). Within possible-worlds theory there is, however, considerable variation regarding the nature and perception of the role of boundaries between worlds. Ryan's formulation of this question focuses on the crossing of world boundaries as part of the process of readerly *immersion*, "which pushes the reader into a new system of actuality and possibility" (1991, 22, see also Ryan 2001). Lewis, however, speaking as a philosopher, sharply defines the boundaries of one world in relation to another: "There are no spatiotemporal relations at all between things that belong to different worlds. . . . Nor do they overlap; they have no parts in common" (1986, 2). Lewis's *world-separatist* approach is echoed in the context of fiction by Doležel's claim that "we insist on a distinction between the actual and the fictional. By setting firm boundaries, we avoid *confusion* whenever our aesthetic desire or cognitive project invite us to transworld travel" (1998, xi, emphasis added).

The setting of rigid world boundaries, however, runs the risk of losing sight of the dynamics of the real reading experience. Critics and philosophers set theoretical boundaries, but the average reader, imaginatively immersed in the fictional world, does not. Doležel's call for the eradication of "confusion" may be desirable for a theoretical analysis, but, as cognitive theory has shown, *confusion*—in the sense of largely unconscious mental operations involving the *blending* of different mental spaces or worlds, a process that Gilles Fauconnier and Mark Turner call "conceptual integration" (1998b, 2003)—is in fact the way the human mind makes sense of complex phenomena. The blurring of ontological boundaries is therefore precisely what happens when the human mind (the reader) deals with representations of alternate worlds, or what Fauconnier and Turner call "the unreal" (2003, 217–47).

Alternate possible worlds are worlds that, considered from the perspective of the actual world, are unrealized possibilities. Theoretically, such *nonactual* worlds cover an infinite range of possible deviations from circumstances in the actual world conceivable by the human mind (Rescher 1975, 168).[2] However, the alternate possible worlds of narrative fiction are more specific. Prince (1988, 1992) proposed the concept of "the disnarrated" to refer to "all the events that *do not* happen though they could have and are nonetheless referred to (in a negative or hypothetical mode) by the narrative text" (1992, 30). Before this, Bremond (1980) defined the triadic structure of action as consisting of events that are actualized and those that are not. Ryan (1991) then explored the role of virtual events in narrative plots. Her examination focuses on virtual worlds generated in the minds of characters: "These constructs include not only the dreams, fictions, and fantasies conceived or told by characters, but any kind of representation concerning past or future states and events" (Ryan 1991, 156).[3]

Ryan's tenet that "the virtual in the narrative universe exists in the thoughts of characters" (1991, 110) produces a theory of plot centering on the conflicts provoked when characters attempt to turn their own virtual wish and intention worlds into reality: "The moves of the game are the actions through which characters attempt to alter relations between worlds. . . . For a move to occur and a plot to be started, there must be some sort of *conflict* in the textual universe" (1991, 119–20). Here Ryan's action-oriented approach follows in the steps of Pavel's (1985) work on drama. However, the action-oriented concept of the move, together with a primary focus on the character domain, effectively backgrounds the process of *how* the alternate worlds are actually woven into the narrative discourse. In fact, these processes are coordinated by the narrator, a figure whose key mediative role has traditionally been seen to constitute the crucial distinction of narrative fiction in comparison to drama (Stanzel 1984). In order, therefore, to provide a full account of the construction of alternate possible worlds in narrative fiction, it is necessary to bring the narrator more centrally into the analytical focus, not least because it is through narratorial sleights of hand that narrative events can be represented as real when they are in fact only virtual.

Focalization, Character Domains, and the Narrator's Power over the Ontological Hierarchy

The heterodiegetic narrator, who is not a character in the narrative world but a voice speaking from outside it (Genette 1980), occupies a supreme position of power in coordinating virtual and actual domains. In sophisticated heterodiegetic narratives such as those of Fielding or Austen, the narrator often exploits this power and creates bogus worlds that are presented as actual for a sizeable portion of the discourse.

Focalization is one key technique used to represent virtual events in a character domain as the actual narrative world.[4] The degree of focalized penetration into the character's domain is variable. In free indirect discourse (Cohn's [1978] narrated monologue), the narrator's presence is closely intertwined with the information from the character's domain (speech or thought). This allows the narrator to imply his authentication of the veracity of information, even if this impression is deceptive. In reported thought (which belongs to Cohn's category of psychonarration), the character domain is presented separately, while in the case of direct thought (Cohn's quoted monologue), the reader is completely submerged in the character domain without narratorial assistance.

The narrator can therefore manipulate the reader's perception of the ontological status of events by granting uncorrected focalized access to a character's domain, that is, by making the reader privy to a character's erroneous thoughts without clarifying their ontological status. For example, in Austen's *Sense and Sensibility*, uncorrected access to the knowledge world of Elinor Dashwood results in the extended construction of a bogus actual sequence of events. Elinor is in love with Edward Ferrars, who unfortunately has a prior commitment to Lucy Steele. In chapter 47 Elinor receives an eyewitness account that Edward and Lucy have married; the servant Thomas tells her: "'I see Mr Ferrars myself, ma'am, this morning in Exeter, and his lady too, Miss Steele as was'" (Austen 1969, 344). Elinor, whose domain is now accessed by free indirect discourse, then responds to this information with her own mental reconstruction of the details of the reported scene and her virtual projection of its continuation: "They were married, married in town, and now hastening down to her uncle's. What had Edward felt on being within four miles of Barton, on seeing her mother's servant, on hearing Lucy's message!" (347). Elinor's construction of these virtual scenarios in response to Thomas's information further establishes the marriage as a real event. However, toward the end of chapter 48 both Elinor and the reader are surprised by Edward Ferrars's appearance and his revelation that the Mr. Ferrars married to Lucy Steele is in fact his brother, Robert, to whom Lucy Steele has opportunistically transferred her affections (349–50). The marriage of Lucy and Edward therefore seems to belong to the actual narrative world for several pages of the novel but then completely evaporates. While this event cannot be said to belong to the story of *Sense and Sensibility*, it makes a crucial contribution to the reading experience of the novel's love plot.

Temporal Orchestration: The Plotting of Multiple Versions of the Past and Future

The term *temporal orchestration*, in contradistinction to Genette's (1980) concept of anachrony, refers to the suggestion of more than one version of the past or future by the text. Genette's (1980, 40) concepts of analepsis (retrospection) and prolepsis (anticipation) do not capture the ontologically intricate network of pathways of virtual and actual time in narrative fiction. This is because Genette's model is tied down to the concept of story; anachrony is thus conceived of as a narrative movement backward and forward along the single sliding scale of the past and future of the story and not—as in an ontologically pluralistic approach—as a portal to different world versions. Genette's approach centers on narrative *order* from the postclosure position, where a single-story version has been established, but it tells us little about how a more chaotic array of worlds is generated during the narrative.[5]

Temporal orchestration can be conceived of metaphorically as a kind of time machine that not only switches between past and future worlds but also switches between parallel worlds. In a multiple-worlds analysis of plot, retrospection (analepsis) and anticipation (prolepsis) can thus involve a journey into the virtual past of the narrative world or the projection of a virtual future that is not part of the story at all. Austen's *Sense and Sensibility* also provides a good example of projections of nonactual future events. Believing that Edward has married Lucy Steele, Elinor constructs a scenario of their future life together that, from the standpoint of the reader confined to Elinor's focalized domain, seems to be a projection of an actual future: "She saw them in an instant in their parsonage-house; saw in Lucy, the active, contriving manager, uniting at once a desire of smart appearance, with the utmost frugality, and ashamed to be suspected of half her economical practices. . . . In Edward—she knew not what she saw, nor what she wished to see;—happy or unhappy,—nothing pleased her; she turned away her head from every sketch of him" (Austen 1969, 347).

An excerpt from Eliot's *Daniel Deronda* illustrates a different form of virtual prolepsis. Here the heroine, Gwendolen Harleth, repeatedly projects alternate futures for herself: "Gwendolen . . . saw the life before her as an entrance into a penitentiary. Wild thoughts of running away to be an actress . . . came to her with the lure of freedom; . . . dimly she conceived herself getting amongst vulgar people who would treat her with rude familiarity" (Eliot 1967, 315–16). In comparison to Elinor's projection in *Sense and Sensibility*, Gwendolen's futures have a *clear virtual status* at the point where they are narrated. They are not, like Elinor's, the product of specific erroneous knowledge but the product of Gwendolen's general lack of orientation concerning her future life.

In a similar fashion, sophisticated past-world plotting can involve trips back into the past of the narrative world in which the ontological status of seemingly actual world versions is revised. Fielding's *Joseph Andrews* (1742), for example, juggles character relationships and identities in a complex temporal orchestration of the coincidence plot. At the beginning of the novel, Fielding's narrator represents Pamela and Joseph Andrews as the daughter and son of Gaffar and Gamma Andrews (1977, 40–41), while Fanny (with whom Joseph falls in love) is a foundling (65). In the novel's final recognition scenes, this past world and its kinship relations are subjected to multiple remodeling. First of all, a peddler provides a new account of Fanny's origins, from which it emerges that she too is the Andrewses' daughter (304–5). A further round of revelations then exposes this second, temporarily actual constellation (in which Fanny and Joseph seem, disastrously, to be siblings) as equally virtual when it is discovered that Joseph is not the Andrewses' son but was himself a foundling. In the novel's games with character relationships, Joseph and Fanny therefore go through several sets of virtual identities and origins before their final, actual identities and origin plots are bestowed upon them. In Fielding, however (in contrast to Austen and Eliot), the virtual worlds of the past are not created through focalization but through a combination of the narrator's reporting discourse and character dialogue.

The failure of the story-discourse approach to perceive the key role of alternate world versions is still evident in Jonathan Culler's (1981) deconstructive revision of the story-discourse model. Culler discusses Sophocles' *Oedipus the King*, a text that is highly relevant for this study, since it is the prototype of all disastrous coincidence plots. An analysis of what Culler's discussion overlooks highlights how ontological plotting can be used to understand the narrative dynamics of the recognition scene (Aristotle's *anagnorisis*) within the coincidence plot.[6] Culler suggests that instead of reading *Oedipus the King* as portraying Oedipus's discovery of a prior story (his birth as the son of Laius and Jocasta and his subsequent unwitting murder of the former and marriage to the latter), the play can be read as constructing a logic of argument that renders this *apparently prior* state of affairs an a posteriori construction of the discourse: "Oedipus becomes the murderer of his father not by a violent act that is brought to light but by bowing to the demands of narrative coherence and deeming the act to have taken place." Culler therefore reverses the causal relationship between the components of the story-discourse distinction: "Meaning is not the effect of a prior event but its cause" (1981, 174).

However, in describing the information coordination leading to Oedipus's discovery of his actual identity, Culler unwittingly highlights the multiple-world structure that is central to play's identity plot and that is in a state of ontological limbo prior to the central recognition scene in which Oedipus discovers his origins. Like many recognition scenes in the traditional coincidence plot, this involves the elevation of one possible version of the past to the status of a single actual world. Here the construction of Oedipus's kinship relations and true identity depends on which version of past events a messenger instates as the actual world: "Everything hangs on the testimony of this witness, whom they await" (Culler 1981, 173). However, in an ontologically sensitive analysis of the narrative dynamics of this scenario, we can rather say that in Oedipus's act of discovery, actuality is conferred on the most catastrophic version of past-world relationships: he has killed his father and married his mother.

The key point here is that Oedipus's discovery of the "facts" of his birth gains its narrative power through the competition for actuality with the alternate happier version of the past world in which Oedipus is *not* the son of Laius and Jocasta but truly a stranger. This narrative power is ultimately engendered by the (literally and metaphorically) blinding force of Oedipus's discovery that the world in which he has blithely believed himself to exist, with its system of normal human relationships, is a virtual construct. Instead, Oedipus finds himself in a new world with a *new identity* that (referring to the forms of causal plotting discussed in chapter 1) is the result of a transformed *causal-progenerative lineage*, in which he is at the center of the worst possible constellation of relationships (patricide and maternal incest) imaginable. The narrative power of recognition in this type of plot therefore has little to do with the relationship between story and discourse and much more to do with the pivotal position of the character experiencing recognition in a process which is the culminatory phase of the temporal orchestration of the alternate worlds of the plot. Recognition thus evokes an experience in which a character is, often traumatically, transferred from a world that he or she has hitherto considered to be actual and thrust into a new alien version of reality.

In such plots of coincidence, the question of *character identity* within changing ontological constellations is therefore central: multiple versions of identity are experienced *successively* by a character within the recognition plot. As the next section will show, counterfactuals also have a key component concerning character identity, but here multiple character identities are presented *concurrently* in different alternate worlds. This centrality of identity in the ontological configurations of the plots of coincidence and counterfactuality confirms Fauconnier and Turner's (2003, 6, 95–96) listing of "identity" as one of the "vital relations" of human thought, that is, as one of the key cognitive parameters with which the mind processes experience.

Counterfactual Worlds

In contrast to the examples discussed above, a counterfactual world is a *consciously virtual* alternate version of the past world constructed in a thought experiment that asks, "What would have happened if . . . ?" Again, the story-based concepts of analepsis or retrospection cannot properly describe the nature of the temporal movement involved in the creation of a counterfactual world, since counterfactuals do not simply return to the past: they alter the past and in doing so construct a new world, one whose ramifications can also create an altered present. While counterfactuals have not yet received sufficient focus in literary studies, they have been discussed extensively in possible-worlds theory (Goodman 1947; Lewis 1973; Rescher 1975) and have stimulated more recent work in the political, social, and cognitive sciences (e.g., Roese and Olson 1995c; Tetlock and Belkin 1996a; Turner 1996; Fauconnier and Turner 1998a, 2003). Examples of counterfactuals from narrative fiction were given in chapter 1 to illustrate how the plotting principle of causation is a key part of their cognitive structuring. The present chapter analyzes their ontological configuration in different genres of narrative fiction and describes the cognitive effects on the reader stemming from this ontological complexity.

Historical counterfactuals are constructed by proposing a hypothetical deviation from real-world history. This alteration often centers on what different conditions would have been necessary to produce an altered outcome in key historical events, such as Napoleon's defeat at Waterloo (Rescher 1975, 174; Fearon 1996, 55; Horne 2001). In narrative fiction the subgenre of alternate history frames similar questions within a fictional format. Thus, the prologue of Keith Roberts's *Pavane* (1966) contains a counterfactual exposition of sixteenth-century history articulated as fact and not as hypothesis: "On a warm July evening of the year 1588, in the royal palace of Greenwich, London, a woman lay dying, an assassin's bullets lodged in abdomen and chest. Her face was lined, her teeth [were] blackened, and death lent her no dignity; but her last breath started echoes that ran out to shake a hemisphere. For the Faery Queen, Elizabeth the First, paramount ruler of England, was no more" (1995, vii). This prologue serves as the historical antecedent to the novel's actional present, which is located in the historical consequent of the counterfactual—a less technologically advanced twentieth-century England that is still dominated by the culture of Catholicism. Here, therefore, the historical counterfactual is used to generate a complex narrative world. Furthermore, the hypothetical status of the counterfactual world is suppressed, and events are articulated as those of the *actual narrative world* for the whole duration of the text.

At the other end of the scale, what I propose to designate as autobiographical counterfactuals represent a different kind of thought experiment. Here a fictional subject reworks events in his or her own life and constructs a brief hypothetical narrative that is embedded into the actual narrative world. In contrast to the more detached speculation of counterfactual history, the altered world created by the autobiographical counterfactual touches the existential and experiential world of a single human being and can articulate a strong sense of missed opportunities. Thus, in the following dialogue from Hardy's *Tess of the d'Urbervilles*, Tess Durbeyfield and Angel Clare jointly construct an alternate autobiography in which they met and married earlier in their lives:

> "Why didn't you stay and love me when I—was sixteen; living with my little sisters and brother, and you danced on the green? . . . " . . .
> "Ah—why didn't I come!" he said. " . . . If I had only known!" (Hardy 1978, 261)

In practice, counterfactuals in narrative fiction can take a broad variety of forms that are located somewhere between the extensive historical frame and the transient embedded autobiographical sketch of the two examples cited above. Various types of biographical counterfactual can be articulated in narrative fiction either by one character speculating about another character's life trajectory or by a heterodiegetic narrator speculating on the possible alternate fates of characters.

The complex ontological structure of counterfactuals means that when used in narrative fiction they also play a key role in the assertion of a narrative world's actuality. A counterfactual can perform an important authenticating function in the realist tradition: character-counterfactual speculations like those by Tess and Angel cited above serve to strengthen the impression that the narrative world is "real" by constructing a further, contrastive "less real" sequence of events that reinforces the apparent reality of the narrative world by *ontological default*. The articulation of a counterfactual thus encourages the reader to think of the actual events in the narrative world as "real" in contradistinction to the "less real" counterfactual sequence. Notwithstanding the fact that theoretically (i.e., from the standpoint of the real world) Tess and Angel's factual and counterfactual love stories are both "fictional," the fact that the reader regards them as having a very different ontological status bears witness to the reality effect created by counterfactuals in fiction.

The same reality effect can be achieved by narratorial counterfactuals. In the following excerpt from an extensive counterfactualizing commentary, the narrator of Austen's *Mansfield Park* (1814) speculates how, if Henry Crawford had acted differently in the final stages of the novel, he might have won the heart of Fanny Price: "Had he done as he intended, and as he knew he ought, by going down to Everingham after his return from Portsmouth, he might have been deciding his own happy destiny" (Austen 1966, 451). The narrator's sense of disappointment in Henry suggests that he is an autonomous human being on the same ontological level as the narrator and not a fictional creation at all. This effect may, of course, be a calculated part of Austen's strategy of narrative realism or, equally, evidence of her own emotional engagement with her characters during the writing process.

Counterfactual events presented in alternate histories like Roberts's *Pavane*, on the other hand, invite the reader to perform a cognitively interesting act of doublethink. The reader will *consciously* view a counterfactual historical world (in which, say, Elizabeth I was assassinated in 1588 and as a result twentieth-century Britain is a Catholic nation) as counterfactual if mentally he remains on the ontological level of his true spatiotemporal coordinates. If, however, the reader crosses the boundary into the narrative world during reading and becomes immersed in the detailed fabric of the counterfactual twentieth-century world depicted in a text like *Pavane*, he will view it as the actual world and suppress its "historical fictionality."

Counterfactuality, Transworld Identity, and World Blending

Transworld identity has been a much-debated concept in possible-worlds theory. This debate concerns differing positions on the question of transworld identification, that is, to what extent is it possible to make connections between, for example, the historical Napoleon in the real world and the Napoleon of a counterfactual world in which he won the battle of Waterloo or invaded England (scenarios that are used both in possible-worlds theory and in an early alternate history like Edmund Lawrence's *It May Happen Yet* [1899]). Discussing transworld identity with reference to narrative fiction, Doležel claims that "fictional individuals are not dependent for their existence and properties on actual prototypes" (1988, 482–83).[7] This statement, however, is only valid in a noncognitive context, since the full enjoyment and effect of the reading experience of an alternate history about, for example, a counterfactual Napoleon lie in the reader's capacity to cross-reference the alternate Napoleon with his real-world original. Upon closer analysis, the question of identity in counterfactuals turns out to be more complex than has been appreciated by possible-worlds theory.[8]

In the philosophical possible-worlds literature, different terminological systems have been proposed to deal with transworld identity. Rescher (1975, 85–89) formulates his solution in a world-linking model. Different *versions* of "a single individual" can be located in different worlds: "Our theory leads to a position where one selfsame individual can reappear in different descriptive guises in different possible worlds. It accordingly becomes necessary to distinguish between two versions of what it is to be a 'single individual'" (Rescher 1975, 88). Lewis, on the other hand, takes a world-separatist position in observing that "'trans-world' identity in the truest sense—overlap of worlds—creates a disastrous problem about the accidental intrinsic properties of the alleged common parts"; he therefore advocates that "we . . . reject [the] overlap of worlds" (1986, 210). He also proposes a different terminology—counterpart theory: "The counterpart relation is our substitute for identity between things in different worlds. . . . Where some would say that you are in several worlds, in which you have somewhat different properties and somewhat different things happen to you, I prefer to say that you are in the actual world and no other, but you have counterparts in several other worlds" (Lewis 1983, 27–28). It should be noted that Lewis's resolute world-separatist approach is not in line with larger trends in theory. The "overlap of worlds" that causes such "a disastrous problem" from a philosophical perspective lies at the heart of much recent thinking in cultural and literary theory, from the juggling of worlds in postmodernist fiction (McHale 1987, 1992) through the foregrounding of the concept of hybridity in postcolonial studies to counter the monolithic and world-separatist versions of culture and identity proposed by (neo)colonial discourse (Bhabha 1994; Young 1995).

In the present context, too, the overlap of worlds and the dynamics of character identities across worlds play a substantial role in complex counterfactual narratives. In order to discuss this process, both Rescher's and Lewis's terms can be utilized. "Counterpart" can be used as a general term to refer to related entities across worlds, while Rescher's "version" can be used more specifically to refer to entities occupying different worlds who also have explicitly different characteristics, for example, in which a counterfactual character is presented as having a perceivable alteration in his or her psychological makeup or personality.[9] In connection with this, the term *real-world original* can be used to distinguish entities located in the real world from their counterparts or versions in fiction. Thus, the counterfactual Napoleon who invades Britain in *It May Happen Yet* has a counterpart *and* real-world original in the real world (the historical Napoleon). By contrast, the two versions of Henry Crawford in *Mansfield Park* are counterparts, but, unlike Napoleon, they have no real-world original (a counterpart in the real world beyond the text). In the following I will illustrate these terms by discussing some variations of transworld identity from narrative in order to illustrate cognitive processes that, I contend, are central to the analysis of character identity and fictional counterfactuals—transworld identification and transworld differentiation.

In some forms of minimal counterfactual world, only plot and not character is at issue because the alternate course of events depicted does not have any repercussions for the representation of the character concerned. For example, after his shipwreck, the eponymous hero of Defoe's *Robinson Crusoe* conceives of a counterfactual scenario in which things could have been even worse:

> Then it occurred to me again, how well I was furnished for my subsistence, and what would have been my case if it had not happened, *which was an hundred thousand to one*, that the ship floated from the place where she first struck and was driven so near to the shore that I had time to get all these things out of her. What would have been my case if I had been to have lived in the condition in which I at first came on shore, without necessaries of life, or necessaries to supply and secure them? Particularly, said I aloud (tho' to my self), what should I ha' done without a gun, without ammunition, without any tools to make any thing, or to work with, without clothes, bedding, a tent, or any manner of covering? (1965, 80–81)

The text constructs a counterfactual version of the initial stages of Crusoe's survival as a castaway but does not explicitly postulate any concomitant effect on his character. Although a strict possible-worlds theorist might claim that Crusoe has constructed a separate counterpart in a counterfactual world, this alternative Crusoe (the one who could rescue nothing from the shipwreck) is not in any way a recognizably different *version* of Crusoe himself—the difference lies only in the altered sequence of events initiated by the antecedent of the hypothetical change in the ultimate location of the ship in relation to the shore. In cognitive terms, therefore, nothing in the text prevents the reader from completely *identifying* the Robinson in the counterfactual scenario with his actual version in the novel. The nontheorizing reader will thus conceive of the counterfactual Robinson and his actual counterpart as the same fictional entity.

By contrast, in the counterfactual plotting of events by the narrator in Austen's *Mansfield Park* cited above, the creation of a different character version is actually the *prerequisite* of the counterfactual. In saying, "could he [Henry Crawford] have been satisfied with the conquest of one amiable woman's affections" (Austen 1966, 451), the narrator briefly constructs an altered version of Henry Crawford, one who is less rakish and more patient. Here, therefore, the brief counterfactual plot is actually generated through a character-based antecedent as opposed to the event-based one in *Robinson Crusoe*. Most importantly, the reader cannot perform automatic transworld identification between the Henry of the actual narrative world of *Mansfield Park* and his counterfactual counterpart in the way she can in *Robinson Crusoe*. There is an explicit *differentiation* by the narrator that the reader too must appreciate in order to follow the resulting causal-counterfactual line of plot development, that is, if Henry had had more self-control, he could have won Fanny's affection.

Counterfactual worlds in twentieth-century fiction create a whole new range of scenarios for games with transworld identity. Science fiction and fantasy texts generate a particularly rich landscape of alternatives precisely because, in terms of genre, they are located in a transitional realm between full realism and antirealism (metafiction). Thus, they use nonrealistic plots based on fantasy or fictional science to engender multiple worlds, but the principles of their characterization techniques remain realistic and differentiated. In texts using counterfactuals, this results in psychologically credible multiple character versions across worlds, and some texts describe "transworld journeys," in which counterparts from different worlds swap places or meet, thereby creating an interesting fictional literalization of the kind of "overlap of worlds" found so philosophically daunting by Lewis (1986).[10]

In Wyndham's story "Random Quest," a scientific experiment goes wrong, and the protagonist and narrator, Colin Trafford, finds himself transferred into a counterfactual version of the mid-twentieth century in which he occupies the body of an alternate version of himself. One of the main themes of the story is the nonidenticality of the two versions of Colin Trafford. As a result of a deviation in history somewhere in the 1920s, World War II and the consequent drive for technological innovation have not occurred, and so the counterfactual Trafford has become a novelist instead of a scientist. In the process he has (in comparison to the protagonist and narrator Trafford) also become not such a nice person: "[This] Colin Trafford looked like me ... But ... things on our different planes must have run differently for us. Environment, or experiences, had developed different qualities in him which, I have to think, lie latent in me.... I found the results somewhat painful, rather like continually glimpsing oneself in unexpected distorted mirrors" (Wyndham 1965, 160–61). The spice of the story is created by the contrast of the two versions of Trafford and the fact that Trafford the narrator must suffer for his counterpart's sins because no one in the counterfactual world is aware of his different identity.

Wyndham's story can, furthermore, be used to illustrate how the world-separatist approach to counterfactuals cannot capture the nature of the readerly processing of counterfactual plots and characters. As reported in the headlines of a counterfactual version of the *Daily Mail*, the events of the counterfactual version of the year 1954 make strange reading for the displaced Colin Trafford from the real-world 1954: "I turned to the middle page, and read: 'Disorders in Delhi. One of the greatest exhibitions of civil disobedience so far staged in India took place here today demanding the immediate release of Nehru from prison....' Then an item in an adjoining column caught my eye: 'In answer to a question from the Opposition front bench Mr Butler, the Prime Minister, assured the House that the Government was giving serious consideration—'" (Wyndham 1965, 144–45). The reading activity of the fictional character Colin Trafford, dislocated from his own real world, is equatable with that of a real-world reader of alternate history. For the full significance of the passage to be realized, the real reader, like the fictional Trafford, must have detailed knowledge of the real-world twentieth century. She will then be in a position to recognize names such as "Nehru" and "Butler" by accessing her real-world encyclopedic knowledge or "common frames" (Eco 1981) of twentieth-century history.

However, the cognitive dynamics here go beyond the automatic activation of previously stored knowledge. As Fauconnier and Turner (1998a) show, the counterfactual construct does not simply involve recognition but the creation of a unique new blend of worlds in which input is taken from a number of real-world "mental spaces." Through the specification of these real-world mental spaces and their new blend in the counterfactual space, it is possible to identify the "emergent structure"—Fauconnier and Turner's (1998a, 286) designation for the structural uniqueness and causal-imaginative implications of the new counterfactual world that is created out of aspects of the old. As Fauconnier and Turner state, the mental processes involved in world blending are "largely unconscious," so that "it seems easy, but it is in fact complex" (1998a, 287, see also 2003, 17–57).

Applied to the passage cited from "Random Quest," this produces the following breakdown of the stages of the reader's mental processing of its counterfactual propositions. The real-world reader recognizes that she comes from a world in which Nehru became prime minister of India as a result of that country's independence in 1947 and in which Rab Butler never became leader of the British Conservative Party or prime minister in postwar Britain. Notwithstanding the fact that this information is not contained in the text, only if the reader possesses this knowledge is she able to perceive the above events as counterfactual deviations from actual history and enjoy the text's full counterfactual-creative scope. Nehru is here patently not the same version as his real-world original, since he is languishing in prison. The Nehru of this text, however, is a blend of two "mental spaces" from real-world Indian history: the first input space is Nehru's acts of civil unrest against the British prior to Indian independence, which are here extended into the counterfactual space of 1954. The second real-world input space is Nehru's becoming prime minister of India as from 1947: while this fact is contradicted in the emergent counterfactual space (in which the imprisoned Nehru is patently not enjoying the privileges of prime minister), it is precisely because of its ironic contrast with the counterfactual scenario that it is a key input feature in the counterfactual construct that the reader is invited to entertain in her mind. Furthermore, the emergent structure of this counterfactual world of 1954 also involves a contradistinctive commentary on the real-world 1940s Indian scenario. This is made through the implicit causal reasoning that only by virtue of India's engagement in World War II did it achieve independence and Nehru become prime minister.

Similarly, the counterfactual scenario of Rab Butler as British prime minister in 1954 is constructed through the blending of input spaces involving the real-world Conservative leader and prime minister in 1954, Churchill, and the real-world Rab Butler, who, despite his ambitions, never actually became British prime minister. Here the emergent structure contains the causal inference that Churchill only became leader through the occurrence of World War II. It is highly interesting and indicative of the complexity of counterfactuals that the name Churchill does not even occur in the text. Nevertheless, alongside the failed political aspirations of the real-world Butler, the real-world premiership of Churchill is one of the most significant input spaces of this historical counterfactual, which the real-world reader must activate in order to understand the full permutations of the counterfactual scenario of Wyndham's story.

The above discussion therefore shows that a world-separatist possible-worlds framework is incapable of penetrating the cognitive dynamics of counterfactuals, which involve the *blending* and not the *separation* of worlds or "input spaces." For the contemporary real-world reader, therefore, the world blending that takes place in the reading of counterfactuals involves a dual process not only of *transworld identification* (the perception that the fictional Nehru and Butler have real-world counterparts) but also of simultaneous *transworld differentiation*: it is necessary to perceive the strategic differences between the input spaces in order to appreciate the emergent structure of the counterfactual world.

By contrast, the reader comprehends Colin Trafford's two different versions in the factual and counterfactual 1954s within a different frame of reference. While an understanding of the ramifications of the absence of World War II is necessary to comprehend the causal reasoning behind the different developmental biography of Trafford's counterfactual self, the reader cannot import any specific real-world space for the mental construction of Trafford himself because he is a fully fictional figure who only exists in the story's two worlds. Therefore, in terms of the cognitive operations necessary to read the text, the figures Nehru, Butler, and Trafford do not have ontological homogeneity. Trafford may seem like a real-world figure on the level of Nehru because he features in a narrative world that contains Nehru too. However, unlike Nehru, Trafford has no real-world original and thus no extratextual space from which the reader can, either identifying or differentiating, import information relating to him. Nehru, on the other hand, has an explicit counterfactual version in the text, an implicit fictional real-world counterpart in the fictional version of the real world that Trafford comes from, and also, on an extratextual level, a flesh-and-blood (as opposed to fictional paper) real-world original. Doležel's claim that "as non-actualized possibles, all fictional entities are ontologically homogeneous" (1988, 482–83) is thus hardly borne out by this example of a complex counterfactual scenario in narrative fiction.

A different type of transworld identity constellation, an *intertextual* or, to be more specific, an *interfigural* one (Müller 1991), splices the real world and the fully fictional in William Gibson and Bruce Sterling's *The Difference Engine* (1990), an alternate history of the nineteenth century. In addition to playfully remodeled versions of real-world figures (the prime minister of Britain is Lord Byron), this counterfactual world also contains Sybil Gerard, a character from the novel *Sybil* (1845) by Benjamin Disraeli, the real-world nineteenth-century prime minister. The Sybil of *The Difference Engine* can also be described as having a real-world original insofar as she is imported from a prior real-world text (*Sybil*) into a new fictional context; she is thus not as fully fictional as Colin Trafford, who has no original outside Wyndham's story. However, she only has a textual original as opposed to a flesh-and-blood one. To use Margolin's (1996) distinctions: Sybil has *intertextual* versions, whereas in Wyndham's story Colin Trafford has *intratextual* versions and Nehru has an *extratextual* original.

In comparison with the complicated identity configurations of the alternate history genre, transworld identity in the alternate worlds generated by the self-reflexive texts of experimental postmodernist fiction does not display the same degree of complexity in the creation of different character versions of transworld counterparts. This is probably one reason why the genre has not proved as interesting to the general reading public. Unlike their semirealistic science fiction counterparts, these antirealist texts exaggerate plot at the expense of character: characters are put through different plot versions, as, for example, in Coover's "The Babysitter," without the altered plots having any substantial effect on character in the way altered history has a crucial effect on character in a text like Wyndham's "Random Quest." This is clearly revealed in one of the most extreme examples of the form, the ending of B. S. Johnson's short story "Broad Thoughts from a Home" (1973), in which "the reader is offered a choice of endings to the piece" (1973, 110). In this concentrated excess of plot options there is absolutely no room for the development of varying character versions within the different alternatives:

Group One: The Religious. . . .

Group Two: The Mundane. (a) Samuel rapes Miss Deane in a state of unwonted elation. (b) Miss Deane rapes Samuel in a state of unwonted absentmindedness. (c) Robert rapes both of them in a state of unwonted aplomb. . . .

Group Three: The Impossible. The next post contains an urgent recall to England for (a) Samuel (b) Robert (c) both; on account of (i) death (ii) birth (iii) love (iv) work. (Johnson 1973, 110)

Neither is it even possible here to talk in terms of the actual versus the counterfactual, since no clear framework can be constructed to distinguish an ontological hierarchy—a concept that will now be considered in concluding this chapter.

Ontological Hierarchies in Realist and Other Fictions

Ontological hierarchy is a concept that can be defined as the system of relationships between alternate possible worlds that emerges in the process of the plot's development (subsequent to the ambiguities and complexities of temporal orchestration). The ontological hierarchies of realist and nonrealist narrative genres vary substantially. In conventional realist narrative, whatever forms of temporal orchestration may take place during the unfolding of the discourse, the final ontological hierarchy can only confer the status of actuality on one version of events. In many denouements, as in the example of Fielding's *Joseph Andrews* discussed above, the final actual world or authenticated story version achieves its narrative power and authoritative status precisely by displacing other potential versions and rising to the apex of the ontological hierarchy.[11]

Realist texts are single-world texts insofar as they do not allow more than one world to assume the level of actuality, notwithstanding the fact that they play games with alternate versions of that narrative world. The creation of ontological clarity is thus a particular feature of conventional realist texts: although *Robinson Crusoe* constructs counterfactual versions of reality and *Joseph Andrews* constructs multiple versions of the past, no more than one version of reality is given concurrent actual status. By contrast, the single-world alternate history, as represented by *Pavane*, constitutes a borderline case in which the multiple-world form is incipient but not yet manifest in the text itself. Cognitively, it may be seen as a multiple-world text because in order to understand it the reader must access real-world history to grasp its counterfactual frame. Ontologically, however, it is a single-world text in the realist tradition, since the counterfactual world is the text's only actual world.[12]

Semirealist and fully nonrealist texts, however, subvert the clear ontological hierarchies of realism by constructing permanently pluralistic multiple-world scenarios. Wyndham's "Random Quest" depicts two different world versions existing side by side without giving either ontological superiority. Nevertheless, in terms of both its characterization and—as seen in chapter 1—its use of causality, Wyndham's story is fundamentally realist. Johnson's "Broad Thoughts from a Home" drives the multiplication of worlds much farther: its closing section spawns multiple-event fragments in which there is no coherent system of worlds at all. The multiple-world structure of Gibson and Sterling's *The Difference Engine* is different again: no single world can emerge as actual in this novel amalgam of worlds that combines metafictional character importation and alternate history.

Key differences in ontological hierarchy also facilitate the distinction between counterfactuals and other forms of alternate world. A counterfactual involves a binary pair of events, the *factual* one and its hypothetical other—the *counter*-factual. The counterfactual is thus an alternate world that is viewed, with hindsight, as an ontologically subordinate event—something that *might* have been but was not. Conversely, possible versions of the future conceived of by a character, as seen in Gwendolen's future imaginings in *Daniel Deronda* cited above, do not contain a single dominant *factual* version that contrasts with less actual ones but simply represent a fan of as yet unrealized possibilities.[13] Likewise, the often bewildering effect of the narration of multiple contradictory versions of events in postmodernist experimental narrative, like that of Johnson, consists precisely in the fact that the reassuring ontological hierarchy of realism, in which only one narrated set of events is ultimately confirmed to be actual, is radically undermined. Here too the alternate worlds of the text do not fall into the clear binary structure of the counterfactual.

In an ontologically sensitive approach to narrative, the *story* therefore loses its exclusive position and becomes just one of the ontological levels of the plot, which is itself the dynamic sum of the alternate possible worlds generated by the text. Seen in this way, plot becomes something much more complex and multifaceted than a chronological story sequence or its anachronic inversion by the discourse (the two approaches that characterized structuralist plot analysis). The domain containing the events that actually occur in the narrative world—in contradistinction to those events that are narrated but prove to be virtual constructs—is thus the *actual narrative world*.[14] This concept clearly has affinities with the traditional structuralist "story" but no longer has that concept's dominant position and automatic emphasis on a single, unilinear chronology that is dechronologized by the discourse, its conceptual Other. In the multiple-world approach to plot, the actual narrative world's conceptual Other is not discourse (in the sense of the rearrangement of story chronology) but the larger, ontologically multifarious realm constituted by the alternate possible worlds generated by the text.

Only when viewed from the postclosure position of knowledge about the nature of *the* story can narrative temporality be defined in terms of a balanced equation between story and discourse, with story seen as "something which exists prior to and independently of narrative presentation and which narrative then reports" (Culler 1981, 171). Viewed in its nonfinalized state as experienced during reading, plot is an ontologically unstable, primordial mass of events and relationships out of which the story is gradually formed; plot is thus not so much a preexistent given (although the reader will ultimately view the actual narrative world as such) as (at least in the realist tradition) the gradual formation of one version from a variety of alternatives.

3. Spatial Plotting
Paths, Links, and Portals

The bodily experience of negotiating and perceiving space underlies many sense-making operations, including the comprehension of time. The negotiation of space is one of the first orientational steps in life any human being must undertake; this knowledge is used to make sense of or metaphorically "map" other experiences. Johnson (1987) and Turner (1991, 68–98) show how human language is structured metaphorically in terms of the bodily experience of space. In this chapter I wish to implement and expand some of Johnson's and Turner's proposals on two distinct levels. In the first section I deal with the metaphorical spatialization of time in narrative theory and in narrative fiction. Here I deal primarily with the representation of time as a path or line. As will be seen in both this chapter and chapter 5, the conceptualization of time as a linear-sequential structure, using spatial metaphors like the path and the fork, is a key means used in realist and semirealist texts to create a sense of the coherence of narrative time. In the second section the focus switches to the representation of space in narrative fiction. I propose a cognitive model for the investigation of the historical development of the fictional depiction of space and illustrate it using examples from the coincidence plot that show how these schemata play a key role in creating narrative immersion. While the predominant tendency in other analyses of fictional space and related issues (Stanzel's [1984] concept of a/perspectivism, Frank's [1945] "spatial form") is to perceive modernism as the key historical moment of change in spatial representation, I show how the analysis of specific spatial schemata in the representation of fictional space produces a more detailed diachronic map.

The Spatial Mapping of Time and Narrative
Time Is a Path

Time is so unfathomable and elusive that the human mind often resorts to the more concrete parameters of space to grasp it. This is true both for theoretical models of narrative, including time and plot, and for the general conceptualization of time.[1] Johnson (1987) explores the cognitive basis for spatial mappings of nonspatial phenomena. In place of theoretical attempts to separate the human spheres of mind and body, bodily experience and mental processes should be seen as inextricably linked: "Imaginative projection is a principle [*sic*] means by which the body (i.e. physical experience and its structures) works its way up into the mind (i.e. mental operations). . . . [A]s animals we have bodies connected to the natural world, such that our consciousness and rationality are tied to our . . . interactions with our environment. Our embodiment is essential to who we are, to what meaning is" (Johnson 1987, xxxvi, xxxviii).

One key manifestation of the geographical contours of bodily experience described by Johnson concerns the interrelated schemata of the *path* and the *link*. On paths Johnson writes: "Our lives are filled with paths that connect up our spatial world. There is the path from your bed to the bathroom[,] . . . from San Francisco to Los Angeles, from the Earth to the Moon. Some of these paths involve the actual physical surface that you transverse, such as the path from your house to the store" (1987, 113). Human beings "can impose directionality on a path" because they "have purposes in traversing paths" (114). Moreover, there is a linear-temporal component inherent in the idea of movement along a path: "Paths can also have temporal dimensions mapped onto them. I start at point A (the source) at time T_1 and move to point B (the goal) at time T_2. In this way, there is a timeline mapped onto the path. . . . Such a linear spatialization of time gives rise to one important way we understand temporality" (114).

Johnson (1987, 117–19) explores the schema of the *link* as related to the path but with much broader connotations. Links can be as basic as that "to our biological mothers by umbilical cords" (117), while they also play a role in the causal conceptualization of time: "As the child develops it learns to experience *temporal connections*. Event A is linked to event B by a series of temporally interceding events. . . . we can experience causal relatedness between temporally linked events" (118). Links can also be conceptualized as "*genetic connections*" and also "make . . . possible our perception of similarity. Two or more objects are similar because they share some feature or features. Those shared features are their cognitive links in our understanding" (118–19).

The concept of the *link* in particular, therefore, represents a spatially emphasized formulation of all the sense-making patterns already considered in chapter 1 under the term *plotting principle*. The key cognitive parameters considered there—sequential causality, biological lineage, and similarity—all have vertical or lateral linking patterns. The *link* schema is thus the most widely applied cognitive framework of all, since the process of sense making in all forms involves the construction of connections.

The spatial metaphor of the link therefore creates a sense of *cohesion*. This cohesive function can be seen in the two cognitive metaphors *time is a path* and *life is a journey*. These metaphors construct an interconnected map of individual points in time in a person's life. Indeed, in citing examples from the Bible, Dante's *Divine Comedy*, Shakespeare's *Macbeth*, and Bunyan's *Pilgrim's Progress*, George Lakoff and Mark Turner conclude: "The life-as-a-journey metaphor is so taken for granted in the Judeo-Christian tradition that we instantly understand that God is a guide, that there are alternative paths of good and evil through life, and that death hangs over us throughout" (1989, 10). The following sections explore several permutations of the metaphors *life is a journey* and *time is a path* in both narrative theory and narrative fiction.

Reading Is a Journey

This spatial metaphor was in fact already applied in the discussion of readerly immersion in chapter 1. The concept of immersion sees the time spent reading not as stationary mental activity but as movement in space. The idea that reading is the cognitive simulation of ontological liberation discussed in chapter 1 describes a process in which, freed by the text, the reader's mind relocates itself into the fictional world. In constructing a mental world out of the words on the pages of a book, the reader experiences a form of release or escape from the real world. Indeed, the *reading is a journey* metaphor is a cogent explanation as to why the fiction market is so successful: it offers readers a holiday from the real world—holidays to places not listed at the local travel agency.

Woody Allen's short story "The Kugelmass Episode" (1977), in which a college professor is actually transported to the world of Gustave Flaubert's *Madame Bovary* (1857) by a machine, is a literal enactment of *reading is a journey*. The same metaphor can be found in J. R. R. Tolkien's (1988) description of the effect of reading fantasy literature, which he saw as offering an escape from what he called the "Primary World" (the real world) into a "Secondary World." In Nell's (1988) metaphor for the pleasurable experience of reading—being "lost" in a book—the journey metaphor becomes even stronger, for what contented holiday maker has not had fantasies of being lost or cut off while on vacation and thus prevented from returning to everyday reality?

Paths and Links in the Mapping of Coincidence and Counterfactuality

In the theoretical mapping of narrative time and plot structure, the *path* and the *link* both play a key role. They can be combined with each other to capture the bold essentials of a particular plot, involving relationships in space and time, and between characters. The plots of coincidence and counterfactuality involve the contrastive spatiometaphorical mapping of convergence versus divergence.

Thus, the coincidence plot can be graphically mapped as a meeting of paths in space and time, whereas counterfactuality can be configured in the depiction of branching paths.

3. The Essential Structure of the Coincidental Encounter within the Traditional Coincidence Plot

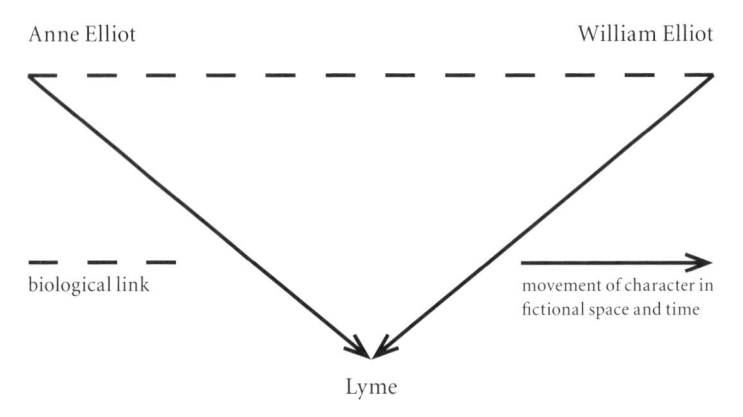

```
Anne Elliot                                William Elliot
    ╲   ─ ─ ─ ─ ─ ─ ─ ─ ─ ─ ─ ─ ─ ─ ─ ─ ╱
     ╲                                 ╱
      ╲                               ╱
       ╲                             ╱
        ╲                           ╱
   ─ ─ ─ ╲                         ╱  ───────▶
 biological link                      movement of character in
                ╲               ╱     fictional space and time
                 ╲             ╱
                  ▼           ▼
                      Lyme
```

The map of the structure of a coincidental encounter in figure 3 uses the example of Anne Elliot's encounter with her (as yet unrecognized) cousin William Elliot on the street in Lyme in Jane Austen's *Persuasion* (1818). The dotted line represents the *biological link* between the two characters and thus expresses the key component—the fact that the characters must have some kind of former relationship in order that their meeting be not a mundane but a remarkable occurrence. The lines with direction arrows describe the characters' separate trajectories toward the moment of spatial and temporal intersection in Lyme.

Counterfactuality and other forms of alternate world construction can also be mapped in terms of the *time is a path* model. Here, however, the paths do not represent those of individual characters but the alternate courses of events on different ontological levels. Ryan (1991) introduced this method of mapping the events of a narrative plot by distinguishing between virtual and actual branches of time.[2] Figure 4 maps the one actual and two virtual courses of events created by embedded counterfactual speculations in the closing chapters of Austen's *Mansfield Park*. In the actual course of events, Edmund eventually marries Fanny; in a counterfactual constructed by Mary Crawford, Fanny accepts Henry's proposal of marriage, which in turn leads to the marriage of Edmund and Mary; in a counterfactual constructed by the narrator herself, the deviation from actuality comes later and centers on Henry's not remaining in London to flirt and then elope with Mrs. Rushworth.

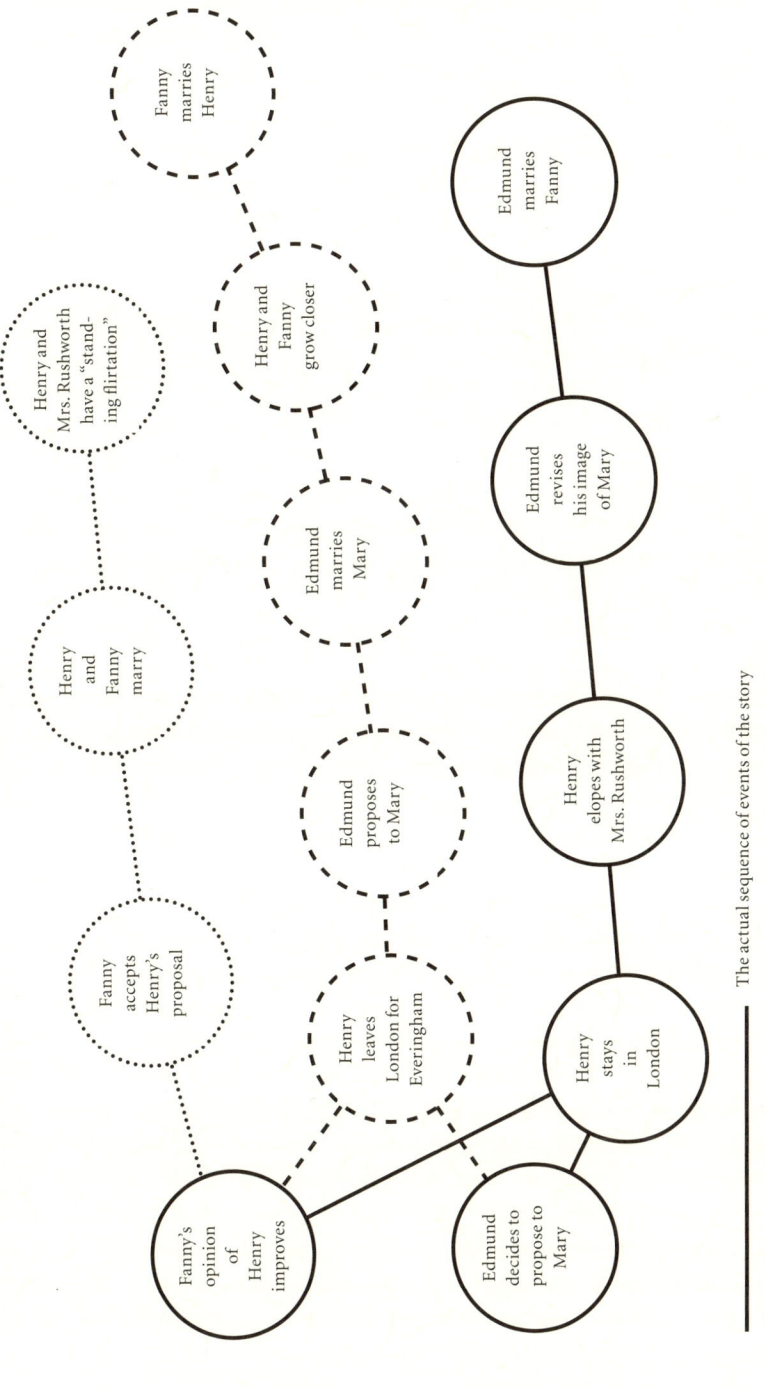

4. Actual and Counterfactual Paths of Time in Austen's *Mansfield Park*

- Henry marries Fanny
- Henry and Mrs. Rushworth have a "standing flirtation"
- Henry and Fanny grow closer
- Henry and Fanny marry
- Edmund marries Mary
- Edmund marries Fanny
- Fanny accepts Henry's proposal
- Edmund proposes to Mary
- Edmund revises his image of Mary
- Henry leaves London for Everingham
- Henry elopes with Mrs. Rushworth
- Fanny's opinion of Henry improves
- Henry stays in London
- Edmund decides to propose to Mary

——— The actual sequence of events of the story
·········· Counterfactual sequence constructed by Mary in chapter 47
— — — Detailed counterfactual-causal steps outlined by narrator in chapter 48

5. Multiple Actual Worlds and the Transworld Journey of the Protagonist in De Camp's "The Wheels of If"

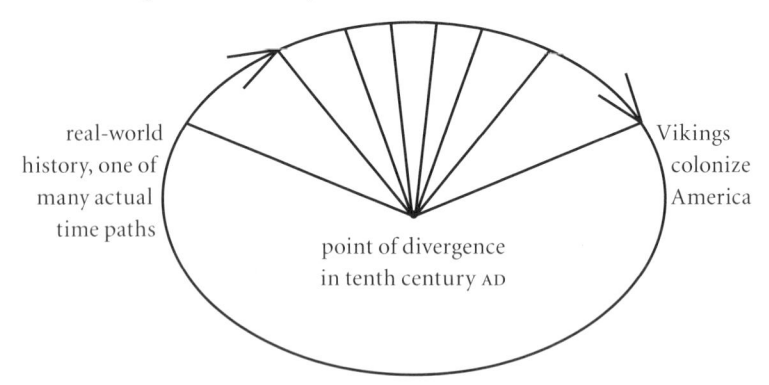

real-world history, one of many actual time paths

Vikings colonize America

point of divergence in tenth century AD

In twentieth-century science fiction, freedom from the constraints of the ontological hierarchy of realism leads to multiple actual paths of time, as in De Camp's story "The Wheels of If," which contains eight different equally actual versions of history existing side by side in a universe that is conceived of, as the story's title indicates, as having a wheel-like structure. In figure 5 the directionality arrow is not used to highlight the passage of time in any one of the alternate worlds but to represent the "sideways" movement taken by the protagonist, who comes adrift from his own particular world and undergoes a transworld journey, successively switching time paths and temporarily inhabiting the bodies of seven alternate versions of himself. In the ontological system of De Camp's story, all worlds are equally actual in that they are conceived of as simultaneously coexisting branches of time. Notably, the closed wheel structure of time constructed by this text is also characteristic of the semirealist genre of science fiction: the narrative universe is closed and coherent as opposed to being enigmatic and fragmentary like the worlds of postmodernist fictions.

It would, of course, also be possible to generate more complex multidimensional maps of the coincidence plot's interweaving of the virtual and the actual in narrative configurations where temporal orchestration creates multiple versions of past-world character relationships and identities, as in Sophocles' *Oedipus the King*, Fielding's *Joseph Andrews*, and Dickens's *Great Expectations*.

The Path and Fork Metaphors in the Mapping of Alternatives

In the diagrams for *Mansfield Park* and "The Wheels of If," the point at which events in the counterfactual world deviate from the factual world is represented spatially as a fork at which two paths diverge. However, the conceptualization of multiple versions of events as branching paths in time is not limited to the theoretical analysis of plot—it also occurs widely in fiction. The fork metaphor is sometimes used to describe two different stages of a decision-making process. In the first stage a character contemplates two (or more) as yet unactualized future alternatives represented by the fork metaphor, which expresses the idea that *decisions are junctions in the road*. Later, when the decision has been made, the unactualized path of the fork becomes a counterfactual branch of "what might have been," now contemplated by the character located on the other actualized path. Robert Frost's poem "The Road Not Taken" (1916) (discussed by Lakoff and Turner [1989, 3] as an example of the *life is a journey* metaphor) describes decision making in life as "Two roads [that] diverged in a yellow wood" (1969, 105). The poem closes with the speaker expressing the realization that much later in life he will look back "with a sigh" because he knows his choice of paths in life will have "made all the difference" (105). The poem's key implication is that whatever choice is made in life, the unactualized counterfactual branch will always, in retrospect, look a little greener in contrast to the path of life actually chosen and experienced.

Three examples from narrative fiction illustrate various uses of the *time is a path* metaphor. In chapter 20 of Sir Walter Scott's *The Bride of Lammermoor* (1819), Ravenswood, the novel's hero, is depicted deliberating whether to give up his romantic interest in Lucy Ashton immediately before he comes to a forking pathway in a wood:

> Ravenswood . . . saw himself at once in the very dilemma which he had for some time felt apprehensive he might be placed in. . . . [H]is honour now required he should take an instant leave of Ravenswood Castle, or become a suitor of Lucy Ashton. . . . "I wish her well," he said to himself, ". . . but I will never—no, never see her more!"
>
> With one bitter pang he adopted this resolution, just as he came to where two paths parted; the one to the Mermaiden's Fountain, where he knew Lucy waited him, the other leading to the castle by another and more circuitous road. He paused an instant when about to take the latter path . . . when young Henry [Lucy's brother] came flying up to him, half out of breath—"Master, Master, you must give Lucy your arm back to the castle, for I cannot give her mine. . . ." . . . And having thus satisfied himself that he was taking not only a wise, but an absolutely necessary step, he took the path to the fatal fountain. (Scott 1991, 204–5)

Ravenswood's internal decision-making processes are reproduced in the spatiality of the forking-path setting: one road literally leads to Lucy, the subject of his dilemma. Lucy's brother then coincidentally appears and influences Ravenswood's choice of paths and thereby the whole story of the novel. The fountain is "fatal" because, far from severing the romantic connection between Ravenswood and Lucy, this meeting cements it. The foreshadowing of future events by the narrator with the adjective "fatal" therefore constructs a causal-progenerative path of time that proleptically creates a *link* between Ravenswood's decision to take the path to Lucy and ensuing events leading to both their deaths.

In Eliot's *Daniel Deronda* the crucial phase in which Gwendolen Harleth must decide whether to accept Grandcourt's proposal of marriage is described in terms of the spatial imagery of *life is a journey*. At a decisive point in their conversation, before she agrees to marry Grandcourt, the narrator comments that "she was conscious of being at the turning of the ways" (Eliot 1967, 347). Subsequently, the narrative emphasizes both the irrevocability of Gwendolen's decision and the fact that from the current temporal perspective her future with Grandcourt still looks promising by using the spatial metaphor of forward movement down a path: "She who had been used to feel sure of herself, and ready to manage others, had just taken a decisive *step* which she had beforehand thought that she would not take—nay, perhaps, was bound not to take. She could not *go backward* now; she liked a great deal of *what lay before her*; and there was nothing for her to like if she *went back*" (Eliot 1967, 355, emphasis added). The repeated metaphors of movement across and contemplation of a terrain now metaphorically enact the consequences of Gwendolen's decision as a walk across a terrain on the path she has chosen.

Similarly but on a metatextual level, the "Author's Note" that prefaces Joseph Conrad's *Chance* (1913) uses the same form of metaphor to describe the author's deliberations about which way he should let his plot develop. Here the creation of narrative is itself described as a boat journey on the path of a stream: "Starting impetuously like a sanguine oarsman setting forth in the early morning I came very soon to a *fork* in the stream and found it necessary to pause and reflect seriously upon the direction I would take. Either presents to me equal fascinations, at least on the surface, and for that very reason my hesitation extended many days. I floated in the calm water of a pleasant speculation, between the *diverging* currents of conflicting impulses" (Conrad 1974, 9, emphasis added).

All the above examples (which conform to the ontological hierarchy of realism, in which only one world can be actual) follow this pattern in only seeing one path as actualizable, whether by a character, as in Scott and Eliot, or by the author himself, as in Conrad. Similarly, on a theoretical level Turner discusses the use of the forking-path schema to represent life's alternatives in terms of real-world ontology: "Metaphorically, meeting a fork corresponds to coming upon alternatives. But the fixity of the fork does not map onto the fixity of the alternatives. . . . We cannot take a step back and be again at the metaphoric fork in the road, *because the fork does not exist anymore*" (1991, 273). Semirealistic and antirealist texts, however, create their plots precisely through the abandonment of such real-world constraints. In spatial terms the subversion of the real-world ontological hierarchy involves creating metaphors of time as *a system of multiple actual forking pathways*. The ontological systems of such fictional worlds are constructed so that no event is irrevocable: the fork is deemed to exist even after an event has occurred or a decision has been made. Consequently, the spatial metaphor of time as a *forking* or *branching* system of pathways occurs frequently in such texts. Jack Williamson's groundbreaking pulp time-war novel *The Legion of Time* (1938) is full of such metaphors, generally used in the characters' dialogue to expound on the ontological principles of his fictional world, in which two different potential versions of the future do battle to decide which version will become actual history. In the following passage the pathway metaphor used is that of a corridor illuminated by time and consciousness: "The world is a *long corridor*, from the beginning of existence to the end. Events are groups in a sculptured frieze that runs endlessly along the walls. And time is a lantern carried steadily through the hall, to illuminate the groups one by one. ... Again and again the corridor *branches*, for it is the museum of all that is possible. The bearer of the lantern may take one *turning*, or another" (Williamson 1952, 22, emphasis added).

The ontological system of Williamson's novel still contains vestiges of the single-world realist hierarchy, since the lantern bearer may only take one turning. Later science fiction narratives depicting advanced technological interference in the flow of time move farther away from real-world constraints. In Isaac Asimov's *The End of Eternity* time-traveling custodians of time routinely calculate the right place in history to strategically intervene and create a new sequence that improves on the previously actual version of history. Thus, Andrew Harlan, a "Technician," calculates that merely "a jammed vehicle clutch would supply the necessary *fork*" to create a desirable "Reality Change" in which a new causal sequence would prevent a war in the 224th century (Asimov 1959, 32–33, emphasis added).

Three years after the publication of Williamson's *The Legion of Time* in 1938, Jorge Luis Borges's "The Garden of Forking Paths" was first published in Spanish. These nearly parallel publications indicate that at this point, in incipient postmodernist culture, a conceptual breakthrough occurred concerning the idea of multiple branching paths of time. Borges drives the same conceptual schema to absurd extremes in his story, which completely explodes not only the ontological hierarchy of realism but also the principle that no literary work is complete (Doležel 1988), by conceiving of a book that contains infinite alternate versions of a story. Over a decade later the same idea infected theoretical physics in the form of the publication of Hugh Everett's (1957) many-worlds interpretation of quantum theory.

The Cognitive Schemata of Bodily Orientation in Fictional Space

The previous section considered the role of a cluster of related spatially based cognitive schemata (paths and links) in the metaphorical expression of the experience of time. This section focuses on the depiction of fictional space by analyzing fiction's use of a number of key schemata shaping the bodily experience of space. Ryan (2001) makes the key distinction between temporal and spatial immersion. Accordingly, whereas chapter 1 of this study described how the immersive text "captures" the reader within the fictional world by preoccupying his mind with aspects of that world's temporality, the following section shows how immersion is created by taking the reader on a mental exploration of the fictional space of the narrative world.

Narrativity has traditionally been defined with reference to temporality, in contradistinction to the spatial arts. However, as David Herman observes, "spatial reference [is] not an optional or peripheral feature of stories, but rather a core property that helps *constitute* narrative domains" (2002, 296). Diachronically oriented studies, notably Joseph Frank's (1945, 1963) concept of spatial form and Franz Stanzel's (1984) work on a/perspectivism, have pinpointed the spatial dimension as an emergent force in the development of narrative. While their approaches are different, the results in diachronic terms are similar: modernism is viewed as the major watershed in the innovative representation of space in art. Other critics have located the advent of spatial innovation at slightly earlier points in narrative history; in particular, there have been contradictory findings regarding innovative spatialization in the work of Dickens.[3]

In his discussion of "spatial form," Frank observes how several simultaneous events are depicted in *Madame Bovary*: Flaubert "dissolves sequence by cutting back and forth between the various levels of action in a slowly rising crescendo. ... [T]he time-flow of narrative is halted" (1963, 15). Frank also calls this method "cinematographic" (14), and other critics have drawn attention to related techniques in the narrative depiction of space. David Lodge (1981) discusses what he sees as innovative cinematic techniques, including the technique of zooming in, in the novels of Thomas Hardy. W. J. Harvey (1965, 95) moves farther back historically to pinpoint cinematic effects in Dickens's *Bleak House* (1853) (see also Chatman 1978, 96–107), whereas Stanzel (1984), using the concept of perspectivism versus aperspectivism, rules Dickens out as innovative in the depiction of space, asserting modernist texts, notably James Joyce's *Portrait of the Artist as a Young Man* (1914–15), as the initiators of spatial innovation. Stanzel's approach centers on the text's ability to map a fully fleshed out spatial environment that creates perspective by setting up clear spatial relationships between objects so that "a graphic sketch might be made of it" (1984, 120; for more detailed work on such "cognitive maps" see Ryan 2001, 123–27, 2003). In the Joyce text, Stanzel finds, perspectivism is achieved through the representation of space via the focalizing consciousness of Stephen, whereas a scene narrated by Esther Summerson in *Bleak House* is found to be all but lacking in spatial description. By contrast, Harvey (1965) points to innovative cinematic techniques in the heterodiegetic narration of *Bleak House*.[4]

A cognitively oriented evaluation of the representation of fictional space produces yet a different account of patterns of innovation. If we see the fictional space into which the immersed reader is transported as a complex virtual world with, if the immersive process is to be a deep one, substantial simulation of real-world components, then we should examine the ability of narrative texts to re-create the schemata of real-world orientation learned and performed by the human mind/body in its cognitive interaction with space. In the following I outline the parameters for such an analysis and then examine a selection of texts for their use of the schemata of bodily orientation in space.

The work of Johnson (1987) and Turner (1991, 1992) provides the basis for such a cognitive exploration of fictional space. Turner provides a succinct description of the basic range of image schemas used in cognitive operations based in spatial experience: "Many of our most important and pervasive image-schemas are those underlying our bodily sense of spatiality. They include our image-schema of verticality, of a path leading from a source to a goal, of forward motion, of a container[,] . . . of such orientations as up/down, front/back, and center/periphery. . . . When we understand a scene, we naturally structure it in terms of such elementary image-schemas" (1992, 728, see also 1991, 171).

An image schema is "a recurring, dynamic pattern of our perceptual interactions and motor programs that gives coherence and structure to our experience" (Johnson 1987, xiv), or, more simply, an "extremely skeletal image[s] which we use in cognitive operations" (Turner 1992, 728). Image schemata are thus basic patterns or sketches stored in the brain that are fleshed out into "'rich' images" (Johnson 1987, 24) in specific situations of vision and cognition, both in bodily orientation in the physical world and in "metaphorical projections" (Johnson 1987, xiv) that map these schemata onto other contexts, as in the case of the *time is a path* metaphor discussed above.

The following image schemata arising from the "orientational feats" (Johnson 1987, 30) performed by the human body in the normal real-world spatial environment are of particular relevance for the exploration of the simulation of space in the narrative texts examined further below.[5]

> 1. Containment-boundedness (in-out). This schema is used to evoke surfaces as walls containing or enveloping further areas of space and their contents: "Our encounter with containment and boundedness is one of the most pervasive features of our bodily experience. . . . We move in and

out of rooms, clothes, vehicles, and numerous kinds of bounded spaces" (Johnson 1987, 21). In narrative fiction the container schema often involves the depiction of rooms, interiors, and other walled structures.
2. Paths (from-to) and links. The path schema involves directionality and purpose, whereas the link is a line only suggesting connection.
3. Center-periphery (inner-outer). "Our world radiates out from *our bodies* as perceptual centers from which we see, hear, touch, taste, and smell our world" (Johnson 1987, 124); notably, this image schema can also occur in combination with the container schema (Johnson 1987, 125).
4. Verticality (up-down). "We grasp this structure of verticality repeatedly in thousands of perceptions and activities we experience every day, such as perceiving a tree, our felt sense of standing upright, the activity of climbing stairs" (Johnson 1987, xiv).
5. Horizontality. This is a more literally spatial formulation of the balance schema, which is the primary focus in the cognitive literature (Johnson 1987, 74); as such it forms a complementary schema to that of verticality. Balance, indeed, is something we often learn with outstretched arms, that is, by transforming the primarily vertical form of our bodies into something more horizontal.
6. Portal or window. I propose that the portal or window, while not discussed by Johnson, is a major schema that occurs in combination with the container schema. Johnson writes of the container schema: "The most experientially salient sense of boundedness seems to be that of three-dimensional containment (i.e., being limited or held within some three-dimensional enclosure, such as a womb, a crib or a room)" (1987, 21–22); surely, therefore, the experience of such three-dimensionality is most acute when portals or windows exist through which interiors and exteriors can be simultaneously perceived. Windows and portals, as breaks or gaps in containers through which people can look or pass through, respectively, therefore have a key function in our experience of the three-dimensionality of space. In narrative fiction, the motif of the doorway to another world has also long been one of the most evocative means of suggesting escape, from Romanticism through science fiction and fantasy (see Dannenberg 2007).[6]

Spatialization in Narrative Fiction

The examples illustrating the use of spatial schemata discussed below all occur in conjunction with the depiction of recognition scenes within the coincidence plot (the scene in which characters with a previous relationship recognize each other's true identity). The observation of the narrative depiction of space is particularly well suited to such scenes because recognition frequently involves both a character's perception of and movement within space. The ubiquity of the coincidence plot thus enables us to take a diachronic field trip to illustrate theoretical parameters and in doing so chart key points in the development of spatial depiction in narrative fiction.

Four key progressions in style and strategy emerge with regard to the representation of fictional space:

1. Three-dimensionalization involving, in particular, the combined use of container-window-portal schemata in order to create a concrete and detailed environment in tandem with the depiction of the cognitive process of recognition (exemplified by Sir Philip Sidney's *New Arcadia* [1590], Charlotte Brontë's *Villette* [1853], and Charles Dickens's *Martin Chuzzlewit* [1843-44]).
2. Omission of the spatial environment to focus entirely on character response and emotions (exemplified by Jane Austen's *Persuasion* [1818]).
3. Modernist sublimination of the spatial environment to focus on character and movement as opposed to depicting a concrete spatial backdrop (exemplified by Ford Madox Ford's *The Good Soldier* [1915]).
4. Physiognomical spatialization, in which the face of a character is perceived as a detailed terrain by a homodiegetic narrator (exemplified by Jeanette Winterson's *The Passion* [1987] and Paul Auster's *Moon Palace* [1989]).[7]

The resulting analysis of the use of cognitive schemata in the presentation of fictional space thus contains a substantially more diversified map of historical development than those previous studies that have tended to perceive modernism as the key site of change.

Sidney's two *Arcadia* versions provide an early example of technical development within the work of one writer. Both *The Old Arcadia* and *The New Arcadia* contain examples of the coincidence plot. However, most of these examples are not represented scenically as recognition scenes but simply reported in cursory fashion. Such nonspatialized representation can be exemplified by the following passage from *The New Arcadia*, in which Pyrocles coincidentally encounters a minor character called Pamphilus: "So began our foot-fight, in such sort that we were well entered to blood of both sides, when there comes by that unconstant Pamphilus whom I had delivered (easy to be known, for he was barefaced), with a dozen armed men after him" (Sidney 1987, 242). Here only the clause in parentheses contains a rudimentary description of the recognition process, but there is no spatial backdrop to the meeting.

There is, however, one passage in *The New Arcadia* that represents recognition in a much more extended and scenic fashion. This concerns a recognition scene between the novel's two heroes, Pyrocles and Musidorus; Musidorus does not recognize Pyrocles immediately because the latter is disguised as an Amazon:

> [Musidorus] lying under the protection of a shady tree... saw a sight which persuaded, and obtained of his eyes, that they would abide yet awhile open.
>
> It was the appearing of a lady, who, because she walked with her side toward him, he could not perfectly see her face... [there follows a long description of the lady's attire].
>
> But this lady walked outright till he might see her enter into a fine, close arbour. It was of trees whose branches so lovingly interlaced one the other that it could resist the strongest violence of eyesight. But she went into it by a door she opened—which moved him as warily as he could to follow her; and by and by he might hear her sing this song... [the song follows].
>
> The ditty gave him some suspicion, but the voice gave him almost assurance who the singer was. And therefore boldly thrusting open the door and entering into the arbour, he perceived indeed that it was Pyrocles thus disguised. (Sidney 1987, 68–70)

While the depiction of the cognitive processes of recognition is, in accordance with the general trends in Renaissance fiction, still underdeveloped, spatial presentation in this scene is sophisticated. The tree under which Musidorus lies is established using both *vertical* and *horizontal* image schemata, verticality being first evoked by the word "tree," while the adjective "shady" suggests the horizontal schema of spreading branches. The description of Musidorus's inability to perceive the lady's face "because she walked with her side toward him," while not evoking any detailed image schema beyond the basic verticality of a human form walking by, is in fact a mild example of Stanzel's perspectivism (which he [1984, 118] attributes to the innovations of modernism) because it sketches physical relationships between two characters and portrays the limitations in Musidorus's field of vision due to his relative position.

It is, however, the depiction of the arbor of trees that establishes the center of this text's strong spatiality. The "fine, close arbour" of "trees whose branches so lovingly interlaced one the other" evokes an intense visual rendition of the *link* schema, so that the arbor is transformed into a *container* schema because the interlinking branches create a dense wall. The lady's disappearance into the arbor "by a door she opened" uses the *portal* schema to establish the three-dimensionality of the container while preserving an external view of it. Finally, the description of Musidorus "boldly thrusting open the door and entering into the arbour" and his recognition of Pyrocles takes us into the container, moving us from one space to another, thus truly rendering the experience of three-dimensionality. When Musidorus penetrates through the door, the wall of the *container*, previously depicted from the outside, now becomes a *peripheral* wall disclosing the *center* of the arbor, where recognition takes place. Moreover, the description of Musidorus following the as yet unknown "lady," first visually and then literally, traces the additional schema of the *path*, which is implicitly traced across the fictional landscape. The spatial description in Sidney's text therefore combines a great number of image schemata to create a bold and immersive visual impression of movement and perception within fictional space.

The passage above is evidence of Sidney's innovative contribution to Renaissance fiction and is significant in the overall context of narrative fiction: such a substantial three-dimensionalization of fictional space is by no means automatic in recognition scenes in subsequent texts. Authors as various as Smollett and Austen do without spatial detail in their depictions of recognition because they focus on the depiction of character sentiment and cognition. In Austen's *Persuasion*, for example, the recognition scene between Anne and her cousin William contains a description of character reaction including facial expression but absolutely no concrete spatial backdrop: "Anne drew a little back, while the others received his [William Elliot's] compliments.... Anne, smiling and blushing, very becomingly shewed to Mr Elliot the pretty features which he had by no means forgotten, and instantly saw, with amusement at his little start of surprise, that he had not been at all aware of who she was. He looked completely astonished, but not more astonished than pleased; his eyes brightened" (Austen 1965, 156).

Examples from two nineteenth-century authors, however, reveal a sophisticated use of spatial image schemata. The following example from Dickens's *Martin Chuzzlewit* shows how the containment schema and the resulting variations in character perception can be used to create narrative suspense in a scene involving staggered recognition. In this scene young Martin Chuzzlewit coincidentally reencounters an old and unloved acquaintance, Montague Tigg, at a London pawnbroker's. Recognition is delayed because both characters are confined within separate booths:

> Entering by a side-door in a court... [Martin] passed into one of a series of little closets, or private boxes, erected for the accommodation of the more bashful and uninitiated customers. He bolted himself in; pulled out his watch; and laid it on the counter.
> "Upon my life and soul!" said a low voice in the next box....
> Martin drew back involuntarily, for he knew the voice at once. (Dickens 1968, 280)

Moving with him through the door (*portal*) into the pawnbroker's shop, the reader then shares Martin's experience of *containment* as confinement (i.e., containment without a window or portal outward to the exterior) in the box, into which only acoustic signals penetrate and by which means Martin recognizes

Tigg's identity. Martin is now trapped within this container, since he has no desire to meet Tigg. A long section of dialogue between the pawnbroker and Tigg follows during which suspense develops as to whether Martin will manage to evade Tigg and avoid bilateral recognition by using his containment as a shield. Finally, however, Tigg's act of recognition is staged through the grotesque intrusion of his body into Martin's own container:

> The shopman was so highly entertained . . . that Mr Tigg himself could not repress some little show of exultation. It vented itself, in part, in a desire to see how the occupant of the next box received his pleasantry; to ascertain which he glanced round the partition, and immediately, by the gaslight, recognised Martin.
>
> "I wish I may die," said Mr Tigg, stretching out his body so far that his head was as much in Martin's little cell as Martin's own head was, "but this is one of the most tremendous meetings in Ancient or Modern History!" (Dickens 1968, 281–82)

This example exemplifies one type of Dickens's many uses of coincidental encounter—that between antagonistic characters. Dickens uses such situations to create an atmosphere of dread and menace when the protagonist meets a character who has previously played a negative role.

Charlotte Brontë's *Villette* stages an even more elaborately extended depiction involving the container and window schemata during the suspenseful buildup to a recognition scene. In this phase of the novel, the heroine and narrator, Lucy Snowe, who works as a teacher in the fictional Belgian town of Villette, has collapsed after a breakdown. She awakes to find herself in strangely familiar surroundings. In the ensuing scene, which lasts for several pages, it gradually becomes clear that, remarkably, she has now woken up in the house of Mrs. Bretton, the woman who once gave her a home in Bretton, England, when she was a child. The buildup toward full recognition of the still absent Mrs. Bretton starts with Lucy's wakening and her gradual visual exploration of the room she finds herself in, leading to the discovery that its contents are very familiar:

> At last I took in the complete fact of a pleasant parlour . . . pale walls over which a slight but endless garland of azure forget-me-nots ran mazed and bewildered amongst myriad gold leaves and tendrils. A gilded mirror filled up the space between two windows. . . . In this mirror I saw myself laid, not in bed, but on a sofa. I looked spectral; my eyes larger and more hollow, my hair darker than was natural, by contrast with my thin and ashen face. It was obvious, not only from the furniture, but from the position of windows, doors, and the fireplace, that this was an unknown room in an unknown house.
>
> . . . [A]s I gazed at the blue arm-chair, it appeared to grow familiar; so did a certain scroll-couch, and not less so the round centre-table, with a blue covering, bordered with autumn-tinted foliage. . . .

Bretton! Bretton! and ten years ago shone reflected in that mirror. And why did Bretton and my fourteenth year haunt me thus? (Brontë 1979, 238, 241)

While we do not have perspectivism in Stanzel's sense here, for we could still only draw an imperfect sketch of the relationships between all the objects in this room from the information, we do have three-dimensionality created by the container and portal schemata. In the passage a *mirror* is used to create a form of visual portal, one that casts back the reflection of the heroine, achieving a three-dimensional sense of space by opening up an inset image of the room.

The buildup to the actual recognition scene is prefaced by a sequence of passages in which Lucy recognizes inanimate objects set in a three-dimensionalized spatial environment using the *container-portal* schemata. Thus, after falling asleep again, she awakes to find herself in an enclosed bed:

> At waking, lo! all was again changed.... I felt sure now that I was in the pensionnat—sure by the beating rain on the casement; sure by the "wuther" of wind amongst trees, denoting a garden outside; sure by the chill, the whiteness, the solitude amidst which I lay. I say *whiteness*—for the dimity curtains, dropped before a French bed, bounded my view.
>
> I lifted them; looked out. My eye, prepared to take in the range of a long, large, white-washed chamber, blinked baffled, on encountering the limited area of a small cabinet—a cabinet with sea-green walls; also, instead of five wide and naked windows, there was one high lattice. (Brontë 1979, 240–41)

This passage is notable for its creation of multiple embedded *containers* and of receding peripheral surfaces away from the *center* established by the bed. First, the existence of a further world beyond the central *containers*—the bed and the room—is introduced not by a visual view from the window ("casement") but through the acoustic information regarding the sound of the rain and the wind. Following this, the passage then successively presents two different interiors when Lucy creates a visual *portal* by parting the curtains. Here the first interior described is in fact a virtual one, that of the pensionnat, which Lucy expects but does not find and which is then replaced by the actual one of Mrs. Bretton's house. Both virtual and actual rooms are again constructed with windows, reinforcing the three-dimensionality of the enclosure by implying visual gateways to a world outside, even if that world is not actually depicted. This passage thus contains four different spaces, all linked by Lucy's perception and the *portal-container* schemata. The three-dimensionalization continues after this passage, with Lucy subsequently moving to the window and surveying the terrain outside as the narrative moves forward slowly to the moment of encounter and bilateral recognition with Mrs. Bretton and her son, Graham (Brontë 1979, 24–51). In this extended sequence, spatial discovery and the cognitive processes of recognition are also protractedly intertwined through Lucy's gradual identification of furniture already familiar from her childhood.

If we now look at a modernist depiction of a recognition scene, a different spatial impression altogether is created. In the following key scene from Ford's *The Good Soldier* the narrator, John Dowell, observes his wife, Florence's recognition of a former acquaintance, Bagshawe, from a distance. Dowell is involved in conversation with Bagshawe in the foyer of the hotel where all the characters are staying when Florence enters through the swing doors:

> He [Bagshawe] was fencing for a topic with which he might gain my affection.
> And then, quite suddenly, in the bright light of the street, I saw Florence running. It was like that—Florence running with a face whiter than paper and her hand on the black stuff over her heart. I tell you, my own heart stood still; I tell you I could not move. She rushed in at the swing doors. She looked round that place of rush chairs, cane tables and newspapers. She saw me and opened her lips. She saw the man who was talking to me. She stuck her hands over her face as if she wished to push her eyes out. And then she was not there any more. (Ford 1946, 96)

What is striking about the depiction of space in comparison to the two previous examples from the nineteenth century is the comparative lack of a firm and concrete spatial scenario. While the passage uses the wall and portal scheme, it has become a transparently impressionistic environment against or rather *through* which events are experienced by Dowell. It is not the solidly three-dimensional container scenario we saw in the previous examples. The wall of the hotel actually seems to be translucent, for Dowell reports that he sees Florence in the street without providing clear information about the nature of the opening (presumably, in a realistic recuperation, large glass windows) through which he is already able to perceive her before she enters. Here solid spatial description gives way to movement and impressions. In the evocation of Florence rushing through the doors, the solid *container-portal* schema dissolves into the atmospheric description of her recognition of Bagshawe. The materialistic evocation of the inside and outside of the *container* (the hotel) has thus been abandoned in favor of the depiction of character-cognitive processes, behind which the spatial description only shimmers rather than existing in a fully concrete, realist fashion.

Recognition scenes from two contemporary novels reveal a further progression. The first passage comes from Auster's *Moon Palace*; it is part of the scene in which Fogg realizes that Barber is his father, which was already discussed in chapter 1: "I found myself studying the contours of his eyelids, concentrating on the space between the brows and the lashes, and all of a sudden I realized that I was looking at myself. Barber had the same eyes I did" (Auster 1990, 296). The second example comes from Winterson's *The Passion*. Here the narrator, Henri, describes a moment of confrontation in which he discovers that an old enemy is also the estranged husband of the woman he has fallen in love with:

> We pulled up against [the] water-gate but, as we prepared to fasten our boat, a silent prow slid from behind us and I was staring into the face of the cook.
> The cook.
> The flesh around his mouth moved into a suggestion of a smile. He was much heavier than when I had known him, with jowls that hung like dead moles and a plump case of skin that held his head to his shoulders. His eyes had receded and his eyebrows, always thick, now loomed at me like sentries. He folded his hands on the edge of the boat, hands with rings forced over the knuckles. (Winterson 1996, 127)

We already saw in the Ford passage how, despite the continuing use of key schemata, spatial description became less concretely tangible and focused more on cognitive processes. In these two passages this progression goes a step farther in that the focus of recognition itself, the face of a human being, becomes the enlarged and expanded site of spatialized description. The facial description is also entirely different from the brief details of facial response contained in the passage from Austen's *Persuasion* cited above. Here the focus zooms in to map facial features as a spatial terrain perceived in detail by the narrator as he performs the act of recognizing another character's identity. Thus, while in the previous forms described spatialization was used to depict the *backdrop* to recognition, here spatialization is used to focus on the *object* of recognition itself.

This effect, which can be called *physiognomical spatialization*, is again created through the use of key spatial schemata. In a few words the Auster passage creates a detailed facial map on three different axes: vertical, horizontal, and the link between perceiver and perceived. *Verticality* is contained in the alignment of eyebrows, eyelids, and lashes, while *horizontality* within the *balance-symmetry* schema is automatically constructed through the doubling of all these features to form the image of a human face constructed within the mind of the reader when she reads the plural designations of "eyelids," "brows," and "lashes." The final aspect is both spatial and cognitive. When Fogg says that he realizes that he is looking back at himself because Barber has the same eyes, this creates both an additional impression of a horizontal *path* or *link* of the gaze traced between the two sets of eyes and also reaches farther to evoke the link of kinship and similarity on both the character-cognitive and the genetic level.

The Winterson passage creates an even more complex facial terrain using a disorienting mix of spatial schemata. At the beginning a *center-periphery* schema is created in the image of the mouth surrounded by flesh. However, the normal visual center of the face, the eyes, is completely negated and remains obscure. Then incongruous *verticality* schemata that evoke a grotesque facial landscape are established by the similes of the hanging jowls as dead moles and the description of the eyebrows as sentries. The latter simile is in particular highly bizarre in its effect precisely because it undermines the normal schema of *horizontality* evoked by the concept of the eyebrow stretching *across* a face in the reader's mind and converts it into the vertical schema of the sentry on guard. Thus, both passages create a new type of spatial environment; the focus is not on a larger portion of actual space as the location for events (the setting) but on the enlarged terrain of a human face as the location of perceptual activity in the act of recognition.

The overall shape of historical development traced by these examples indicates four major shifts in the representation of fictional space. Realist narrative, as represented by Brontë and Dickens and preempted by Sidney, employs spatial schemata to achieve an effect of three-dimensionalization. This substantiates the physical environment in which the characters act and their cognitive acts of recognition take place. Here spatial obstruction and enclosure, particularly as represented by the use of the *container* schema, can also be used to create suspense. A different approach to spatial representation within realism can be seen in Austen's *Persuasion*. The heightened depiction of cognitive processes entails the backgrounding of the spatial environment. The modernist text, as represented by Ford's *The Good Soldier*, backgrounds three-dimensional space in favor of cognitive processes in a fashion different from that of Austen. The spatial environment is not actually omitted but constitutes a less concrete evocation of the spatial backdrop, which blends impressionistically with the description of the cognitive responses to recognition. By contrast, in the examples of physiognomical spatialization from Winterson's *The Passion* and Auster's *Moon Palace*, the face of a character is represented using a "zoom" effect that depicts facial features themselves as a spatial terrain. These contemporary examples represent the ultimate progression in the backgrounding of "real" fictional space and the foregrounding of cognitive processes and the act of perception already noted in Austen and Ford, since now spatialization is utilized to render the visual experience of a figure's perception of facial characteristics.

The textual examples discussed in this chapter have considered two different aspects of *spatial plotting*. First, in investigating the *spatial mapping of time* in both narrative theory and narrative fiction we saw how the human mind, located within the body, applies spatial concepts to describe the more abstract component of time. Second, in investigating the *mapping of fictional space* itself we saw how narrative fiction makes use of key schemata from the bodily experience of real-world space to create fictional environments. Nevertheless, the example of the recognition scene from Austen's *Persuasion* indicates that detailed spatial environments are not a prerequisite of immersive or "realist" fiction but only one major option. Austen's immersive technique takes the reader straight into the minds and experience of characters without providing so many opportunities for the reader to sojourn in the virtual space of the narrative world outside those minds. Thus, just as temporal orchestration can be seen in the historical development of narrative fiction to be facilitating increasingly immersive states in the mind of the reader, so does the fictional representation of space create a variety of strategies to take the reader into both the three-dimensional environments and the cognitive spaces of narrative worlds.

Theorizing Coincidence and Counterfactuality

2

4. The Coincidence Plot

Coincidence in Literature and Science

The use of coincidence is a widespread phenomenon in narrative fiction. However, despite a sizeable body of contributions on the topic, what has hitherto been missing is a systematic analysis and definition of the *plots* of coincidence as they occur in fictional narratives—a poetics of coincidence. By contrast, the scientific study of real-world coincidence offers incisive observations on the structure and cognitive effects of coincidence and therefore provides useful input for the analysis of fictional narratives. In the literary research into coincidence, a number of papers have focused on the phenomenon in the work of individual authors, notably in the Victorian novel. However, there has as yet been no attempt to propose a comprehensive definition and theory of coincidence or undertake a historical survey. The following section gives an overview of previous work on coincidence before presenting a theory of coincidence in narrative fiction.

Literary Research

There is a striking lack of consensus about what coincidence actually is. Some literary discussions of coincidence assume that the term is self-explanatory and offer no explicit definition (Goldknopf 1969; Forsyth 1985; Lodge 1992; Ickstadt 1994). Other contributions have provided ad hoc definitions and present a fascinating semantic spectrum. "Coincidence" is thus (among other things) "the violent connection of the unconnected" (Van Ghent 1961, 223); "a convergence through contiguity or similarity of causally unconnected events" (Hannay 1988, 89); "a convergence of several elements: agent(s) and/or object(s), time and/or space" (Yacobi 1991, 464); "the coinciding of events and of the physical presence of persons at the same point of time and space" (Dessner 1992, 162).[1] Such definitions emphasize the interconnective function of coincidence, centering either on the bringing together of characters or on the creation of chains of relationship.[2] The term is also sometimes used loosely as a synonym for chance and not to refer to a specific narrative plot (see Hornback 1971; Bell 1993; Monk 1993; Richardson 1997); thus, in discussing biblical narrative, Sternberg observes that "in a God-directed world there is no room for coincidence" (1985, 142).[3] Bert Hornback's definition, referring to the novels of Thomas Hardy, treats coincidence as an umbrella term that allows any accident or twist of chance or fate to qualify: "Coincidences come about either as chance occurrences or through the operation of causal relationships. An example of the first is Tess's placing a note under the door and Angel's failing to find it because it has slipped—by accident—under the carpet.... More interesting, however, is such coincidence as that of the height of Michael Henchard's ambitions being crossed by the return of the wife he sold to realize those ambitions" (Hornback 1971, 6).

In a comprehensive poetics of coincidence, the examples cited by Hornback can be distinguished as distinct phenomena. The first example (from *Tess of the d'Urbervilles*) concerns nonconvergence or *negative coincidence*, in which the intended intersection of objects in the narrative world is randomly thwarted. The second example (from *The Mayor of Casterbridge*) concerns what this study designates as the *traditional coincidence plot* and in this case involves a particularly complex configuration of kinship reunion with an extended and ultimately tragic *recognition plot* because the daughter with whom Henchard believes himself to be reunited ultimately turns out to be another man's child. Recognition within coincidence is, indeed, one of the most neglected aspects in literary research; only Neil Forsyth (1985) and Werner Wolf (1993) have focused on this aspect.

Exceptionally, an overall definition proposed by Thomas Vargish (1985) in his study of Providence in the Victorian novel offers a more substantial definitional framework. Vargish defines "*coincidence* in its basic meaning [as] merely the concurrence or juxtaposition in time and space of two or more events or circumstances" (1985, 7). However, he also observes: "But coincidence in its common and most important literary use carried with it an element of surprise or astonishment that derives from the lack of apparent causal connection.... [C]oincidence is not necessarily a failure in realism or (as is sometimes implied) a cheap way out of difficulties in plot and structure—though of course it can be both in a bad novel. Instead, coincidence is a symbol of providence" (Vargish 1985, 7, 9).

Here Vargish highlights two important points: the fact that fictional plots of coincidence and coincidence in real life are not automatically equatable with each other and that the coincidence plot has an important *cognitive effect* on the reader in stimulating the desire for *explanation* (an aspect that is also manifested in the scientific literature on coincidence).

To date, no attempt has been made to study coincidence in an extensive diachronic framework.⁴ Its ubiquity in narrative has largely been ignored, and discussions have focused on coincidence in the nineteenth century, particularly in the novels of Dickens and Hardy.⁵ As a result, instead of being approached as a fundamental narrative strategy, coincidence has sometimes been treated as an example of Victorian excess, even accompanied by critical indignation at authors' persistence in using the device.⁶ The varied nature of approaches to coincidence can of course also be attributed to the fact that in examinations restricted to single authors, definitions are molded to the practice of the novelist concerned. Coincidence in twentieth-century fiction has received comparatively little attention (James Joyce, Isak Dinesen, Boris Pasternak, and Don DeLillo have been considered), and the general resurgence of coincidence in postmodernist texts has not received commensurate attention.⁷ The specifically postmodernist form of the coincidence plot is mentioned in studies discussing historiographic metafiction's tendency to use connecting structures across different temporal levels (see Stanzel 1995). Ansgar Nünning (1995b, 335) observes that the search for correspondences and analogies in Salman Rushdie's *Midnight's Children* (1981) is a major structural principle in the presentation of history; in fact, interestingly, these "correspondences" are referred to as "historical coincidences" in the novel itself (Rushdie 1982, 27).

The continuing use of the traditional coincidence plot in the contemporary novel (e.g., in Auster's *Moon Palace*, Don DeLillo's *Libra* [1988], or Louis Sachar's *Holes* [1998]) also proves the fallaciousness of Ian Watt's simple generic distinction between the romance and the novel, in which he claims that the novel "replaces the reliance of earlier narratives on . . . coincidences" with "a causal connection operating through time" (1987, 22). In fact, far from being a disused plot remnant from the romance, this prerealist plot form was carried to new heights in the nineteenth century (the purported age of realism), and this indicates the generic complexity involved both in coincidence and the novel as a whole. Equally fallacious is the idea (Burkhardt 1983, 282) that coincidence is a fundamentally premodernist narrative device and that the modernist rejection of Victorian literary conventions heralded its demise as a narrative strategy.⁸ The greatest diachronic insight into coincidence is in fact offered by a postmodernist novel. The metanarrative discourse on forms of coincidence by the narrator of Barnes's *Flaubert's Parrot* (1985, 66–73; see the discussion in chapter 6) is unique in its observation of a continuity of tradition between traditional and postmodern forms.

Research into Real-Life Coincidence

The analysis of real-life cases of coincidence, notably the work of Alice Johnson, Paul Kammerer, and Carl Jung, offers a number of useful parameters for the definition of coincidence absent in literary research. This research has considered coincidence as a real-life narrative plot involving a sequence or constellation of events and has in particular focused on the deep human need to make sense of the bizarre and miraculous constellations involved. Johnson defines a coincidence as "any conjunction of circumstances that would primarily be regarded as accidental, but in which a special aspect is involved, suggesting a causal relation" (1899, 159). Her definition therefore emphasizes the important fact that coincidence, although ostensibly a random occurrence, is so striking and special that it produces a strong desire in the human mind for an explanation, often one using the connecting patterns of causation. In her full investigation, Johnson then subdivides "coincidences" in terms of three different explicative models: "Causation," "Design," and "Chance." Kammerer's *Gesetz der Serie* (The Law of Series) (1919) investigates striking series of chance repetitions in everyday life, for example, the bizarre recurrence of numbers or names. Kammerer (36) defines *seriality* as the repetition of the same or similar things and events in time and space that cannot be linked by a mutual causal factor. The concept of seriality thus highlights coincidence as a phenomenon stretching across time (in effect, a narrative sequence). Kammerer (71–75) discusses different types of repetition (*Wiederholung*) or clustering (*Häufung*) within the series due to phenomena such as similarity, affinity, and analogy. While Kammerer's approach is narrative-sequential, his evaluation of coincidence in terms of the governing principles of repetition moves away from the search for larger orchestrating systems that characterized Johnson's model. Later in the twentieth century, Jung's (1985) definition and analysis of coincidence (a configuration that he calls both "synchronicity" and "meaningful coincidence") goes one step farther: it circumvents both the construction of causal connections and sequentiality. Jung understands coincidence not as a narrative-sequential plot at all but as "the simultaneous occurrence of two meaningfully but not causally connected events" (1985, 36). Jung's consideration of "synchronicity" focuses precisely on modes of understanding that transcend previous temporal-linear forms of thought. Indeed, for Jung the concept of objective time is not relevant to synchronicity, precisely because the unconscious mind functions outside the physical framework of space-time (42).

In these three approaches we can therefore observe various manifestations of the *cognitive desire* to explain the remarkable in coincidence. These explanations move from a heavily causal orientation (Johnson) to the backgrounding or rejection of causal connections (Kammerer and Jung). Moreover, while Kammerer still treats examples of analogical coincidence (series of repetitions) as a sequence, analogical coincidences in Jung are no longer studied as a linear narrative. Notably, this increasing emphasis on analogical patterns, the foregrounding of the human mind itself as a key factor in the coincidental constellation, and the backgrounding of causal explanations also all feature in twentieth-century fictional representations of coincidence.

Beyond these significant scientific studies, the continuing desire to narrate and explain coincidences from real life is documented by the steady flow of books on the subject for the general reader; a significant early example that also influenced Kammerer and Jung is Camille Flammarion's *L'inconnu* (1900).[9] Such works represent the ongoing attempt to classify and define the phenomenon of coincidence in real life while also illustrating the cognitive relativity of categorical systems (well demonstrated by Lakoff [1987]).[10] Modern popular interpretations of coincidence generally take a demystifying, statistical approach (Krämer 1996) or, alternatively, preserve the marvelous element by interpreting coincidence in terms of paranormal and psychic phenomena (Tanous and Ardman 1976; Mardorf 1997). In addition, a number of more serious journalistic works give an overview or history of the human preoccupation with coincidence (Koestler 1972; Hardy, Harvie, and Koestler 1973; Inglis 1990).

These scientific and popular works, which document the extent of mankind's extraliterary preoccupation with coincidence, are clear evidence of the strong desire to construct sense-making patterns out of coincidence and out of life itself, phenomena already discussed in chapter 1 in terms of the plotting principle. The literary analyst who treats fictional coincidence as a hackneyed device fails to appreciate this deeper dimension. In fact, when its fictionality is disguised by the kind of immersive textual strategies described in the first three chapters of this study, the coincidence plot effectively becomes a real-world event for the reader, prompting the same sense of the remarkable and stimulating the *cognitive desire* for an explanation.

The Traditional Coincidence Plot in Narrative Fiction

A basic definition of coincidence that incorporates elements of the scientific definitions discussed above can be formulated as follows: *Coincidence is a constellation of two or more apparently random events in space and time with an uncanny or striking connection.* In the traditional coincidence plot of narrative fiction, the connection is one of a *previous relationship* between the coinciding (i.e., intersecting) characters. In analogical coincidence, the connection is that of *similarity*. While this basic definition constructs parameters in time and space, the most crucial elements in the realization of coincidence in narrative fiction that transform it into a truly complex plot are the *cognitive* components of *recognition* and *explanation*.

This study's model of coincidence in fiction constructs a detailed "three-dimensional" analytical matrix of the coordinates of space, time, and mind operative within the coincidence plot in order to chart the variations and developments in its individual realization over an extended period of literary history. This cognitive poetics of coincidence incorporates the theoretical parameters presented in the initial chapters of this study into a historically framed account of its features and forms.

In the traditional coincidence plot, the paths of characters with a previous connection intersect in the space and time of the narrative world in apparently random and remarkable circumstances and through no causal intent of their own. This plot consists of three main phases in terms of the story sequence:

A. The *previous relationship* (prehistory).
B. The *coincidental encounter* (intersection) of the characters in the time and space of the narrative world.
C. A cognitive process involving the characters' *recognition* (discovery) of each other's identity.

It is the events occurring between phases B and C that constitute the narrative power of the coincidence plot. Nevertheless, phase A, the previous relationship between the characters (however sketchily it is portrayed in the actual narrative), remains the sine qua non of the traditional coincidence plot. Without it, the recognition phase cannot occur. In addition, phase A can in no way give rise to phase B in a direct, causal fashion; that is, the characters with the previous relationship must in some way be separated or estranged prior to their renewed intersection. The essential uncanniness of the coincidence is constituted by the fact that the events of phases A and B are random and unconnected.

While this basic story pattern constitutes the prerequisite framework of the traditional coincidence plot, narratives that stimulate readerly interest and immersive states are created by additional features that involve both character- and reader-cognitive levels centering on the processes of *recognition* and *explanation*. Recognition in the traditional coincidence plot achieves the greatest cognitive and emotional impact when it involves *kinship reunion*. This plot has been used by many key texts, such as Sophocles' *Oedipus the King*, Greene's *Pandosto*, Defoe's *Moll Flanders*, Brontë's *Jane Eyre*, and Auster's *Moon Palace*.[11] The narrative strategies that generate highly immersive versions of the traditional coincidence plot include, notably, temporal orchestration, suspense, sophisticated forms of narrative explanation, and the complex spatial depiction of the recognition scene.

The Previous Relationship

In traditional coincidence, relationships between characters constitute a *prehistory* created by the *links* of friendship, love, kinship, or enmity that exist between characters prior to the coincidental encounter. Variations in the specific types of relationship are thus one significant variant in the history of fictional coincidence.

The centrality of the family in human relationships and the emotional power latent in the links between parents, children, and siblings means that the scenes accompanying kinship reunion are most intense, making this the most narratively intense form of previous relationship in the coincidence plot. Sibling or parent-child reunions facilitated by coincidence can take the form of positive *euphoric* or negative *dysphoric* patterns, and the latter in particular are created by plots of *hidden kinship*. The list of texts using the age-old motif of joyous family reunion is extensive and includes Greene's *Pandosto*, Smollett's *Roderick Random*, Fielding's *Joseph Andrews* and *Tom Jones*, Brontë's *Jane Eyre*, Dickens's *Oliver Twist* (1837–38), Margaret Drabble's *The Realms of Gold* (1975), and David Lodge's *Small World* (1984). Thus, while the novel has been theoretically defined as constructing new plots as opposed to reusing old ones (Watt 1987), in the case of coincidence, the novel has extensively recycled a plot from romance.

At the dysphoric or tragic end of the pole, the Oedipus story, with its double destruction and perversion of the child-parent relationship, is the most consummately disastrous version of the traditional coincidence plot. Oedipus is caught up in a double set of phase B: in separate incidents he is coincidentally reunited with both his father and mother, whom he unwittingly kills and marries, respectively, leading subsequently to the most horrendous recognition phase conceivable. Plots of incest through delayed recognition occur in particular in Renaissance fiction and in the early modern novel in various forms. Greene's *Pandosto* only ultimately achieves felicitous family reunion because unwitting father-daughter incest is averted by last-minute recognition. The eighteenth-century novel uses the plot in a variety of forms. In Defoe's *Moll Flanders* delayed recognition leads to the incestuous marriage of siblings, while Fielding's *Joseph Andrews* and *Tom Jones* contain seemingly real but ultimately bogus incestuous relationships that are constructed by the narrator's manipulation and suppression of information concerning the characters' prehistory. The gothic novel is also notable for its use of the coincidental incest plot: Matthew Lewis's *The Monk* (1796) contains brother-sister rape, while in Ann Radcliffe's *The Romance of the Forest* (1791) the heroine escapes rape by her uncle prior to the discovery of their family links.

By contrast, coincidental encounters involving characters with nonblood ties represent a less emotionally charged but quantitatively substantial form of coincidence. Several different trends can be distinguished within this form. First, the coincidental encounter reuniting both friends and enemies plays a major role in narratives in the picaresque tradition. Manifestations of this can be seen from Thomas Nashe's *Unfortunate Traveller* (1594) in the Renaissance through Smollett's *Roderick Random* and Fielding's *Joseph Andrews* and *Tom Jones* in the eighteenth century and on to Dickens (e.g., in *Martin Chuzzlewit*) in the nineteenth century. In its basic form in picaresque narrative this involves a single coincidental encounter between the protagonist and another character from an earlier phase in his or her life that loosely connects two episodes. However, a less episodic and more integrative form of the coincidental encounter takes place when a character coincidentally recurs in new contexts, as in the characters with multiple identities in Dickens's *Martin Chuzzlewit*, for example, Montague Tigg (alias Tigg Montague) and Young Bailey.[12]

Modernist fiction represents a different trend in the use of nonblood relationships in coincidence. Contrary to some assumptions (Burkhardt 1983, 282), modernist plots do not abandon the use of coincidence, but they do reject the kinship reunion plot as part of their rejection of previous literary conventions. Instead, previous acquaintances and amorous liaisons (Virginia Woolf's *Mrs Dalloway* [1925], Forster's *A Room with a View*, Ford's *The Good Soldier*) supersede blood connections as the form of previous relationship. Notably, too, Jane Austen—a forerunner of modernism in terms of her innovative use of consciousness representation and portrayal of quotidian reality—also largely avoids the kinship reunion form of coincidence.

A further type of nonblood relationship in the traditional coincidence plot is that in which lovers are reunited. In the romance and in earlier novels, coincidental romantic reunions are frequently used, such as the reunion of Oroonoko with Imoinda in Aphra Behn's *Oroonoko* (1688) and that of Moll with Jemmy in Defoe's *Moll Flanders*. This use of coincidence as a deus ex machina to achieve romantic union, usually at closure, can be contrasted with its absence in the more recent novel, which requires an emotional, consciousness-oriented and not simply plot-oriented solution to the love plot. In some novels romantic reunions through coincidence form the *initial device* for bringing together an estranged couple (as in Austen's *Persuasion* and Forster's *A Room with a View*). This can be seen as symptomatic of the changing cultural construction of love and marriage: felicitous closure in the love plot is no longer reached through external mechanisms but by a process of growing understanding and deepening of affection on the part of the characters concerned (as pioneered in Richardson's and Austen's love plots).[13]

The coincidental encounter involving enemies is the least widely used but nevertheless narratively highly effective combination, since it can evoke extreme states of fear and menace. Dickens frequently exploits this scenario, for example, in *Great Expectations* and *Martin Chuzzlewit*, while in Winterson's *The Passion* Henri's unexpected reencounter with the cook is staged in a darkly grotesque and horrific scenario.

Postmodernism's freedom from the constraints of realism and its reengagement with the literary past means that the novels of this period make free with all forms of previous relationship, including family configurations with bizarre antirealist symmetry or fairy-tale structures: Auster's *Moon Palace* backgrounds maternal links completely and reconnects a male family chain across three generations in a discordant plot of delayed recognitions. Winterson's *The Passion* uses a coincidental love triangle set in Napoleonic Europe that stretches across France, Russia, and Italy. Sachar's *Holes* orchestrates an even more fantastic interlinking of characters and life plots in its coordination of realist and fantastic elements in the family history of its hero, Stanley Yelnats.

Coincidental Relationships and Double Identity

In *coincidental relationships*, as opposed to the coincidental encounter, the emphasis is on a network of *links* between characters who are uncannily connected by the existence of multiple relationships. Here, accordingly, recognition takes the form of the discovery of connections by a character. This moment of discovery generally involves the revelation of the fact that characters who are connected in an apparently random fashion on a primary level are connected by additional links that are not causally related to the first set of connections. These primary and secondary layers of relationships mean that at least one character in the chain turns out to have a *double identity*.

6. Coincidental Relationships and Double Identity in Austen's *Persuasion*

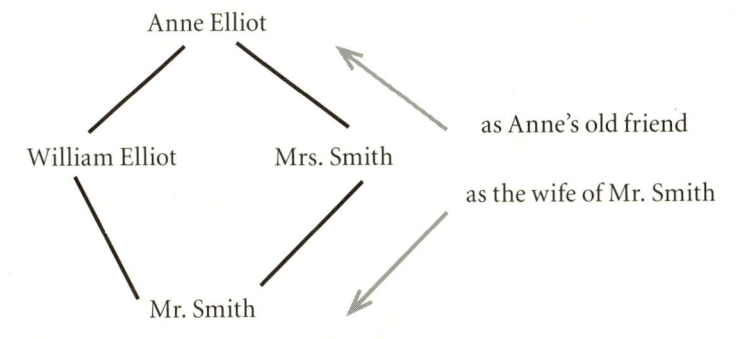

```
          Anne Elliot
          /        \
         /          \
        /            \
William Elliot    Mrs. Smith      as Anne's old friend
        \            /
         \          /             as the wife of Mr. Smith
          \        /
          Mr. Smith
```

Dickens's novels in particular use complex systems of character interrelationships and multiple double identities. However, Austen's *Persuasion* offers a good small-scale illustration (see figure 6). Toward the end of the novel, Anne Elliot must make a choice between two suitors, Captain Wentworth and William Elliot. Her decision is facilitated by information indicating that William's interest is materially motivated. This information comes to Anne via a chain of hitherto hidden connections: her old friend Mrs. Smith turns out to be the widow of a man who was cheated by William Elliot. Mrs. Smith's dual identity constitutes the closing link in this convergent chain of relationships. Depending from which direction in the chain she is approached, Mrs. Smith is either Anne's old friend or the wife of William Elliot's former business associate. Recognition in the plot of coincidental relationships thus involves the discovery of an additional identity or character relationships as opposed to the fundamental recognition of identity in the coincidental encounter.

The Narrative Dynamics of Recognition

The most crucial phase of the traditional coincidence plot—the recognition scene in which characters discover each other's true identity—was already explored in many aspects in part 1. As discussed in chapter 1, the prospect of recognition between the coinciding characters can create considerable narrative suspense, while recognition within the framework of family reunion can trigger powerful vicarious states of emotion in the reader due to the overriding cognitive power evoked by the *links* of kinship in the human mind. In addition, as discussed in chapter 2, the temporal orchestration of different identity constellations and past-world versions can make the recognition of actual kinship links (as in Oedipus) a particularly harrowing one in which relationships, and with them the character's whole world, are turned upside down. Chapter 3 showed how the spatialization of the recognition scene, in particular the use of *containers* and *portals*, can facilitate, delay, or underline the cognitive processes involved within the recognition process.

Recognition within the kinship form of the coincidence plot establishes a character's biological identity, allowing the tracing of a network of blood links and relationships in which the character can locate himself or herself. As Sternberg observes in discussing narrative temporality in the Bible, "there is more even to genealogy than the genealogical imperative with its procession-like chronology" (1990, 115). The recognition scene within the coincidence plot exemplifies this fact: the discovery of kinship involves the mapping of a multidirectional network of *links* through time and family.

Recognition in the coincidence plot is a manifestation of what Aristotle calls *anagnorisis*, and it is indeed notable that in discussing anagnorisis in *The Poetics* Aristotle mentions *Oedipus*. Aristotle's discussion of anagnorisis does not foreground the coincidence plot, but it still formulates some important analytical parameters. The most relevant passage is the following:

> *Recognition* . . . is a change from ignorance to knowledge, disclosing either a close relationship or enmity. . . . Recognition is best when it occurs simultaneously with a reversal, like in the *Oedipus*. There are indeed other kinds of recognition. . . .

> Since the recognition is a recognition of some person or persons, some involve the recognition of one person only on the part of the other, when it is clear who the other is; but sometimes there must be a recognition on both sides. (Aristotle *Poetics* 52a30–52b6, 1996, 18–19)

Aristotle's observations on the possibility of *unilateral* or *bilateral* recognition on the character level are central to the consideration of the recognition process in the coincidence plot: as we saw in chapter 1, unilateral recognition is a key device for creating suspense.

Aristotle's subsequent listing of kinds of recognition (*Poetics* 54b19–55a21, 1996, 26–27) concerns the question of how recognition is brought about, for example, by tokens such as Odysseus's scar (55a16–20, 1996, 27). The example of Odysseus, who returns to Ithaca not by coincidence but by his own design and who knows the identity of his wife and son from the outset, allows us to highlight key differences in recognition between the coincidence plot and other plots of discovery. In the coincidence plot there must be a *zero level* of character knowledge regarding the forthcoming meeting because the characters are brought together through unforeseen circumstances. By contrast, in noncoincidental recognition plots like that of Odysseus's return, Odysseus himself anticipates recognition because, although long thwarted, he intends the approaching reunion with his wife and son, and they in turn anticipate his return, although with considerably less certainty about its occurrence.

Aristotle highlights recognition as part of the culmination of a tragic plot in conjunction with *peripeteia*. Recognition in coincidence in narrative fiction can also occupy this *culminatory position* and can thus involve a *denouemental insight*, as, for example, the stages of recognition undergone by Pip in Dickens's *Great Expectations* (see Forsyth 1985) or by Henchard in Hardy's *The Mayor of Casterbridge*. In narrative fiction, however, as a form of the epic genre, which, as Aristotle observes, "contains a multiplicity of stories" (*Poetics* 56a13, 1996, 30), recognition can also occur in all phases of the story, to all manner of characters, and at all levels of emotional and cognitive intensity. Minor episodic scenes depicting coincidental encounters do not involve the kind of monumental form of recognition that Walsh (1966, 35) calls "illumination" but use brief encounters with the instantaneous *perception of identity* rather than a complex act of *discovery*.

Such basic forms of coincidental encounter can be designated as *ad hoc coincidence*. Here, intersection (phase B) and recognition (phase C) are more or less simultaneous and involve little or no character-cognitive detail or suspense. By contrast, the complex and hence strongly immersive use of the coincidence plot involves the deferral of recognition—often creating suspense if the reader is aware of the previous relationship—and culminates in a narratively powerful recognition scene. Two eighteenth-century novels both attributed to the picaresque tradition—Defoe's *Moll Flanders* and Smollett's *Roderick Random*—in fact use very different configurations of coincidence. In *Moll Flanders* the central coincidence plot extends over a substantial period of discourse and story time, stretching from Moll's marriage to a man she meets in London and accompanies to North America, to her discovery of the previous relationship, which transforms her husband into her brother and her mother-in-law into her own estranged mother, to a protracted narrative of suppressed recognition while she lives for several years in a state of unilateral knowledge before revealing the truth first to her mother and finally to her brother. By contrast, coincidental encounters in *Roderick Random* are generally brief and episodic. For example, Roderick one day happens to come along the road at the right time to save his beloved Narcissa from the violent and unwanted attentions of a neighboring squire: "What were the emotions of my soul, when I beheld Narcissa, almost sinking beneath the brutal force of this satyr! I flew like lightening [sic] to her rescue" (Smollett 1981, 229). Here recognition is instantaneous ("I beheld") with the intersection.

These two examples illustrate a further distinction. While the coincidental encounter involves the intersection of characters in both the space and time of the narrative world, it is also possible to distinguish between primarily spatial or temporal coincidence. Moll's encounter with her brother from halfway round the other side of the world is an example of predominantly spatial coincidence (the "small world" effect), while the example from *Roderick Random* is predominantly temporal, since it is the *timing* of Roderick's intersection with Narcissa that is crucial.[14] Nevertheless, if a narrative constructs further causal-progenerative plot repercussions, a primarily temporal coincidence can create a more complex emplotment of events. In Thomas Hardy's novels, for example, the precise timing of the intersections by characters in the fictional space of Egdon Heath often has calamitous results, as in "The Closed Door," book 4 of *The Return of the Native* (1878), which culminates in the death of Mrs. Yeobright.

Recognition on the part of characters can thus be instantaneous or delayed, bilateral or unilateral. The nature of the previous relationship (kinsman, friend, or foe) can give rise to a variety of emotional reactions on the part of the coinciding characters, which, depending on the extent of internal focalization, can in turn represent the emotional affects of the recognition upon the character(s) in a variety of ways. Furthermore, the speed of recognition on the story level in the case of coinciding kinspeople can be crucial. Belated recognition by close relatives may lead to unwitting incest, where subsequent recognition takes the most negative form. Without the incest factor, however, the reunion of estranged relatives can constitute the most positively emotional scenes of recognition.[15]

The Point of Intersection and Deferred Recognition

The mediated nature of the genre of narrative fiction, in which events and relationships as well as the characters' internal emotional and cognitive processes both prior to and during recognition are described by a narrator, make the dynamics of recognition within the coincidence plot a particularly multifaceted phenomenon. Thus, as Sternberg emphasizes in discussing the manifestations of surprise within the dynamics of recognition, surprise for the fictional character and surprise for the reader are two distinct processes: "The two may, but need not, run parallel: theirs derives from the living, ours from the telling about their living" (1992, 508).[16]

In the dynamics of recognition in traditional coincidence, knowledge communicated or withheld by or simply not available to the narrator has a substantial effect on the dynamics of the coincidence plot. The following three examples of the point of intersection, all using deferred recognition, show different variants in the extent of narrator versus reader knowledge regarding the relationship between the coinciding characters. A passage from Dickens's *Martin Chuzzlewit* describes a coincidental brush between two characters caught up in a network of coincidental relationships. It plays off maximal and overt narrator knowledge against minimal character and reader knowledge:

> Mr Nadgett might have passed Tom Pinch ten thousand times; might even have been quite familiar with his face, his name, pursuits, and character; yet never once have dreamed that Tom had any interest in any act or mystery of his. Tom might have done the like by him, of course. But the same private man out of all the men alive, was in the mind of each at the same moment; was prominently connected, though in a different manner, with the day's adventures of both; and formed, when they passed each other in the street, the one absorbing topic of their thoughts. . . . Why Tom had Jonas Chuzzlewit in his mind requires no explanation. Why Mr Nadgett should have had Jonas Chuzzlewit in his, is quite another thing. (Dickens 1968, 661–62)

This passage playfully leaves the reader in a multileveled state of anticipation regarding recognition and prehistory. The reader is alerted to the existence of a hidden coincidental relationship in the past of the narrative world, about which she may begin to speculate, anticipating both the characters' and her own discovery of the implied links at some point in the future.

In the following passage from Austen's *Persuasion* there is, as in Dickens, minimal character knowledge, but here the narrator is more covert and gives no indication at this stage of the narrative that the scene depicted is a coincidental encounter at all: "When they came to the steps, leading upwards from the beach, a gentleman at the same moment preparing to come down, politely drew back, and stopped to give them way. They ascended and passed him" (Austen 1965, 124). No sense of anticipation is created in the reader here, so that the subsequent revelation that the gentleman Anne briefly encountered is her cousin William has a greater effect of surprise.

The effect is similar in autodiegetic narrative in which the knowledge of the narrating self in the story's future is suppressed. For example, when Moll Flanders describes her identification of a promising suitor in London, his true identity as her half-brother remains completely unmentioned: "I, who had a subtle game to play, had nothing to do but to single out . . . the properest man that might be for my purpose. . . . I picked out my man without much difficulty, by the judgment I made of his way of courting me. I had let him run on with his protestations and oaths that he loved me above all the world; that if I would make him happy, that was enough" (Defoe 1978, 93).

In all of the above scenarios, recognition is deferred well beyond the point of the character's intersection in the coincidental encounter, but only in Dickens does the information supplied by the narrator prompt the reader to recognize that a coincidence plot exists at the actual point of intersection, thereby creating anticipatory suspense.

The Explanation of Coincidence

In the question of the narrative explanation of coincidence, a similar plurality of critical voices reveals itself to those noted in the question of its overall definition. Some studies have focused on coincidence only in the context of one particular explanatory system (e.g., Vargish [1985] on Providence or Bell [1993] on chance), thereby automatically producing a selective picture. Other approaches consider the interplay of different explanatory systems.[17]

The complexity of the issue of explanatory systems is indicated by the contradictory maps of the nineteenth-century worldview that emerge in the discussions of the narrative explanation of coincidence in Hardy (1964), Harvey (1965), Goldknopf (1969), Reed (1975), Forsyth (1985), Bell (1993), and Monk (1993). While all commentators concur in seeing late-nineteenth-century narratives, notably those of Thomas Hardy, as depicting "the absence of Providence" (Hardy 1964, 71), the steps down the road to this point are subject to various readings. Hardy makes the general claim that Providence is "plainly outworn and discredited" in Dickens, Eliot, and George Meredith. For Goldknopf the narrative demise of Providence comes in the mature work of Dickens (*Bleak House* and *Great Expectations*), while in *Hard Times*, as in Brontë's *Jane Eyre* and *Villette*, "Providence [still] takes command" (1969, 44). Reed sees providential explanations dominate for much of the period, exemplified in the novels of Dickens and Wilkie Collins, while the novels of Eliot and Meredith expose

Providence as an individual interpretation involving an "egoistic confusion of the convenient and the ordained"; later still, he finds, "Providence... is replaced by Destiny" (1975, 135, 137). A more binary picture is created by critics who focus on chance or randomness as replacing providential explanations (Monk 1993; Bell 1993). However, both cultural processes (the replacement of Providence by determinism or, alternately, by chance) are seen to crystallize fully in modernist texts.[18] The interpretation of the significance of coincidence in the work of Dickens in particular is highly contradictory, and the plurality of interpretations is indicative of the cultural complexity of conflicting worldviews seething under the surface of the fictional coincidence plot in its individual narrative manifestations.[19]

The contradictory configurations of explanatory systems in the critical literature offer strong evidence that an approach that seeks to force narrative texts and literary periods to conform to one explanatory system constructs a one-sided picture that neglects what might be called the *explicative polymodality* within individual novels, not to say the complete works of an author and indeed any period. The desire to interpret in terms of a static worldview (something, indeed, that real humans, as opposed to critical constructs of the author, rarely tend to have) overlooks the more interesting opportunity to explore the plurality of perspectives (and the conflicts they give rise to) that are present within any author, culture, or period.

The pluralistic cognitive model proposed in chapter 1 for the analysis of explanatory systems is capable of registering explicational diversity. Hence it is possible to map explanatory systems as establishing links of causation but also instating the lack of causation, that is, randomness. The suggestion of *causal links* between events forms the major strategy used by realist narratives to suggest that the world of the story is an autonomous one that conforms to the major explanatory system the reader uses in everyday life and is therefore a "real" one. However, within causality there is a variety of different cognitive types (as suggested by Turner 1987) that enable us to differentiate much more precisely between the different, culturally variable forms of this key realist explicational strategy. This model therefore allows us to examine each work of fiction for its own individual use and combination of explanatory systems and avoids the tendency toward oversimplistic mapping.

Negative Coincidence

The traditional coincidence plot therefore consists of a range of variations of the coincidental encounter and coincidental relationships. However, two additional, less widespread plots should also be considered and defined in relation to these major forms. Negative coincidence, generally treated as a form of "chance" in previous literature (see Hornback 1971, 6), is a plot structure different from the coincidence plot and involves a situation of thwarted convergence. It is used in tragedies of circumstance such as the novels of Thomas Hardy.[20] In *Tess of the d'Urbervilles*, for example, Tess's attempt to tell Angel about her past relationship with Alec before their wedding is accidentally thwarted because the letter she pushes under his door gets wedged under the carpet and never reaches him. Negative coincidence is therefore an *inversion* of the structure of the coincidental encounter because it involves the *nonconvergence* of an *intended* intersection in space and time that is the result of random circumstances. In the coincidental encounter, characters meet without intending to do so; in negative coincidence, the reverse is the case: things that are intended to meet or intersect do not.

In addition, because negative coincidence involves a negative outcome in which a desired set of events is thwarted, it also automatically implies a counterfactual version of events in which the intersection did actually take place. For this reason, negative coincidence and counterfactuality are closely connected phenomena, above all in tragic plot structures. The narrative interaction of negative coincidence and counterfactuality will be discussed in chapter 5.

The Coincidence of Dates

This minor form has an analogical component—the repetition of the same date—but is sequential rather than synchronic, since the repeated dates form part of a narrative sequence in the fashion of the phenomena observed in Kammerer's (1919) "law of series." As represented in narrative fiction, this plot involves significant events in the life of a character repeatedly occurring on the same date, leading the character to draw conclusions (which, in turn, vary according to the period and the character's worldview) about the significance of these repetitions. For example, Defoe's Robinson Crusoe makes the following observations in reviewing the repetition of dates in his life:

> And first by casting up times past, I remember that there was a strange concurrence of days in the various providences which befell me; and which, if I had been superstitiously inclined to observe days as fatal or fortunate, I might have had reason to have looked upon with a great deal of curiosity.
>
> First, I had observed that the same day that I broke away from my father and my friends, and run away to Hull, in order to go to sea, the same day afterwards I was taken by the Sallee man of war, and made a slave.
>
> The same day of the year that I escaped out of the wreck of that ship in Yarmouth roads, that same day-year afterwards I made my escape from Sallee in the boat.
>
> The same day of the year I was born on, viz. the 30th of September, that same day I had my life so miraculously saved twenty-six year after, when I was cast on shore in this island, so that my wicked life and my solitary life begun both on a day. (1965, 143–44)

In using the term "providences" Crusoe implies that the repetitive patterns in his life are the manifestation of a form of divine symmetry or organizational principle. His rational and providentially oriented mindset rejects an interpretation based on pure superstition. By contrast, John Dowell, the narrator of Ford's *The Good Soldier*, offers a more ambivalent interpretation of the strange fact that August 4 has always been a significant date in his wife, Florence's life: "There is a curious coincidence of dates, but I do not know whether that is one of those sinister, as if half-jocular and altogether merciless proceedings on the part of a cruel Providence that we call a coincidence. Because it may just as well have been the superstitious mind of Florence that forced her to certain acts, as if she had been hypnotized" (1946, 75). Providence may be cited as a possible reason here, but it is no longer an expression of religious faith. Dowell immediately replaces this interpretation with a more modernistically subjective one—that Florence herself is creating the pattern.

The device is used with a magic realist touch in Salman Rushdie's *Shame* (1983): "At the end of the first year of civilian rule, General Raza Hyder became a grandfather. Good News [his daughter] gave birth to fine, healthy twin sons.... Exactly one year later Good News became a mother again; this time she produced triplets.... Precisely twelve months later Good News brought forth a beautiful quartet of baby girls.... Five more granddaughters turned up one year later to the day" (1984, 206). Here the preposterous accumulation of repeated birthdays in combination with the steadily increasing number of children born each year exposes the constructedness of the story, pointing to the causal-manipulative influence of the author as storyteller, combined with characteristically Rushdian humor: "And now Hyder had to say something. 'Fourteen kids with the same birthday,' he told the couple as sternly as he could manage, 'what do you think you're up to?'" (206).

Analogical Coincidence

A distinctly different form of the coincidence plot becomes notable in twentieth-century fiction. This shift involves a change in the type of relationship between the characters or objects within the coincidence. Traditional coincidence involves actual physical or biological relationships between characters across the space and time of the narrative world. By contrast, both the specifically modernist and postmodernist forms of coincidence are constructed through an *indirect* or *figurative system of connection*: relationships are no longer story based through plots of kinship or friendship but are *only* cognitively constructed through the perception of correspondences. This development away from story-based traditional coincidence is a correlate of the change in focus of the scientific coincidence research noted in the work of Kammerer (1919) and Jung (1967) cited above.[21]

The difference between modernist and postmodernist forms of analogical coincidence also concerns the narrative level from which these analogous relationships are *recognized*. Modernist coincidence often underlines the subjectivity of human perception by foregrounding a character's own pluralistic or relativizing interpretations of analogous relationships. In postmodernist coincidence the analogous relationships on multiple levels create causal conundrums about the interpretation of relationships not for the characters but for the reader.

Modernist Coincidence

In modernist coincidence, analogous relationships link characters and objects on the same spatial and temporal level. Thus, in Conrad's *Chance* two unrelated men who share the surname Powell come together near the beginning of the story. Modernist coincidence can also take a purely perceptual form; for example, in James Joyce's *Ulysses* (1922), Leopold Bloom's thoughts frequently dwell on his perception of analogical relationships between objects and people. Here the intersection takes place in Bloom's mind and not in space and time because he creates a link between otherwise separate elements.

Postmodernist Coincidence

Postmodernist coincidence creates networks of relationships between characters across narrative time, but, unlike the traditional coincidence plot (which also occurs in postmodernist fiction), it does not do this by giving these characters a previous relationship in the form of spatial and temporal contiguity but by creating networks of uncanny correspondences between characters who are distributed across more than one temporal or ontological level. One frequent form of this type of relationship is the *constellational resemblance* in which analogous groups of characters repeat themselves across narrative levels. For example, in Prawer Jhabvala's *Heat and Dust* the constellation of a central female protagonist who has a relationship with one Indian and one Englishman repeats itself on two time levels (India in the 1970s and in 1923). Barnes's *Flaubert's Parrot* uses intertextual analogies: a correspondence exists between the narrator (a doctor), his wife and her extramarital relationships, and the main characters of Flaubert's novel *Madame Bovary*. Repeated story patterns can also be part of these analogical links: in *Heat and Dust* both the narrator and her alter ego on the 1923 time level become pregnant by their Indian lovers in the same location, and both subsequently contemplate abortion.

Since these analogically linked characters do not generally become spatially or temporally contiguous within the narrative world itself, it is generally the reader on the extradiegetic level who is the one capable of performing the act of *analogical recognition*, while the characters themselves exist in benign ignorance of the fact that they are figures in an interlocking constellation of correspondences. For example, Peter Ackroyd's *Chatterton* (1987) creates a multiple network of analogical links between characters on three different time levels in the eighteenth, nineteenth, and twentieth centuries.[22] However, only the reader is capable of performing the cognitive act that links the different figures and levels into an interconnecting matrix. In Barnes's *Flaubert's Parrot*, on the other hand, a form of recognitional process does take place on the character level when Geoffrey Braithwaite compares his wife and the fictional character Madame Bovary. The comparison does not actually constitute a recognition of the full constellational correspondences, but it may provoke recognition of the analogical relationships in the reader: "Did she [Ellen, Braithwaite's wife] display the cowardly docility which Flaubert describes as characteristic of the adulterous woman? No. Did she, like Emma Bovary, 'rediscover in adultery all the platitudes of marriage'? We didn't talk about it" (Barnes 1985, 164).

In postmodernist coincidence the concept of *relationship* (or *links*) is therefore a completely different one: relationships are not constructed through the temporal-linear, causal-progenerative, story-based links of human connections taken from the experience of real life (as in traditional coincidence) and cannot be traced back in a linear fashion to an *originary* relationship between the characters. Connections constitute links that form bridges across several worlds and ontological levels: they are links *between* stories and not links *within* the story (as in traditional coincidence).

In postmodern coincidence, therefore, the recognition of correspondences by the reader generally takes the place of spatial intersection in the narrative world: the corresponding trajectories of the characters intersect in the reader's mind when he activates the plotting principle of similarity. (Some historiographic metafictions, however, use fantastic transtemporal meetings between characters from different levels to create a greater convergence—see chapter 6.) Even if the discourse of the novel itself is completely immersive with no metafictional interruptions, as is the case in Ackroyd's *Chatterton* and Prawer Jhabvala's *Heat and Dust*, the existence of such relationships suggests an underlying constructedness that subtly undermines the autonomy of the fictional world by giving it the causal-manipulative fingerprint of an orchestrating author. This author may be either an intradiegetic character, like the nameless narrator on the 1970s level of *Heat and Dust* (whom the reader is inclined to suspect of manipulating either events or her own text to create analogical links), or the real-world author, who, in the case of a novel like *Chatterton*, can be the only possible manipulator behind the novel's complex story matrix. In either case, the reader's identification of the system of uncanny correspondences creates a completely different trans- or extradiegetic, causally manipulative pattern of links to the causal-progenerative links of biological relationships within one story that are constructed in the traditional coincidence plot.

The key differences between the different forms of coincidence can be summarized as follows. In traditional coincidence, recognition *between* characters stabilizes conceptions of identity by clarifying family relationships, restoring children to their parents, and establishing the characters' *origins* within a clear and stable framework. Particularly in its more euphoric forms, this form of plot creates narrative pleasure for the reader through a convergent pattern that evokes the experience of homecoming, belonging, and the clarification of identity. These links are also often backed up in the text's explanatory framework by satisfying networks of causality. Moreover, in traditional coincidence the clarification of mysteries in the past world of the story in conjunction with the assertion of character identity means that the assertion of one actual world creates a cognitive stability that replaces the uncertain virtual flux of possible relationships that has existed beforehand. The postmodernist form, on the other hand, leaves the narrative in a permanent state of flux in which the relationships of analogical links are never replaced by definitive connections within the story.

In modernist coincidence, by contrast, the reader's participation is much more limited, since he is witness to the depiction of single analogical relationships, often occurring or perceived within one narrative episode. By contrast, both traditional coincidence and the postmodernist use of analogical relationships stretch across the time sequence or time zones of the fictional world, constituting much larger and complexly organized plots that stimulate the reader's own interconnecting cognitive faculties in different ways.

The coincidence plot in its complex traditional and postmodernist manifestations is therefore a matrixlike structure and truly a "plot" in the sense of an intricate design. From the crucial point of the characters' intersection in the narrative world, the traditional coincidence plot can harness the reader's attention by radiating backward in narrative time to unresolved issues and events in the prehistory of the characters' relationships and forward in story time to the possibility of recognition, thereby creating curiosity or suspense. At the same time it can provoke in the reader a questioning or curious response regarding the existence of hidden forces or systems existing in or beyond the narrative world that may explain the marvelous or strange constellation of events. The postmodernist coincidence plot creates a similar cross-temporal matrix, but one that connects character groups across multiple levels and that subverts the causal-linear structures of traditional coincidence, replacing them with analogous links that can, ultimately, only be causally traced back to the manipulative level of an author.

5. Counterfactuals and Other Alternate Narrative Worlds

> Perhaps the best argument for the significance of counterfactual reasoning in everyday life comes from its prevalence in works of popular art. The reactions of characters in plays, books, and movies frequently turn on thoughts about what might have been.
>
> David Dunning and Scott F. Madey,
> "Comparison Processes in Counterfactual Thought"

Counterfactuals across the Disciplines

The statement above comes from an essay in the most comprehensive psychological study of human counterfactualizing to date—Neal J. Roese and James M. Olson's *What Might Have Been: The Social Psychology of Counterfactual Thinking* (1995). The authors cite texts such as Charles Dickens's *A Christmas Carol* (1843) and Frank Capra's movie *It's a Wonderful Life* (1946) as evidence of their claim that the urge to counterfactualize is an intrinsic mode of human thought.[1] While nonliterary scholars are well aware of the prevalence of counterfactuals in novels and movies, counterfactuals have not yet attracted commensurate attention in literary studies, nor has the extensive nonliterary research into counterfactuals, which offers great potential for application in literary analysis, been capitalized upon.

Chapter 2 already incorporated Fauconnier and Turner's (1998a, 2003) cognitive work on counterfactuals into the analysis of the readerly *identification* and *differentiation* of transworld character versions in fictional counterfactuals. (Earlier philosophical work on counterfactuals [Goodman 1947; Lewis 1973; Rescher 1975] was also reviewed there.) This section reviews further key aspects of cross-disciplinary research into counterfactuals before assembling a full model for the analysis of counterfactuals in narrative fiction.

Counterfactuals in the Psychological, Cognitive, and Political Sciences

The essays in Roese and Olson (1995c) represent a range of contributions dealing with both the empirical study and the theoretical modeling of counterfactualizing in human thought:[2]

> Counterfactual thinking is an essential feature of consciousness. Few indeed have never pondered a lost opportunity nor regretted a foolish utterance. And . . . it is from articulations of better possible pasts that individuals may realize more desirable futures. . . . Counterfactual thoughts represent an empirically definable and measurable feature of individuals' mental lives; research examining these thoughts may therefore be uniquely poised to shed new light on the very essence of human consciousness. (Roese and Olson 1995a, 46–47)

The ubiquity of counterfactuals in human thought is also emphasized by Fauconnier and Turner: "Our species has an extraordinary ability to operate mentally on the unreal" (2003, 217). Counterfactual thinking is therefore not simply a field for philosophical speculation, as practiced in possible-worlds theorizing (e.g., Lewis 1973), but a fundamental thought pattern in human consciousness and a key part of the way we narrativize what happens in our lives.

People tend to construct counterfactual narratives in the everyday course of events. These can range from minor counterfactual responses formulated when the daily schedule goes wrong ("if I had not gotten stuck in a traffic jam, I would have arrived on time" [Fearon 1996, 50–51]) to the counterfactuals generated, often at times of personal crisis, to review one's life trajectory and formulate long-term regrets about missed opportunities (Gilovich and Medvec 1994; Kahneman 1995). Such alternate life scenarios are an everyday manifestation of the human urge for *narrative liberation* from the real world discussed in chapter 1. Human beings' tendency to construct alternate worlds to the one they live in already begins with such natural counterfactual narratives.

Recent research defines counterfactuals as theoretical alterations or *mutations* of a past sequence of events made in order to construct a different version of reality that counters the events of the "real" or factual world. Roese and Olson's definition concurs with other earlier philosophical definitions (e.g., Goodman 1947):

> The term *counterfactual* means, literally, contrary to the facts. . . . For present purposes, we restrict our use of the term counterfactual to alternative versions of past or present outcomes, although we are aware that others have also used the term to describe future possibilities. . . . Thus, in the present analysis, an essential feature of a counterfactual conditional is the falsity of its antecedent, in that it specifies a prior event that did not occur. (1995a, 1–2)

A counterfactual is generated by creating a nonfactual or false *antecedent*. This is done by *mentally mutating* or "undoing" a real-world event in the past to produce an *outcome* or *consequent* contrary to reality (see Roese and Olson 1995a, 1–2; McMullen, Markman, and Gavanski 1995). If we apply the spatial metaphor of the fork discussed in chapter 3, the *antecedent* thus refers to the point in the past at which reality is altered and a new hypothetical branch in time is created. The term *consequent* or *outcome* refers to the result of that alteration farther on down the counterfactual time path. A counterfactual therefore involves a clear contrastive relationship between a real event belonging to a factual world and a hypothetical one that counters this fact: "With its assertion of a false antecedent, the counterfactual sets up an inherent relation to a factual state of affairs" (Roese and Olson 1995a, 11).

Daniel Kahneman and Dale T. Miller's norm theory established key patterns in counterfactual formation, pinpointing the specific kinds of situations in which humans tend to generate counterfactuals: "The mental representation of a state of affairs can always be modified in many ways, [but] some modifications are much more natural than others, and ... some attributes are particularly resistant to change" (1986, 142–43). Thus, everyday human counterfactual thinking generally restricts itself to the laws of the real world concerning mutations: "For the average person, some things are very mutable (e.g. effort), whereas other things seem relatively immutable (e.g. gravity)" (Roese and Olson 1995a, 7). Significantly, research has found that people are more inclined to mentally mutate exceptional events than routine ones: "The more abrupt or discontinuous the change, the more likely people are to notice it, to try to explain it, and generate counterfactual scenarios in which they 'mutate' the departure from normality to the more customary and expected default value" (Tetlock and Belkin 1996b, 33; see also Kahneman and Miller 1986). Counterfactuals are therefore often generated in dramatic or exceptional situations, and traumatic or negative outcomes in particular tend to trigger counterfactuals. This is also borne out by research in political science: "Negative events are also more likely to capture the attention of scholars in world politics than positive events" (Olson, Roese, and Deibert 1996, 300). These points will be highly relevant for counterfactuals in narrative fiction relating both to the representation of personal tragedy and to wider historical scenarios.

Regarding the definition of counterfactuals, it should be noted that, in contrast to the body of research referred to above, Fauconnier and Turner's (2003, 217–47) cognitive exploration of counterfactuals uses an understanding of counterfactual within their concept of "the Unreal," which broadens its application to other hypothetical constructions. Instead of being viewed as a clear narrative sequence involving an antecedent and a consequent and that can be distinguished from a factual proposition, "counterfactuality is not an absolute property. A space will be counterfactual depending on the point of view one takes" (Fauconnier and Turner 2003, 230).[3] Fauconnier and Turner's particular focus is on striking conceptual blends taken from contemporary linguistic culture, such as "if Clinton were the *Titanic*, the iceberg would sink," a "counterfactual that circulated inside Washington, D.C., during February 1998" (221; this was a wry comment on Bill Clinton's political resilience despite the Lewinsky affair). This example, which contains a striking *metaphorical hypothesis* but is not the same kind of counterfactual narrative sequence discussed by Roese and Olson (1995c), illustrates Fauconnier and Turner's much broader use of the term (compare, however, Turner 1996, which still uses "counterfactual" in the more traditional sense).

Many of the theoretical models describing everyday human counterfactualizing formulated in the psychological literature are highly applicable to the patterns of counterfactualizing by characters and narrators in narrative fiction. A key distinction is that between *downward* and *upward* counterfactuals (sometimes also formulated as *direction*): "We have termed counterfactuals that improve on reality ('. . . it could have been better') upward counterfactuals and those that worsen reality ('. . . it could have been worse') downward counterfactuals" (McMullen, Markman, and Gavanski 1995, 134).[4] The same authors also make a distinction between self-focus versus external focus. This distinction refers to counterfactuals in which the self is the central focus but either as a perpetrator (self-focus) or as a victim (external) of circumstances (149–50). This will prove relevant in narrative fiction for what I call the *counterfactualizing agent*. A further distinction—that between *behavioral* and *characterological counterfactuals*—is also important, since it concerns whether a person's behavior or character is the focus of the counterfactual mutation: characterological counterfactuals "merely condemn the self rather than provide insight into specific actions by which the outcome might be changed" (McMullen, Markman, and Gavanski 1995, 150; see also Janoff-Bulman 1979). Applied to narrative fiction, this distinction can be extrapolated to refer to story versus character-based counterfactuals.

Beyond these formal distinctions, by far the most fascinating aspect, relevant both for real-world and fictional contexts, is the question of *counterfactual emotions*. *Satisfaction* and *regret* about the actual course of events are two key responses linked to the *direction* of counterfactual comparisons (Gilovich and Medvec 1995). Upward counterfactuals constructing a better possible world stimulate regret, whereas downward counterfactuals of a world that could have been much worse create satisfaction.[5] Moreover, in an analysis of the way people counterfactually review their own life stories, Thomas Gilovich and Victoria Husted Medvec uncover a "temporal pattern" in which "regrettable inactions loom larger in the long run than they do in the short term" (271)—that is, looking back on their lives, people are more likely to regret things they *didn't* do. In addition, Kahneman (1995, 391) suggests a powerfully expressive distinction between *hot regret* and *wistful regret*. This depends on whether regret is experienced intensely but briefly in response to a transiently important event that is then quickly forgotten or whether a deeper emotion is harbored as a result of a long-term preoccupation with "roads not taken" in life.

In briefly discussing some literary examples, Roese and Olson (1995b, 189–92) designate what they call "*counterfactual fiction*" as fulfilling a *definitional* function: "Counterfactual suppositions may serve to define and clarify a state of affairs by pointing to a contrasting yet plausible alternative state of affairs. By considering the points of convergence, one may obtain a clearer sense of the nature of actuality" (189). They point to "the self-serving nature," that is, the actuality-enhancing quality, of such fictions, since they portray overwhelmingly downward counterfactual worlds (e.g., Nazi victory in World War II), whereas, they claim, "upward counterfactual comparison[s], which may suggest points of improvement to actuality, are rare in popular fiction" (190). Roese and Olson point to Capra's movie *It's a Wonderful Life* (a fantasy in which the hero finds himself in a downward counterfactual world where he was never born; see also Dannenberg 2004b) as an example of how the definitional function involves a "useful dialectic by which the individual comes to grasp more completely his or her particular lifespace" (191–92). However, as the examples in the third section of this chapter show, there is in fact a more variable spread of counterfactual directions in narrative fiction than those in the texts to which Roese and Olson refer.

The plotting principle of *causation* applied to counterfactuals from narrative fiction was already discussed in chapter 2. The question of *causality* also recurs across recent research. Roese and Olson state quite categorically that "all counterfactual conditionals are causal assertions" (1995a, 11), and this link is also seen as intrinsic in research within the political and historical sciences: "We can avoid counterfactuals only if we eschew all causal inference and limit ourselves to strictly noncausal narratives of what actually happened (no smuggling in causal claims under the guise of verbs such as 'influenced,' 'responded,' 'triggered,' 'precipitated,' and the like)" (Tetlock and Belkin 1996b, 3); "causal claims are the stuff of historical analysis, and counterfactual claims are implicit in all causal assertions" (Breslauer 1996, 72).[6] By contrast, Fauconnier and Turner, as part of their less narratively oriented definition of counterfactuals, challenge this claim: "Great ranges of counterfactual thought are directed at important aspects of understanding, reason, judgment, and decision that are not concerned principally with causality" (2003, 219). Their example "if Clinton were the Titanic, the iceberg would sink" (221) illustrates how their broader understanding of the term *counterfactual* leads to the inclusion of propositions that lack causal connections. Here the metaphorical aspect (Clinton as a political heavyweight capable of sinking icebergs) overrides any literal-causal sequence (the actual-world physical capacity to cause an iceberg to sink).

The key role of causation within counterfactuals is certainly confirmed by its role in narrative fiction. As we saw in chapter 1, the use of causally based arguments within counterfactuals is a key strategy in the creation of immersive narrative, which simulates real-world cognitive explanatory patterns in the presentation of fictional events. Many counterfactuals thus satisfy the basic human *cognitive desire* for systems of causal connection, and this can be seen as a contributory factor to "the significance of their pervasive presence in people's mental lives" (Roese and Olson 1995b, 169). Counterfactuals are thus deeply "meaningful" mental operations precisely because they enable the human mind to construct cogent causal connections within narrative sequences that "make sense" of life.

In the political sciences the analysis of the construction of causal patterns in counterfactual models of history distinguishes between several types of causal connection: *simple chains* versus *complex networks* of interaction (*mono*-versus *multicausality*). Richard Lebow and Janice Stein contrast "simple, monocausal counterfactual arguments," in which one antecedent leads to an outcome, with "the long chain of causal reasoning that connects small events to large consequences" (1996, 120). A radical example of how "distant trivial events can have far-reaching consequences" (120) is Blaise Pascal's (1960, 118) speculation about the effect a counterfactually shorter version of Cleopatra's nose might have had on world history. James Fearon contrasts such "butterfly-effect 'causes'" (the reference is to chaos theory's analysis of the potential of a single butterfly to influence weather systems) with other forms of antecedent-outcome linkage, distinguishing between "legitimacy" and "plausibility" (1996, 57). For example, the counterfactual "if Napoleon had had Stealth bombers at Waterloo, he would not have been defeated" is in itself plausible (Stealth bombers would have given Napoleon victory), but in terms of its antecedent (Stealth bombers existing in the early nineteenth century), it is a more "illegitimate" counterfactual claim than a counterfactual like that of Cleopatra's nose, which is "plausible even though [it] seem[s] intuitively wrong" (54–55). Such implausible counterfactuals, however, while of little use to historical analysts, are used to great effect in history-alteration narratives in science fiction. As the historical overview in chapter 7 will show, such narratives demonstrate an increasingly anarchic attitude to the master narratives of history and thus pave the way for the historical relativism of the genre of historiographic metafiction.

If we apply the key concepts from Turner's (1987, 140–42) typology of causation discussed in chapter 1 to these different forms of causal modeling, we can see that the causation patterns constructed by counterfactuals center particularly on the *causal-progenerative* form. The empirical observation of counterfactualizing in psychological studies highlights the mind's construction of causal-progenerative connections linking the antecedent to the consequent—for example, long-term regret is experienced through a sense of a lost better life that the counterfactualizing individual has *failed to cause* because of a key omission (Gilovich and Medvec 1994). By contrast, the distinction in the political sciences between monocausal linear patterns or "path dependence" (Kiser and Levi 1996, 196) and more complex and chaotic causal networks (Fearon 1996; Kiser and Levi 1996) centers precisely on the *inability to discern* connections: perceivable causal-progenerative paths dissolve and are replaced by the inference of complex networks of causal interaction, which are inscrutable to the human mind. This is in fact one reason why counterfactualizing in the political sciences is a controversial methodology and has even been disclaimed as "the *fallacy of fictional questions*" and a "methodological rathole" (Fischer 1970, 15, 18; cf. the discussion in Tetlock and Belkin 1996b, 3). However, notwithstanding such methodological objections, the counterfactual approach to history in the political sciences as practiced by the contributors to Philip Tetlock and Aaron Belkin's *Counterfactual Thought Experiments in World Politics* (1996a) and the genre of the counterfactual historical essay collected in anthologies by J. C. Squire (1932), Niall Ferguson (1997), and Robert Cowley (2001) certainly documents the insuppressible cognitive urge of many historians and political scientists to construct counterfactual narratives.

Counterfactuals in Narrative Studies

In narrative theory, counterfactuals have been discussed under a variety of names.[7] In his investigation of urban oral narratives, Labov identifies a particular type of "comparator" that only tends to occur in "the narratives of older, highly skilled narrators" (1972, 386). All the examples of this kind of "comparator" in fact involve evocations of what might have happened; Labov's observation that this form of "comparator" occurs in more sophisticated oral narratives correlates with the present study's finding that counterfactuals occur in tandem with the novel's development of more complex forms of narrative discourse (see chapter 7). In the literary study of narrative, the most notable treatment of counterfactuals is Prince's (1988, 1992, 28–38) discussion of the larger phenomenon of the *disnarrated*, a concept that refers to "all the events that do not happen" but "are nonetheless referred to (in a negative or hypothetical mode) by the narrative text" (1992, 30); it "can pertain to the future, the present, or the past.... [I]t frequently consists of hopes, desires, imaginings and pondering, unreasonable expectations and incorrect beliefs" (34–35). The disnarrated therefore includes counterfactuals articulated in a hypothetical mode but would not include counterfactuals articulated in the genre of alternate history, since here counterfactual events are narrated as actual events within the ontological hierarchy of the narrative world. Ryan (1991, 166–69) evaluates Prince's "disnarrated," and reduces it to a tripartite typology in order to correlate it with her own concept of the *virtual*. Ryan's understanding of the virtual does not cover the full spectrum of counterfactuals in fiction as her main focus is on the private worlds of characters as opposed to narratorial constructions. In Margolin's (1996) typology of the different forms of character version, the intratextual and extratextual forms concern counterfactuals. The intratextual form involves "a branching or divergence of worlds" where a character has "several alternate life histories" (114). The "extratextual" form involves historical counterfactuals, that is, "revisions of actual individuals, where initial phases of the actual individual's history are preserved, while successive ones are replaced, to diverge emphatically from accepted public facts" (131). Margolin's example is Richard Chesnoff, Edward Klein, and Robert Littel's *If Israel Lost the War* (1968), an alternate history of the 1967 Arab-Israeli War. Herman's (1994, 2002, 309–30) discussion of "hypothetical focalization" uses the concept of the "counterfactual witness" (1994, 238). In its simplest form, this refers to the postulation of a hypothetical observer—as in the phrase "an observer might have speculated" (taken from A. S. Byatt's *Possession*)—used in narrative description. The concept thus refers to the *hypothetical observation* of a single-world narrative event that gives the recipient "as it were, illicit access to the aspects of the storyworld" (Herman 2002, 310).[8] Indeed, there is certainly a fuzzy borderline between outright counterfactuals and the divergent versions of events narrated from different character perspectives that can be observed in texts such as Samuel Richardson's *Clarissa* (1747–48) through to Julian Barnes's *Talking It Over* (1991).

A further relevant area of research concerns the reader's construction of counterfactuals in response to narrative plots. Gerrig proposes the term *replotting* to refer to the process whereby "once readers are made privy to particular outcomes, they mentally begin to comment on them" (1993, 90). Gerrig's work is thus related to the psychological literature on counterfactualizing. This becomes particularly clear in his claim that "it is easiest to observe these replottings when an outcome has been particularly negative" (90). This corroborates similar claims in the psychological literature (see Tetlock and Belkin 1996b, 33).

Research into Literary Genres that Use Counterfactuals

Counterfactuals and other forms of alternate-world construction have been discussed in genre-focused studies of twentieth-century narrative fiction.[9] Within the field of science fiction studies, counterfactual historical narratives are generally designated as *alternate* (sometimes "alternative") *history* (see, e.g., Wolfe 1986, 6; Malmgren 1991, 149; Adams 1994; Alkon 1994; Schenkel 1996). "Alternate history" is sometimes used in contradistinction to "parallel history" (Adams 1994; Alkon 1994) or "parallel worlds" to refer to a "frame in which many alternate worlds can be simultaneously held, sometimes interacting with each other" (Clute and Nicholls 1993, 23).[10] The spatial metaphors "alternate time stream" (Scholes and Rabkin 1977, 177), "multiple time tracks" (Harrison 1976, 108), and "alternate probability time lines" (Malmgren 1991, 93) are all used as terms to refer to the alternate paths of time constructed in such narratives.[11] Jörg Helbig (1988) proposes the term "parahistorical novel" in a study of historical counterfactuals in English and American fiction. He explores how alternate histories are a specifically national literature that processes a nation's historical traumas by transforming a positive historical moment (e.g., the Allies' victory in 1945) into a negative scenario (a postwar world ruled by a German Reich) (Helbig 1988, 102–3). He also distinguishes between discursive and narrative forms of alternate history. The former, manifest in the counterfactual essay, seeks historically logical interpretations and closed causal chains, while the latter deals with more entertaining aspects of counterfactual speculation.[12] Paul Alkon contrasts the postmodern staging of the "disappearance of the past" (1994, 65) in contrast to "classical" alternate history, which creates an authenticated and distinctive world of the counterfactual past by "giving historical information or references to orient readers with respect to points of divergence and congruity between the fictional and real worlds" (81). Postmodernist alternate histories, on the other hand, merge past and present through the "abolition of historical distance by . . . importing features of our present into the past" (80). Christoph Rodiek (1997) considers counterfactual historical narratives outside English studies using the term "uchronie," coined in French literature by Charles Renouvier (1988). Notably, Rodiek highlights the nature of the reception process of the uchronie, in which the counterfactual text must be able to activate the contrastive real-world history in the mind of the reader (61); he also distinguishes between texts depicting counterfactual history and those focusing on counterfactual biographies (49). Karen Hellekson (2001) studies the interweaving of narrative and history in key texts of the alternate history genre by authors such as Philip K. Dick and Ward Moore. In a recent and fascinating work Gavriel D. Rosenfeld (2005) undertakes a comprehensive study of the wide body of genres that represent counterfactual versions of Nazism and analyzes their contribution to the cultural and historical memory of the Third Reich.

Multiple plot versions and alternate histories in postmodernist fiction have also received extensive attention. Patricia Waugh and Brian McHale designate

Borges's story "The Garden of Forking Paths" as the initiator of "textual contradictions" (Waugh 1984, 137) or "realizations of the forking-paths principle" (McHale 1987, 108).[13] Doležel (1988, 491–93) discusses "incompatible alternate plots" in Alain Robbe-Grillet's *La maison de rendez-vous* (1965) and in a substantially earlier text—O. Henry's "Roads of Destiny" (1903). Ursula Heise (1997, 77–175) traces "time forks and time loops" in postmodernist texts.

The role of alternative historical narratives in the genre that is generally referred to as "historiographic metafiction" (a term proposed by Linda Hutcheon [1988]) has been widely discussed (see Engler and Müller 1994; Engler and Scheiding 1998; Nünning 1995a, 1995b). McHale's observations on the genre, which he calls the "postmodernist historical novel," remain incisive: the traditional historical novel fills in the "dark areas" of history, that is, "those aspects about which the 'official' record has nothing to report" (1987, 87) without contravening actual written history. By contrast, the postmodernist use of history and of real-world historical figures involves "stark contradiction of the historical record," "illicit mergings of history and the fantastic," and the use of blatant anachronisms (89). The postmodernist contradiction of history can occur in two ways: "Either it *supplements* the historical record, claiming to restore what has been lost or suppressed; or it *displaces* official history altogether" (90). McHale therefore uses the term "alternative history" to refer to a specifically "postmodernist strategy" (90) as opposed to a larger narrative phenomenon; a major example of a text dealing in the "postmodernist revision of official history" (92) is Carlos Fuentes's *Terra Nostra* (1975), which, for example, "has Felipe II of Spain marrying Elizabeth Tudor of England" (92). In a more recent study, Suzanne Keen (2001, 142—53) discusses manifestations of "the counterfactual imagination" as part of her study of the "romance of the archive," a subgenre of contemporary British fiction.

The above survey shows how previous studies have focused on many different aspects related to counterfactuality. In doing so, however, they have seldom provided a broader historical or generic picture. The following theoretical model, in combination with the historical overview in chapter 7, aims to consolidate these fragmented areas of research on theoretical, textual, and historical levels.

A Theory of Counterfactuals in Narrative Fiction

In its basic form a counterfactual is a narrative sequence, but in narrative fiction characters play an essential role within its structure and effect. This was already seen in the cognitive-ontological exploration of multiple character versions and transworld identity in chapter 2. Fictional characters are the correlates of the real-world human subjects of empirical psychological study. This is one key aspect of the narrative power of autobiographical counterfactuals in fiction—they tap into the counterfactualizing capacity of the real reader, reminding her of personal counterfactual narratives and making the fictional narrative seem more "real." The psychological study of counterfactuals thus helps us to better understand the representation of counterfactual thinking in fictional characters as the simulation of an authentic human consciousness.

In terms of the *definition* of counterfactuality, this study uses a clearly delimited understanding of the term as practiced by Roese and Olson (1995c) and Tetlock and Belkin (1996a). This is because a clear distinction between counterfactuals and other forms of fictional alternate worlds enables us to chart and analyze the historical mutations of counterfactuals, particularly those involved in postmodernist writing. Historically, an overall development can be observed involving the destabilization of the clear ontological hierarchy of counterfactuality, in which *fact* is clearly distinguished from a "less real" *counterfact*, and the construction of more ambivalent hierarchies of alternate worlds.

Definition and Structure

A *counterfactual* is a hypothetical alteration in a past sequence of events that changes the events in a *factual* sequence in order to create a different, *counter*factual outcome. The term *antecedent* refers to the event in the past where the alteration is made. The *consequent* (or *outcome*) refers to the result of the alteration. *Upward* counterfactuals construct a better consequent, improving on circumstances in the factual world, whereas *downward* counterfactuals construct a worse version of the factual world (McMullen, Markman, and Gavanski 1995).

The Counterfactualizing Agent

Self-focused counterfactuals are made by a character who responds subjectively, and often emotionally, to events in his or her own life. *Externally focused* counterfactuals analyze events, life stories, or history outside the speaker's own life. They can be articulated by one character about another or by a heterodiegetic narrator about a character's life or larger framework of events, in which case the counterfactuals are generally more detached and do not involve *counterfactual emotions*.

The Counterfactual Context and Scope

A *historical* counterfactual is a proposition that alters real-world history. A *biographical* counterfactual focuses on a character's life story as opposed to a larger framework of events, and, when this is self-focused, it becomes an *autobiographical counterfactual*. A biographical counterfactual can, of course, still be part of a larger historical framework. Purely fictional (nonhistorical) biographical counterfactuals, by contrast, create or imply multiple versions of a character who does not have a real-world historical *counterpart*.

In *behavioral* counterfactuals alterations concern the story or character actions but not the personal qualities of the character itself. By contrast, *characterological* counterfactuals alter character in order to create a counterfactual course of events, thereby creating a new *version* of that character (see *transworld identity* below). Characterological counterfactuals therefore change a character's personality in order to create the counterfactual antecedent. Conversely, in behavioral counterfactuals the antecedent is created purely through an altered event.[14]

Counterfactual Emotions

Self-focused autobiographical counterfactuals often create *counterfactual emotions*. *Satisfaction* is generally expressed through the construction of a downward counterfactual, in which a character imagines how his or her life might have been worse. *Regret* is typically expressed through the construction of an upward counterfactual, in which a character constructs an improved version of reality. *Hot regret* is a short-term counterfactual emotion, while *wistful regret* applies to long-term counterfactual retrospectives of autobiographical development (Gilovich and Medvec 1994; Kahneman 1995).

Ontological Hierarchy

The *ontological hierarchy* is the hierarchy of relations between worlds in counterfactuals and other narrative scenarios that create alternate worlds. Basic counterfactuals generate a binary hierarchy of events, in which *fact* is contrasted with a hypothetical *counterfact*. However, counter-counterfactuals—a counterfactual version of a counterfactual proposition (see Helbig 1988, 90–91)—already destabilize this binary relationship between fact and counterfact. Other forms of alternate-world scenario construct a much more ambivalent and less rigid hierarchy of relations between worlds. The possible worlds of the future, for example, are conceived of not retrospectively but anticipatorily, so that no single possibility can be ontologically and hierarchically dominant.

There are *single* and *multiple-world* forms of ontological hierarchy, depending on whether the ontological system of the fictional world admits the possibility that more than one world can be actual. The different uses of counterfactuals in the genres of narrative fiction can be mapped in terms of three main tendencies:

1. *The realist ontological hierarchy.* Realism is based on the premise that the text depicts a "real" world, and therefore only a single world can be represented as actual. In this form, counterfactuals are always hypothetical worlds embedded within the real world, that is, they are the product of speculations made by narrators or characters. Similarly, in the most

realistic form of counterfactual history, the single-world alternate history, the counterfactual world is the only actual world of the text.
2. *The semirealist ontological hierarchy* (major example: science fiction). The narrative world or universe can consist of several actual worlds, but these are organized into a plausibly coherent, interconnected system of worlds using realist explanatory strategies such as causation.
3. *The antirealist ontological hierarchy* (comprising postrealist texts such as radical metafiction and historiographic metafiction but also more radical works of science fiction). The multiple worlds are not part of a coherent and unified system. If connections are made between worlds, *analogical* as opposed to *causal* relationships predominate. Hierarchical distinctions between these multiple worlds, such as the distinction between fact and counterfact, become fuzzy or disappear altogether.

A further distinction can be made between a *static* versus *dynamic* ontological hierarchy. Sophisticated alternate-world plotting is dynamic in all its different generic manifestations (from realism through to metafiction), involving changes in the ontological hierarchy that generate narrative interest. In realist narrative this is achieved through temporal orchestration (discussed in chapter 2). In science fiction texts the ontological hierarchy of the narrative universe is, for example, restructured by time travelers in history-alteration narratives. In experimental postmodernist metafiction narrative sleights of hand convert seemingly actual events into virtual ones. In historiographic metafiction apparently factual representations of history are revealed to be fakes or subjective constructions.

The ontological hierarchy and the reader's relationship to history can also give rise to *historical relativity*. The ontological hierarchy of a counterfactual history is identical for author and reader, both of whom can view events as counterfactual because they mutate events from a mutual past history. By contrast, the ontological hierarchy of a future history will change according to the temporal point at which the reader accesses the text. As soon as the reader is located beyond the fictional future date of the text, it effectively becomes an a posteriori counterfactual world: a reader reading George Orwell's *Nineteen Eighty-Four* in 1985 (published in 1949) will no longer see the text as a possible future but as a de facto counterfactual historical narrative.

Transworld Identity

The question of transworld identity arises in counterfactuals when characters have counterparts in another world (be it in real-world history, in another work of fiction, or in the same fiction). In realist fiction counterparts are hypothetical versions of characters constructed (or merely implied) by counterfactual speculations; in science fiction counterparts can be alternate versions of a fictional character in a transworld journey narrative; in historical counterfactuals a counterfactual historical figure's counterpart is located in real-world history. The reader's processing of transworld identity centers on the *identification* of and *differentiation* between different character versions and their factual (real-world) versus counterfactual life stories.

Characterological counterfactuals automatically generate different character versions, since the antecedent itself concerns a hypothetical alteration in character. In this case there can be no full transworld identicality between a character and his or her counterfactual counterpart. Conversely, behavioral (pure plot-based) counterfactuals do not alter character and thus create an identical version of the actual character in the counterfactual scenario.

The Role of Causation and Spatialization in Counterfactuals

As we saw in chapter 1, the reader is encouraged to think of narrative worlds that use the plotting principle of causation as "real" because the construction of causal links is a fundamental sense-making pattern in human cognitive operations. In addition, as we saw in chapter 2, counterfactual speculations in realist narrative create a reality effect by *ontological default*: the suggestion that things could have happened differently reinforces the *apparent* reality of actual events in the fictional world, making it seem to be an autonomous system as opposed to a fictional construct.

The links between causal reasoning and realism also become evident in the spatial mapping of time in narrative fiction. In realist and semirealist texts, time is conceived of metaphorically as a continuous and linear-sequential spatial network through the use of metaphors like the path and the fork or branch in time. These metaphors create an additional sense of the *coherence* of narrative time. In radical metafiction, however, where plot versions are presented fragmentarily and not as an autonomous narrative world, there is a marked absence of the spatialization of time to create coherence: events exist as an array of unconnected fragments, between which analogical and not linear-causal relations predominate.

Key Forms of Counterfactual in Narrative Fiction

The following examples illustrate the analytical parameters presented above but also reveal that in practice narrative texts are more complex combinations of the basic theoretical distinctions.

Autobiographical Counterfactuals

Realist counterfactuals are generally brief speculations inserted into the narrative by a character or a narrator. Many early forms in eighteenth-century fiction are the equivalents of the real-life counterfactual thought experiments studied in the psychological literature. A character—the fictional correlate of a real-world person—constructs an autobiographical counterfactual and in doing so often generates counterfactual emotions, thereby creating the impression of an authentic human consciousness.

The following example from Defoe's *Moll Flanders* illustrates short-term *hot regret*; here Moll blames herself for giving in to a suitor's amorous advances: "Had I acted as became me, and resisted as virtue and honour required, this gentleman had either desisted his attacks . . . or made fair and honourable proposals of marriage; in which case, whoever had blamed him, nobody could have blamed me" (Defoe 1978, 48). Here Moll constructs two alternate upward counterfactuals, intensifying her sense of lost opportunity in contrast to the actual event—the rapid loss of her virginity. The following example from Samuel Richardson's *Pamela* (1740) has a different effect: "'Now, my Pamela, I would have you think, and I hope you will have reason for it, that had I married the first lady in the land, I would not have treated her better than I will you'" (1980, 464). Here the upper-class Mr. B. constructs an, in social terms, upward counterfactual, since, counterfactually, he marries a socially superior bride. This counterfactual, however, does not frame an introspective or emotional speculation regarding his own life but functions *rhetorically* to underline both his magnanimity and fairhandedness in marrying the socially inferior Pamela.

Counterfactuals by a Heterodiegetic Narrator

When the narrator is emotionally engaged in the style of Jane Austen or George Eliot, externally focused counterfactuals by a heterodiegetic narrator can also have emotional undertones. The following counterfactual from Austen's *Mansfield Park* shows the narrator responding to a character with a mix of analytical detachment and personal engagement: "Would he [Crawford] have deserved more, there can be no doubt that more would have been obtained. . . . Would he have persevered, and uprightly, Fanny must have been his reward—and a reward very voluntarily bestowed—within a reasonable period from Edmund's marrying Mary" (1966, 451). Here exasperation is implied in the repeated "would" of the narrator, creating the emotional undertones of an observer who seems to be on the same ontological level as the character. The implication is that Crawford is a real person whose behavior has created an empathetic but exasperated response in the narrator. Whether the narrator's counterfactual is to be considered an upward or downward one is, however, a more complex and interesting question that strikes at the heart of the moral complexity of Austen's novel. From the narrator's perspective, sympathizing with Henry Crawford at this point, the counterfactual is an upward one (the alternative scenario would have been a better one for Crawford). However, from the perspective of the heroine's desires it is a downward counterfactual, for Fanny does not seek Crawford's love but that of her cousin Edmund.

The above counterfactual is a characterological one: the counterfactual *antecedent* is created by an alteration in Henry's *character* (Henry is more persevering), leading to a different *outcome* (Henry marries Fanny). Other variants are also possible. For example, in the following narratorial counterfactual from William Makepeace Thackeray's *Vanity Fair* (1848), altered character is the *consequent* as opposed to the *antecedent*: "O Vanity Fair—Vanity Fair! This might have been, but for you, a cheery lass: Peter Butt and Rose a happy man and wife, in a snug farm, with a hearty family; and an honest portion of pleasures, cares, hopes, and struggles: but a title and a coach and four are toys more precious than happiness in Vanity Fair" (1968, 119). Here the vain materialism of society, which Thackeray designates "Vanity Fair," is counterfactually wished away in order to postulate happier and more contented versions of the characters Peter Butt and Rose.

The above examples illustrate the overall tendency of counterfactuals in realist narrative to create a reality effect. The following example from Anthony Trollope's *Barchester Towers* (1857) follows a different strategy. The narrator uses an upward counterfactual to comment on a scene of misunderstanding in the love plot: "As she [Eleanor] spoke she with difficulty restrained her tears; but she did restrain them. Had she given way and sobbed aloud, as in such cases a woman should do, he would have melted at once, implored her pardon, perhaps knelt at her feet and declared his love . . . and Eleanor would have gone back to Barchester with a contented mind. . . . But then where would have been my novel? She did not cry, and Mr Arabin did not melt" (1995, 267–68).[15] This narratorial counterfactual is mildly characterological but essentially ironic: the counterfactual version of Eleanor conforms to the tearful Victorian female stereotype, whereas the actual one does not. However, the narrator's final comment draws attention to the extradiegetic level of plot construction. Counterfactual speculations by a heterodiegetic narrator can therefore have a destabilizing effect on the reader's belief in the actuality of the narrative world if, as here, they draw attention to the fact that events might have been *created* otherwise by the author.[16]

The fact that the examples cited are predominantly upward counterfactuals shows that realist fiction by no means adheres to the downward pattern observed by Roese and Olson (1995b) in their brief assessment of "counterfactual fiction" (twentieth-century counterfactual histories and biographies). The imitation of real-life counterfactualizing in realist fiction presents an array of upward and downward forms.

Counterfactuals and Negative Coincidence

As the psychological research reveals, radical changes from expected outcomes provoke counterfactual scenarios (Tetlock and Belkin 1996b, 33); furthermore, "negative events are also more likely to capture the attention . . . than positive events" (Olson, Roese, and Deibert 1996, 300). These findings have their fictional correlates in the striking conjunction of counterfactuals and negative coincidence. The following example of a narratorial counterfactual from Hardy's *Tess of the d'Urbervilles* illustrates this phenomenon. Destitute after her husband, Angel, has abandoned her, Tess goes to Emminster intending to seek help from her parents-in-law. However, she abandons this plan at the last minute, owing to a conversation between Angel's brothers she coincidentally overhears on the street (Hardy 1978, 376–77). At this point the narrator emphasizes the lost potential of the situation with an explicit upward counterfactual: "And she went her way without knowing that the greatest misfortune of her life was this feminine loss of courage at the last and critical moment through her estimating her father-in-law by his sons. Her present condition was precisely one which would have enlisted the sympathies of old Mr and Mrs Clare" (378). This narratorial counterfactual orchestrates the sense of tragic discordance and nonconvergence in Tess's life, in which, despite good intentions, things always take the worst course.

Such externally focused narratorial counterfactuals can therefore function to intensify the reader's emotional response to tragic plots. Character counterfactuals in response to negative coincidence can articulate a stronger emotional response. In Auster's *Moon Palace* Marco Fogg reviews the negative convergence within the novel's coincidence plot with a counterfactual expressing not only *wistful* but also *bitter regret*:

> I . . . felt frustration, bitterness over the years that had been lost. For if Victor had answered Barber's second letter instead of running away, I might have discovered who my father was as far back as 1959. . . . It was all a matter of missed connections, bad timing, blundering in the dark. We were always in the right place at the wrong time, the wrong place at the right time, always just missing each other. (1990, 249)

The fact that the human urge to counterfactualize in tragic contexts is strong is also proved by the responses of literary critics to tragic plots. Thus, in a discussion of Shakespeare's *Romeo and Juliet*, T. McAlindon constructs a whole string of counterfactuals to prove his point that "asynchrony is almost the determining principle of the action": "If the wedding of Juliet to Paris had not been brought forward from Thursday to Wednesday; if Friar Lawrence's message had reached Romeo in time; if Romeo had reached the vault a minute later, or Juliet awakened a minute earlier; or if the Friar had not stumbled as he ran to the vault[,] ... then the tragedy would not have occurred" (1991, 67). This example of a reader's response to negative coincidence in a literary text well illustrates how such a "mistimed" (67) tragic plot provokes a counterfactual response or "replotting" (Gerrig 1993, 90) in the recipient, even if no counterfactual is articulated in the fictional discourse itself. The interplay of negative coincidence and the counterfactual represents one of several key narrative intersections of the two plot patterns of coincidence and counterfactuality.

Historical Counterfactuals

Historical counterfactuals in narrative fiction frequently take an ontologically different form in which the counterfactual premise engenders a whole narrative world instead of, as in the examples from realist fiction above, being limited to hypothetical inserts embedded in the main actual world of the narrative text.

Biographical-Historical Counterfactuals

Nathaniel Hawthorne's short story "P.'s Correspondence" (1845) is an early example of the use of counterfactual history in fiction. P.'s narrative, which depicts an alternate nineteenth-century England, is produced through counterfactual biographies as opposed to wider counterfactual historical events. The text is full of references to the counterfactual biographies of real-world figures such as Charles Dickens and Napoleon Bonaparte. The following is P.'s description of Lord Byron's counterfactual longevity: "His early tendency to obesity having increased, Lord Byron is now enormously fat; so far as to give the impression of a person quite overladen with his own flesh. . . . Would that he were leaner; for, though he did me the honor to present his hand, yet it was so puffed out with alien substance, that I could not feel as if I had touched the hand that wrote Childe Harold" (Hawthorne 1903, 169–70). A satirical effect is produced through the contrast between Byron's real-world youth and counterfactual old age, and this is the result, in terms of the reader's transworld identification, of a very clear act of *differentiation* between the historical and counterfactual versions of Lord Byron. Such playfully counterfactual historical biographies are a notable feature of some alternate histories. Other works, such as Peter Ackroyd's *Milton in America* (1997), which depicts John Milton's counterfactual biography when he seeks refuge from the English Restoration in Puritan New England, undertake a more detailed exploration of counterfactual biography.

Counterfactual Historical Worlds

The genre of alternate history and the related science fiction narratives of history alteration use a counterfactual-historical premise to construct a detailed narrative world with a significantly altered historical framework. In ontological terms these are fully autonomous counterfactual worlds: counterfactual events are articulated as fact by the narrator and not as hypothesis.

Academic historical counterfactualizing (Tetlock and Belkin 1996a) centers on the construction of coherent and linear *causal-progenerative* chains leading from antecedent to consequent. In fictional forms of counterfactual history, however, the full details of the historical antecedent may only be implied because the major focus is on the imaginative narrative creation of the counterfactual world of the historical consequent. For example, in Roberts's *Pavane* a clear causal link is implied between Elizabeth I's assassination in 1588 and the technologically retarded, Catholic-dominated, twentieth-century England in which the novel's main action takes place, but this link is not strongly substantiated by the narrative. Traditional alternate histories in science fiction do, however, rely, implicitly or explicitly, on this causal-linear justification for the credibility of the counterfactual world. In contrast to such "classical" (Alkon 1994) alternate histories, science fiction texts with a marked postmodernist agenda tend to background or suppress historical paths of causation.

A key strategy used by some texts involves the temporary suppression of the historical antecedent, thereby playing with the *cognitive desire* of the reader for a causal explanation. Here the reader is plunged in medias res into a defamiliarized version of history and must read on in order to discover the causal-progenerative clues that point to the historical antecedent. In the following example from Philip K. Dick's *The Man in the High Castle* (1962) the historical antecedent is covertly introduced:

> "Listen. One of those two Zippo lighters was in Franklin D. Roosevelt's pocket when he was assassinated...."
> "Gee," the girl said, awed. "Is that really true? That he had one of those on him that day?"...
> The girl now stood at the window, her arms folded, gazing out at the lights of downtown San Francisco. "My mother and dad used to say we wouldn't have lost the war if he had lived," she said. (1965, 66)

In alternate histories where only one counterfactual world exists as the actual world, events are generally narrated by a narrator who is (apparently) unaware of the existence of worlds beyond that of the world of the text. This narrator is usually a covert heterodiegetic one (as in Robert Harris's *Fatherland* [1992]) but can, less commonly, be homodiegetic (as in Christopher Evans's *Aztec Century* [1993]). Despite their counterfactual premise, such texts fulfill the basic conditions of traditional realist narrative in instating only one world as the actual one. It is the reader herself who brings the historical frames to the text and undertakes the cognitive operations of differentiation and identification of transworld relations between the explicit counterfactual world of the text and the implicit real-world one from which it deviates.

Beyond these most realist forms, there is a rich spread of ontological variation across texts using alternate history within the science fiction tradition. Key variations can be pinpointed according to differences in the ontological hierarchy:

1. In the *single-world alternate history*, in accordance with the conventions of realism, only events in a single historically counterfactual world are narrated in the text, generally by a covert heterodiegetic narrator (Harris's *Fatherland*).
2. In the *dual-world alternate history*, a more overt heterodiegetic narrator describing the counterfactual historical world of the text also acknowledges the existence of the real world of the reader. Phillip Mann's *Escape to the Wild Wood* (1993) commences: "Welcome to the Earth. . . . But this is not quite the Earth which you and I know. . . . In this world the Roman legions never quit Britannia" (1994, 7).
3. In the *time-war* story, representatives of different versions of history wage war against each other and, by means of history manipulation, attempt to establish their own version of history as actual (Williamson's *The Legion of Time*).
4. In the *time-travel* story with *history alteration*, a time traveler either intentionally (i.e., causal-manipulatively) or accidentally (i.e., causal-progenratively) creates an antecedent that leads to a new version of history. This can involve the historically subversive substitution of real-world history with a new version (as in L. Sprague de Camp's *Lest Darkness Fall* [1939], where the alteration prevents the onset of the Dark Ages in the sixth century). Notably, such narratives do not conform to the overall tendency to use downward counterfactuals to glorify the course of real-world history observed by Roese and Olson (1995b). By contrast, the historically more conservative *correction* of a counterfactual version of history restores real-world history (as in Ward Moore's *Bring the Jubilee* [1953], which reestablishes the real-world result of the American Civil War).
5. In the *time-travel story* with *history multiplication*, a new branch of history is created, but the old branch is still explicitly featured in the text as a parallel world. For example, at the close of Gregory Benford's *Timescape*, two different versions of the late twentieth century are portrayed.
6. In the *multiple-worlds* alternate history, there is an a priori plurality of worlds in the narrative universe and usually some form of commerce or communication between them. Here a transworld traveler may meet or

exchange places with an alternate version of himself (as in Wyndham's "Random Quest").

7. The *multiple-world future history* is a related variant. Here the narrative world is set in the future and either consists of an a priori multiplicity of alternate worlds (Philip K. Dick's *Now Wait for Last Year* [1975]) or creates different versions of history through successive history alteration (Ursula K. Le Guin's *The Lathe of Heaven* [1971]).

These forms therefore represent a plethora of different world mixes and ontological hierarchies. Despite their postmodern ontological playfulness, their multiple-world structure is made more realistically cohesive and logical by virtue of intradiegetic connections between worlds. The following examples, from John Wyndham's "Opposite Number" (1956) and Joanna Russ's *The Female Man* (1975), illustrate how the fictional discourse echoes scientific discourse (in particular Everett's [1957] many-worlds interpretation of quantum theory) to make their multiple-world structure more credible:

> So every "instant" an atom of time splits. The two halves then continue upon different paths and encounter different influences as they diverge.... The pattern of it is the radiating ribs of a fan; and along each of the ribs, more fans; and along the ribs of those, still more fans; and so, *ad infinitum*. (Wyndham 1959, 129–30)

> Every choice begets at least two worlds of possibility.... Every displacement of every molecule,... every quantum of light that strikes here and not there—each of these must somewhere have its alternative. It's possible, too, that there is no such thing as one clear line or strand of probability, and that we live on a sort of twisted braid, blurring from one to the other without even knowing it. (Russ 1985, 6–7)

In these examples the metaphorical spatialization of time as a line or path—here the images of the "ribs of a fan" and the "twisted braid"—is used to evoke a cohesive spatiotemporal framework and interlinking system of worlds. Other causal aspects of counterfactual plots can also create a cohesion of worlds: time travelers are depicted as introducing *causal-manipulative* antecedents that trigger *causal-progenerative* changes in history, linking the multiple paths of history into a holistic spatiotemporal fabric.

Counterfactual History Blended with Postmodernist Relativity

Historiographic metafiction (Hutcheon 1988) (the postmodernist historical novel [McHale 1987]) also uses historical counterfactuals but with significant alterations to the clear ontological hierarchy of fact versus counterfact. Here a far less coherent historical narrative undermines the construction of an objective historical map or ontological hierarchy because the alternate versions of history are disconnected fragments and only *possible representations* of historical events. In these texts an ambivalent ontological structure, the fragmentary nature of world versions, and the suppression of causality are dominant strategies that can be contrasted with the cohesive counterfactual time lines of conventional science fiction. Thus Ackroyd's *Chatterton* incorporates many contradictory narratives, including counterfactual narratives about the historical poet Chatterton. Similarly, DeLillo's *Libra*, a novel about Lee Harvey Oswald and the Kennedy assassination, constructs a dense fabric of possible historical reconstructions. Part of the novel concerns retired CIA analyst Nicholas Branch, who has been "hired . . . to write the secret history of the assassination of President Kennedy" (15). Branch is shown evaluating the seemingly endless influx of evidence and documents that could potentially form the basis for any number of interpretations of history. DeLillo's text therefore implies that, if the precise nature of the true *facts* remains unknown or indeed is unknowable, there can also be no clear *counter*factual but only multiple configurations of data.

Historiographic metafiction thus does not depict *actual history* but shows how historical narratives are received by subsequent generations as authoritative narratives of a past world that is no longer accessible by any other means than textual reference. These multiple alternate historical worlds are an expression of the assertion that there is no clear *hierarchy of history* with one universal, transhistorically valid master version positioned authoritatively at the top. Here, therefore, the ontological hierarchy is culturally constructed *and* eroded: all historical narratives are virtual because they are generated within a particular epoch and culture.

Beyond the *Counter*factual: Multiple Alternate Worlds

As discussed above, a counterfactual involves a clear contrastive relationship between a *factual* sequence of events and a *counter*factual proposition that changes the factual by creating a new antecedent and an altered outcome. By contrast, in some narratives the ontological hierarchy is so blurred that it is no longer possible to use the designation *counter*factual. The discussion of historiographic metafiction above already reached the border zones of the counterfactual. The following discussion highlights some related alternate worlds in narrative fiction that fall well beyond it.

Multiple Alternate Futures

In psychologically complex realist texts, characters sometimes conceive of their possible future lives as well as their counterfactual autobiographies in an alternate past. Such techniques also mirror real-world human thought processes and strategies: "People have an innate ability to build scenarios, and to foresee the future" (Schwartz 1998, 29). The detailed interweaving of multiple virtual futures is, for example, a notable technique in the novels of George Eliot. In the rich tapestry of intertwined character lives in *Middlemarch*, a key structural principle is the juxtaposition of different characters' conceptions of what the future will or should bring. Eliot depicts her disastrous marriage plots in terms of the contradictory attitudes and visions of the future entertained by Dorothea as opposed to Casaubon and Lydgate as opposed to Rosalind. Like the evolution of the counterfactual, the representation of subjective character futures marks a significant departure from the previous conventions of realism because it foregrounds the subjective *virtual* character worlds in combination with the actual.[17]

Alternate Story Plotting

The narration of multiple actual versions of events constitutes a subversive stand against the traditional ontological hierarchy of realism (in which an authoritatively singular actual world exists in contradistinction to other subordinate virtual worlds). In terms of their ontological hierarchy, such texts do not generate counterfactuals but have a more ambivalent structure because they present more than one version of events without clearly indicating which version is to be viewed as actual.

The ending of Charlotte Brontë's *Villette* constitutes an early rebellion against the ontological hierarchy of realism. The closing narration suggests the reader should select whichever ending she feels happier with, one in which Lucy Snowe marries M. Paul, the man she loves, and one in which he is drowned at sea and does not return to marry her (Brontë 1979, 596). In radical postmodernist metafiction, the technique pioneered by Brontë reached new extremes in the often bewildering and disorienting narration of multiple story versions. One of the most extreme examples of this form is Coover's short story "The Babysitter," which consists of numerous contradictory and highly fragmentary episodes and culminates in a selection of contradictory endings. Here the lack of any clear markers concerning an ontological hierarchy sabotages the reader's ability to interact with the narrative world. The emphasis is on the antirealistic *exaggeration* of plot, while the detailed depiction of character (a key realist technique) is avoided: characters are merely duplicated, albeit performing different actions, in each story version.

In conclusion, some key distinctions can be made between the different genres using either counterfactual or multiple alternate versions of (hi)story in terms of their different uses of the plotting principle of causation. In realist texts counterfactuals are *linked* to the actual fictional world by being embedded in the discourse of characters or narrators. However, in the radical postmodernist alternate story text, the reader can only impose coherence on the story fragments by identifying the causal-manipulative role of an *extradiegetic* author who must ultimately be seen as the source of the contradictory story fragments. Conversely, while authorship also plays a key role in the generation of the multiple textual versions of history in historiographic metafiction, authorship here is essentially *intradiegetic*: on the story level, many writers and researchers are depicted generating versions of history. History and cultural memory are depicted as a maze of causal-progenerative textual tracks. By contrast again, the science fiction text has a range of intradiegetic strategies that interlink the text's different versions of history, such as the spatial metaphors of the interconnected branching paths of history that create the impression of a narrative universe that is a coherent whole.

Coincidence and Counterfactuality in the History of Narrative Fiction

3

The diachronic mapping of coincidence and counterfactuality in the following two chapters reads the history of these plots in two different ways—as a developmental "narrative of progress" for each plot pattern and, where relevant, as a history of the interaction of the narrative forces of convergence and divergence within individual texts and genres. Thus, some texts dealt with for their use of coincidence in chapter 6 are viewed in a new light for their use of counterfactuality in chapter 7. This dual perspective aims to reveal the richness and complexity of plot structures in individual novels as well as trace the changing cultural and generic pressures that influence the development of narrative fiction from the Renaissance to the present day.

In its entirety this evolutionary map of the novel and of the gradual transformation of narrative fiction for a period of over four centuries has two key aspects. It reveals the growth and development of innovative narrative strategies that give key texts of the novel heightened narrativity (in its qualitative sense), and it shows how age-old narrative traditions are reconfigured and formed anew as narrative fiction evolves. This developmental line ends in a survey of postmodernist fiction, showing how contemporary fiction is very much alive and innovative but also locating contemporary fiction within a much bigger historical picture of diachronic development and generic cross-fertilization. In pinpointing key developmental phases of the novel, the following two chapters use the analysis of the plots of coincidence and counterfactuality to evaluate the status of key writers from particular periods. In doing so, they underscore the innovative status of writers such as Philip Sidney, Daniel Defoe, Jane Austen, Samuel Richardson, Henry Fielding, Charlotte Brontë, Charles Dickens, Thomas Hardy, George Eliot, Joseph Conrad, Henry James, Philip K. Dick, Julian Barnes, Paul Auster, Jeanette Winterson, and Don DeLillo in the evolution of narrative fiction.

The two chapters thus function as a laboratory for the observation of the historical growth of narrative fiction. This way of charting a centuries-long period of growth involves the undermining and rewriting of simple analytical dichotomies such as that of the romance versus the novel and their replacement by the observation of branching structures of increasing generic plurality in the dense and diversifying network of subgenres and forms taken on by the developing plots of coincidence and counterfactuality. In terms of the diachronic picture it produces of the narrative manifestations of the love plot, this transhistorical perspective also allows us to observe the interaction of coincidence and counterfactuality in the historical trajectory of the representation of female developmental narratives as traced through the work of Jane Austen, Ann Radcliffe, Charlotte Brontë, George Eliot, Joanna Russ, and Jeanette Winterson.

In terms of the analysis of novelistic discourse, this larger diachronic picture of the changing techniques for the representation of coincidence and counterfactuality—as already indicated in the theoretical accounts of chapters 1 to 3—allows us to observe, over several centuries, precisely how the novel evolves increasingly more sophisticated strategies of immersion to enthrall the reader, thereby establishing the novel as the most successful and widely enjoyed form of print literature. The development of coincidence and counterfactuality and their interactive relationship can be seen as a complex and shifting dialogue between realism, romance, and other non- or antirealistic forms of narrative. The history of the novel and its subgenres reveals a sequence of changing positions, generic cross-dressing, and alternating impulses. Coincidence—a plot strategy used extensively by Renaissance romance—establishes itself as a major convention within key writers of the eighteenth-century novel (Daniel Defoe, Henry Fielding) and subsequently escalates into heightened forms of narrative convergence from the Romantic period (Ann Radcliffe but also Jane Austen) onward, particularly taking hold as a key strategy in the major period of "narrative realism" in the nineteenth century, for example, in the works of Charlotte Brontë, Charles Dickens, George Eliot, and Thomas Hardy. These developments prompt the inference that, over and above the continuing legacy of the genre of romance, Romanticism and its cultural aftermath constitute key influences in the continuing proliferation of the coincidence plot in nineteenth-century fiction. While it is originally a plot from the genre of romance, coincidence nevertheless establishes itself as a "realist" convention, renewed both by the evolution of immersive narrative strategies and by the cultural impulses of Romanticism.

This transfer of romance into the "realism" of novelistic discourse can primarily be attributed to the growing ability of the novel to represent coincidence using the sophisticated immersive strategies discussed in chapters 1 to 3. The heightening of narrative suspense, the cognitive reinforcement of patterns of kinship, the deepening of spatialized representation, the use of sophisticated causal plotting and of mystery plots made more complex and immersive through temporal orchestration of different story versions all transform the coincidence plot of romance into new immersive forms of representation. The coincidence plot, therefore, not only survives the transition from Renaissance romance but undergoes a rebirth, becoming a key plot of realist fiction despite its unlikely configurations of space and time, which potentially implicate the manipulating hand of the author. It is not until the more radical aesthetics of modernism, including its programmatic break with previous literary conventions, that we really see narrative consequences being drawn from the realization that the coincidence plot, above all, the kinship reunion plot, is not the stuff of quotidian reality but an age-old convention. Following this, however, the generically eclectic impulses of postmodernism lead to the reembracing of coincidence with all its former excesses and implausibilities.

Even more so than coincidence, counterfactuality can be seen working in various forms and directions within the novel, ranging from its use to create a narrative "reality effect" to forms that displace realism or subvert the concept of "the real" completely. In Renaissance fiction the counterfactual largely features as a rhetorical device in the speeches of characters. Then, in the eighteenth century it is increasingly used as a key realist strategy both in the representation of characters' consciousness and in heterodiegetic narration. While this trend is continued in the realist narratives of the nineteenth century, it is at this point that, as a result of key changes in the ontological and cultural mindset, counterfactuals begin to evolve and proliferate into other forms. In narratives of alternate history, autonomous counterfactual worlds are constructed that contradict historical fact, thereby moving counterfactuality into a new phase of ontological pluralization. This trend radically intensifies in the twentieth century in many different forms. The ontological hierarchies of alternate worlds in science fiction become increasingly convoluted and contradict the concept of the real through their creation, among other things, of multiple versions of history and the sabotage of official history through the actions of time travelers in history-alteration narratives. In radical postmodernist fiction, counterfactuality and alternate-world construction fully break out of the framework of realism by narrating multiple contradictory story lines. In historiographic metafiction the concept of subjective or manipulated alternate versions of history is used to destabilize the idea of historiographic authority. Thus, in the history of these two plot forms, the novel taps into the romance tradition of coincidence for additional narrative impulses and in order to create convergent story structures, while counterfactuality, at first a prop of realism, increasingly develops into nonrealistic forms of narrative.

The nineteenth century is a key site in the development of the plots of coincidence and counterfactuality. In one cultural-historical context these developments can be seen as dual reflections of Darwin's plots (Beer 1983): the branching structure of Darwin's evolutionary maps are reflected in the divergent patterns of counterfactual narrative, while Darwin's establishment of links of kinship between different forms of life on the planet is mirrored, on a smaller scale, in the extensive kinship plots of coincidence in Victorian fiction. In the dialogic history of coincidence and counterfactuality, however, the nineteenth century is also the site of a struggle between the opposing forces of romantic convergence and the divergent plot paths of counterfactuals. In some writers there is an underlying sense that the convergent pressures on plot to depict harmonious conclusions and happy marriages are in fact inimical to *social realism* and the representation of the position of women, since such euphoric resolutions follow the utopian plot agendas of comedy and romance. Novelists such as Charlotte Brontë, George Eliot, and Thomas Hardy all use forms of alternate-world construction and counterfactuality to emphasize and orchestrate the discordant, desolate, and nonconvergent life plots of their heroines. Brontë's *Villette* ultimately excludes the heroine from the convergence of kinship and romantic love that was staged in the coincidence plot of *Jane Eyre* and subverts the literary convention of romantic closure through its divergent ending, which suggests two contradictory versions of the love plot. George Eliot goes one step farther and partitions her novel *Daniel Deronda* into convergent and divergent plot patterns according to the gender of the protagonist, while Thomas Hardy's *The Return of the Native* and *Tess of the d'Urbervilles* subvert the tradition of "realism" constructed by convergent plots by using a combined strategy of negative coincidence and counterfactual commentaries to create and then orchestrate discordant event patterns. By contrast, Dickens's *Great Expectations* uses coincidence itself as a device to undermine a sense of harmony through the creation of a menacing sense of convergence in which the novel's criminal underworld emerges everywhere and a network of coincidental relationships becomes the means to expose the hero's illusory picture of Victorian society.

Later, in the postmodernist period, as John Barth envisaged, the "novel . . . somehow rise[s] above the quarrel between realism and irrealism" (1996, 283). To a large extent, therefore, postmodernist fiction brings an end to the confrontation and juxtaposition of forms and the beginning of a period of more pluralistic coexistence of narrative strategies. Thus, coincidence in the postmodernist period can be neoromantic (Drabble's *The Realms of Gold*), parodistically metafictional (Lodge's *Small World*), or tragic (Auster's *Moon Palace*). Counterfactuals abound across all genres—in realism, in science fiction, in fantasy, and in historiographic metafiction. Particularly, texts belonging to the latter genre (Ackroyd's *Chatterton*, DeLillo's *Libra*, Winterson's *The Passion*, and Barnes's *Flaubert's Parrot*) feature the interesting and fruitful merging of the strategies of postmodernist coincidence and counterfactuality.

The wide prevalence of the plots of coincidence and counterfactuality in narrative fiction precludes an all-inclusive approach in the selection of texts. The following two chapters discuss key examples to highlight important stages in the development of the two plot forms, above all focusing on innovative narrative strategies, change, variety, and development within each literary period. If the resulting picture is necessarily incomplete, this is only the nature of narrative itself, including that of literary history. The aim is not to create a detailed synchronic panorama within any one period but to give an account of the variegated developmental history of narrative fiction seen through the transhistorical analytical perspective of the plots of coincidence and counterfactuality.

6. The Metamorphoses of the Coincidence Plot

Discordant and Euphoric Recognition in the Renaissance Romance

Seen through the investigative lens of the coincidence plot, the history of the novel reveals a continuity rather than a dichotomy between romance and realism. The analysis of the coincidence plot in the development from romance to novel thus produces the "destabilization of generic categories" formulated by Michael McKeon (1987); it challenges Watt's (1987) dichotomous genre model and confirms Frye's observation that "the novel ... had few structural features peculiar to itself"; rather, it "use[s] much the same general structure as romance, but adapt[s] that structure to a demand for greater conformity to ordinary experience" (1976, 38–39). The modern novel takes the coincidence plot from romance and installs it in a contemporary narrative world, reinventing it by using immersive techniques such as temporal orchestration, suspense, cognitive stratification, and complex narrative explanations.

In Renaissance fiction the coincidence plot is most prevalent in the genre of pastoral romance. Paradoxically, it is in these—in terms of setting and plot—nonrealistic works that we can observe features that preempt later technical developments in the novel. Conversely, Elizabethan prose fiction located in a more contemporary and therefore "realistic" setting only makes very rudimentary and episodic use of coincidence. Thomas Nashe's *The Unfortunate Traveller* (1594) and Thomas Deloney's *Jack of Newbury* (ca. 1597) contain only occasional ad hoc coincidental encounters (cf. Nashe 1987, 237, 299 and Deloney 1987, 380–81) but do not use coincidence as an extended plot to create narrative suspense through the deferral of recognition—a strategy practiced both by the Renaissance romance and by the modern novel.

Sidney's *Old Arcadia* (ca. 1580) uses concealed identity and deferred recognition within a kinship reunion plot to drive events to the brink of catastrophe.

The fifth and final book of *The Old Arcadia* contains a protracted sequence of thwarted recognition between King Euarchus, his son Pyrocles, and his nephew Musidorus. Pyrocles and Musidorus have been imprisoned and put on trial for their attempts on the honor of the princesses Philoclea and Pamela and for their complicity in the apparent death of Duke Basilius. Unaware of their identity, King Euarchus—who arrives, coincidentally, to visit his old friend Basilius—agrees to judge the case. While Euarchus's arrival triggers the prospect of a momentous kinship reunion scene (the two princes have been away from home for many years), this only occurs at the very end of book 5 after many delays and multiple reversals of expectation. The extended trial scene (Sidney 1994, 325–53) takes place in a suspenseful situation of bilateral ignorance on the character-cognitive level and culminates in Euarchus condemning Pyrocles and Musidorus to death (352–53). Even when the princes' identities are revealed through a last-minute deus ex machina—the arrival of Musidorus's "trusty servant" Kalodoulos (353)—and a conciliatory recognition scene seems imminent, this expectation is frustrated because, in the name of impartial injustice, Euarchus regretfully but steadfastly refuses to reverse his judgment. Moreover, while Euarchus technically acknowledges the princes' *identity*, he is not inclined to recognize them as his *kin* because their recent behavior and multiple disguises have created a sense of estrangement: "Nay, I cannot in this case acknowledge you for mine; for never had I shepherd to my nephew, nor never had woman to my son. Your vices have degraded you from being princes, and have disannulled your birthright" (356). Unlike Greene's *Pandosto* (which was discussed in chapter 1), *The Old Arcadia* does not succumb to the temptation of a tritely joyous reconciliation scene but maintains the darker discordance of thwarted kinship recognition to the very end.

The New Arcadia (1590) remained unfinished and thus has no denouement to parallel the scenes discussed above. However, Sidney substantially altered his narrative strategy in this text, creating innovations in his presentation of coincidence.[1] The narration brings the action much closer to the reader by widely dispensing with overt heterodiegetic narration, by using characters as focalizers, and by using sections of embedded first-person retrospective narrative. This means that the narrative can now create surprises not only on the character-cognitive level but also for the reader, and this process is intensified by the disguises and false names assumed by the two princes. A major example of Sidney's innovative technique is an extended spatialized coincidental encounter between Musidorus and the disguised Pyrocles in which the reader accompanies Musidorus in his observation of an apparently female figure into the enclosed space of an arbor and there experiences the surprise of recognition with him (Sidney 1987, 68–70; see the discussion in chapter 3). A further example comes in a scene in which Musidorus attempts to rescue his Arcadian host's son from a group of Helots only to discover that the captain of the Helots is none other than Pyrocles himself. This transformation surprises Musidorus and reader alike: "'What!' said the captain, 'hath Palladius [Musidorus] forgotten the voice of Diaphantus [Pyrocles]?'" (Sidney 1987, 38). Moreover, in *The New Arcadia* the narrative episode of the princes' exploits to assist the beleaguered Princess Erona of Lydia is now told by an unwitting Philoclea to Pyrocles himself (who is, at this point, disguised as the Amazon Zelmane). Within a chain of coincidental relationships, Philoclea has heard the story from Plangus, who was also involved in the Lydian episode. Philoclea's narration of the arrival of the two heroes to save Erona is therefore full of *cognitive stratification*: Pyrocles enjoys the narration of his own exploits by the woman he loves, who herself is completely unaware that her seemingly female addressee and the heroic male subject of her narrative are the same person:

> There came thither . . . two excellent young princes, Pyrocles and Musidorus[,] . . . two princes, as Plangus said (and he witnessed his saying with sighs and tears), the most accomplished both in body and mind that the sun ever looked upon.
> While Philoclea spake those words, "Oh, sweet words!" thought Zelmane [Pyrocles] to herself, "which are not only a praise to me, but a praise to praise itself, which out of that mouth issueth!" (206)

Sidney's experimentation with focalization and embedded narratives in *The New Arcadia* thus creates a much more complex configuration of coincidence.

Thomas Lodge's *Rosalynde* (1590) stages a nimbly intricate sequence of coincidental encounters in the Forest of Arden, interlinking kinship and love plots. The novel's suspenseful orchestration of delayed recognition and its use of cognitive stratification and identity games in combination with innovative character-cognitive effects make it a significant text.[2] When Gerismond, the rightful king of France, is usurped by his brother Torismond, he flees to the forest. Subsequently, many other characters with previous relationships also take refuge there. The coincidental encounter of Rosalynde (disguised as the page Ganymede) with Rosader, the man with whom she has previously fallen in love (Lodge 1971, 67), and Rosader's final recognition of Rosalynde (158) are separated by more than half of the text. In contrast to Sidney's practice in book 5 of *The Old Arcadia*, Lodge uses *unilateral* recognition to heighten the suspense and create identity games: Rosalynde recognizes her beloved Rosader but does not reveal her identity to him. The reader thus enjoys complicity in Rosalynde's games with Rosader while experiencing suspense as to when Rosader will discover that Ganymede is Rosalynde.

The first encounter between Rosalynde (accompanied by Torismond's daughter, Aliena) and Rosader (67–73) employs a variety of techniques to heighten both the reader's complicit inclusion and Rosader's ignorance. When their paths cross in the forest, the two women discover Rosader reciting a sonnet he has written to none other than Rosalynde:

> Rosader did every day eternize the name of his Rosalynde; and this day especially when Aliena and Ganymede, enforced by the heat of the sun to seek for shelter, by good fortune arrived in that place, where this amorous forester registered his melancholy passions. They saw the sudden change of his looks, his folded arms, his passionate sighs: they heard him often abruptly call on Rosalynde, who, poor soul, was as hotly burned as himself, but that she shrouded her pains in the cinders of honourable modesty....
>
> Reading the sonnet over, and hearing him name Rosalynde, Aliena looked on Ganymede and laughed, and Ganymede looking back on the forester, and seeing it was Rosader, blushed; yet thinking to shroud all under her page's apparel, she boldly returned to Rosader, and began thus:
> "I pray thee tell me, forester, what is this Rosalynde for whom thou pinest away in such passions?" (67–68)

The cognitive stratification is here intensified because the reader is given signals to decode concerning the women's cognitive response to the encounter that are lost on Rosader: Aliena's and Ganymede's (i.e., Rosalynde's) external displays of recognition ("laughed," "blushed") and their reported exchange of looks upon meeting him heighten the reader's sense of complicity and anticipation.

Parallel to this love plot, scenes of coincidence and recognition play themselves out within a separate sibling rivalry plot between Rosader and his brother Saladyne (93–101) in which the brothers are finally reconciled. The narrative then moves toward a climax of multiple recognition when Ganymede/Rosalynde is reunited with her father and recognized by Rosader. When the disguised Rosalynde is brought before her father, the text uses character-cognitive details to signal her unilateral recognition of him: "Ganymede coming in, and seeing her father, began to blush, nature working affects by her secret effects. Scarce could she abstain from tears to see her father in so low fortunes.... The consideration of his fall made Ganymede full of sorrows; yet ... she smothered her melancholy with a shadow of mirth, and very reverently welcomed the king" (150). The passage contains both the external detail of emotional reaction ("blush") and detailed information concerning Rosalynde's state of mind upon seeing her father. This detailed creation of the anticipatory stages of recognition marks Lodge's text as more innovative in the representation of character-cognitive details than its contemporary, Greene's *Pandosto* (1588).

Recognition and Identity in the Developing Novel

In the research into the developmental history of the novel before the eighteenth century, critics have increasingly drawn attention to Aphra Behn as a significant writer.[3] Behn's status is confirmed by her representation of coincidence. While William Congreve's *Incognita* (1692) uses an elaborate coincidence plot, its representation of recognition is still very much in the style of Renaissance texts like *Pandosto* (see, e.g., Congreve 1991, 525). In Behn's colonial novel *Oroonoko* (1688), by contrast, a single coincidental encounter reveals a marked development in the spatial and cognitive depiction of recognition.

This recognition scene describes the reunion of Oroonoko and Imoinda, the woman he loves, in Surinam after they have both separately been transported there from Africa as slaves. For Oroonoko (here called by his slave name, Caesar), recognition is particularly powerful because he believes that Imoinda (whose slave name is Clemene) is dead. The recognition scene begins as Oroonoko and Trefry (a British character who has befriended him) approach Imoinda's dwelling:

> They had no sooner spoke, but a little shock dog . . . ran out, and she [Imoinda], not knowing anybody was there, ran to get it in again, and bolted out on those who were just speaking of her, when seeing them, she would have run in again, but Trefry caught her by the hand and cried "Clemene, however you fly a lover, you ought to pay some respect to this stranger," pointing to Caesar. But she, as if she had resolved never to raise her eyes to the face of man again, bent 'em the more to the earth . . . and gave the prince the leisure to look the more at her. There needed no long gazing or consideration to examine who this fair creature was; he soon saw Imoinda all over her: in a minute he saw her face, her shape, her air, her modesty, and all that called forth his soul with joy at his eyes, and left his body destitute of almost life; it stood without motion and, for a minute, knew not that it had a being, and I believe he had never come to himself, so oppressed he was with overjoy, if he had not met with this allay: that he perceived Imoinda fall dead in the hands of Trefry. This awakened him, and he ran to her aid, and caught her in his arms, where, by degrees, she came to herself, and 'tis needless to tell with what transports, what ecstasies of joy they both awhile beheld each other without speaking, then snatched each other to their arms, then gaze again, as if they still doubted whether they possessed the blessing they grasped; but when they recovered their speech, 'tis not to be imagined what tender things they expressed to each other, wondering what strange fate had brought 'em again together. (Behn 1998, 42–43)

First, a specific spatial framework is evoked through the use of the *container* schema: the prepositions connoting movement "into" and "out of" Imoinda's (unspecified) dwelling establish a basic spatial location in which the recognition scene is played out. Then the passage follows Oroonoko's gaze in detail as he perceives and takes in Imoinda's appearance and qualities ("her face, her shape, her air, her modesty") in the act of recognition, using original and detailed language to describe its effect upon him, particularly the frozen shock of recognition. The depiction of Oroonoko's response is followed by the narration of its effect on Imoinda and then culminates with the extended description of their actual embrace and the external manifestations of joy. *Oroonoko*'s single coincidence therefore contains a significantly extended depiction of a recognition scene.

In the eighteenth-century novel the *discovery of identity* within the kinship plot becomes a recurrent feature, either in the representation of the mental processes of the figure at the center of the identity plot, as in Defoe, or through the temporal orchestration of identity in *mystery genealogy plots*, as in the novels of Fielding. Both these strategies lead to the more immersive harnessing of the reader's attention within the narrative world.

It is in Defoe's *Moll Flanders* (1722)—the fictional autobiography of a serial wife, bigamist, and thief—that we find a truly extended and deep plotting of coincidence. Defoe's most significant innovation is the highly suspenseful multiphased representation of staggered recognition that commences when Moll discovers that she has unwittingly married her half-brother. Accessing events from the perspective of Moll's experiencing self, the reader shares both Moll's own discoveries and her anticipations concerning possible futures. In the first stage of this process, Moll describes her own secret, silent, and unilateral recognition during a conversation with her (ostensible) mother-in-law:

> Here she went on with her own story so long, and in so particular a manner, that I began to be very uneasy; but coming to one particular that required telling her name, I thought I should have sunk down in the place.... [A]nd let any one judge the anguish of my mind, when I came to reflect that this was certainly no more or less than my own mother, and I had now had two children, and was big with another by my own brother, and lay with him still every night. (Defoe 1978, 101)

Moll is "now the most unhappy of all women in the world" (102). The text suspensefully describes her fears about the consequences of recognition in her still incognizant mother and brother, depicting her mind turning over and discarding alternate future events and actions:

> I had now such a load on my mind that it kept me perpetually waking; to reveal it, which would have been some ease to me, I could not find would be to any purpose, and yet to conceal it would be next to impossible; nay I did not doubt but I should talk of it in my sleep, and tell my husband of it whether I would or no. If I discovered it, the least thing I could expect was to lose my husband, for he was too nice and too honest a man to have continued my husband after he had known I had been his sister; so that I was perplexed to the last degree.... If I had discovered myself to my mother, it might be difficult to convince her of the particulars, and I had no way to prove them. On the other hand, if she had questioned or doubted me, I had been undone. (102)

After deciding not to reveal the truth, Moll states that she "lived with the greatest pressure imaginable for three years more" (102). Then, as the tension of her unilateral state of recognition rises, she finally resolves to reveal the truth to her mother, leading to a lengthy bilateral recognition scene between the two women (107–8). After this the narrative enters its final phase of prerevelatory tension, focusing on Moll's horror at the situation she finds herself in and on her fears about her brother's possible reaction and slowly building up to her resolution to tell him the truth (112–14). When she finally does this, she sees "him turn pale and look wild" (114), and he twice attempts suicide as a result of the discovery (115). The recognition sequence is concluded when Moll leaves for England again.

Here, therefore, the revelation of identity is structured to make recognition a long-drawn-out nightmare as opposed to a single scene. More favorable coincidences occur later in the novel, when Moll twice reencounters her "Lancashire husband," Jemmy, the second meeting leading to their permanent reunion. These, while comparatively brief, are also notable for their use of spatialization with a *container* framework and their representation of Moll's silent and unilateral identification of Jemmy, which only later culminates in bilateral recognition (see 183–84, 264, 277–78).

In terms of the plotting principle, Moll's incestuous marriage and her later, more fortuitous encounters with Jemmy are *implicitly* instated within a twofold causal principle. The first coincidence is implied to be the result of punitive providential action for Moll's earlier behavior in Colchester, and the second is a reward for Moll's (apparent) spiritual improvement later on in the narrative. The fact that Moll's incestuous marriage is an apt punishment for her previous deeds is implied by the foreshadowing of the incest motif in the episode with the two brothers at Colchester at the beginning of the novel. Here she states explicitly that, having married one brother but still desiring the other, "I committed adultery and incest with him every day in my desires" (77). This complex form of providential explanation involves both causal-progenerative (Moll brings events on herself through her actions) and causal-manipulative levels (God punishes Moll for her actions by orchestrating the incestuous marriage and rewards her good behavior by bringing her together with Jemmy again).[4]

As Alessandro Vescovi (1997) points out, a number of features in *Moll Flanders*, including the recurrence of Jemmy, create "the cohesion of the picaresque"; this is confirmed by Defoe's use of the coincidence plot. The overall spatial-geographical pattern of the major stages in Moll's life draws a double loop, passing from Newgate (birth) to Virginia (incestuous marriage) back to Newgate after she is arrested followed by transportation to Virginia with Jemmy at the end of the novel. Each of these phases is structured by coincidence. Coincidence is therefore truly *plotted* in Defoe and used in a way quite different from the loose, ad hoc string of episodes in Smollett's *Roderick Random* (1748), whose stereotypical descriptions, emotional overkill, and farcically fast recognition scenes give it a style of coincidence completely different from Defoe's.[5]

In *Tom Jones* (1749) Fielding does not, like Defoe, concentrate on the extended psychology of recognition but creates a hitherto unrivaled narrative network of coincidental encounters and relationships that uses temporal orchestration to create suspense, curiosity, and surprise. At the center of *Tom Jones* is the mystery genealogy plot concerning the eponymous foundling Tom around which the novel sets up a seemingly chaotic array of characters and gradually imposes order on them by revealing the true nature of their relationships with each other. It is the prospect of this imposition of order on chaos that constitutes a major source of the novel's readerly fascination and anticipation.[6] The novel is full of coincidental meetings and recurrent characters, and even the minor characters Tom encounters are part of a complex interweaving of coincidences and prove significant for the orchestration of his story and character.[7] The Upton episode in books 9 and 10 is the coincidental nexus of the novel (Fielding 1966, 444–93) and draws together a number of interrelated characters in a complex knot of coincidental meetings and negative coincidences that heighten the mystification of Tom's genealogy plot. Tom arrives at the inn in the company of a woman called Mrs. Waters, whom he has just met. Characters subsequently arriving at the inn include Partridge, whom Tom has previously encountered (and who is suspected of being Tom's father), Sophia Western (in search of Tom, having run away from her father's house), and Squire Western himself (who coincidentally lights on the right place to find his daughter but only after her departure). Despite their intersection and contiguity at the inn, not all these characters actually encounter each other. Sophia departs from the inn upon learning that Tom has spent the night in Mrs. Waters's room, and, most significantly, the narrative powers that be do not allow Partridge and Mrs. Waters to come face to face (thereby delaying a significant recognition scene); only later, however, does this negative coincidence become a meaningful absence.

On the face of it, therefore, the major negative coincidence (or nonconvergence) at Upton is that of Tom and Sophia. In its subsequent narrative remodeling, however, the crux of the Upton episode is transformed. Mrs. Waters's real identity is later discovered during a conversation between Tom and Partridge: she is Jenny Jones, the woman rumored to be Tom's own mother. Tom's dalliance with a random female acquaintance is now transformed into a tragically incestuous plot of coincidental family reunion:

> Partridge came stumbling into the room with his face paler than ashes, his eyes fixed in his head, his hair standing on end, and every limb trembling. In short,

> he looked as he would have done if he had seen a spectre, or had he indeed been a spectre himself. . . . "Why then the Lord have mercy upon your soul, and forgive you," cries Partridge; "but as sure as I stand here alive, you have been a-bed with your own mother." . . . Upon these words Jones became in a moment a greater picture of horror than Partridge himself. He was indeed, struck dumb with amazement and both stood staring wildly at each other. (814–15)

Typical of Fielding's comic style and low level of focalization, recognition is here depicted with a cartoonlike plasticity of dramatically exaggerated external appearance and body language.[8]

Tom and Partridge's discovery is, however, simply a further illusory detour in the narrative's ongoing manipulation of information. The metanarrative commentaries of the narrator also play a role in the novel's complex interweaving of the coincidence plot: the narrator repeatedly comments on his narrative strategy and the concepts of probability and possibility shortly before or after accelerations of coincidence (cf. 361–67 and 777–78). The revelations at the end of the text establish the actual world of the story and uncover the authoritative set of coincidental relationships, allowing the reader, finally, to plot Tom's true genealogy. The overall effect of the novel's plot is therefore achieved by the temporary frustration of the reader's causal-progenerative mapping of Tom's life story. Used with considerable effect by Fielding, coincidence plots woven round a character's enigmatic genealogy were later consolidated by Dickens (e.g., in *Bleak House*) and Wilkie Collins (*The Woman in White*) in the nineteenth century.

In contrast to Fielding's playful treatment of the motif, the coincidental incest plot is at its most negative and traumatic in the gothic novel. The archetypal gothic constellation of innocent female threatened by evil male is intensified when coincidence transforms the threatening male figure into a close relative of the heroine.[9] Thus, in Lewis's *The Monk* (1796) Ambrosio, having first murdered his mother without realizing it, rapes and kills his sister before discovering her identity. Within its romantic-gothic reasoning, this recognition scene depicts the deeper workings of the blood links Ambrosio has just defiled. Immediately after he has raped her, Ambrosio intuitively senses Antonia's identity as his sibling, and his former sexual attraction turns to repulsion: "He dropped [her hand] again as if he had touched a serpent. Nature seemed to recoil at the touch. He felt himself at once repulsed from and attracted towards her, yet could account for neither sentiment. There was something in her look which penetrated him with horror; and though his understanding was still ignorant of it, Conscience pointed out to him the whole extent of his crime" (Lewis 1959, 371).

In the developmental trajectory of coincidence, Radcliffe's *The Romance of the Forest* (1791) is significant for its complex temporal orchestration of character relationships and transformations of identity. The heroine, Adeline, abandoned by her supposed father at the beginning of the novel, is imprisoned and oppressed by the marquis de Montalt, who ultimately turns out to be both her uncle and her father's murderer. At the center of this process is a series of metamorphoses in Adeline's own family relations that gradually transforms her from an apparent outcast without an identity into a figure interlocked in a network of positive versus negative and real versus figural kinship ties. In its working out of the concealed kinship plot and in the networking of characters, Radcliffe's text creates a double movement: the negative kinship reunion plot within Adeline's own family is balanced by a positively convergent pattern regarding another family group. Having escaped from de Montalt, she is welcomed into the home of a stranger, M. La Luc (Radcliffe 1986, 259), whose son Theodore turns out to be the man who has previously aided her and with whom she has fallen in love. These progressively positive coincidental relations, which provide Adeline with a new and better family, are counterpointed and intensified by the parallel sequence of negative discoveries concerning Adeline's own causal-progenerative identity. This discovery plot passes through multiple stages of transformation, constructing two virtual levels of relationships—that Adeline is the daughter of a man called St. Pierre who abandons her at the outset of the novel or that she is "the natural daughter of the Marquis de Montalt" himself (333)—before finally revealing that she is the daughter of Montalt's half-brother Henry (341).

The discovery plot of *The Romance of the Forest*, with its parallel movement of negative and positive family coincidences, is historically significant because it constitutes an early example of the positive networking of characters into euphoric family units that, in the wake of Romanticism, characterizes many nineteenth-century novels. Radcliffe's novel thus stands poised between the traditions of the two centuries: like many eighteenth-century novels, it uses the negative plot of incest to destabilize and destroy the links of kinship, but its final euphoric family constellation celebrates and restabilizes the family motif.[10]

The parochial nature and apparent verisimilitude of the worlds of Jane Austen's novels mean that her use of coincidence has none of the flamboyance or drama of Fielding or Radcliffe. Nevertheless, it is a clear indication that coincidence has become an established plot strategy in the developing realist novel that it is also a recurrent feature in Austen's quotidian worlds. Austen, however, transforms and naturalizes coincidence so that it tones in with the environment of her novels. Coincidence here also reflects the necessities and constraints of the world of the English gentry, in which minor chance encounters with acquaintances are a vital form of social interaction. Coincidence thus also plays a key role in Austen's love plots because, in a world of social constraints upon the single woman, the chance encounter represents a major opportunity for furthering romantic inclinations and interests.

Persuasion (1818) involves three separate phases of coincidence. Austen uses coincidence to connect the different spatial locations (on and off the narrative stage) of its "scattered and diffused world" (Tanner 1986, 244). At the beginning of the novel Austen uses coincidental relationships to bring about the reencounter of Anne and Wentworth (whose initial proposal of marriage Anne has previously been "persuaded" to reject). Kellynch Hall is rented by Captain and Mrs. Croft, and the latter turns out to be Captain Wentworth's sister, bringing Anne's former suitor back into her geographical sphere.

A different form of coincidence using a mild form of kinship reunion (the only time Austen uses this device) structures the central chapters of the novel. The intersection takes place when Anne, accompanied by Wentworth, passes a gentleman on the steps leading from the beach in Lyme. This scene shows Austen's skill with character-cognitive detail, capturing a moment of brief but intense three-way nonverbal communication between the two intersecting strangers and Wentworth: "As they passed, Anne's face caught his eye, and he looked at her with a degree of earnest admiration, which she could not be insensible of. . . . It was evident that the gentleman, (completely a gentleman in manner) admired her exceedingly. Captain Wentworth looked round at her instantly in a way which shewed his noticing of it" (Austen 1965, 124–25). After his departure from Lyme, the gentleman's identity is discovered (he is Anne's own estranged cousin William), and this creates anticipation about a possible future recognition scene. When Anne and William then actually meet in Bath, the narrative exploits the cognitive imbalance between them:

> It was the same, the very same man, with no difference but of dress. Anne drew a little back, while the others received his compliments. . . . Sir Walter talked of his youngest daughter . . . and Anne, smiling and blushing, very becomingly shewed to Mr Elliot the pretty features which he had by no means forgotten, and instantly saw, with amusement at his little start of surprise, that he had not been at all aware of who she was. He looked completely astonished, but not more astonished than pleased; his eyes brightened. (156)

The representation of recognition extends more clearly into the depiction of the characters' minds: character reactions are finely traced in the detail of facial response and are also explicitly linked to internal thought processes. The passage describes William Elliot's surprise at discovering that Anne was the stranger he passed in Lyme while portraying Anne's cognitively superior enjoyment of his surprise. Anne's superior gaze in this recognition scene confirms Robyn Warhol's observation that "Anne's gaze, as well as her visibility within the text, are sources of unprecedented power for the heroine" (1996b, 27).

In Austen's plotting of the "two suitors convention" (Kennard 1978), William Elliot constitutes the alternative and ultimately undesirable suitor. Wentworth's perception of Elliot's unspoken admiration of Anne in the coincidental encounter in Lyme already functions to catalyze his renewed feelings for her. For Anne's part, her rejection of William Elliot (which leaves her free to reaffirm her feelings for Wentworth) is achieved by a final phase of coincidence in which Austen implements multiple sets of coincidental relationships.[11] Anne learns that William Elliot was "the intimate friend" (Austen 1965, 206) of her friend Mrs. Smith's late husband, and this connection serves to bring highly negative information about William to light. Then, through a further chain of relationships, Mrs. Smith provides Anne with information indicating that Elliot's motivation is predominantly pecuniary: "'Mr Elliot talks unreservedly to Colonel Wallis of his views on you. . . . Colonel Wallis has a very pretty silly wife, to whom he tells things which he had better not, and he repeats it all to her. She, in the overflowing spirits of her recovery, repeats it all to her nurse; and the nurse, knowing my acquaintance with you, very naturally brings it all to me'" (211). In Austen's world, therefore, coincidental relationships take the form of convergent chains of gossipmongers within a limited social sphere.[12]

Austen's narrative justification of coincidence is also striking in its quotidian contextualization. She repeatedly naturalizes coincidence by having her characters explicitly comment on coincidental events as the occasional bizarre quirks of life.[13] These character responses function as a lightning conductor and work to counteract any sense of incredulity in the reader. For example, the key word "extraordinary" is used to describe the coincidental meeting between Anne and William Elliot by three different characters: Wentworth (127), Mary Musgrove (147), and twice in the representation of Anne's thoughts (200). Likewise, Mrs. Smith remarks how "curious" (207) her separate and unconnected acquaintance with both Anne and her cousin William is. Similarly (but with greater comic effect), in *Emma* Harriet comments on the strangeness of a (rather less unlikely) coincidental meeting with her admirer, Mr. Martin: "'Only think of our happening to meet him!—How very odd! It was quite a chance, he said, that he had not gone round by Randalls. He did not think we ever walked this road. . . . So very odd we should happen to meet!'" (Austen 2005, 31–32). In Austen's very material narrative world, therefore, we find absolutely no sign of any causal-manipulative deity but only the affirmation of the random quirkiness of space, time, and human relationships.

The Hyperconvergence of the Fictional Victorians

The continuing expansion of the coincidence plot in the nineteenth-century novel reflects a fundamental paradox in Victorian fiction, in which the depiction of the "real" interacts with the continuing influence of Romanticism. Victorian fiction, like Victorian painting, uses realism in combination with Romantic elements. Thus, rather than representing the culminating phase in the development of narrative realism, the "Romantic impulse release[s] the creative energies in many... Victorian novelists" (Stone 1980, 3).[14] The same synergy of realism and Romanticism characterizes the Victorian use of euphoric coincidence, reflecting Romanticism's utopian urge to network all things into a unified and interconnected whole. The hyperconvergent coincidence of family connection in Victorian fiction can, however, also be seen to be additionally fueled by other cultural forces. The frequency of euphoric family reunions across the nineteenth-century canon reflects—in comparison to the eighteenth-century dysphoric or ambiguous presentation of the family reunion plot—the growing establishment of the family as the supreme and mystically enshrined social unit in Victorian culture.[15] Furthermore, the interconnection of a multitude of characters—as practiced particularly by Dickens—preempts the wider historical narrative of Charles Darwin's *Origin of Species* (1859), in which, similar to the hyperconvergent coincidence plot of fiction, life is mapped as a deeply interrelated structure across the time and space of the planet and man is "[restored] to his kinship with all other forms of life" (Beer 1983, 62). Moreover, the frequent staging of the coincidence plot in terms of the discovery of genealogy reflects the intensification of interest in the question of *origins* manifested in Darwinian thought.

Victorian fiction is rife with coincidence (Reed 1975). Just as the nineteenth century is the breeding ground for a rich variety of narrative genres, so does coincidence diversify noticeably within this period. The novels of four authors—Charlotte Brontë, Charles Dickens, George Eliot, and Thomas Hardy—reveal a substantial plurality of forms. Coincidence is not only formed anew by each author, it is also often used with considerable variation across each author's works.

Similar in many ways to Radcliffe's *Romance of the Forest*, the romantically euphoric kinship plot of Brontë's *Jane Eyre* (1847) saves the heroine from an inimical family unit (the Reeds) and instates her within a protective network (the Rivers family). In *Jane Eyre* the reader is invited to interpret coincidence as a sign of the workings of a benevolent universe that protects the heroine from harm. The coincidences of *Jane Eyre* are an expression of the novel's romantic-causal plotting principle, which postulates the existence of "sympathies... between far-distant, long-absent, wholly estranged relatives asserting... the unity of the source to which each traces his origin" (Brontë 1966, 249). This is the underlying explanation of the central kinship recognition scene in *Jane Eyre*, when Jane discovers that the Rivers family, who have taken her in as a destitute stranger, are actually her cousins: the forces of mind and genealogy, it is implied, have worked together to exert a powerful force of attraction. Both in terms of content and presentation, this recognition scene ("Glorious discovery to a lonely wretch!" [411]) is the antithesis of Moll Flanders's protracted nightmare of incestuous sibling reunion.

Within the novel's romanticized world order, "coincidence" is also used in the sense of the perfect meeting and understanding of minds. Before she discovers they are her relatives, Jane says of Diana and Mary Rivers: "Thought fitted thought, opinion met opinion: we coincided, in short, perfectly" (377). It is interesting to note that, by contrast, the same sense of coincidence is suggested to be dogmatic and unsound in Austen's skeptical representation of Romanticism, as articulated in more dogmatic terms by Marianne Dashwood in *Sense and Sensibility*: "I should not be happy with a man whose taste did not coincide with my own. He must enter into all my feelings" (Austen 1969, 51).

The coincidence of the sympathy of minds is also at the heart of the novel's denouement, in which Jane and Rochester hear each other's voices even though they are spatially separated in different areas of England. Jane's appeal for help to a higher power: "'Show me, show me the path!' I entreated of Heaven" is answered by Rochester's voice, and she subsequently calls this event a "coincidence... too awful and inexplicable to be communicated or discussed" (Brontë 1966, 444–45, 472). This event, indeed, does not follow the normal pattern of the traditional coincidental encounter but borders on Jungian synchronicity, in which minds and not bodies connect.

Discussions of coincidence in *Jane Eyre* have sometimes ignored the romantic context of the novel and judged it according to the dictates of verisimilitude (Goldknopf 1969, 41–42; Craik 1968, 86–87). However, it is more useful to see coincidence in *Jane Eyre* as the vehicle for a fairy-tale wish-fulfillment plot powered by a romantically optimistic sense of the sympathetically convergent workings of the universe. Indeed, the plotting principles suggested in the novel's two major coincidences point to a multileveled metaworld created out of a synthesis of orthodox religion and pantheistic impulses that act in tandem with the human mind and soul. The unseen powers operating upon the novel's mundane world are variously called "God," "Providence," "mother," "nature," and the latter two aspects are combined in the personified figure of the moon. It is important to note that these figures constitute a more complex and diversified metaworld than that presided over by an orthodox Christian God and thus reveal Brontë's remodeling of the singularly masculine and patriarchal deity of traditional Providence.[16]

Sandra Gilbert and Susan Gubar note the similarity of the coincidence plot of *Villette* (1853) to that of *Jane Eyre*: "Brontë charts a course of imprisonment, escape, and exclusion until the heroine, near death from starvation, fortuitously discovers a family of her own" (1984, 419). However, *Villette* can also be seen as Brontë's counternarrative to the romantic coincidence of *Jane Eyre*. The working out of the coincidence plot in *Villette* involves thwarted convergence leading to the exclusion of the heroine. While characters from an earlier phase of Lucy Snowe's life coincidentally reappear with transformed identities in the town of Villette, the heroine herself remains outside the romance constellations, for it is Paulina who marries Graham Bretton. *Villette* thus inverts the procedure of *Jane Eyre* completely: Lucy Snowe remains excluded from the convergent, integrated social unit into which characters like Jane Eyre are admitted.

Moreover, because of key differences in the personality of *Villette*'s heroine, the presentation of recognition is also completely different from *Jane Eyre*. Whereas Jane Eyre, as narrator, immediately shares the emotional responses of her experiencing self with the reader, the secretive Lucy Snowe withholds information. When Lucy is coincidentally reunited with her godmother, Mrs. Bretton, and the latter's son, Graham, the recognition process expresses the heroine's disorientation rather than any euphoria when her mind slowly registers familiar objects from Mrs. Bretton's former home (Brontë 1979, 238–41). Subsequently, while describing her own detailed recognition of Graham Bretton's face, Lucy coolly informs the reader that she has in fact long recognized that Dr. John is Graham Bretton:

> The discovery was not of to-day, its dawn had penetrated my perceptions long since. Dr John Graham Bretton retained still an affinity to the youth of sixteen: he had his eyes; he had some of his features; to wit, all the excellently-moulded lower half of the face; I found him out soon. I first recognized him on that occasion, noted several chapters back, when my unguardedly-fixed attention had drawn on me the mortification of an implied rebuke.... To say anything on the subject, to *hint* at my discovery, had not suited my habits of thought, or assimilated with my system of feeling. On the contrary, I had preferred to keep the matter to myself. I liked entering his presence covered with a cloud he had not seen through. (247–48)

Here Lucy reveals the fact that she *enjoyed* the experience of unilateral recognition, which has given her a sense of power over Dr. John. Quite unlike Jane Eyre, Lucy indulges in power games that go beyond pure narratorial unreliability and can be interpreted as an expression of the insecurity of her position as a single woman in Victorian society.

It would probably be difficult to discover a novelist more consummate in the art of coincidence than Dickens. *Martin Chuzzlewit* (1843–44) and *Great Expectations* (1861) represent two stylistic extremes: playful versus somber coincidence. Despite darker sides, *Martin Chuzzlewit* is a comic work, and this is apparent in the often effervescent juggling of coincidental relationships and encounters among a panoply of characters. The novel does not so much progress in a linear, causal-progenerative manner but follows a pattern of gradual convergence created by coincidental encounters, multiple recurrent characters, and coincidental relationships, so that by the end of the novel an extended "megafamily" of characters has formed from which the evil characters (notably, Jonas Chuzzlewit and Pecksniff) are expelled.

As part of this strategy, Dickens elevates the minor ad hoc coincidental encounter into a major structural device. For example, in chapter 37 Tom Pinch encounters Charity Pecksniff in London outside the Monument:

> "My gracious!" cried a well-known voice behind Mr Pinch. "Why, to be sure it is!"
>
> At the same time he was poked in the back by a parasol. Turning round to inquire into this salute, he beheld the eldest daughter of his late patron. (Dickens 1968, 652)

This example shows how Dickens even uses the ad hoc form with effect: suspense is briefly provoked regarding the identity and intentions of the character poking Pinch in the back. Moreover, on a metastructural level this scene functions collectively with many others like it to gradually integrate the novel's teeming cast of characters, parallel events, and locations.

The recurrent characters that coincidentally turn up again and again with new identities in different contexts also have a major cohesive function. Bailey's recurrence is so widespread that "the whole novel flow[s] through him" (Furbank 1968, 17). He starts off as the boy at Todgers's and ends up as Tigg Montague's cabdriver but is also a lodger at Poll Sweedlepipe's house in London and thus links different strands of the narrative. Similarly, from his role as servant to Chevy Slyme in chapter 4, Montague Tigg reappears briefly in a coincidental encounter with Martin junior in the London pawnshop in chapter 13 and then reemerges as the restyled Tigg Montague, the mastermind of the fraudulent Anglo-Bengalee Disinterested Loan and Life Assurance Company, in chapter 27. These transformations are part of Dickens's playfully nonmimetic style: the characters' natures, personalities, and movements are transformed, contorted, and manipulated at will.

A more complex form of coincidence used by Dickens is that created out of hidden coincidental networks of relationships and identities that run invisibly underneath the narrative's surface, waiting to be exposed. The detective Nadgett also has a dual identity in the novel, but, unlike the recurrent characters, his multiple personae are not sequential but simultaneous. Initially, Tom Pinch's landlord and the investigator Nadgett appear to be just two of the novel's many characters, each belonging to entirely different areas of the action. Then, starting in chapter 40, these two entities are melted into one character, surprising the reader and forcing him to reconstruct his mental map of the novel. Dickens is therefore highly innovative in his use of coincidental relationships: characters like Nadgett are not simply given additional identities when chains of relationships are revealed but are dramatically reconfigured through the merging of two seemingly separate characters.

The fact that the comic world of *Martin Chuzzlewit* has some fundamentally nonmimetic tendencies becomes particularly apparent in the narrative justification of coincidence. Far from feeling the compulsion to naturalize its coincidences in realist fashion, the novel self-consciously celebrates them without resorting to any causal-explanatory plotting. Thus, when Mark and Martin's friends from Eden, America (who, in chapter 33, were last seen on the other side of the Atlantic in the grips of swamp fever), miraculously appear on a London street at the close of the novel so that they too can be absorbed into the euphorically extended Chuzzlewit family, this outrageous final coincidence is ostentatiously and cheekily proclaimed by the novel's discourse, in the words of Mark Tapley, to be a "'coincidence as never was equalled!'" (Dickens 1968, 911). Similarly, earlier in the novel Tigg calls a coincidental meeting with Martin junior in London "'one of the most tremendous meetings in Ancient or Modern History!'" (281). The comic, softly antirealistic world of *Martin Chuzzlewit* is therefore not apologetic about its subversion of the laws of verisimilitude but asserts its right to exist on its own terms.

Whereas coincidence is used intensively and exuberantly in the comic world of *Martin Chuzzlewit*, *Great Expectations* stages coincidence as a somber, mystifying, and sometimes threatening network of relationships. The reader accompanies the narrator, Pip, on a bewildering journey of discovery in which he gradually unravels a constellation of hidden coincidental relationships in which the convict Magwitch, and not Miss Havisham, turns out to be his hidden benefactor and also Estella's father, and a second convict, Compeyson, turns out to be the man who jilted Miss Havisham. Particularly in the case of the central question of the identity of Pip's mysteriously anonymous benefactor, these discoveries of *actual* relationships often supplant erroneous *virtual* constructions made by Pip when he "misread[s] the plot of his life" (Brooks 1992, 130).

As Forsyth comments, Pip's process of discovery "has much of the tragic irony with which Sophocles invested Oedipus's discovery of the implausible coincidences that shaped his destiny" (1985, 164). The fact that criminal connections lurk below seemingly pristine surfaces transforms Pip's understanding of his role in society and gives him an insight into his own social prejudices. From the point where Magwitch appears in Pip's apartments in London and confronts Pip with a strange new version of his life (Dickens 1965, 336–37), the discovery process in *Great Expectations* takes on a relentless dynamic in which Pip uncovers the additional networks of uncanny links between Jaggers, Pip, Miss Havisham,

Magwitch, Estella, and Compeyson. In keeping with the novel's labyrinthine structure, this information is revealed in disjointed and fragmentary fashion. It is a key part of Dickens's narrative strategy of disorientation and surprise that the information leading to these discoveries always comes in an unexpected context and transforms previous conceptions of characters' identities and roles. Thus, as Pip and Herbert Pocket listen to Magwitch's narrative of his life, they realize that the characters in the account—Arthur and Compeyson—are actually Miss Havisham's brother and "the man who professed to be Miss Havisham's lover" (367). Moreover, the central traumatic event of Miss Havisham's life story—being jilted on her wedding day—is now narrated in defamiliarized form by Magwitch (362–63). Here the reader, along with Pip, turns a corner in the narrative and discovers that she has emerged at a point she has passed through before but that she has now approached from a completely different and unsuspected direction. Similarly, the discovery of Estella's biological identity (which establishes yet another link between Miss Havisham and Magwitch) brings together two apparently separate strands of the narrative as facets of one and the same story. Here Pip realizes by an associative, analogical contemplation of her facial characteristics that Molly, the housekeeper at Jaggers's house, is Estella's mother: "I looked at those hands, I looked at those eyes, I looked at that flowing hair; and I compared them with other hands, other eyes, other hair, that I knew of, and with what those might be after twenty years of a brutal husband and a stormy life.... And I felt absolutely certain that this woman was Estella's mother" (403). Notably, recognition is here presented as Pip's cognitive processing of analogical genetic features created by family lineage.

The final stage in the unraveling of the hidden chain of relationships is Pip's discovery that Magwitch himself is Estella's father. This deduction is made as Pip hears Herbert Pocket renarrate sections of Magwitch's story (419). Dickens, however, does not follow up this discovery with any further euphoric convergence: while the reader may liminally plot a father-daughter reunion scene between the dying Magwitch and Estella, this is not actualized by the story, and Estella's discovery of her true identity remains a virtual event beyond the horizon of the novel's closure. In contrast to *Martin Chuzzlewit*, therefore, *Great Expectations* rejects positive convergence and refuses to tie off all the loose ends in its entanglement of life stories.

In *Great Expectations*, furthermore, individual coincidental encounters have nothing of the effervescent coincidence of *Martin Chuzzlewit* but become vehicles for the creation of a deep sense of menace when Pip finds himself repeatedly reconnecting with figures from the novel's criminal underworld in scenes of suspenseful unilateral recognition. On a journey from London Pip coincidentally finds himself in the same coach as two convicts, one of whom he recognizes as the man who, many years before, was sent by Magwitch to give him a present of two pound notes. Dickens gives the scene a further uncanny twist, dramatically heightening the level of coincidence, when the convict actually begins to narrate the episode of the two pound notes to his companion:

> It is impossible to express with what acuteness I felt the convict's breathing, not only on the back of my head, but all along my spine.... I dozed off.... The very first words I heard them interchange as I became conscious were the words of my own thought, "Two One Pound notes." ... "So he says," resumed the convict I had recognized—" ... Would I find out that boy that had fed him and kep his secret, and give him them two one pound notes? Yes, I would. And I did." ... [T]he coincidence of our being together on the coach was sufficiently strange to fill me with a dread that some other coincidence might at any moment connect me, in his hearing, with my name. (250–51)

Dickens intensifies Pip's sense of dread by explicitly making him fear the uncanny power of coincidence and the convergence of the novel's criminal world upon him. This and other similar scenes (see 397–99, 434–40) create a sense of ubiquitous criminal menace in the world of *Great Expectations*. While there are, therefore, key differences in the style of coincidence that Dickens uses in *Great Expectations* and *Martin Chuzzlewit*, Dickens's strategy is similar in both insofar as coincidence does not form part of any metaphysical or providential system of explanation but is used for narrative effect.[17]

Preempting later developments in modernist fiction, George Eliot's novels reveal a key development: the relativizing and foregrounding of the explanation of coincidence. *Middlemarch* (1871–2) uses coincidence in a subsidiary plot in which the moralistic Bulstrode's shady past catches up with him due to the chance reading of a piece of paper by Raffles, a figure from Bulstrode's past who coincidentally arrives in Middlemarch (Eliot 1965, 451–52). *Middlemarch* is shot through with the philosophical observations of its heterodiegetic narrator concerning the self-deceptive nature of humanity's egocentric view of the universe.[18] As the coincidence plot unfolds, this theme is expanded in Bulstrode's obsessive use of providential explanations. Until Raffles's appearance, Bulstrode sees his life as having "been sanctioned by remarkable providences" (666), while to him other less worthy lives lie "outside the path of remarkable providences" (666, cf. 668 and 735). By placing this providential explanation so often in Bulstrode's mouth, the novel's discourse ironically discredits the traditional causal-manipulative plotting principle of divine intervention. Moreover, instead of suggesting any metaphysical causality, *Middlemarch* traces the causal-progenerative effects on Bulstrode's life of the accidental miscarriage of a piece of paper that in due course significantly influences the lives of Lydgate, his wife, Rosamond, and Will Ladislaw.

In *Daniel Deronda* (1876), an intricate coincidence plot involves the hero in a double plot of kinship connections. The novel contains two parallel narratives of development: that of Gwendolen Harleth and her disastrous marriage to Grandcourt and that of Daniel Deronda, who is the focus of a genealogical mystery plot. Contrasting narrative strategies for each character mark the novel out as particularly innovative: Gwendolen's narrative is characterized by multiple futures and wistful counterfactuals (see chapter 7), while Deronda's story of cultural and genealogical self-discovery is a convergent narrative of coincidental encounters across Europe.

Deronda's story is set within a double-phased network of coincidences. He is instrumental in the reunion of a Jewish brother and sister, Mordecai and Mirah, in London. While Daniel's initial meeting with Mirah is a random event insofar as they have no personal previous relationship, since Deronda himself turns out to be Jewish, it is a "cultural coincidence," and this first meeting sets off a causal-progenerative series of encounters that lead to Daniel's discovery of his Jewish identity and a reunion with his estranged mother.

In contrast to Eliot's ironic treatment of coincidence in *Middlemarch*, *Daniel Deronda* has a more complex stance. The convergence of Jewish connections in Deronda's life is repeatedly represented in romantic terms, for example, in Mordecai's deep and intuitive belief that Deronda is Jewish and that they are linked by "invisible fibres" (Eliot 1967, 633). This sense of links is also reinforced by repeated references to the search for facial resemblances and the sense of instinctive sympathies in Daniel's meetings with Mirah and Mordecai. When he first encounters Mirah, Deronda feels "a great outleap of interest and compassion towards her" (228), her accent suggests "foreignness and yet was not foreign" (230), while Mordecai sees in Deronda "a face and frame which seemed to him to realize the long-conceived type" (536).[19] The representation of the perception of facial characteristics as part of the instinctive recognition of affinity or kinship takes up a motif used by two other authors writing during or in the wake of Romanticism—Ann Radcliffe and Charlotte Brontë.[20] However, the deeply emotive staging of romantic convergence is absent in *Daniel Deronda*: the recognition scenes are markedly noneffusive and noneuphoric. Mirah and Mordecai's reunion is more cerebral than emotional: "They looked at each other, motionless. It was less their own presence that they felt than another's; they were meeting first in memories, compared with which touch was no union" (643). Likewise, Deronda's own reunion with his mother much later in the novel is highly unsentimental and has him "wondering at his own lack of emotion" (687).[21]

From the seeds of the chance encounter with Mirah in London the novel constructs a dual network of causal-progenerative plot links and mystical suspicions of identity that end in Deronda's discovery of his Jewish genealogy and his true cultural home. Deronda's reunion with his mother is the causal-progenerative result of his meeting with Mirah and Mordecai because, motivated by his interest in Mirah, he visits a synagogue in Frankfurt and encounters a Jewish stranger who recognizes his resemblance to his mother (415–17). Significantly (and in contrast to Gwendolen's sustained wistful upward counterfactual plotting of her life), Deronda stresses the causal links in this positively coincidental chain of events in a satisfied, downward counterfactual: "'To me the way seems made up of plainly discernible links. If I had not found Mirah, it is probable that I should not have begun to be specially interested in the Jews'" (573).

However, while the emotional and perceptional experiences of the characters suggest the existence of a network of intuitive connections and sympathies that the reader should take seriously rather than ironically, the novel's multifarious stances on coincidence undermine a consistent reading of the plot in this spirit. Thus, in discussing Mordecai's prescience, the narrator makes an ambivalent "apology for inevitable kinship" in which she affirms the "knowledge" of "second-sight" but also concedes that it is "a flag over disputed ground" (527–28). In addition, the figure of Deronda's guardian, Hugo Mallinger, represents the rational "negative whisperings" (568) that counter Mordecai's mysticism. Moreover, the narrator undercuts any wholehearted spirit of romanticism by placing Deronda's identity quest plot within an intertextually relativistic framework that stresses the power of the narrative construction of the romantic: "And, if you like, he was romantic. That young energy and spirit of adventure which have helped to create the world-wide legends of youthful heroes going to seek the hidden tokens of their birth and its inheritance of tasks, gave him a certain quivering interest in the bare possibility that he was entering on a like track" (573–74).[22]

As well as this undermining of full-blown romanticism, the novel's pluralistic responses to coincidence range from the naturalistic to the metafictional. Thus, as in Austen, coincidence is defused when the characters themselves discuss its remarkableness (cf. 784). At the other extreme, the novel's discourse covertly draws attention to the pleasure created by the uncovering of *links* in a narrative: when two minor characters, Amy and Mab, discuss a coincidence, Amy exclaims, "'Oh, this finding out relationships is delightful! . . . It is like a Chinese puzzle that one has to fit together'" (718). Therefore, just as the novel's overall plotting structures are split between its two protagonists, so is its coincidence plot torn between the split impulses of rationality, mysticism, and even occasionally metafiction, ultimately occupying a relativistic position founded in shifting modes of interpretation. The mystical aspects look backward to Romanticism, while Eliot's explicational relativism preempts modernism.

Thomas Hardy's use of coincidence demonstrates a key shift away from Victorian conventions and the euphoria of interconnectedness. Negative coincidence—or what Albert Pettigrew Elliott calls "malignant Coincidence" (1966, 59)—creates plots of tragic mistiming in which the representation of space and time takes on innovative forms. *The Return of the Native* (1878) is constructed around a series of meetings and failed meetings, and the spatial environment through which the characters move toward points of convergence or nonconvergence is depicted with plasticity and detail. Egdon Heath is repeatedly mapped as a terrain crisscrossed by paths, often from the perspective of one character perceiving the movement of another across the landscape (see, e.g., Hardy 1974b, 37, 174).

Hardy's detailed mapping of complex coincidental junctures from a multiple spatial and character-cognitive perspective is particularly notable in the novel's fourth book, "The Closed Door," which narrates a series of events culminating in the death of Mrs. Yeobright. Seeking a reconciliation with her son and his wife, Mrs. Yeobright sets out on a hot August day to visit Clym and Eustacia. The protractedly nonconvergent train of events commences with Mrs. Yeobright's trajectory almost but not quite converging with that of her son.

> Mrs Yeobright . . . tried one ascending path and another, and found that they led her astray. Retracing her steps she came again to an open level, where she perceived at a distance a man at work. She went towards him and inquired the way.
>
> The labourer pointed out the direction, and added, "Do you see that furze-cutter, ma'am, going up that footpath yond?"
>
> Mrs Yeobright strained her eyes, and at last said that she did perceive him.
>
> "Well, if you follow him you can make no mistake. He's going to the same place, ma'am." (297)

The "furze-cutter," as the reader suspects, is Clym himself, and the ensuing section suspensefully intensifies the anticipation of a possible meeting, emphasizing the combination of distance and proximity between mother and son by describing the mutual spots they each pass by in succession: "His [Clym's] progress when actually walking was more rapid than Mrs Yeobright's; but she was enabled to keep at an equable distance from him by his habit of stopping whenever he came to a brake of brambles, where he paused awhile. On coming in her turn to each of these spots she found half a dozen long limp brambles which he had cut from the bush during his halt and laid out straight beside the path" (297). Mrs. Yeobright follows in the track of the "furze-cutter" for some way before recognizing him as her son and seeing him "enter his own door" (298). At this point, Wildeve, Eustacia's admirer, coincidentally appears to complicate the situation. Events occurring inside and outside are now represented in a complex narrative of shifting spatial perspectives and time levels. In these divided but proximate locations the two doorways and a window of Clym's cottage become key *portals* in the evocation of narrative space that connect the different character perspectives but also demarcate the internal space of Clym's home as a *container* from which Mrs. Yeobright remains tragically excluded.

Resting on top of a knoll at one side of Clym's house (298), Mrs. Yeobright observes Wildeve's arrival before deciding to approach the cottage herself. This section ends with her visual perspective on the cottage door's exterior: "By the door lay Clym's furze-hook and the last handful of faggots she had seen him gather" (299). The next section then retraces time to depict events from Wildeve's perspective before taking him through the door and into the cottage: "The key turned in the lock, the door opened, and Eustacia herself confronted him" (300). During the ensuing conversation between Eustacia and Wildeve as they stand before the sleeping figure of Clym, the reader is suspensefully conscious that this scene is taking place parallel to the description of Mrs. Yeobright outside the cottage. The temporal strands are brought together when "a click at the gate was audible, and a knock came to the door. Eustacia went to a window and looked out" (303–4). Fearing being discovered in conversation with Wildeve, Eustacia hesitates to open the door to her mother-in-law, subsequently believing that Clym has answered it because she hears him utter "the word 'Mother'" (304). The chapter ends with Eustacia's discovery that Clym is not, after all, awake, and her dismayed glance out of the other door of the cottage again picks up the spatial markers that had previously been given from Mrs. Yeobright's perspective: "Nobody was to be seen. There, by the scraper, lay Clym's hook and the handful of faggot-bonds he had brought home; in front of her were the empty path, the garden gate standing slightly ajar; and beyond, the great valley of purple heath thrilling silently in the sun. Mrs Yeobright was gone" (305).

The next section retells the same section of time from Mrs. Yeobright's retrospective point of view as she walks away from the cottage under the impression that she has been spurned by her daughter-in-law. The inside-outside portal perspectives of the two cottage doors and the window, which form the barrier to communication and convergence, are reiterated yet again in Mrs. Yeobright's thoughts: "Clym's mother was at this time following a path which lay hidden from Eustacia by a shoulder of the hill.... Her eyes were fixed on the ground; within her two sights were graven—that of Clym's hook and brambles at the door, and that of a woman's face at a window" (305). The multiple temporal, spatial, and cognitive perspectives used in "The Closed Door" episode illustrate how in his novelistic discourse Hardy demonstrates an acute sense of the temporal and spatial dynamics of character trajectories in his staging of the interplay of negative and positive coincidence.[23]

Analogous and Traditional Coincidence in Modernist Fiction

In his two influential essays on the changing impulses operating in twentieth-century literature, John Barth (1977, 1996) contrasts the "exhaustion" of modernist literature with the "replenishment" of postmodernism. As Barth subsequently emphasized, this was "the 'exhaustion' not of language or of literature, but of the aesthetic of high modernism" (1996, 286). By contrast, the "ideal postmodernist novel will somehow rise above the quarrel between realism and irrealism" (283). Barth's observations are mirrored by the development of the coincidence plot in twentieth-century fiction. The restrained use of coincidence in modernist fiction reflects the self-imposed limitation of narrative possibilities created by the rejection of previous literary conventions. By contrast, in postmodernist fiction the coincidence plot is taken up again and reinvented in all manner of forms, and it constitutes a key source of the narrative replenishment of postmodernism.

Coincidence in modernist texts is used in a much more restrained fashion. If characters are now brought together in a coincidental encounter, the previous relationship is the less dramatic and more verisimilar one of acquaintance and not of kinship. Analogous coincidental constellations also replace the traditional coincidence plot, while the tendency to relativize and pluralize explanatory systems is a recurrent feature.

Joseph Conrad's *Chance* (1913) is a key example of this new trend. The novel's title alone draws attention to the overall shift within modernism to "systems of thought that make chance, accident, arbitrariness, and coincidence their centers" (Caserio 1999, 6; see also Monk 1993). *Chance* is certainly concerned with the random but also with the *causal-progenerative results* of the random. However, while a Victorian text like Eliot's *Daniel Deronda* traces causal-progenerative consequences in a linear narrative of the protagonist's development, Conrad's *Chance* creates a dense entanglement of chance events on the double levels of the novel's story and its narration.

At the beginning of the novel a character called Charles Powell tells the novel's two main narrators (a nameless frame narrator and Marlow) how, when he was a young man visiting the shipping office in search of a post, he was caught up in a strange analogical coincidence:

> Our new acquaintance advanced now from the mantelpiece with his pipe in good working order.
> "What was the most remarkable about Powell," he enunciated dogmatically with his head in a cloud of smoke, "is that he should have had just that name. You see, my name happens to be Powell too." (Conrad 1974, 19)

This "coincidence" (25) involves the analogical link of *similarity*—a shared surname. In Conrad's text this analogical relationship is even used to *simulate* a biological relationship: the other Mr. Powell allows the captain of the *Ferndale*, Captain Anthony, who is in urgent search of a first mate, to believe that he and young Powell are related in order to get the job. *Chance* then traces the ultimate random consequence of this coincidence of names in the life of the novel's heroine, Flora, when she finds herself caught in a conflict between her husband, Captain Anthony, and her father, the ex-banker de Barral. It is only because of Powell's presence on board the *Ferndale* that Captain Anthony survives the trip at all: on deck one night Powell looks, by chance, through a skylight onto the ship's interior and witnesses (and subsequently foils) an attempt by the disgruntled de Barral to poison his son-in-law's drink (339–57). As Caserio observes: "The reader is left with the sense of something arbitrary at the heart of the precision that might have arranged things very differently, either more conjunctively or disjunctively because the wonderful linking up is only accident" (1999, 43). Interestingly, Caserio's observation, which is framed as a counterfactual, reveals how counterfactual plotting on the part of the reader can be prompted not only by negative coincidence (as in Hardy) but in general by constellations of randomness. This suggests that historically, as discussed below in chapter 7, the rise of counterfactual thinking is linked to the demise of providential coincidence and the sense of a divinely ordered world.

The novel's discourse repeatedly emphasizes the causal-progenerative link between the initial coincidence of names and Powell's saving of Anthony's life: "Mr Powell, whom the chance of his name had thrown upon the floating stage of that tragi-comedy"; "Mr Powell, the chance second officer of the ship *Ferndale*" (Conrad 1974, 229, 237, cf. 357 and 359). A longer commentary from Powell's perspective stresses the sequence more overtly: "He was full of his recalled experiences on board the *Ferndale,* and the strangeness of being mixed up in what went on aboard simply because his name was also the name of a shipping master, kept him in a state of wonder which made other coincidences, however unlikely, not so very surprising after all" (260). In its plotting of coincidence, *Chance* therefore *inverts* the pattern of traditional coincidence. Whereas in the traditional coincidence plot the coincidental encounter constitutes a subsequent link in a previous constellation of events, the analogical coincidence in *Chance* is presented as the initial event out of which other consequences can be traced into the future. Powell's role in the sequence is not that of a purposeful agent, that is, that of the premodernist, conventional narrative hero; he merely constitutes a link in a causal-progenerative chain. In addition to this emphasis on consequences, *Chance* is also pluralistic about explanatory systems. The presence of a rope on deck, which makes Powell stoop and observe de Barral's attempted poisoning through the *portal* of "the lighted skylight of the most private part of the saloon," is ascribed to "chance, fate, providence, call it what you will!" (338). This relativism is further consolidated by the novel's insistently broad semantic spectrum applied to the word "chance" itself; the term is used, variously, in the sense of "opportunity" ("her only chance" [161]), "luck" ("a most extraordinary chance" [34]) or "randomness" ("merest chance" [200]).

Chance also uses coincidental relationships on the level of its narration: the novel's representation of the organized plot of Flora's life is presented as having been called into being by an arbitrary process of connecting characters and oral links. These links and relationships are only gradually unraveled during the novel and also create suspense, as, for example, when the unnamed frame narrator asks Marlow: "How do you know all this?" whereupon Marlow replies, "You shall see by and by" (223). Marlow forms the linchpin in this system of coincidental narrative relationships ("Yes, I know their joint stories which Mr Powell did not know" [258]). He knows Mr. Powell at the Shipping office (18); he knows Captain Anthony (41); he has an "accidental acquaintance" (44) with the Fynes family, with whom Flora grew up (Mrs. Fynes's brother is Captain Anthony), and so he turns out to know the younger Flora herself. Flora's story can therefore only be constructed as a coherent narrative due to the network of coincidental relationships existing between the narrators and their sources of information.

Other modernist texts still use the traditional coincidental encounter. In Ford Madox Ford's *The Good Soldier* (1915), a dramatic coincidental encounter lies at the center of the novel's story of romantic intrigue, in which the narrator's wife enters a hotel lobby to see her husband in conversation with Bagshawe, a man who witnessed her juvenile sexual exploits many years before. Characteristically, however, Dowell's meandering narrative does not contextualize the significance of the encounter, only communicating his visual impressions of the dramatic moment of encounter: "I tell you, my own heart stood still; I tell you I could not move. . . . She looked round that place of rush chairs, cane tables and newspapers. She saw me and opened her lips. She saw the man who was talking to me. She stuck her hands over her face as if she wished to push her eyes out. And then she was not there any more" (Ford 1946, 96). It is up to the reader to reconstruct the significance of this incident by untangling Dowell's temporally convoluted narrative.

By contrast, Woolf's *Mrs Dalloway* (1925) contains run-of-the-mill coincidental encounters in the small central London world of Westminster. Near the beginning of the novel, Mrs. Dalloway bumps into Hugh Whitbread in St. James's Park: "And who should be coming along with his back against the Government buildings, most appropriately, carrying a despatch box stamped with the Royal Arms, who but Hugh Whitbread" (Woolf 1992, 5). The novel also uses different strategies to connect its characters: for example, the novel's Regent's Park scene depicts unconnected characters from the different plot strands in random spatial contiguity (71). Nevertheless, Mrs. Dalloway still succumbs to a looser form of narrative convergence in its final scenes, bringing Sir William Bradshaw, the Harley Street doctor who has been treating Septimus Warren Smith, to Mrs.

Dalloway's party in the evening and reuniting Mrs. Dalloway with her childhood girlfriend Sally Seton.

Like *Chance*, many modernist texts are relativistic in their explanation of coincidence. Forster's *A Room with a View* contrasts two characters' interpretations of coincidence, either as "Fate" or as mundane causality (1978, 147; see the discussion in chapter 1); in Ford's *The Good Soldier* Dowell equivocates about possible explanations for the "curious coincidence of dates" in his wife's life (1946, 75). The role of human subjectivity in the explanation of coincidence is taken to more comic extremes in Joyce's *Ulysses* (1922), in what might be called "paranoid coincidence." Bloom sees, or thinks he sees, Blazes Boylan crossing his path several times in the course of the day. The fact that Bloom is heavily preoccupied by his wife's relationship with Boylan means that his mind actually seems to be creating minor coincidental encounters with the "spectre" (Ackerley 1997, 46) of Boylan, such as when he thinks he sees Boylan passing in a car: "He eyed and saw afar on Essex bridge a gay hat riding on a jaunting car. It is. Again. Third time. Coincidence" (Joyce 1986, 217). The reader is privy to Bloom's mental meanderings as he tries to evaluate the significance of coincidence—or what he believes is coincidence—in his life. This effect is even stronger for Bloom's preoccupation with analogical coincidences. He wonders whether it counts as a coincidence to see someone just after you have thought of their brother: "Now that's a coincidence. Course hundreds of times you think of a person and don't meet him" (135). *Ulysses'* extreme form of character-cognitive subjectivity thus foregrounds the fallacious nature of perception and redefines coincidence as an act of the mind.

The Postmodern Renaissance of the Coincidence Plot

The postmodernist fascination with literary conventions, its renewed dialogue with the past, and the pluralization and playful hybridization of literary forms mean that the coincidence plot is revived in all its previous manifestations. Kinship reunion plots are again rife because, in the literature of an age that can mix "realism and irrealism" (Barth 1996, 283) without compunction, there is no longer a literary tabu on the use of less realistic forms but a playful sense that anything goes. The result is a literature full of coincidence that, as well as reversing the restrictive modernist aesthetic, also builds on modernism's use of analogical coincidence to produce new and original postmodernist forms.

Coincidence occurs across the genres of narrative fiction in the postmodernist period, both in texts that display a marked *antirealist* tendency by infringing on or destroying a sustained immersive process through blatant self-reflexivity and intertextuality and in more immersive texts that use a postrealist combination of fantastic elements or historical narrative alongside the representation of quotidian reality.²⁴ Texts that belong to the field of historiographic metafiction (Hutcheon 1988) use coincidence in a variety of different ways: DeLillo's *Libra* and Winterson's *The Passion* use traditional coincidence, while Ackroyd's *Chatterton* and Barnes's *Flaubert's Parrot* use the postmodernist coincidence plot of multiple analogical relationships.

The Postmodernist Coincidence Plot in Historiographic Metafiction

Postmodernist coincidence builds on the analogical form used in modernist coincidence but expands it by creating a network of analogical relationships across multiple time levels in which it is, above all, *the reader* who performs an act of *recognition*—the perception of a system of correspondences across the textual fabric. By contrast, the characters, isolated on their individual cultural and temporal levels, are incapable of any such "omniscient" perspective—in this way omniscience itself is revealed to be a textual construct. However, the reader's ability to construct causal-progenerative relationships across the temporal levels is also undermined, and this frustration of *causal-cognitive desire* is one aspect of historiographic metafiction's antirealist agenda. While narrating events in an immersive fashion, the genre nevertheless sabotages the coherence that traditional realist texts create through the plotting principle of causation.

Ackroyd's *Chatterton* (1987) constructs a multifarious network of analogical connections across three time levels. This transhistorical matrix of artistic and literary connections—a new form of *coincidental relationships*—can only be surveyed as a meaningful whole by the reader. The analogical system that interconnects these characters is that of artistic activity, research, and forgery. On the eighteenth-century time level, the poet Chatterton (a real-world literary figure) is a celebrated imitator. On the nineteenth-century time level, the (real-world) artist Henry Wallis is painting the (real-world) portrait of Chatterton's death scene using the (real-world) writer George Meredith as a model for Chatterton. On the twentieth-century time level, further characters are researching the past: Charles Wychwood discovers manuscripts and a painting that indicate that Chatterton faked his own suicide and lived on, but these are later exposed as forgeries by Wychwood's friend Philip Slack; Sarah Tilt is studying Wallis's painting of Chatterton in her book project, "The Art of Death"; Andrew Flint is writing a biography of George Meredith; Philip Slack later decides to write an alternate biography of Chatterton himself. A further analogical relationship exists between Chatterton and Charles Wychwood, that of death: toward the end of the novel, Charles dies unexpectedly from a brain tumor, and the text then closes with a tour-de-force description of Chatterton's violent death throes in what (in this version) is posited to be accidental arsenic poisoning (in opposition to the traditional account that he died by suicide). *Chatterton*'s covert heterodiegetic narrator coordinates these multiple scenarios, switching back and forth across the different time levels and textual versions.[25]

In particular, the intermediate nineteenth-century time level, lodged between the eighteenth-century level of the "real" Chatterton and the twentieth century, contains several considerations of the paradoxical analogical relations between art and the cultural creation of history. Thus, for subsequent generations the nineteenth-century figure Meredith will become the eighteenth-century figure Chatterton:

> "The poet does not merely recreate or describe the world. He actually creates it. And that is why he is feared." Meredith came up to Wallis, and for the first time looked at the canvas. "And that is why," he added quietly, "this will always be remembered as the true death of Chatterton." (Ackroyd 1993, 157)

Meredith, standing in as an image for the original (Chatterton himself), *becomes the original* for subsequent generations. The key idea that texts create "reality" for subsequent epochs instead of mediating the actual past thus underlies the novel's network of analogical relationships. The relationship between different epochs is one based on approximate similarity (as in the relationship between the red-headed young men Chatterton and his stand-in Meredith) and not one of continuous, causal-progenerative connections over time and history. As Philip Slack comments: "'And if you trace anything backwards, trying to figure out cause and effect, or motive, or meaning, there is no real *origin* for anything. Everything just exists'" (232). In such a disconnected and discontinuous temporal panorama, the only kind of relationships or sense-making pattern that can be activated is that of analogies.

The textual levels of Ackroyd's text do, however, succumb to a postrealist form of convergent plotting through the strategic use of *transtemporal encounters*, in which characters from different time levels meet through dreams and hallucinations.[26] Meredith reports having "passed Chatterton on the stairs" (156), while a more complex series of transtemporal meetings takes place between Charles (who is hallucinating due to his brain tumor) and Chatterton (47, 234). This culminates in the novel's concluding narration of Chatterton's death by arsenic. The scene closes by including the figures of Charles Wychwood and Meredith in the dying Chatterton's field of vision, bringing the characters from the separate time levels together in one unified dreamscape: "[Chatterton] sees ahead of him an image edged with rose-coloured light. It is still forming, and for centuries he watches himself upon an attic bed, with the casement window half-open behind him, the rose plant lingering on the sill, the smoke rising from the candle, as it will always do. I will not wholly die, then" (234). In this epiphanic passage Chatterton is given temporal omniscience in his moment of death: he sees the birth and subsequent predominance of his fictional pictorial image in future ages (the rose tones refer to the colors of Wallis's painting), and he joins Meredith and Charles to survey literary posterity:

> Two others have joined him—the young man who passes him on the stairs and the young man who sits with bowed head by the fountain—and they stand silently beside him. I will live for ever, he tells them. They link hands, and bow towards the sun.
>   And, when his body is found the next morning, Chatterton is still smiling. (234)

In this postrealist form of fiction, such transhistorical convergence is not given causal justification within the discourse; in its fantastic implausibility, it offers itself to be interpreted as the artistic construct of the author, made in order to create a closing convergence of the multiple levels of the text.

In many respects Barnes's *Flaubert's Parrot* (1984) represents the zenith of the postmodernist coincidence plot, since it combines a complex and multifarious fabric of analogical coincidences with extensive metanarrative comments on coincidence.[27] Analogical relationships exist between characters in the main narrative and fictional ones on an intertextual level: as the novel progresses, the reader gradually perceives that, like Emma Bovary, the narrator's wife had a hidden life, was unfaithful to her husband, and eventually committed suicide; furthermore, like Madame Bovary's husband, Geoffrey Braithwaite is a doctor. The text offers no causal-progenerative explanation for these correspondences; the reader is left to wonder whether Braithwaite's fascination with Flaubert began because *Madame Bovary* reminded him of his own life, or whether Braithwaite is too obsessed with the literary to even pay enough attention to his personal life, or to draw the submerged metafictional inference that Braithwaite's life must itself be a fictional game created by Julian Barnes. Braithwaite himself hardly acknowledges this primary analogical coincidence, but the text resounds with other correspondences, such as the parallels between Eleanor Marx (who, we are informed, was the publisher of the first English translation of *Madame Bovary*) and Madame Bovary herself, which are used to demonstrate the potential for distortion and selectivity in the construction of analogical relationships (Barnes 1985, 176).

An analogical conundrum also involves the novel's eponymous parrot: the original Flaubertian causal-progenerative parrot is indistinguishable from its less historic fellows.[28] In France Braithwaite tries to identify the original stuffed parrot that served as the model for the parrot Loulou in Flaubert's *Un coeur simple*. This turns out to be an impossible endeavor because the original parrot cannot be distinguished from a whole collection of stuffed parrots, and identification is complicated by the fact that more than one cultural monument claims to possess the authentic parrot (184–90). This conundrum underlines the novel's central historically metafictional thesis: the present is a cultural zone incapable of reconstructing the distant landscape of the past.

In a chapter tellingly entitled "Snap!" (66), Braithwaite also indulges in a metanarrative that focuses extensively on coincidence: "I don't much care for coincidences. There's something spooky about them: you sense momentarily what it must be like to live in an ordered, God-run universe. . . . I prefer to feel that things are chaotic, free-wheeling, permanently as well as temporarily crazy" (66). Having indicated that his response to real-life coincidence is characterized by a discomfort about its implication of causal-manipulative plotting from a higher metaphysical level, Braithwaite then goes on to find literary coincidence equally suspect because of its suggestion of authorially "divine" manipulation. "And as for coincidences in books—there's something cheap and sentimental about the device[:] the sudden but convenient Dickensian benefactors; the neat shipwreck on a foreign shore which reunites siblings and lovers. I once disparaged this lazy stratagem to a poet I met, a man presumably skilled in the coincidences of rhyme. 'Perhaps,' he replied with a genial loftiness, 'you have too prosaic a mind?'" (67). However, the phrase "coincidences of rhyme" highlights the fact that in the form of *repetition* and *analogical relationships*, coincidence is a major structuring principle of art. The novel's discourse therefore contradicts Braithwaite's own representation of coincidence as a "lazy stratagem" by suggesting that all art, insofar as it is an arrangement of variations on a theme or acoustic effect, is intrinsically "coincidental," and—unlike the raw, random material of the real world—all texts are causally manipulated and arranged by the author.

Braithwaite then changes tack and broadens the field by reinventing coincidence as "irony": "One way of legitimising coincidences, of course, is to call them ironies. That's what smart people do. Irony is, after all, the modern mode, a drinking companion for resonance and wit. . . . I wonder if the wittiest, most resonant irony isn't just a well-brushed, well-educated coincidence" (67). In a section entitled "Dawn at the Pyramids" (69–70) Braithwaite elaborates the thesis that irony is the coincidence of the modernist age by narrating a complex anecdote concerning an "irony" in the life of Flaubert. This event also turns out to be a construction, with Flaubert and his friend Maxime du Camp as the joint manipulators of a seeming coincidence whose playful but complex intertextual reverberations extend as far as an analogical coincidence of names in Nabokov's *Lolita* ("perhaps Nabokov had read Flaubert's letters before writing *Lolita*" [73]). In its entirety, Braithwaite's commentary therefore constitutes a brief history of coincidence, swiftly covering key literary forms and combining playfulness with incisiveness.

Toward the end of the novel Braithwaite then focuses on a different type of analogical irony—the pitfalls of constructing correspondences between art and life: "Ellen. My wife: someone I feel I understand less well than a foreign writer dead for a hundred years.... Books say: she did this because. Life says: she did this. Books are where things are explained to you; life is where things aren't. I'm not surprised some people prefer books. Books make sense of life. The only problem is that the lives they make sense of are other people's lives, never your own" (168). The fact that Braithwaite does not even seem to perceive the analogical relationship between his own life situation and that in *Madame Bovary* is of course an additional irony, particularly as, since he and his wife "never talked about her secret life," he says that he has to "fictionalize" in order to "invent [his] way to the truth" (165). This more personal perspective reinforces the text's historiographically metafictional message: the causal networks constructed in narrative fiction that give the reader cognitive satisfaction by "making sense of life" are far removed from the raw experience of life itself.[29]

Traditional Coincidence in Postmodernist Fiction

The postmodernist replenishment (Barth 1996) of narrative fiction is good news for the traditional coincidence plot. After the literary downgrading of coincidence in modernism, postmodernist fiction both revives and reinvents the older forms and conventions. After dormancy in modernism, kinship reunion plots return in force, while plots of coincidental relationships occur in new forms. Postmodernism's rediscovery of the coincidence plot mirrors Charles Jencks's definition of the postmodern in terms of architectural style as "a double coding—the combination of modern techniques with something else (usually traditional building)" (1991, 4). Within the architecture of fiction, the coincidence plot is the "traditional building" and is thus a key manifestation of postmodernism's "complex relation to the past" (16), especially in contrast to modernism's programmatic break with previous conventions.

Signaling this literary reengagement with the past, texts from the earlier postmodernist period in particular are marked by an awareness of coincidence as a literary convention. Margaret Drabble's *The Realms of Gold* (1975) stages a neo-Romantic coincidence plot of kinship reunion blended with social realism and soft metafiction. During the novel the protagonist, Frances Wingate, is reunited with two separate branches of her estranged family (her cousins David Ollerenshaw and Janet Bird) and reestablishes roots in rural Tockley, the village of the Ollerenshaws' origins. The coincidence plot is used to present contrasting images of women's social positions in twentieth-century Britain when the world of Frances Wingate, a successful, independent, and divorced academic based in London, collides with that of her cousin Janet Bird, tied to her home, her one-year-old baby, and an awful husband, in rural middle England. Wingate thus has the role of "hero" in a romanticized narrative of contemporary female success and mobility (see Homans 1983, 201); as an archaeologist, she is famous for her intuitive discovery and subsequent excavation of the ancient Saharan city of Tizouk (Drabble 1977, 35–36).

The novel's overt heterodiegetic narrator presides over the action, as in the following passage narrating the first intersection of the unsuspecting cousins at an international conference, which emphasizes narratorial omniscience in contrast to the characters' noncognizance: "There sat, though she did not know it, her distant cousin David Ollerenshaw, geologist. David Ollerenshaw did not know that he was her cousin, nor did he know much about her" (31). Later, this self-conscious narratorial style becomes fully self-reflexive in a metanarrative on the novel's use of negative coincidence. Here the nonconvergence of lovers' letters—a postcard bearing the message "I love you" that Frances sends to her estranged lover, Karel, at the beginning of the novel but that only reaches him at its end—is the fault of the postal services: "Its journey from box to bag had taken nine months.... And to those who object to too much coincidence in fiction, perhaps one could point out there is very little real coincidence in the postcard motif, though there are many other coincidences in this book" (224). The narrator not only refers to Hardy as a major model in the narrative tradition of negative coincidence but also (justifiably, in view of the key aspect of nonconvergence in this example) quibbles on the categorization of the device as a "coincidence": "These days, the post being what it is, it would have been more of a miracle if the postcard had arrived on time, as Frances (unlike Tess of the d'Urbervilles) should have been sensible enough to realize, though (in this sense like Tess of the d'Urbervilles) her judgement too was clouded by emotion" (224).

While Drabble's novel combines neo-romanticism and social realism with narratorial playfulness, David Lodge's *Small World: An Academic Romance* (1984) indulges in a more singularly parodistic game with the literary convention of coincidence. The novel recounts the meetings and coincidental encounters of international academics. Its crowning coincidence is a burlesque working of the kinship reunion plot: twin foundlings discovered in the toilet on a transatlantic flight are reunited with their real mother, the Cambridge bluestocking Sybil Maiden (Lodge 1985, 335), while their father turns out to be the aging doyen of American literary criticism, Arthur Kingfisher.[30] The novel's subtitle already directs the reader to its model for the use of coincidence—the romance. Accordingly, its imitation of prenovelistic textual traditions is noticeable in the presentational style of its numerous coincidental encounters, which invariably take the ad hoc form with a minimum of character-cognitive detail in the recognition scene (see, e.g., 213). In *Small World* Lodge is at overt play in the *recycling* of the coincidence plot and not aiming at literary innovation.[31]

More recent works have abandoned self-conscious intertextuality and parody in their use of the traditional coincidence plot, and they have developed more innovative and original forms. Jeanette Winterson's *The Passion* (1987) contains one starkly dramatic constellation of coincidental relationships. The novel is a four-cornered love story set in Napoleonic Europe and alternately narrated by two of its characters, Henri and Villanelle.[32] In the first section Henri tells of his life in Napoleon's army. One of the many characters he mentions is a cook in the kitchens who first befriends him and then becomes his "sworn enemy" (Winterson 1996, 19) when Henri is preferred to the cook, who is found "blind drunk" when Napoleon carries out a surprise inspection (17). The cook is then forgotten by the reader after Henri makes the seemingly insignificant comment that "it was a long time before we met again because the Captain had him transferred to the stores outside Boulogne" (19). In the second section Villanelle tells the story of her life in Venice. While her narrative focus concerns the passion she develops for another woman, Villanelle also mentions the attentions of a rich suitor, a "large man with pads of flesh on his palms like baker's dough" (55) at the casino where she works, and later describes with resigned repulsion how he forces himself on her: "he . . . squashed me flat against the wall. It was like being under a pile of fish" (64). In the third section, when Villanelle and Henri meet during Napoleon's Russian campaign, she continues her story, telling Henri how she finally married the "rich man with fat fingers" (96), how he caught up with her when she ran away from him and then sold her to a French general (99).

When Henri and Villanelle reach Venice, a dark scene of discovery and recognition is narrated from Henri's perspective:

> I saw my reflection in the window. . . . Beyond my reflection I saw Villanelle backed up against the wall with a man standing in front of her blocking her way. . . . He was very wide, a great black expanse like a matador's cloak. . . . She pushed him, swiftly and suddenly, and just as quickly his hand flew from his pocket and slapped her. . . . [S]he ducked under his arm and ran past me down the stairs. (125–26)

The ensuing passage reveals that Winterson is reinventing Dickens's technique of merging dual identity in a plot of coincidental relations; the long-forgotten cook and Villanelle's husband are one and the same character:

> "It's him," she said. . . .
> "Your husband?"
> She spat. "My greasy, cock-sucking husband, yes."
> I sat up. "He's following us." . . .

> We pulled up against her water-gate but, as we prepared to fasten our boat, a silent prow slid from behind us and I was staring into the face of the cook.
> The cook.
> The flesh around his mouth moved into a suggestion of a smile.... "Henri," he said. "My pleasure." (126–27)

Both the configuration of the coincidental situation and the recognition scene itself are strikingly original. Recognition is introduced using a window as a *portal* for spatialization; however, in this case the window becomes a dark mirror, reflecting the scene taking place behind Henri. The scene surprises the reader by suddenly superimposing the character of the cook over the seemingly separate character of Villanelle's husband. An ironic causal twist crowns the coincidence when it is revealed that the transformation of the coarse cook into Villanelle's wealthy suitor can be traced back to the day Henri was promoted and the cook was disgraced: the latter made his fortune because he was "drummed out of Boulogne and sent to Paris to mind the Stores" (127).

Winterson's plot of triangular coincidental relations across Napoleonic Europe is one of the starkest and most original versions encountered in this study. The coincidence is so bizarre that it covertly seems to proclaim its fictionality. However, the dramatic framing of the recognition scene and the overpoweringly repulsive depiction of the cook/husband divert the reader's attention from a potentially *expulsive* response born of incredulity to one of horrified *immersion* in the unfolding scene. Before being merged into one character, both the cook and Villanelle's husband have been described as aggressive men who arouse violent feelings of repulsion in both the novel's narrators; these feelings are merged and intensified when the two seemingly separate figures combine to become one character.

Don DeLillo's *Libra* (1988), a novel about Lee Harvey Oswald and the Kennedy assassination, has generally been classified as historiographic metafiction.[33] However, it uses a more original configuration of traditional and analogical coincidence than the "standard" postmodernist coincidence of multiple analogical relationships and links. The version of the Kennedy assassination narrated in *Libra* involves "a proliferation of conspiracies whose plots interweave and acquire lives of their own" (Michael 1994, 146). Oswald is recruited by a group of (largely) ex-CIA men, disgruntled after the Bay of Pigs fiasco, to shoot at the president: Win Everett and Larry Parmenter plan that Oswald should miss Kennedy but that the attempt should be traceable, via Oswald, back to Cuba and Castro ("'We couldn't hit Castro. So let's hit Kennedy'" [DeLillo 1991, 28]). However, other conspirators, led by a man called T. J. Mackey, want Oswald to actually hit the president, and they post additional marksmen in Dallas to ensure that the assassination is successful.

Oswald's recruitment by the conspirators is represented as an ironic plot of coincidental relations because Oswald independently comes into contact with various members of the group. The first link is to Captain David Ferrie, a man whom Oswald already knows as a teenager (42–46); the second link is to George de Mohrenschildt, who gives Oswald a "friendly debriefing" (56) after his temporary defection to the Soviet Union and subsequently brings him to Parmenter's attention (55). Further links in the chain of relationships exist between Mackey and Guy Banister, "a former FBI agent who ran a detective agency in New Orleans" (28). David Ferrie is also associated with Banister's agency (29)—a link that closes the coincidental network around Oswald.

Oswald's entry into the conspiracy takes place at Banister's agency and involves a further coincidence, that of timing and intentions, for the conspirators are already trying to locate Oswald in order to recruit him (118) when he enters Banister's office with the idea of becoming an undercover agent. This ironic convergence of aims—the fact that Oswald appears when already sought—on top of the closing network of coincidental relationships is symptomatic of the novel's intricate construction of coincidental conjunctions that ultimately stress the conspirators' lack of causal-manipulative control over events.

The scene at Banister's agency that closes the chain of coincidental relationships is framed as a coincidental encounter with unilateral recognition between David Ferrie and Oswald. In an adjacent room in Banister's offices, Ferrie by chance hears Oswald's voice in the next room and then looks out of the window after Oswald leaves, trying to remember where he has heard his voice before: "David Ferrie . . . looked out the street-side window, trying to catch a glimpse of the young man whose voice he'd just been listening to. Had he caught something familiar in the tone? Would he be able to match a body to the voice? He looked at the swarm of people moving down the street. Dark folks aplenty, he thought. But no sign of the sweet-voiced boy who wants to be a spy" (130–31). Depicting Ferrie in the first stages of unilateral recognition, the scene uses the window as a *portal* to frame Ferrie's search of the scene outside and of his own memory.

Beyond this configuration of coincidental character relationships, *Libra* also uses analogical relationships and repetitive series to reflect Oswald's unbalanced state of mind; Ferrie even encourages Oswald to think that these are signs that he is predestined to shoot the president (384). As the assassination date draws closer, Oswald's own compulsive observation of analogical coincidences escalates:

> Coincidence. Lee was always reading two or three books, like Kennedy. Did military service in the Pacific, like Kennedy. Poor handwriting, terrible speller, like Kennedy. Wives pregnant at the same time. Brothers named Robert. (336)

> October was his birthday. It was the month he enlisted in the Marines. He shot himself in the arm, in Japan, in October. . . . He arrived in Russia in October. It

was the month he tried to kill himself. He'd last seen his mother one year ago October. October was the missile crisis. (370)

Within the novel's metahistorical framework, analogical coincidences and links of all kinds are used to order the vast body of data that constitute history. Interpolated between the sections narrating Oswald's biography and the conspiracy are scenes from another, later time level in which Nicholas Branch, "a retired senior analyst of the Central Intelligence Agency, hired on contract to write the secret history of the assassination of President Kennedy" (15), sifts the evidence that has accumulated over the years and reviews the plots and patterns that emerge from it.[34] Branch's perspective on his almost infinite data conveys the novel's message about the infinity of interpretational patterns in the study of history, including coincidental relationships: "There is enough mystery in the facts as we know them, enough of conspiracy, coincidence, loose ends, dead ends, multiple interpretations. . . . Branch sees again how the assassination sheds a powerful and lasting light, exposing patterns and links, revealing this man to have known that one, this death to have occurred in curious juxtaposition to that" (58). Coincidental relationships, therefore, just like all patterns of interpretation, are created by arranging data centripetally for its relevance to a single event—in this case, the Kennedy assassination.[35] As Branch sifts through the data, becoming aware of myriad analogical relationships, he is depicted gradually losing his patience and control under the sheer "suggestiveness" of so much historical information: "Branch has become wary of these cases of cheap coincidence. He's beginning to think someone is trying to sway him toward superstition. . . . The Curator sends a four-hundred-page study of the similarities between Kennedy's death and Lincoln's" (379). From the historical "center" of the Kennedy assassination, the potential for analogical connections—here between the deaths of two presidents—radiates out into historical infinity. *Libra* therefore shows how characters' attempts to be causal manipulators of events, and even of historiographic narrative, are frustrated by the chaotic mass, and mess, of events that is referred to as "history." History has no clear plot, but the material of history can be formed into multiple plots, particularly, here, ones in which forms of coincidence provide a pattern.

The bizarre plot of kinship reunion in Auster's *Moon Palace* (1989) may defy the reader's sense of credibility, but the novel is nevertheless a fundamentally immersive narrative. After abandoning college, the novel's main narrator, Marco Stanley Fogg, finds a job in which he works for an eccentric old man called Thomas Effing, taking dictation of his memoirs. After Effing dies, Fogg seeks out Effing's estranged son, Barber, to hand over the memoirs. When he meets Barber, the strange truth is gradually discovered: Barber, who was not even aware he had a son, is Fogg's own father, and so the old man, now dead, was in fact Fogg's grandfather. The protracted recognition sequence between Fogg and Barber begins when, traveling with Barber, Fogg decides to visit his mother, Emily's grave:

> The two of us were side by side in front of my mother's grave, and when I turned my head in his direction, I saw that tears were pouring down his cheeks. . . . He went on staring at my mother's grave, weeping under the immense blue sky as if he were the only man left in the universe.
> ". . . Sweet, darling, little Emily . . . It's all such a terrible waste, such a terrible waste." (Auster 1990, 291–92, ellipses in speech in original)

The text then evokes the dramatic shift in worldview that comes with the moment of recognition; identities are reconfigured, the past world is transformed, and a stranger becomes a kinsman:

> I listened to him as though the earth had begun to speak to me, as though I were listening to the dead from inside their graves. Barber had loved my mother. From this single, incontestable fact, everything else began to move, to totter, to fall apart—the whole world began to rearrange itself before my eyes. . . . [A]ll of a sudden I knew. I knew who he was, all of a sudden I knew everything. (Auster 1990, 292)

This recognition scene, however, turns into a catastrophe because Fogg nevertheless obstinately refuses to acknowledge Barber as his father:

> I felt nothing but anger, a demonic surge of nausea and disgust. "What are you talking about?" I said. . . . Blind to everything around him, [Barber] lurched down the row of graves . . . howling and sobbing as I continued to scream at him. . . . [T]hen, as he came to the edge of the grave that had been dug that morning, he began to lose his balance. . . . I heard his body land at the bottom with a sharp thud. (292–93)

The text frustrates the reader's desire for a positive recognition scene and turns the moment of revelation into a travesty. The son does not embrace the father; instead, his emotional mismanagement of the scene leads to the latter's death. The *container/portal* schema, which in many other texts is the background or the visual vehicle to recognition, here—in the form of a grave and the opening to it—destroys the prospect of kinship reunion.

Moon Palace also ironically juxtaposes explanatory models. Fogg's statement that "it seemed as though fate was watching out for me, as though my life was under the protection of benevolent spirits" (53) becomes, ultimately, an ironic misperception of his life story in the light of the "missed connections" (249) of his family narrative. Moreover, it contrasts wildly with his grandfather's claims that coincidental events are the result of electrical charges in human bodies: "'There are no coincidences. That word is used only by ignorant people. Everything in the world is made up of electricity, animate and inanimate things alike. Even thoughts give off an electrical charge. If they're strong enough, a man's thoughts can change the world around him. Don't forget that, boy'" (104–5). *Moon Palace* thus foregrounds and ironizes the deep human need for explanations but does not itself provide a coherent and streamlined system of justification.[36]

While Auster's *Moon Palace* ultimately destroys the convergence of the coincidence plot in a tragic narrative of mishandled recognition, Louis Sachar's *Holes* (1998) combines a fairy-tale narrative of marvelous convergence with a brutal contemporary scenario. When a pair of shoes miraculously falls on his head as he walks along the street, Stanley Yelnats is arrested and subsequently found guilty of the theft of the shoes. He is sent to a boys' correction center at Camp Green Lake, where the boys are forced to dig the novel's eponymous holes out of dry, compacted earth as a form of punishment. Here Stanley befriends a boy called Zero, and together they eventually manage to escape the camp's cruel and corrupt regime. Combined, however, with this quotidian plot is a fabulistic narrative: ultimately, it turns out that Zero is the great-great-great-grandson of Madame Zeroni, who once put a curse on Stanley's great-grandfather, Stanley Yelnats I, for not carrying her up a mountain as he had promised. When the two boys attempt to escape from the camp, Stanley carries the exhausted Zero up the same mountain and unwittingly breaks the curse. The novel's coincidences multiply when it is discovered that a more recent previous relationship also links the two boys: Zero was actually involved in the episode of the stolen shoes for which Stanley was unjustly sent to Camp Green Lake.

The plot of *Holes* therefore combines double layers of coincidence: two different forms of previous relationship exist between Stanley and Zero before they meet. A plot of parallel causal-progenerative family origins is mapped in the joint history of their families. Additionally, Stanley and Zero, the respective representatives of the contemporary generation, have an analogical relationship to the characters in the earlier generation of their families' lineage, Stanley Yelnats I and Madame Zeroni (as the repetition of names indicates). The novel's complex and slowly unfolding coincidence plot contrasts with its simple narrative style and the magical-realist innocence of the discourse, which has no need to rationalize the fantastic elements: "As Stanley stared at the glittering night sky, he thought there was no place he would rather be. He was glad Zero put the shoes on the parked car. He was glad they fell from the overpass and hit him on the head. . . . When the shoes first fell from the sky, he remembered thinking that destiny had struck him. Now, he thought so again. It was more than a coincidence. It had to be destiny" (Sachar 2000, 187). This most recent example of the coincidence plot shows how contemporary postrealist fiction, merging realism and fantasy, utilizes all manner of forms of relationship in the networking of characters within a coincidence plot.

The texts by Winterson, DeLillo, Auster, and Sachar are all substantial indications that, despite its very long developmental history, in the current stage of the novel's development the coincidence plot is as rife and as multifarious as ever. In these contemporary novels, new levels in the state of the art of coincidence are attained by combining an immersive narrative style with fantastic elements or with uninhibitedly implausible contortions of probability. These techniques, together with the pluralistic explanation of coincidence (Auster and DeLillo) and its magically realist fabulation (Sachar) or strikingly original depictions and stagings of the recognition process (Winterson and Auster), constitute the ongoing narrative renewal of the coincidence plot in narrative fiction.

7. The Narrative Evolution of Counterfactuals

From Renaissance Rhetoric toward Realist Counterfactuals

Counterfactuals in narrative fiction grow from modest beginnings. Whereas the traditional coincidence plot is an established strategy that the novel appropriates from the romance, counterfactuals only become fully fledged plots when the novel "rises" to become a dominant literary genre. To trace counterfactuals from these early beginnings is to watch the gradual evolution of a rhetorical device into a diverse range of plots and genres.

While an early "bourgeois novel" (Stemmler 1992) like Deloney's *Jack of Newbury* (ca. 1597) only uses counterfactuals in very occasional ad hoc fashion, we again find much more strategic plotting in Sidney's *The Countess of Pembroke's Arcadia*.[1] Here counterfactuals are used both as a systematic means of characterization and as a device to comment on key events in the narrative. *The Old Arcadia* (ca. 1580) begins with Duke Basilius's retreat into pastoral seclusion with his family as a result of the prediction he solicited from the Delphic oracle. At this point, Basilius's advisor, Philanax, admonishes him for his tardy request for advice. He does this by constructing a counterfactual in which Basilius consults him *before* going to Delphos instead of only seeking his advice *after* receiving the disastrous prophecies:

> "Most redoubted and beloved prince, if as well it had pleased you at your going to Delphos, as now, to have used my humble service, both I should in better season and to better purpose have spoken, and you perhaps at this time should have been, as no way more in danger, so undoubtedly much more in quietness. I would then have said unto you that wisdom and virtue be the only destinies appointed to man to follow, wherein one ought to place all his knowledge.... I would then have said the heavenly powers to be reverenced and not searched into, and their mercy rather by prayers to be sought than their hidden counsels by curiosity; these kinds of

soothsaying sorceries (since the heavens have left us in ourselves sufficient guides) to be nothing but fancies wherein there must either be vanity or infallibleness.... But since it is weakness too much to remember what should have been done, and that your commandment stretcheth to know what shall be done, I do, most dear lord, with humble boldness say that the manner of your determination doth in no sort better please me than the cause of your going." (Sidney 1994, 6–7)

Philanax's counterfactual underscores Basilius's unwise haste—a fact that is confirmed as the narrative unfolds: the pastoral seclusion enforced by Basilius actually triggers the events of the novel because it makes Pyrocles and Musidorus adopt deceitful strategies to gain access to the princesses Philoclea and Pamela. Moreover, as is revealed in book 5, Pyrocles' father, King Euarchus, intended all along to "provide the marriage of Basilius's two daughters for his son and nephew" (310)—a statement that itself implies a counterfactual storyline in which the two couples' love plots are not hindered by Basilius's actions. Philanax's counterfactual therefore emphasizes the *causal-progenerative* role of Basilius's actions in the fulfillment of the oracle's prediction that his daughters will be "stolen" (5) from him. Sidney therefore uses counterfactual discourse both to characterize Philanax's more considered mind style and to comment on Basilius's causal complicity in the unfolding events.[2]

Significantly, Philanax's speech also concludes with a metacommentary on the pointlessness of counterfactualizing ("it is weakness too much to remember what should have been done"). This insight conforms to the text's deterministic plot structure, in which counterfactuals in the sense of truly *alternative possibilities* are unrealizable (even if they may be imagined by characters) within the irreversible movement of the action toward the telos of the oracle's prediction. As Philanax himself emphasizes, in this classically modeled world, causal-manipulative attempts on the part of individuals like Basilius to steer the plot of life are represented as pointless stands against the authority of the gods: "Wisdom and virtue be the only destinies appointed to man to follow."[3]

In the narrative's climax in book 5 (already discussed for its use of coincidence in chapter 6), counterfactuals are then used to great rhetorical effect by Musidorus when, in verbal combat with Philanax, he defends the princes' actions at their trial:

"But mark, I pray you, the ungratefulness of the wretch [Philanax]; how utterly he hath forgotten the benefits both he and all this country hath received of us. ... Were not we the men that killed the wild beasts which otherwise had killed the princesses if we had not succoured them? Consider, if it please you, where had been Timopyrus's [Pyrocles' other pseudonym] rape, or my treason, if the sweet beauties of the earth had then been devoured? Either think them now dead, or remember they live by us." (346–47)

It is, of course, highly fitting that Philanax should be challenged with his own rhetorical strategy by Musidorus. Characteristically, Musidorus's style of counterfactualizing is more youthfully vigorous and rhetorically aggressive. He uses imperatives to the audience, compelling them to envisage the alternate scenario in which the princesses would be long dead if the princes had not saved their lives: "Think them now dead."

Counterfactuals are thus used by Sidney to highlight the intellectual and rhetorical sophistication of key characters and to focus attention on the role of individual characters' actions within the overall development of the plot. These and other examples (see also Sidney [1994, 320] for counterfactuals of wistful regret between the two imprisoned princes) show Sidney's ability to generate alternate worlds in his narrative discourse to be relatively advanced. This is also evident in his use of other alternate-world scenarios, such as a scene in *The New Arcadia* (1590) in which Princess Erona, fearing for the death of Antiphilus, envisages multiple futures. Erona's mind is depicted caught at the "fork" of a difficult decision-making process and torn backward and forward between multiple alternatives (Sidney 1987, 208–9). Thus, despite *The Arcadia*'s classically deterministic plot scheme, the narrative fabric of Sidney's two versions, with its repeated suggestions of alternate worlds, marks him out as a key figure in the evolution of an ontologically pluralistic novelistic discourse.

It is, however, noteworthy that all the examples of counterfactuals from Renaissance texts referred to above occur in the characters' discourse and are not articulated by the texts' heterodiegetic narrators. They thus imitate the real-world framing of counterfactuals by individuals studied in the psychological literature. However, as the novel develops, heterodiegetic counterfactuals become increasingly evident. Behn's *Oroonoko* (1688) is a significant early text in this context. While Behn's novel does not have a heterodiegetic narrator, its homodiegetic witness narrator (purportedly the author herself) is so covert that many passages read like heterodiegetic narration. This is also reflected in the novel's counterfactuals. The most significant example is a comment by the narrator in an episode describing Oroonoko's attempts to catch a giant eel—a scene at which the narrator is not physically present. Nevertheless, the counterfactual commentary reads as if she were a close observer of the scene, that is, as if she were a heterodiegetic narrator who is not embodied in the story world at all: "At last the sought-for fish came to the bait as he stood angling on the bank, and instead of throwing away the rod, or giving it a sudden twitch out of the water, whereby he might have caught both the eel and have dismissed the rod, before it could have too much power over him, for experiment's sake he grasped it but the harder, and fainting fell into the river" (Behn 1998, 51). The episode illustrates one of the main features of Oroonoko's character (which is in keeping with his literary role as a figure "in the tradition of heroic romance" [Brown 1987, 48]): the tendency to take the more desperate and heroic course. The counterfactual is notable because of its evaluation of multiple possibilities: two alternative counterfactuals are framed, including a detailed specification of the consequence of the second one (in which the eel is caught before it gains "too much power"). A further counterfactual that narrates how the governor would have died in the battle between the rebelling slaves and the British colonizers if he had not received help also takes the same form of an externally focused commentary: "She [Imoinda] wounded several, and shot the governor into the shoulder, of which wound he had like to have died, but that an Indian woman, his mistress, sucked the wound, and cleansed it from the venom" (Behn 1998, 61).[4]

These counterfactuals are symptomatic of the ambivalent position of *Oroonoko*'s narrator, who is ostensibly a homodiegetic witness figure but who in fact often lapses into the more privileged style of heterodiegetic narration. These examples can be seen as prototype forms of the privileged "authorial" counterfactuals that develop in the eighteenth and nineteenth centuries and that create a reality effect by asserting the actuality of the narrated course of events in contrast to the less "real" counterfactual alternatives. The fact that heterodiegetic counterfactuals are by no means automatic discourse features is indicated by their absence in another key seventeenth-century text that is often cited as a prototype novel (see Bonheim 1993)—Congreve's *Incognita* (1692).

Autobiographical Counterfactuals in Eighteenth-Century Fiction

The eighteenth century is seen as the point at which the modern novel establishes itself as a major literary genre. One manifestation of this phenomenon is the emergence of fictional autobiographical narrative: the eighteenth century's "conceptualisation of 'autobiography' as a recognizable set of practices, distinct from other kinds of writing" (Nussbaum 1989, xi) results in fiction using forms of real-life first-person narratives such as the journal (Defoe's *Robinson Crusoe*); the autobiography, confessional (Defoe's *Moll Flanders*) or otherwise (Smollett's *Roderick Random*); and the letter (Richardson's *Pamela* and *Clarissa*). Within this narrative form, self-focused counterfactuals simulate the cognitive processes of an *autobiographical consciousness* by framing the kind of retrospective evaluations that are part of authentic autobiographical reflection. In the eighteenth-century novel that uses homodiegetic narration, characters are depicted formulating both short-term emotional responses to exceptional circumstances and long-term evaluations of "roads not taken."

Just as Defoe's use of the coincidence plot in *Moll Flanders* singles him out as a significant innovator, so does his use of extended counterfactuals reveal a more complex narrative structure. *Robinson Crusoe* (1719) repeatedly depicts its protagonist contemplating alternate possibilities. Trying to look on the bright side of life after his shipwreck, Crusoe imagines a worst-case scenario in which he salvages absolutely nothing from the wreck of the ship:

> All our discontents about what we want appeared to me to spring from the want of thankfulness for what we have.
> Another reflection was of great use to me . . . and this was, to compare my present condition with what I at first expected it should be; nay, with what it would certainly have been, if the good providence of God had not wonderfully ordered the ship to be cast up nearer to the shore, where I not only could come at her, but could bring what I got out of her to the shore, for my relief and comfort; without which, I had wanted for tools to work, weapons for defence, or gun-powder and shot for getting my food.
> I spent whole hours, I may say whole days, in representing to my self in the most lively colours how I must have acted if I had got nothing out of the ship; how I could not so much as got any food except fish and turtles; and that as it was long before I found any of them, I must have perished first; that I should have lived, if I had not perished, like a meer savage; that if I had killed a goat or a fowl, by any contrivance, I had no way to flea or open them, or part the flesh from the skin and bowels, or to cut it up; but must gnaw it with my teeth and pull it with my claws like a beast. (Defoe 1965, 141)

The passage (an excerpt of which was already referred to in chapter 1) constructs, in its entirety, an extensive downward counterfactual. The antecedent is brief ("if I had got nothing out of the ship"), but its consequences are very substantially depicted as Crusoe creates a detailed speculative scenario of his alternate existence without the tools from the ship using the minute detail that is characteristic of Defoe's practically oriented narrative realism.

Crusoe's downward counterfactual also functions as a sober reflection in keeping with the novel's religious ethics and the theme of "thankfulness" for God's providence. Crusoe uses counterfactual rhetoric to convince himself that the actual version of events was *caused* by God for Crusoe's special benefit. This rhetoric has important permutations for the novel's colonial ideology: believing that he is under the special protection of God, Crusoe transfers providential authority to his own person in order to become the island's "sovereign, monarch, and patriarch" (Hulme 1986, 217).

A counterfactual from *Moll Flanders* (1722) further corroborates the fact that Defoe's innovative narrative ability to create character-cognitive depth is facilitated through the strategic use of counterfactuals depicting a reflective consciousness. Having swiftly and readily sacrificed her virtue to the amorous advances of the unnamed elder brother of the family who has given her a home, Moll speculates in detail about what would have happened if she had been less free with her favors:

> Nothing was ever so stupid on both sides. Had I acted as became me, and resisted as virtue and honour required, this gentleman had either desisted his attacks, finding no room to expect the accomplishment of his design, or had made fair and honourable proposals of marriage; in which case, whoever had blamed him, nobody could have blamed me. In short, if he had known me, and how easy the trifle he aimed at was to be had, he would have troubled his head no further, but have given me four or five guineas, and have lain with me the next time he had come at me. And if I had known his thoughts, and how hard he thought I would be to be gained, I might have made my own terms with him; and if I had not capitulated for an immediate marriage, I might for a maintenance till marriage, and might have had what I would; for he was already rich to excess. (Defoe 1978, 48)

The variety of upward variants seen with the wisdom of hindsight is part of Moll's characterization as opportunistic and calculating. In contrast to the passage from *Crusoe*, which only framed counterfactual actions and events, this passage is tendentially more characterological in its suggestion of two alternative versions of Moll and the amorous brother. In the first section, Moll is virtuous as opposed to lascivious and is accordingly rewarded either with her virtue intact or with marriage, depending on the brother's counterfactual response to the counterfactually chaste Moll. The subsequent commentary then creates epistemically superior versions both of the brother and of Moll in which each character can counterfactually mind-read the other's true designs ("if I had known his thoughts") and analyzes how both characters could have acted more productively. However, these counterfactuals are not truly characterological if we read them more as calculating reflections on how Moll should have behaved to achieve her goals as opposed to the expressions of a true desire to be more virtuous; this distinction lies at the heart of Moll's ambivalent characterization in the novel. Be that as it may, this passage is innovative for its spate of counterfactual clauses, which creates a diversified matrix of branches, character versions, and responses.

Richardson's groundbreaking epistolary narratives further expand the use of the autobiographical counterfactual. *Pamela* (1740) is strewn with many minor counterfactuals (Richardson 1980, 103, 214–15, 217, 305, 334) but contains one very extensive counterfactual articulated by Mr. B. after he and Pamela have been officially betrothed.[5] In it Mr. B. explores an alternative marriage scenario to a counterfactual wife, who, unlike Pamela, is his social equal:

> "Now, my Pamela, I would have you think, and I hope you will have reason for it, that had I married the first lady in the land, I would not have treated her better than I will you; for my wife *is* my wife....
>
> "Had I married with no other views than most men have, on entering into the state, my wife might have been a fine lady, brought up pretty much in my own manner, and accustomed to have her will in every thing.

"Some men come into a compromise; and, after a few struggles, sit down tolerably contented. But, had I married a princess, I could not have done so. Indeed, I must have preferred her to all her sex, before I had consented to go to church with her; for even in this *best* case, differences are too apt to arise in matrimony....

"Then I must have been morally sure, that she preferred me to all men; and, to convince me of this, she must have lessened, not aggravated, my failings; she must have borne with my imperfections; she must have watched and studied my temper; and if ever she had any points to carry, any desire of overcoming, it must have been by sweetness and complaisance; and yet not such a slavish one, as should make her condescension seem to be rather the effect of her insensibility, than that of her judgment and affection....

"In all companies, she must have shewn, that she had, whether I altogether deserved it or not, an high regard and opinion of me....

"I should have expected, therefore, that she would draw a kind veil over my faults; that such as she could not hide, she should endeavour to extenuate....

"Now, my Pamela, this is but a faint sketch of the conduct I must have expected from my wife, let her quality have been what it would; or I must have lived with her on bad terms....

"... For here is my misfortune; I could not have been contented to have been but *moderately happy* in a wife." (464–66)

Mr. B.'s very lengthy counterfactual (here quoted only in excerpts), with its plethora of detail concerning the hypothetical behavior and qualities of his counterfactually upper-class bride and depicting his own character traits and expectations in marriage, amounts to a brief alternate life story inserted into the narrative. It is probably unequaled, in terms of its scope, as an autobiographical counterfactual in the novel at this stage of its development. The passage has the combined purpose of emphasizing Mr. B.'s magnanimity in marrying Pamela, confirming Pamela's own suitability as a bride notwithstanding her social status, and also providing her with very precise guidelines about how to behave toward Mr. B. when they are married. The counterfactual is thus a key articulation of Mr. B.'s characterization both as an authoritarian eighteenth-century squire and patriarch and as a man who marries for love despite considerable class differences.

The heroine of *Clarissa* (1747–48) is of an entirely different class background to Pamela. Like her main epistolary confidante, Anna Howe, Clarissa Harlowe is a highly educated and articulate young woman. Richardson's class-based mind styling in *Pamela* (not implying intrinsically different intellectual capacities but reflecting Pamela's and Clarissa's different educational backgrounds) gives only Mr. B. the rhetorical sophistication of extensive counterfactualizing. Conversely, in *Clarissa* both the heroine and Anna Howe are given a marked capacity for counterfactualizing. The two most significant plot developments of the novel—Clarissa's "escape" from her domineering family into a new form of captivity with Lovelace and, much later, her rape and subsequent escape from him—are followed in Clarissa's letters by extensive counterfactual analysis.

Under pressure from her family to marry the hideous but rich Mr. Solmes, Clarissa is manipulated by Lovelace into a meeting in which he tricks her into thinking that they have been discovered, with the result that, in a heat-of-the-moment decision, she puts herself in his power. In subsequently narrating these events in a letter to Anna Howe, Clarissa constructs a long and syntactically complex counterfactual in which she retrospectively assesses her own mistakes:

> To have it to reflect, that I should so inconsiderately give in to an interview which, had I known either myself or him, or in the least considered the circumstances of the case, I might have supposed would put me into the power of his resolution and out of that of my own reason.
>
> For might I not have believed that *he*, who thought he had cause to apprehend that he was on the point of losing a person who had cost him so much pains and trouble, would not hinder her, if possible, from returning? That he, who knew I had promised to give him up for ever, if insisted on as a condition of reconciliation [with her family] would not endeavour to put it out of my power to do so?—In short, that he, who had artfully forborne to send for my letter . . . would want a device to keep me with him till the danger of having our meeting discovered might throw me absolutely into his power to avoid my own worse usage [by her family], and the mischiefs which might have ensued, perhaps in my very sight, had my friends and he met? . . .
>
> How much more properly had I acted, with regard to that correspondence, had I once for all when he was forbid to visit me, and I to receive his visits, pleaded the authority I ought to have been bound by, and denied to write to him! . . . now that it is too late, I plainly see how I ought to have conducted myself. (Richardson 1985, 381, letter 94, Tuesday night)

Clarissa constructs a self-focused upward counterfactual to frame her own self-reproach. She postulates a wiser and more insightful version of herself ("For might I not have believed") who would have better seen through Lovelace's strategies and perceived the dangers of the meeting in advance. Following this, as another means of "undoing" the past, Clarissa generates a different counterfactual antecedent in which she complies with the dictates of her family and thus does not allow communication with Lovelace to slip out of her control ("How much more properly had I acted"). The full passage (of which only excerpts are quoted) is an even more dense and intricate montage of counterfactual clauses that, precisely through its torrent of thoughts, creates a most authentic-seeming example of a human consciousness racked by the pangs of *hot regret* at an exceptional moment of crisis.

The above passage, which expresses short-term regret and self-reproach, contrasts markedly with a passage much later in the novel, when, having been raped by Lovelace and close to death (but finally free of her captivity), Clarissa contemplates alternate possible versions of her relationship with him:

> I am more grieved (at times however) for *others*, than for *myself*. And so I *ought*. For as to *myself*, I cannot but reflect that I have had an escape, rather than a loss, in missing Mr Lovelace for a husband: even had he *not* committed the vilest of all outrages [i.e., the rape].
>
> Let anyone who knows my story collect his character from his behaviour to *me, before* that outrage; and then judge whether it was in the least probable for such a man to make me happy. But to collect his character from his principles with regard to the *sex in general*, and from his enterprises on many of them ... together with the high opinion he has of himself, it will be doubted that a wife of his must have been miserable; and more miserable if she loved him, than if she could have been indifferent to him.
>
> A *twelvemonth* might, very probably, have put a period to my life; situated as I was with my friends; persecuted and harassed as I had been by my brother and sister; and my very heart torn to pieces by the *wilful*, and (as it is now apparent) *premeditated* suspenses of the man whose gratitude I wished to engage, and whose protection I was the more entitled to expect, as he had robbed me of every other, and hating my own family had reduced me to an absolute dependence upon himself. This once, as I thought, all his view; and uncomfortable enough for me, if it had been all....
>
> Have I not reason, these things considered, to think myself happier without Mr Lovelace than with him?—My will too unviolated; and very little, nay, not anything as to him, to reproach myself with? (Richardson 1985, 1161–62, letter 379, Sunday, July 30)

In a sober assessment of the major events of the novel, Clarissa constructs a downward counterfactual to create a sense of the preferability of the actual version of events. The counterfactual contains a detailed evaluation of Lovelace against which Clarissa draws conclusions about her fate as his counterfactual wife. She imagines herself dead within a year from a combination of the emotional stress of marriage to Lovelace and the sadness of alienation from her family and friends. In the concluding downward counterfactual, she then assesses the materialistic aspects, rejoicing that no further ill will has been created by Lovelace gaining access to her fortune through marriage. This passage therefore constructs a compact but eventful alternate version of the novel in which marriage to Lovelace is postulated as involving greater suffering and harm than the heroine's actual life. Clarissa's counterfactual evaluation of her autobiography is therefore a crucial passage that asserts the calmness of her heart in the face of both her life and her actual death. The passage is a particularly good fictional example of counterfactuals functioning as an "important component of psychological adjustment" by creating a "useful dialectic by which the individual comes to grasp more completely his or her particular lifespace" (Roese and Olson 1995b, 191–92).

While on one level Clarissa's conclusions reflect a providential value scheme, from a cultural and feminist perspective the counterfactual demonstrates the impossible nature of Clarissa's situation and the fact that she is "painfully constrained by the pressure of other people" (Damrosch 1985, 218). This "history of a young lady" (the novel's subtitle) in the mid-eighteenth century is presented, in stark contrast to *Pamela*'s Cinderella-style optimism, as a "no way out" situation: Clarissa is intelligent and financially endowed, but her potential is obstructed by the oppression of patriarchal family structures, the pressure to marry, and the largely unrestrained power of (unlike *Pamela*'s Mr. B.) untamable upper-class rakes like Lovelace.

Counterfactuals in Eighteenth-Century Heterodiegetic Narration

Externally focused counterfactuals are a significant part of the overt heterodiegetic narratorial style of Henry Fielding. In *Tom Jones* (1749) a steady flow of counterfactual asides draws attention to possible alternative branches in the action; for example: "The mistress would have turned away her maid for a corrupt hussy, if she had known as much as the reader" (Fielding 1966, 490), and "Mr Western and his nephew were not known to one another; nor indeed would the former have taken any notice of the later, if he had known him" (490). These minor counterfactuals have a cumulative effect: they subtly reinforce the comparative *actuality* (reality) of the narrative world in contradistinction to less actual possibilities; by sketching unactualized possibilities, they assert that events "really *did* happen" like this and not in any other way.

It is, however, symptomatic of the playfully ambivalent stance of Fielding's narrator with reference to the reality of the world of *Tom Jones* that he also uses counterfactuals to foreground his role as world-creating author. This can be seen in the treatment of a strategically engineered case of nonconvergence in the Upton episode (already discussed in chapter 6 for its use of coincidence): Partridge only meets Mrs. Waters/Jenny Jones after Tom Jones has slept with her at Upton and is therefore unable to warn Tom that he may be committing incest. At the beginning of chapter 2 of book 18, Partridge counterfactually laments his nonconvergence with Mrs. Waters at Upton: "'Nay, sir,' cries Partridge, '. . . what I have said is most certainly true—that woman who now went out is your mother. How unlucky was it for you, sir, that I did not happen to see her at that time, to have prevented it? Sure the devil himself must have contrived to bring about this wickedness'" (815). Partridge's reference to a "devil" can be read as a playful reference to the world and speech-manipulating presence of the author behind the discourse. This "devil" then draws attention to himself more clearly when the narrator comments, tongue in cheek:

> If the reader will please to refresh his memory, by turning to the scene at Upton in the ninth book, he will be apt to admire the many strange accidents which unfortunately prevented any interview between Partridge and Mrs Waters, when she spent a whole day there with Mr Jones. Instances of this kind we may frequently observe in life, where the greatest events are produced by a nice train of little circumstances; and more than one example of this may be discovered by the accurate eye, in this our history. (815–16)

The phrase "many strange accidents which unfortunately prevented" is itself a veiled counterfactual amounting to "but for these strange accidents, Partridge and Mrs Waters would have met." The narrator thus combines softly metafictional authorial self-congratulation with an ironic statement concerning the ostensible similarity of his plot construction to the reality of life. This involves a paradoxical playoff between two different forms of causality: in the first sentence the narrator-as-author covertly draws attention to himself as the *external* causal-manipulative force controlling the novel's events; in the second he then switches strategies and asserts the reality of the narrative world of *Tom Jones* by stressing its *autonomous* structure of causal-progenerative chains of events ("a nice train of little circumstances"). In Fielding counterfactuals thus both support and playfully subvert narrative realism.

Austen's *Mansfield Park* (1814) undertakes a more concerted form of counterfactualizing, in which both the characters and the narrator separately map out counterfactual versions of the concluding phase of the novel's love plot (see also figure 4 in chapter 3). The twin romance constellations involving Edmund Bertram/Mary Crawford and Fanny Price/Henry Crawford are brought very close to becoming actual marriages. Even when Fanny has refused Henry's proposal, a possible future reversal is suggested when Fanny perceives a "wonderful improvement . . . in Mr Crawford. . . . [S]he was quite persuaded of his being astonishingly more gentle, and regardful of others, than formerly" (Austen 1966, 405). Crawford's elopement with Mrs. Rushworth then finally sabotages this possible development. However, at this point the discourse not only becomes exceedingly vague about the details of the newly budding romance between Fanny and Edmund but also explores repeatedly different possibilities.[6] The first counterfactual is articulated by Mary Crawford (but reported in Edmund's words to Fanny) in what Edmund himself calls a "retrospect of what might have been—but what never can be now":

> "'He [Crawford] has thrown away,' said she [Mary], 'such a woman as he will never see again. She [Fanny] would have fixed him, she would have made him happy for ever.'...
>
> "... 'Why, would she not have him? It is all her fault. Simple girl!—I shall never forgive her. Had she accepted him as she ought, they might now be on the point of marriage.... He would have taken no pains to be on terms with Mrs Rushworth again.'" (441–42)

Mary thus constructs a causal-progenerative counterfactual sequence that places the blame for Henry's elopement with Mrs. Rushworth on Fanny herself. Since Mary's dubious moral response to Henry's elopement leads Edmund to withdraw his affection from her, Mary's counterfactual is actually instrumental in this subsequent process.

In the next chapter, a different counterfactual review by the narrator herself provides a counter-counterfactual to Mary's:

> Henry Crawford, ruined by early independence and bad domestic example, indulged in the freaks of a cold-blooded vanity a little too long.... Could he have been satisfied with the conquest of one amiable woman's affections, could he have found sufficient exultation in overcoming the reluctance, in working himself into the esteem and tenderness of Fanny Price, there would have been every probability of success and felicity for him. His affection had already done something. Her influence over him had already given him some influence over her. Would he have deserved more, there can be no doubt that more would have been obtained; especially when that marriage had taken place, which would have given him the assistance of her conscience in subduing her first inclination, and brought them very often together. Would he have persevered, and uprightly, Fanny must have been his reward—and a reward very voluntarily bestowed—within a reasonable period from Edmund's marrying Mary.
>
> Had he done as he intended, and as he knew he ought, by going down to Everingham after his return from Portsmouth, he might have been deciding his own happy destiny. But he was pressed to stay for Mrs Fraser's party; his staying was made of flattering consequence, and he was to meet Mrs Rushworth there. (451–52)

This counterfactual differs significantly from Mary's in its apportioning of blame and its more intricate causal-progenerative dynamics: Henry counterfactually continues the "wonderful improvement" observed by Fanny in an earlier chapter (405) and has enough self-control not to elope with Mrs Rushworth. The key result of this is that Edmund is *not* disillusioned with Mary Crawford, he proposes to and is accepted by her; in turn, Fanny gradually changes her attitude to Henry and marries him. The narrator's counterfactual lamentations regarding Crawford's behavior have a tone of sympathetic impatience that intensifies the novel's reality effect by suggesting that Crawford is an autonomous human being who should have known better. Austen's *emotionally engaged* narratorial counterfactualizing is thus very different from the rhetorical games played by Fielding's more detached narrator.

Austen's insertion of two different counterfactual alternatives into the concluding discourse of her novel is highly significant because it is an early example of a more intricate nonbinary counterfactual narrative fabric: *Mansfield Park* creates an *ontologically pluralistic landscape* of multiple possible worlds. Moreover, the counterfactual endings to *Mansfield Park* suggest a more interesting dynamics of romantic interaction between Henry and Fanny than is to be found in the actual ending of *Mansfield Park*, awakening the impression that, even if Fanny's first choice is Edmund, Austen herself could not fully let go of the idea of the alternative constellation of a marriage between Fanny and Henry.

Alternate Lives and Loves in Nineteenth-Century Fiction

DuPlessis argues that the nineteenth-century novel (just as Miller [1980] does for the eighteenth century) is still the preserve of the romance plot (in the sense of the love plot): "Once upon a time, the end, the rightful end, of women in novels was social—successful courtship, marriage—or judgmental of her sexual and social failure—death" (1985, 1). It is thus only in twentieth-century fiction that, parallel to real-world emancipation, more varied narrative trajectories beyond these rigidly generic "alternate endings in marriage and death" (4) really become available to female characters. There is, however, as DuPlessis observes, a partial watershed in the latter part of the nineteenth century (15). This development is also heralded by a change in the use of counterfactuals and other forms of alternate world. Counterfactuals are now used rhetorically (as in the eighteenth century) not only to create a "reality effect" but also as part of a strategy that challenges the hegemony of the convergently romantic or fairy-tale storylines that still characterize texts of the nineteenth-century "realist" canon like Brontë's *Jane Eyre* and Dickens's *Martin Chuzzlewit*.

The ending of Brontë's *Villette* (1853), narrated by the heroine, Lucy Snowe, is a significant development in the treatment of romantic closure.[7] Deviating from the tendency of other autodiegetic narrators of the period, Lucy does not provide a definitive statement about her ultimate fate in life but offers the reader a choice of two possible versions—marital "union" with M. Paul or his death in a storm at sea while returning to marry her.

> The wind takes its autumn moan; but—he is coming. . . . I know some signs of the sky; I have noted them ever since childhood. God, watch that sail! Oh! guard it! . . . That storm roared frenzied for seven days. . . .

> Here pause: pause at once. There is enough said. Trouble no quiet, kind heart; leave sunny imaginations hope. Let it be theirs to conceive the delight of joy born again fresh out of great terror, the rapture of rescue from peril, the wondrous reprieve from dread, the fruition of return. Let them picture union and a happy succeeding life.
>
> Madame Beck prospered all the days of her life; so did Père Silas; Madame Walravens fulfilled her ninetieth year before she died. Farewell. (Brontë 1979, 595–96)

This passage is not framed hypothetically as a counterfactual—it evokes two alternate versions of the novel's ending. Readers can, however, divine that the more actual ending (which is not actually narrated but only suggested) involves M. Paul's death at sea and that the more explicitly narrated ending involving "union and a happy succeeding life" is a fictitious sop for those readers in need of a more conventional romantic closure. Paradoxically, therefore, the text narrates the virtual and only implies the actual. Nancy Cervetti observes that *Villette* is "a continually self-reflexive text [and] is all about reading" (1998, 72); this is nowhere more true than at the end, where the focus is on the reader's expectations of closure and not on its authoritative narration. *Villette* is an early experimental and prototypically interactive text that invites the *reader* to select and imagine her own preferred ending out of two possible versions.

Villette's divergent ending therefore reinforces Brontë's rebellion against the romantically convergent structure of her earlier novel, *Jane Eyre* (1847) (see also the discussion in chapter 6), by drawing attention to its infringement of the standard narrative conventions of the period. In refusing to narrate positive romantic closure in the heroine's own story, the novel silently addresses the social reality of the many Victorian women who remained outside the convergent, integrated family units of male-driven society. Lucy Snowe is not swept up and carried away by the forces of fictional convergence but follows a divergent path that reflects social reality at the same time as rebelling against the fictional norms of the period.[8]

Later in the nineteenth century, George Eliot deploys divergent plot patterns to analyze the reality of marriage by representing the deep conflicts of aims, wishes, and values that create unsuccessful and unhappy marriages. Eliot's innovative narrative technique represents her characters' consciousness as located in a self-spun network of possible futures and counterfactual past worlds.[9] *Middlemarch* (1871–72) creates an ontologically complex narrative fabric of the divergent virtual future worlds constructed by its characters. Notably, the marriage of Tertius Lydgate and Rosamund Vincy illustrates the negative dynamics caused by antagonistic future wish-worlds. Thus, Rosamond has already "woven a little future" after Lydgate's arrival in Middlemarch: "A stranger was absolutely necessary to Rosamond's social romance" (Eliot 1965, 145). By contrast, Lydgate is represented as having no equivalent intentions: "Not that, like her, he had been weaving any future in which their lots were united" (155). In time, Rosamond's future imaginings of marriage with Lydgate take on the detail of her materialistic inclinations: "Her thoughts were much occupied with a handsome house in Lowick Gate which she hoped would by-and-by be vacant.... [S]he imagined the drawing-room... with various styles of furniture" (300). In a key passage, the narrator then contrasts the potentially reality-generating plasticity of Rosamund's future intentions with Lydgate's own lack of a counterstrategy:

> To Rosamond it seemed as if she and Lydgate were as good as engaged.... It is true, Lydgate had the counter idea of remaining unengaged; but this was a mere negative, a shadow cast by other resolves which themselves were capable of shrinking. Circumstances was [sic] almost sure to be on the side of Rosamond's idea, which had a shaping activity and looked through watchful blue eyes, whereas Lydgate's lay blind and unconcerned as a jelly-fish which gets melted without knowing it. (304–5)

Rosamund is here presented as having the necessary will to form an actual version of her wish-world by manipulating the materials provided by reality. By contrast, Lydgate is depicted as leaving the outcome of events to "chance," disdaining to indulge in strategic thinking, which for him means being "in the grasp of petty alternatives" (210). Indeed, one key overall comparative thread in *Middlemarch* concerns characters' attitudes toward the future. Thus, the sensible Mary Garth long declines to even entertain the prospect of a marriage to Fred Vincy, while both Fred himself and Mr. Brooke are negatively characterized as having a far too lax or irresponsible attitude to their respective futures: Vincy possesses an unfounded optimism about his personal future (261), while Brooke is "elated with an influx of dim projects" (326).

In *Daniel Deronda* (1876) Eliot constructs a highly innovative network of virtual time paths in her depiction of Gwendolen Harleth's mental world. However, Eliot's final novel contains a bold interplay between convergence and divergence. Each of the parallel lives of its two protagonists is dominated by a different plot pattern. Expressive of the more fortunate social position of men in nineteenth-century society, Deronda's life is steered by an ultimately euphoric version of the traditional coincidence and identity plot, ending in marriage, causal-pro-generative clarity, and a meaningful role in society (see chapter 6). By contrast, Gwendolen's life narrative is structured around a pattern of unrealized virtual futures and retrospective wistful counterfactualizing.[10] This clear separation of the life plots of the female and male protagonists subversively indicates that *convergence* is a plot driven by a particularly masculine agenda. In Gwendolen's more socially and emotionally insecure existence, there is no comforting and convergent "coming home" experience but a continual sequence of disappointment and readjustment.

Just as, at the beginning of the novel, Gwendolen is depicted as a player surveying the multiple possibilities of the roulette wheel (Eliot 1967, 35–39), so does she, in the early stages of the novel, entertain a range of possible futures. These reflect the dilemma facing nineteenth-century middle-class women in general: in a world offering little scope to earn an independent income, marriage necessarily constitutes the major future scenario in "visions of possible happiness" (333). Thus, when faced with financial destitution, Gwendolen contemplates two alternate professional futures: a conventional one as a governess (at Bishop Mompert's family) or life as an actress.

> There was always to be Mrs Mompert's supervision; always something or other would be expected of her to which she had not the slightest inclination. . . . Gwendolen . . . saw the life before her as an entrance into a penitentiary. Wild thoughts of running away to be an actress . . . came to her with the lure of freedom; . . . dimly she conceived herself getting amongst vulgar people who would treat her with rude familiarity. . . . Some beautiful girls, who, like her, had read romances where even plain governesses are centres of attraction and are sought in marriage, might have solaced themselves a little by transporting such pictures into their own future. (315–17)

While Gwendolen's mind wavers between these two future projections, the narrator's additional sketch of a *Jane Eyre*–style scenario, which ironically disparages the convergently utopian scenarios of other nineteenth-century fictions, adds a further intertextually virtual dimension against which the grim reality of her position is measured.

The crux comes for Gwendolen when she must decide whether to accept a proposal of marriage from the rich Mr. Grandcourt. In the suspenseful mental tour de force leading up to the moment when she must accept or reject Grandcourt's proposal, her internal decision-making processes are depicted as a consciousness veering helplessly between divergent possibilities: "The alternate dip of counterbalancing thoughts begotten of counterbalancing desires had brought her into a state in which no conclusion could look fixed to her" (341). Before she finally agrees to marry him, the narrator states that "she was conscious of being at the turning of the ways" (347). The crossroads metaphor underlines the fact that Gwendolen has reached a crucial life-decision scenario. When Gwendolen later experiences the actual conditions of marriage to her dictatorial husband, the ontological focus of her autobiographical reflections shifts away from imagining virtual futures, and this "turning of the ways" then becomes the retrospective point of no return for her own wistful counterfactualizing.

Gwendolen's counterfactuals have a marked spatiality in their representation of plural pathways through time and contain imaginary dialogues between Gwendolen and alternate versions of herself. In the following example Gwendolen's thoughts retrace a counterfactual path before briefly contemplating a new virtual future (which, ironically, again concerns gambling) that may distract her from her unhappy marriage:

> She often pursued the comparison between what might have been, if she had not married Grandcourt, and what actually was, trying to persuade herself that life generally was barren of satisfaction, and that if she had chosen differently she might now have been *looking back* with regret as bitter as the feeling she was trying to argue away.... By-and-by she promised herself that she should get used to her heart-sores, and find excitements that would *carry her through life*.... There was gambling: she had heard stories ... of fashionable women who gambled in all sorts of ways. It seemed *very flat* to her *at this distance*, but perhaps if she began to gamble again, the passion might awake. (Eliot 1967, 483, emphasis added)

The phrases "looking back," "at this distance," and "carry her through life" all contain the spatial mappings of the *life is a journey* metaphor: Gwendolen turns round to survey previously trodden but irretraceable terrain and looks forward to view the grim monotony of the path ahead. In contrast to Gwendolen's earlier vivid and imaginative future projections, this future terrain has little life and looks "very flat." Notably, the passage evokes a counterfactual Gwendolen (one who did not marry Grandcourt) who is engaged in counter-counterfactualizing ("she might now have been looking back"). This ontologically complex scenario also articulates the inscrutable relativism of autobiographical counterfactualizing: the actual Gwendolen has no way of knowing what kind of comparable regrets her counterfactual self might have experienced had she chosen otherwise because her hypothetical alternate self treads a path unknown to her. In keeping with Eliot's overall tendency to relativize, this passage avoids overt upward counterfactualizing. Gwendolen's dialogue with different imaginary versions of herself is continued elsewhere (see 496).

Moreover, instead of, in the fashion of other nineteenth-century novels, achieving romantic convergence after Gwendolen is conveniently freed from her marriage by Grandcourt's drowning, her relationship with Deronda remains the subject of wistful counterfactualizing to the end.[11] Gwendolen believes that it is her own morally lax gambling away of her future by marrying Grandcourt that has permanently thrown her off the pathway leading to romantic convergence with Deronda: "When he [Deronda] had left her [Gwendolen] she sank on her knees, in hysterical crying. The *distance* between them was too great. She was a banished soul—beholding a possible life which she had sinned herself away from" (767, emphasis added). In turn, a final counterfactual from Deronda's perspective articulates his own sense that a relationship with Gwendolen has been thwarted by the interception of other priorities: "If all this had happened little more than a year ago, he would hardly have asked himself whether he loved her [Gwendolen]: the impetuous determining impulse which would have moved him would have been to save her from sorrow, to shelter her life for evermore from the dangers of loneliness" (835). In the unconventional structure of Eliot's novel, therefore, a love plot between the novel's two main characters is only achieved in the final convergence of their counterfactual thoughts but not in the actual story.

Thomas Hardy's tragic plots, which abound in implicit and explicit counterfactuals generated in response to a world full of missed opportunities, are the fictional embodiment of the human tendency to construct positive outcomes in response to tragic events observed in the psychological research on counterfactualizing (Roese and Olson 1995b). Hardy's novels contain a complete plotting of coincidental encounters and mistimed nonconvergences (see the discussion of *The Return of the Native* in chapter 6); the interaction of counterfactuals and negative coincidence, however, can best be seen in *Tess of the d'Urbervilles* (1891). In contrast to texts like *Villette* and *Mansfield Park* that only contain alternate endings in the closing discourse, *Tess* already evokes the upward counterfactual version of its tragic love plot at the beginning. At a May Day dance Angel Clare sees Tess from a distance but does not dance with her: "As he [Angel] fell out of the dance his eyes lighted on Tess Durbeyfield, whose own large orbs wore, to tell the truth, the faintest aspect of reproach that he had not chosen her. He, too, was sorry then that, owing to her backwardness, he had not observed her; and with that in his mind he left the pasture.... He wished that he had asked her; he wished that he had inquired her name." (Hardy 1978, 54–55). This initial scenario already invites the reader to plot a counterfactual version of events in which Angel and Tess begin a friendship at the May Day dance. Counterfactuals are implied in the "reproach" in Tess's eyes that Angel did not choose her and half-formulated in Angel's wish that he had danced with Tess and inquired her name.

The first scene later receives more extensive counterfactual commentary when Tess and Angel reencounter each other:

> "Why didn't you stay and love me when I—was sixteen; living with my little sisters and brother, and you danced on the green? O, why didn't you, why didn't you!" she said, impetuously clasping her hands....
>
> "Ah—why didn't I stay!" he said. "That is just what I feel. If I had only known! But you must not be so bitter in your regret—why should you be?"
>
> With the woman's instinct to hide she diverged hastily—

> "I should have had four years more of your heart than I can ever have now. Then I should not have wasted my time as I have done—I should have had so much longer happiness!" (261)

Here Tess's desperately felt upward counterfactual intensifies the tragic sense of the story's divergence from a positive path. Moreover, a further unspoken counterfactual powers the scene, something that Tess here still hides from Angel but that the reader knows is the source of Tess's deeper regret: if she and Angel had become a couple earlier, then the causal-progenerative chain of events that commences with her seduction by Alec would have been avoided.

At the center of his tragic orchestration of events, therefore, Hardy weaves an upward counterfactual into the narrative to intensify the sense of tragedy. These counterfactuals also stress the nature of the world of Hardy's novels, in which convergence is the stuff of fiction (i.e., of counterfactuals) and actuality is full of the lost potential of his characters' lives. This sense of loss is brought out in a counterfactual of strong, wistful regret that Tess articulates concerning her own personal development:

> "Why do you look so woebegone all of a sudden?" he [Angel] asked.
> "Oh, 'tis only—about my own self," she said, with a frail laugh of sadness.
> ... "Just a sense of what might have been with me! My life looks as if it had been wasted for want of chances! When I see what you know, what you have read, and seen, and thought, I feel what a nothing I am!" (182)

Hardy's plots of tragic nonconvergence, orchestrated by counterfactuals, are therefore also the expression of the social conventions and cultural forces conspiring to constrict and suppress the potential in the individual—in *Tess* especially in women—in the late nineteenth century.

The Multiplication of Time: Alternate History in Nineteenth- and Twentieth-Century Fiction

In the fictional genre of alternate history, realism and the impossible meet, producing a new hybridization of romance and realist impulses. Robert Scholes has summarized the significant changes in the human mindset that led to the rise of new nineteenth-century genres of fiction as follows:

> The consciousness that history is an irreversible process led man inevitably to a new view of the future.... The idea that the future might be radically different in its social or economic organization was unthinkable until some time in the seventeenth or eighteenth century, and the impact of irreversible technological change did not become apparent until the nineteenth. The result of these and other developments was that man could finally conceive of the future historically. (1975, 14)

The rising nineteenth-century genres of *future history* and *alternate history* are the result of this change in the conception of historical time. In its basic form, however, *future history* involves a single linear extrapolation from the real-world present that creates a conjectural vision of the near future (George Chesney's *The Battle of Dorking* [1871]) or distant future (the anonymous *Annals of the Twenty-ninth Century; or, The Autobiography of the Tenth President of the World-Republic* [1874]). Counterfactual history, however, involves a more complex ontological structure and conceptual framework because of its idea that the present might have been "radically different."[12] The demise of a widespread belief in Providence is clearly one factor in this conceptual change: if history is no longer following a divinely preordained course, then *divergence* from the actual historical course of events becomes more conceivable (cf. Rodiek 1993, 266; Köhler 1973). The emphasis on the nonuniformity and *branching variability* of life in Darwin's narrative of evolution in *The Origin of Species* (1859) can also be seen as a key influence in awakening a sense of the multiple potentialities of history.[13] Darwin's theory did for the earth's evolutionary map, in spatial and temporal terms, what complex counterfactual narratives do for history. Darwin highlighted how the evolution of mammalian life took on different, *alternate* forms on different continents. His claim that there is "no law of necessary development" (1968, 348–49) was the result of his observation of the *divergent* development of species in different geographical regions.

The first nineteenth-century fictions in English using counterfactual history are conceptually cautious. Shaped by the ontological constraints of realism, they do not attempt to construct fully autonomous alternate worlds. An enduring uneasiness about asserting the full autonomy of a counterfactual world distinct from real-world history means that these texts adopt strategies that naturalize the counterfactual narrative by constructing a link to real-world history.

Four different texts from the period illustrate different permutations within this initial phase of ontological conservatism in the conceptionalization of alternate history. Nathaniel Hawthorne's "P.'s Correspondence" (1845) is an ironical counterfactual fantasy. The story's humor stems from P.'s descriptions of the counterfactual real-world figures he reports meeting while (believing himself) in nineteenth-century England. In this world many English Romantic poets have had their life counterfactually extended and must endure all the indignities and inconsistencies of old age instead of dying young and unblemished. However, the reality of the world P. describes is undermined by a frame narrator who emphasizes the dubious status of P.'s narrative, warning the reader that "his unfortunate friend P. has lost the thread of his life" with the result that "the past and present are jumbled together in his mind" (Hawthorne 1903, 166).

Edward Everett Hale's "Hands Off" (1881), a fantasy that rewrites biblical history, is more innovative on two counts. It depicts a fictional agent actively interfering in history and then traces the counterfactual history that is created by that interference. An unspecified (and clearly superhuman) homodiegetic narrator who is "free from the limits of Time" (Hale 1910, 318), witnesses biblical history on the earth and is moved by a strong desire to free "Joseph, son of Jacob" (320) after the narrator sees Joseph being sold into slavery by his brothers.[14] In order to demonstrate the dangers of interfering in history, a "Guardian" takes the narrator to a "region which the astronomers call the starless region" (320), where he is allowed to experiment in history alteration on a copy of biblical history. He frees Joseph, who returns to his family instead of being taken as a captive to Egypt (which he, according to the biblical narrative, then saved from famine). The catastrophic results of the narrator's minor alteration are then depicted: famine overtakes the region, the whole course of history is changed, and the development of civilization is ultimately thwarted. The causal plotting in this historical counterfactual is particularly notable: the story asserts that *causal-manipulative* interference in history is ill judged (the narrator only wishes to free Joseph but causes the end of civilization), precisely because the *causal-progenerative* multiplications of any action are incalculable. The Guardian's commentary makes this clear: history is a system in which any event will, in butterfly effect fashion, have far wider effects than envisaged:

> "You wanted to save your poor Joseph alone—all sole alone."
> "Yes," I said. "Why should I not want to?"
> "Because he was not alone; could not be alone. None of them were alone.... Why, you know yourself that not a raindrop in that shower yonder but balances against a dust-grain on the other side of creation.... None of us are alone.... Even He is in us, and we are in Him." (335–36)

The text's butterfly effect message is therefore articulated within a religious framework: ultimately, the story advocates a providential vision of history that confirms the desirability of the actual world.[15]

Mark Twain's *A Connecticut Yankee at King Arthur's Court* (1889) stages an attempt to create counterfactual history in the real world that ultimately fails. Here the nineteenth-century Hank Morgan, a skilled weapons-smith, falls asleep and miraculously wakes up in King Arthur's court in the year 513. Morgan's skill in weaponry enables him to cause an anachronistic scenario of nineteenth-century warfare being waged in sixth-century England. However, these anachronisms do not lead to a *permanent deviation* in history because, despite Morgan's superior scientific knowledge, "the entire feudal structure . . . turns and destroys him" (Klass 1974, 18).[16] Morgan therefore attempts to create a historical counterfactual *antecedent*, but its *consequences* are culturally undermined. The fact that Morgan's interference in history produces no causal-progenerative results for posterity is indicated by the fact that he returns to an unaltered version of the nineteenth century after falling into a thirteen-century sleep induced by Merlin.

Edmund Lawrence's *It May Happen Yet: A Tale of Bonaparte's Invasion of England* (1899) narrates a counterfactual version of early-nineteenth-century history in which Napoleon invades England instead of confining his military activities to continental Europe. Lawrence's text is significant in terms of its ontological framing of the counterfactual. Here counterfactual history is narrated as an *actual* sequence of events: chapter 5 of the novel narrates Napoleon's landing at Harwich in the year 1805 with a force of forty thousand, and subsequent chapters narrate the success of the invasion, which reaches the outskirts of London. Nevertheless, the author's position toward the ontological status of his text is characterized by a cautiousness that leads him ultimately to reembed the counterfactual events within real-world history. The narrator's ontological position changes when, toward the end of the narrative, he becomes a voice speaking from the world of real-world historical fact. He claims that the events narrated actually happened but have been forgotten again because the invasion was repelled:

> The non-mention of an event by historians, when there is a very general consensus in ignoring that event, is not a demonstration that the event did not happen. It is held by some eminent historical critics that a conspiracy of silence is a proof that there is something to be silent about. . . . During the latter years of Louis Napoleon's reign, we spent some time in the east of France. There we made the acquaintance of two old gentlemen, who were the first to tell us what we have adopted as the real history of the year 1805. (83)

Lawrence's counterfactual history thus also succumbs to the urge operative in all the nineteenth-century texts discussed so far—the realist need to ontologically harmonize the counterfactual by blending it into a real-world framework. Here counterfactual history is a "secret history" that is parenthetically inserted into the larger frame of official history. The deviating branch of history created by the counterfactual is "bent back" to rejoin real-world history at a later point and, like Twain's *Connecticut Yankee*, is not allowed to create a permanently divergent historical path. In the course of the twentieth century, however, this ontological narrative caution is thrown to the winds.

The Advent of Ontological Pluralization

In the tradition of alternate history, Winston Churchill's "If Lee Had Not Won the Battle of Gettysburg" (1931) is a significant early twentieth-century text that plays games with counterfactual worlds and historical figures and—in contrast to the nineteenth-century texts considered above—portrays a counterfactual world that permanently deviates from real-world history. Churchill's text is a hybrid, combining the fictional genre of alternate history with the counterfactual historical essay. The text is prefaced by a paragraph that summarizes the real-world Battle of Gettysburg (which Lee lost), but the essay that follows is written by a fictional "Winston S. Churchill, M.P." who inhabits a world in which Lee *did* win the Battle of Gettysburg and who therefore narrates counterfactual events as actual. This "Churchill" maps the intricate causal reverberations of the "famous Confederate Victory of Gettysburg" (Churchill 1932, 175) as a factual outline of nineteenth-and early-twentieth-century European and North American history. The victory of the Confederacy has, among other things, led to an ironic reversal of roles in British politics: Gladstone is "a Tory and authoritarian to his finger-tips" (184) whose (real-world) "radical and democratic courses" (184) are postulated as strategies that never developed because of his sealing of an "abiding alliance between Great Britain and the Southern States" (183). By contrast, Disraeli has left the Conservative Party to join "the Radical masses" and is the architect "of those great schemes of social and industrial insurance" (185). The historical narrative continues, optimistically, with the signing of "the Covenant of the English-speaking Association" in 1905, the avoidance of World War I despite tensions in 1914, and a "forthcoming Pan-European Conference in Berlin in 1932" (195). Churchill's narrative therefore blends fictional narrative with the counterfactual historical essay and is a different type of text compared to the drier academic historical essays contained in anthologies such as Ferguson (1997) and Cowley (2001). Churchill's text displays characteristics of the genre of fiction both because of the reversal of the ontological position of his narrator, who, posing as an essay writer, in fact speaks as an inhabitant of a counterfactual world, and because of its construction of counterfactual character versions of historical figures such as Disraeli and Gladstone.

It is, however, in the genre of science fiction that more radical ontological developments in fictional counterfactual narratives take place in the first half of the twentieth century. McHale (1987, 60) designates science fiction as the sister genre of high postmodernist fiction because of its depiction of a multiplicity of worlds. Studies of postmodernism have, however, not sufficiently acknowledged the fact that a significant process of radical ontological pluralization in fact occurs in science fiction *before* the postmodernist period—and also well before the publication of related developments in theoretical physics, notably the many-worlds interpretation of quantum theory (Everett 1957).[17] Ontological pluralization in science fiction sets in with the depiction of multiple counterfactual versions of history within one fictional text. Murray Leinster's "Sidewise in Time" (1934) is probably the first full-blown science fiction text to stage such an innovatively radical multiple-world scenario.[18] In this story the world is hit by a kind of "timequake" that transforms it into a temporally desynchronized terrain in which each geographical region is in a different counterfactual historical phase. The story's multiple-worlds premise is summed up by an insightful scientist who, fortunately, is on hand to explain what has happened: "'There has been a shaking and jumbling of space and time.... [W]e ordinarily think of time as a line, a sort of tunnel perhaps.... We assume that the future is a line instead of a coordinate, a path instead of a direction.... But the futures we fail to encounter, upon the roads we do not take, are just as real'" (Leinster 1974, 552). The sequence of spatial metaphors to describe time—the line, the tunnel, the path, and particularly the multiple roads of different possible futures—indicates the coalescence of the conceptualization of multiple alternate worlds.

Toward the end of the 1930s, at the beginning of the "golden age" of science fiction, these ideas were further developed in Jack Williamson's *The Legion of Time* (1938), which stages a "time war" between two possible future civilizations, Jonbar and Gyronchi. Here the battle for historical supremacy centers on which civilization from the future can favorably influence a crucial event in the twentieth century and hence become the actual future rather than only a potential one. Despite its incipient ontological pluralism, however, Williamson's text still clings to the ontological hierarchy of realism because, within its "conflicting infinitude of possible worlds, only one ... can ever claim physical reality" (1952, 28).

Following these beginnings, the work of L. Sprague de Camp more wholeheartedly indulges in the playful multiple-worlds spirit of postmodernism. In *Lest Darkness Fall* (1939) Padway, a twentieth-century archaeologist on an expedition in Italy, is transferred to the sixth century AD, where he permanently diverts the course of history and the otherwise ensuing Dark Ages by introducing printing, newspapers, and modern military strategies. In contrast to Twain's more cautious *Connecticut Yankee*, De Camp's protagonist is thus rendered capable of causally manipulating the course of history and creating a permanent new causal-progenerative strand of time that *contradicts* established history. Such history-alteration narratives are significant because they preempt the conceptual thrust of historiographic metafiction: both genres represent the *man-made construction of history*—in historiographic metafiction through the act of writing, in science fiction by direct interference. In De Camp's text the paradox created by this new version of history is not avoided but celebrated in the text's expositional pseudoscientific discourse, articulated by another professor in a theoretical discussion:

> "Sounds like a paradox," said Padway.
> "No-o.... We continue to exist, but another history has been started. Perhaps there are many such, all existing somewhere.... History is a four-dimensional web. It is a tough web. But it has its weak points. The junction places—the focal points, one might say—are weak." (De Camp 1955, 1–2)

Again, spatial metaphors—first that of the branching tree and then that of the junction—are used to express the concept of divergent versions of time.

De Camp's "The Wheels of If" (1940) goes one step farther by plotting a narrative universe in which multiple branches of time and history exist side by side a priori. The narrative is an early and highly amusing version of the transworld journey narrative. Allister Park, an attorney from a world representing the contemporary United States, travels through successive versions of twentieth-century North America, each of which is the result of a different history of New World colonization: in one version the Union Jack still flies and "David the Fuist" rules; in another "His Majesty Napoleon V [is] emperor of New York City" (De Camp 1970, 15). Real-world history (the world Park originally comes from) is therefore represented as just one of many equally actual alternatives. This *decentered* ontological hierarchy is metaphorically expressed in the image of the wheel in the story's title. The spatial metaphor of the wheel is significant because it *downsizes* the real-world version of history, representing it as just one of many spokes within a larger structure (see figure 5 in chapter 3). In his transworld journey Park successively occupies the bodies of different versions of himself in each alternate historical reality. This is a bewildering and comic process, since in each world he has to adjust to new versions of his physical appearance, different female companions, a new career, and new versions of the English language. By virtue of its detailed and colorful delineation of the alternate society produced by a different historical outcome, De Camp's text is therefore a key founding text of the alternate history genre as distinct from academic historical counterfactualizing. In De Camp's text the most detailed of these multiple versions of North America colonized by different European cultures is the world in which Park finally chooses to remain and in which the Celtic as opposed to the Roman branch of Christianity is the dominant religious-cultural force.

From these beginnings, fictional worlds using historical counterfactuals proliferate in the mid-twentieth century, producing a multiplicity of different forms of history generation, alteration, and destruction. In these fictions the counterfactual antecedent, that is, the point from which history deviates, is generally a turning point in real-world history that allows the creation of dramatically transformed societies and historical narratives. Such strategic points of evolutionary and historical change include the extinction of the dinosaurs (Brian G. Aldiss's *The Malacia Tapestry* [1976], Harry Harrison's *West of Eden* [1984], Stephen Fry's *Making History* [1996]), the English Reformation (Kingsley Amis's *The Alteration* [1976]), the English civil wars (John Whitbourn's *A Dangerous Energy* [1993]), the sixteenth-century Spanish-English conflict (Keith Roberts's *Pavane* [1966], John Brunner's *Times without Number* [1962]), the American

Civil War (Ward Moore's *Bring the Jubilee* [1953]), and the Second World War (Philip K. Dick's *The Man in the High Castle* [1962], Robert Harris's *Fatherland* [1992]) (see Helbig [2000] for a truly comprehensive list of counterfactual texts, classified according to their historical focus).

Following in the footsteps of the early innovations of Leinster and De Camp, many of these texts completely abandon the realist ontology by admitting, a priori or a posteriori, more than one counterfactual world as an actual world within their fictional universe. Other texts have a more conservative bias toward real-world history; in this case, the manipulative alteration of history *restores* real-world history rather than deviating from it. For example, in John Boyd's *The Last Starship from Earth* (1968) a time traveler from a downward (in this case truly dystopian) counterfactual version of the twentieth century creates an antecedent in the past of that world that creates the Christian religion and thus steers history back to its conventional pattern in the novel's denouement. History-alteration narratives also thematize patterns of causation. Ray Bradbury's "A Sound of Thunder" (1953) is a literalization of "butterfly-effect 'causes'" (Fearon 1996, 57). Here a tourist on a "time safari" to a prehistoric age disobeys instructions to keep to the path and accidentally treads on a butterfly. Returning to his own era in 2055, the tourist finds that the political reality he earlier left and even the English language have been transformed into new, unfamiliar versions. The story thus enacts the inscrutable network of escalating causal-progenerative links created by one small event within a larger system that is postulated by chaos theory. The butterfly is "a small thing that could upset balances and knock down a line of small dominoes and then big dominoes and then gigantic dominoes, all down the years across Time" (Bradbury 1953, 113). A more recent history-alteration narrative, Stephen Fry's *Making History*, centers on the unreliable causal-progenerative consequences of attempts to manipulate history: a wholly more negative and enduring version of the Nazi domination of Europe is created when Hitler is prevented from being born.

Major effects are achieved in these texts through the incorporation of real-world historical figures, allowing the reader to perform complex acts of transworld *identification* and *differentiation*. Some texts construct playfully incongruous biographies for real-world figures: in Amis's *The Alteration*, where there has been no Reformation, previous popes include Martin Luther (Germanian I) and Thomas More (Hadrian VII) (1976, 28). Boyd's *The Last Starship from Earth* creates a clever denouemental twist by unexpectedly transforming an apparently fictional character into a historical one. In the last chapter the protagonist, Haldane IV, who has traveled back in time to sabotage the historical sequence that has led to a dystopian twentieth-century theocracy, turns out to be none other than Judas Iscariot—here the crucifixion itself is deemed to be the necessary antecedent to create a less tyrannical religious culture (Boyd 1972, 182). In Gregory Benford's *Timescape* (1980) the interplay of references to real-world and fully fictional figures is more intricate. Here scientists from a terminally polluted 1990s manage to send a message warning scientists in the 1960s of the dangers to come, thereby initiating a new branch of history from the 1960s. In the novel's ontological system, this new strand remains valid alongside the other (real-world) version of history, and the novel's discourse switches between these two versions, using authenticating strategies based on real-world historical figures and events. Thus, TV reports of the Kennedy assassination with the media figure Walter Cronkite and even a reference to Dick's *The Man in the High Castle*, a key 1960s alternate history (Benford 1982, 213), clearly identify the 1960s passages of the novel as the real-world 1960s. At first sight, the newly created branch of history represented toward the end of the novel by a scene from the year 1974 also seems to be as authentic and verisimilar as the world of 1963 by virtue of references to media figures such as Doris Day (396). However, counterfactual markers ultimately indicate this world's nonhistorical status. Most significantly, the American president is "Scranton" and not Ford (in the real world Nixon resigned on August 9, 1974). The historical time path in which the global ecological catastrophe is averted is therefore clearly marked as a counterfactual version of history, whereas the 1990s world in which society collapses in terminal pollution and food poisoning is implied (seen from the perspective of the book's publication date in 1980) to be real-world future history.

Postmodernist Agendas in Counterfactual Science Fiction

The more "classical" (Alkon 1994) alternate histories described above are built on clear causal and pseudoscientific premises such as mechanized time travel and the manipulative interference in history. From the mid-twentieth century, however, some science fiction texts adopt a more radically postmodernist agenda by substituting the mechanical-causal plotting of history alteration with the more ambivalently subjective force of the human mind itself. Philip K. Dick is the key initiator in these developments. In novels such as *Eye in the Sky* (1957) and *Flow My Tears, the Policeman Said* (1974) consensual reality is depicted as being the creation of the human mind. In *Now Wait for Last Year* (1975) the mechanism for time travel and transworld movement is also cerebral: the drug "JJ-180," and not a machine, allows the taker to journey to the past or to alternate versions of the present and future. These altered plot dynamics, in combination with the repeated play on the indistinguishable borderlines between authenticity, fakery, simulation, and reality, mark Dick's novels out as early texts in the tradition of historiographic metafiction.[19]

Dick's novel *The Man in the High Castle* (1962) is both a seminal text of twentieth-century alternate history *and* a highly significant deviational representative of the genre due to its complex and ambivalent hierarchy of worlds. The novel's primary counterfactual world inverts the geopolitical situation of the historical postwar world: the victory of the Axis powers in World War II has led to the United States being partitioned into German and Japanese spheres of interest.[20] The novel's action takes place in the Japanese-controlled P.S.A. (Pacific States of America), and much of the detail of this alternate postwar civilization depicts the interaction of the dominant Japanese and subordinate American cultures.

However, Dick's novel is not constructed on the simple binary of counterfactual versus historical world. The text avoids setting up a clear relationship between fact and counterfact by introducing additional alternate worlds. These additional worlds are not, though, created using the conventional methods of the science fiction genre. Many characters in *The Man in the High Castle* are reading a contemporary best seller, a subversive alternate history called *The Grasshopper Lies Heavy* by the author Hawthorne Abendsen, which has been banned in the Nazi-dominated areas because it describes a world in which the Axis powers lost the war. The narrative presence of *The Grasshopper* is substantial: its plot is repeatedly discussed by the novel's characters, passages are quoted from it, and it is also used to self-reflexively thematize the classification of alternate history within the science fiction genre (Dick 1965, 109).[21]

The real reader may expect *The Grasshopper* to depict the "correct" version of history, but the embedded novel in fact turns out to describe a third possibility, as the following commentary by a character who has read the text shows:

> Abendsen's theory is that Roosevelt would have been a terribly strong President. As strong as Lincoln. He showed it in the year he was President, all those measures he introduced. . . . Roosevelt isn't assassinated in Miami; he goes on and is re-elected in 1936, so he's President until 1940, until during the war. . . . He makes America strong. Garner was a really awful President. A lot of what happened was his fault.(68)

Roosevelt is therefore given a counterfactual biography different from that of the main world of *The Man in the High Castle* (in which he is assassinated), and a different but equally counterfactual president is in power: "And then in 1940, instead of Bricker, a Democrat would have been elected. . . . His theory is that instead of an isolationist like Bricker, in 1940 after Roosevelt, Rexford Tugwell would have been President" (68). The world of *The Grasshopper* is therefore a counter-counterfactual (see Helbig 1988, 90–91), and in order to appreciate the full texture and constellation of the different worlds within Dick's text, the reader must be capable of fine transworld identification *and* differentiation when reading the characters' comparisons of their own counterfactual world and that of *The Grasshopper*.

Through this device Dick suggests a potentially infinite landscape of possible counterfactual worlds. Moreover, yet another level of reality is suggested when Mr. Tagomi, a Japanese character, undergoes a hallucination in which he briefly finds himself in what appears to be a real-world version of San Francisco (Dick 1965, 222–24); Tagomi's subjective experience briefly opens up an additional window onto real-world history and further complicates the text's already ambivalent constellation of alternate worlds.

A structural reciprocity also characterizes the real and fictional reading processes in the novel. For example, "Freiherr Hugo Reiss, the Reichs Consul in San Francisco" (118), is depicted surreptitiously reading the banned text of *The Grasshopper* in his office. As he does so, the real reader "looks over his shoulder," glimpsing fragments of the *Grasshopper*'s counter-counterfactual world:

> How that man can write, he thought. Completely carried me away. Real. Fall of Berlin to the British, as vivid as if it had actually taken place. Brrr. He shivered.
>
> Amazing, the power of fiction, even cheap popular fiction, to evoke. No wonder it's banned within Reich territory; I'd ban it myself. Sorry I started it. But too late; must finish, now. (125)

This scene is notable because it depicts the *immersive power* of counterfactual narrative, highlighting how such "unrealistic" story lines can exert strong narrative fascination; Reiss is totally absorbed by the depiction of the trial of Hitler by the Allies:[22]

> Now he found himself unable to stop; he began to read the scene out of sequence, the back of his neck burning....
>
> ... The quivering, shambling body jerked taut; the head lifted.... Shudders among those who watched and listened, the earphones pressed tightly, strained faces of Russian, American, British, and German alike....
>
> ... Reiss realized that his secretary had entered the office. "I'm busy," he said angrily.... "I'm trying to read this book, for God's sake!" (125)

The mirroring of the real and the fictional reading process intensifies toward the end of the novel when another character, Juliana Frink, is in the process of finishing *The Grasshopper*. When Juliana then seeks out *The Grasshopper*'s author, Abendsen, to warn him of a Nazi plan to murder him, he reveals to her that the novel was written by consulting the *I Ching*. When Juliana then asks, "Oracle, why did you write *The Grasshopper Lies Heavy*?" the *I Ching* replies, "Inner Truth" (247):

Raising his head, Hawthorne scrutinized her. He had now an almost savage expression. "It means, does it, that my book is true?"

"Yes," she said.

With anger he said, "Germany and Japan lost the war?"

"Yes." (247)

This denouement completely destabilizes the novel's already complex ontological hierarchy by suggesting that the counter-counterfactual is "more real" than the main world of the novel and depicting *The Grasshopper*'s ostensible author, Abendsen, as reacting hostilely to the undermining of his own authority by a text (the *I Ching*). The fact that the historical "truth" asserted by the *I Ching* is a further counterfactual version of history subverts the concept of a single "truth" or authoritative world version, fulfilling the central tenet of historiographic metafiction: "There are only *truths* in the plural, and never one Truth" (Hutcheon 1988, 109).[23] As in historiographic metafiction, reality is here shown to be constructed in and by texts—*The Grasshopper* and the *I Ching*.

The Man in the High Castle therefore stands out as a groundbreaking and complex configuration of counterfactual history within the alternate history genre. Subsequent texts continue this innovation. In Ursula K. Le Guin's *The Lathe of Heaven* (1971) alternate history is created by the protagonist's dreams. George Orr's capacity for "effective dreaming" means that the dreams he has at night become objective reality the next morning. As the novel progresses, multiple versions of (near-future) history succeed each other.[24] Within these transformations, Le Guin stages a much more chaotic form of transworld identity between alternate character versions than conventional science fiction texts like Wyndham's "Random Quest": bizarre and abrupt changes in characters' traits with each reality change involve nonlinear, lateral jumps without any of the detailed causal-progenerative reconstructions of characters' alternate biographies. The same chaotic principle applies to the cumulative effect of the reality changes on Orr. Burdened with multiple memories of each successive version of history and character, George comes to experience his own identity as constituted by multiple layers of contradictory experiences: "There were by now so many different memories, so many skins of life experience, jostling in his head, that he scarcely tried to remember anything" (Le Guin 1974, 109). Le Guin's "effective dreaming" plot thus articulates one of the key concerns of postmodernism by portraying reality as the changing creations of the human mind and identity as discontinuous and fragmented.

Joanna Russ's *The Female Man* (1975) uses counterfactuals and future history with a clear feminist agenda; alternate character versions are used as a "splitting tactic [that] allows Russ to explore the tensions between rage and despair, passivity and aggression, fear and hope, that underlie feminist utopianism"

(Crowder 1993, 239). Here four female characters from different realities are brought together in a transworld journey plot and represent the potential of the character "woman" in multiple social environments. Joanna, a contemporary female (and feminist) persona, is from a twentieth-century real-world scenario; Jeannine, a passive dreamer in pursuit of romance, comes from a world in which the nonoccurrence of World War II has led to the retardation of the emancipation of women; Janet, a strong and competent woman, comes from a future era where men have died out; Jael, a violently vociferous feminist, comes from a different alternate future in which there has been a literal war between the sexes, so that the planet is divided into separate male and female territories. When one of the novel's narrators says, "I live between worlds" (Russ 1985, 110), on the science fiction story level this refers both to the transworld encounters of the four female protagonists, but on the feminist level it refers to the position of women in contemporary society, caught between partial emancipation and continuing domestication.

The counterfactual world of William Gibson and Bruce Sterling's *The Difference Engine* (1990) can be seen as an embodiment of the postmodernist intensification of interreferentiality (see Bolter 1991, 163–64). The novel depicts a Victorian dystopia that combines a sardonically grim vision of nineteenth-century society with the counterfactually accelerated onset of computerization, including widespread surveillance by a "Central Statistics Bureau" (Gibson and Sterling 1992, 103).[25] The novel is an intricate construct of inverted and refracted elements from both historical and literary nineteenth-century worlds. The text playfully experiments with the transworld nonidenticality of counterfactual and historical figures: the prime minister of Britain is Lord Byron, Lord Engels is a textile magnate, Samuel Houston is the exiled president of Texas, and John Keats is employed in "kinotropy," the counterfactual nineteenth-century equivalent of cinema. However, in addition to this historically counterfactual level, the novel also imports characters from a real-world nineteenth-century novel, Benjamin Disraeli's *Sybil* (1845). (For a discussion of the novel's intertextuality see Hellekson 2001, 81–83.) The ultimate irony within this complex interreferentiality is that in this world, Byron (a real-world poet) is prime minister, while Disraeli (a real-world nineteenth-century prime minister) is (in addition to having his characters stolen and recycled by the real-world authors Gibson and Sterling) a second-rate writer and alcoholic, a "bit of a madcap. Writes sensation novels. Trash. But he's steady enough when he's sober" (Gibson and Sterling 1992, 111). The novel is therefore a dense network of counterfactual, historical, and what might be called *counterfictional* cross-referencing that requires very detailed acts of transworld identification and differentiation by the reader.

Counterfactual Fantasies, Metafictions, and Metahistories in Twentieth-Century Fiction

Counterfactual Fantasies

The twentieth-century conceptual breakthrough reflected in the rapid growth of counterfactual worlds in science fiction is also observable in a different type of narrative fiction that focuses on multiple character biographies. Different forms of counterfactual (auto)biographical fantasy develop from modernist through postmodernist fiction. An early innovative text is O. Henry's story "Roads of Destiny" (1903). The story begins with a literalization of the *life is a journey/decisions are junctions in the road* metaphor. Having left home, the protagonist, David Mignot, is faced with three possible roads to follow. The story's major innovation is that it does not have a realistically hierarchical fact versus counterfact structure but narrates three equally actual versions of what happens to David when he takes each of the roads. Each story version, however, ultimately holds the same melodramatic destiny for David: death caused by a shot from the same pistol, although in the intricate weavings of the stories, the pistol is fired in three different locations by three different characters.[26] The story's essentially fatalistic rather than pluralistic thrust is therefore in keeping with Thomas Weissert's definition of the modernist period as being shaped by "determinism" and "closure and textual unity" in contrast to postmodernism's "self-conscious narrative convolutions" (1991, 224).

O. Henry's story preempts the presentation of multiple *story* variants with no focus on variations of *character* that can also later be found in experimental postmodernist fiction. Henry James's "The Jolly Corner" (1908) follows the inverse strategy. The story narrates fifty-six-year-old Spencer Brydon's preoccupation with the man he might have become if he had stayed in New York instead of migrating to Europe at the age of twenty-three. Brydon's counterfactual obsession is initiated when he returns from Europe to New York—an environment that, as his friend Miss Staverton suggests, is more economically competitive and inventive than Europe: "If he had but stayed at home he would have anticipated the inventor of the sky-scraper" (James 1984, 316).

At first, Brydon's thoughts produce shapeless counterfactual musings about a vague but wistfully upward counterfactual life:

> What would it have made of me, what would it have made of me? I keep for ever wondering, all idiotically; as if I could possibly know! I see what it has made of dozens of others, those I meet, and it positively aches within me, to the point of exasperation, that it would have made something of me as well. Only I can't make out *what*. . . . It comes over me that I had then a strange alter ego deep down somewhere within me, as the full-blown flower is in the small tight bud, and that I just took the course, I just transferred him to the climate, that blighted him for once and for ever. (320–21)

Brydon's speculations about his counterfactual self are intensified when the story develops into a neogothic scenario in which he is haunted by a physical embodiment of his counterfactual self. Miss Staverton tells Brydon that she has twice seen his other self in her dreams (322), and subsequently Brydon finds himself face to face with his counterfactual self in the deserted New York house he has inherited:

> Rigid and conscious, spectral yet human, a man of his own substance and stature waited there.... [H]e could but gape at his other self in this other anguish, gape as a proof that *he*, standing there for the achieved, the enjoyed, the triumphant life, couldn't be faced in his triumph.... Horror, with the sight, had leaped into Brydon's throat, gasping there in a sound he couldn't utter; for the bared identity was too hideous as *his*.... The face, *that* face, Spencer Brydon's—he searched it still, but looking away from it in dismay and denial.... Such an identity fitted his at *no* point, made its alternative monstrous.... [T]he face was the face of a stranger. (334–35)

This scene presents the encounter with the counterfactual self as an experience of absolute otherness and strangeness: Brydon meets and comprehends his alter ego only with a sense of difference and alienation and not of *identification*. James's story makes no attempt to construct a logical, causal-progenerative developmental background to solidify the alternate character biography but only focuses on Brydon's own state of mind in response to the counterfactual specter.

The encounter with the alternate other also marks a transformation in Brydon's attitude: he now becomes triumphant in the knowledge of his own *actuality* ("*he*, standing there for the achieved, the enjoyed") in contrast to the other's virtuality. He no longer has a wistful sense of lost potential but affirms his own life for what it is. Brydon's psychological development is therefore structured by a shift from upward to downward counterfactualizing: the counterfactual scenario of professional success, which Brydon initially thinks of in positive terms, turns out to be a negative one that has marked the face of his counterfactual self and produced an "awful beast" (328); as Miss Staverton comments: "He has been unhappy, he has been ravaged.... [H]e's grim, he's worn" (339–40). However, Miss Staverton's admission that she could have liked Brydon's counterfactual self (339), along with Brydon's switch from upward to downward counterfactualizing, gives the story an ambivalence that underscores the subjective and potentially self-delusional nature of autobiographical counterfactualizing.

In more recent fiction, Philip Roth's *The Counterlife* (1986) is a highly intricate exploration of counterfactual biographical narrative that moves well beyond the binary oppositions of character in James's text. Here successive chapters depict multiple variants of the lives of Roth's fictional alter ego, Nathan Zuckerman, and his brother Henry. The successively different counterfactual scenarios of one or other of the brothers' lives create a series of surprising and ironic reversals. For example, the Henry of chapter 1 is an established New Jersey dentist whose midlife crisis involves a clash between his sex life and medication for a heart problem and ends in his death after bypass surgery, whereas the Henry of chapter 2 is very much alive, having deserted his family in America and immigrated to Israel. The successive scenarios also put Nathan in different versions of his life in the United States, Israel (in his search for Henry), and England, where he encounters and experiences multiple versions of what it is to be Jewish in different cultural contexts. Chapter 4 then has Nathan die after bypass surgery (because in this variant it is Nathan and not Henry who suffers from heart disease); after Nathan's funeral Henry discovers the manuscripts of the chapters that the real reader has been reading; he then (rather paradoxically, since the real reader is actually reading them) destroys them because he resents what he calls Nathan's fictional "distortion" (Roth 1989, 205) of their family life in his novels. Chapter 5 then ushers in a further variant in which Nathan is alive and living in England. In this constant process of counterfactual reversals, therefore, the reader struggles to determine which sections of the novel represent actual character versions and which are to be understood as counterfactual fantasies written by the novelist, Nathan; the novel itself does not provide a clear key to its ontological hierarchy. *The Counterlife* therefore uses the device of the counterfactual to depict male sibling rivalry and to explore different versions of Jewish cultural identity as well as—in terms of its structure—constructing a complex and ontologically inscrutable narrative of multiple counterfactuals in which the actual version of events and characters remains elusive.

In Winterson's *The Passion* (1987), the wistful regret of the autodiegetic narrator, Villanelle, about her own life is expressed in one key counterfactual. Like *Daniel Deronda*, *The Passion* practices a gender-specific segregation of the plots of coincidence and counterfactuality: the novel's love triangle of heterosexual passion between Villanelle, Henri, and the cook culminates in a dramatic and deadly coincidental encounter (see chapter 6). However, for Villanelle herself this heterosexually and coincidentally powered love plot is not of overriding importance because her deepest emotions are for another woman. This stronger passion is voiced most clearly in a counterfactual after she has seen the woman she loves again but has decided not to renew the relationship: "The wild card. The unpredictable wild card that never comes when it should. Had it fallen earlier; years earlier, what would have happened to me? I looked at my palms, trying to see the other life, the parallel life. The point at which my selves broke away and one married a fat man and the other stayed here, in this elegant house to eat dinner night after night from an oval table" (Winterson 1996, 144).

The antecedent in this counterfactual biography is clearly marked as the point where Villanelle married the "fat man" (the cook) instead of pursuing her relationship with the woman (who was herself then still married). Villanelle's strong sense of destiny concerning her relationship with the unnamed woman makes her feel that another version of her self must truly exist somewhere: "Sometimes, drinking coffee with friends or walking alone by the too salt sea, I have caught myself in that other life, touched it, seen it to be as real as my own. And if she had lived alone in that elegant house when I first met her? Perhaps I would never have sensed other lives of mine, having no need of them" (Winterson 1996, 144). Villanelle's sense of having had "other lives" evokes the style of the fantastic that, as a whole, intermittently marks *The Passion* out as a postrealist text. Another section of this passage then more strongly echoes the genre of science fiction, using the spatial metaphor of the fan to express a sense of multiple realities and versions of the self: "Is this the explanation then when we meet someone we do not know and feel straight away that we have always known them? That their habits will not be a surprise. Perhaps our lives spread out around us like a fan and we can only know one life, but by mistake sense others" (Winterson 1996, 144). The sense here of a semiconscious *emotional link* to alternate versions of the self (a kind of psychic as opposed to physical transworld journey across alternate selves) is highly reminiscent of a passage from Russ's *The Female Man*: "It's possible, too, that there is no such thing as one clear line or strand of probability, and that we live on a sort of twisted braid, blurring from one to the other without even knowing it" (1985, 6–7).

Like George Eliot before her, Winterson therefore segregates plot strategies according to gender, using coincidence for the male-dominated plot of heterosexual love and counterfactuality within the lesbian love plot. But unlike the nineteenth-century *Daniel Deronda*, which still operates under the cultural and intertextual pressure to provide some form of love closure, *The Passion* does not end with any closure in its love plot. Instead of celebrating heterosexual romance, the novel's denouement kills or imprisons the key male figures (Henri is imprisoned for murdering the cook) and uses counterfactual plotting to orchestrate a sense of wistful regret concerning the lesbian love plot. This regret is, however, tempered by Villanelle's insight that passion consumes identity and that romantic nonconvergence is in fact the best way to safeguard the self: "If I give in to this passion, my real life, the most solid, the best known will disappear and I will feed on shadows again" (Winterson 1996, 146).

Multiple Alternate Worlds in Radical Metafiction

Radical metafictions, which were mainly produced in the 1960s and 1970s, use contradictory story versions to sabotage the teleological linearity of closure (see Waugh 1984; McHale 1987; Moosmüller 1993; Fludernik 1996a).[27] While historical contexts shape both science fiction and historiographic metafiction (see below), the areferentiality of radical metafiction leads it to focus on more mundane fictional events. These fictions are generally characterized by an excess of events coupled with antirealistic character delineation, which means that there is no or little transworld differentiation between characters across the different story versions. Radical metafiction moves beyond the clear ontological hierarchy of counterfactuals by constructing multiple actual or multiple virtual versions of the story, often created through multiple bifurcations. While the multiple worlds of science fiction are presented as a coherent narrative universe (or multiverse) bound together by scientific and causal justification, the chaotic alternate worlds of radical metafiction can only be recuperated into a coherent narrative by explaining them as fragments penned by the real-world author.

Robert Coover's "The Babysitter" (1970) is one of the most extreme examples of the form: narrative chaos pervades the whole discourse, which consists of numerous fragmentary episodes depicting contradictory versions of events taking place one evening at the Tucker family's house and at a nearby party where Mr. and Mrs. Tucker spend the evening. As the narrative progresses, more and more different versions are spawned, and the story closes with a number of alternate endings in which, variously, the Tuckers' babysitter is raped and murdered, she accidentally drowns the baby, or the Tuckers come home to find all is well. All these versions are given actual status, although additional virtual character fantasies further complicate the reader's struggle to navigate the ontological zones of the story (see Dannenberg 1998c). The story's distortion of temporal sequentiality is so great that the reader is rendered incapable of even identifying the points of bifurcation.[28] The textual chaos is also heightened by the repeated phrase "the phone rings"; since scenes describing characters deciding to make a phone call recur with regularity (Coover 1970, 216, 221, 222, 224, 225, 229, 232, 233, 234, 235, 236), this phrase becomes a frantic leitmotif, referring potentially to any number of events. Coover's story is therefore a narrative labyrinth from which no coherent story line can liberate the bewildered reader and in which the story's characters themselves remain undifferentiated puppets.[29] While narratives like "The Babysitter" have provided fascinating material for narrative theorists, their concerted sabotaging of narrative immersion has not rendered them sufficiently interesting for many readers; this indicates that the character-cognitive dimension and human experientiality (Fludernik 1996a), which are missing in the representation of alternate worlds in these texts, are indeed key features that contribute to qualitative narrativity.

In John Fowles's *The French Lieutenant's Woman* (1969) alternate story versions are used more imaginatively in conjunction with the representation of character (see also the discussion in Ryan 1991, 164–66). The novel contains two key bifurcations, each of which differs in its ontological nature. The first bifurcation is a narrative hoax played on the reader when the narrator describes what seems to be a concluding sequence to the novel, in which the hero, Charles Smithson, is reconciled to his planned marriage with Ernestina instead of pursuing Sarah Woodruff. The narrator then belatedly admits that this has been one of the "fictional futures" that "we all" construct: "The last few pages are ... what he [Charles] spent the hours between London and Exeter imagining might happen" (Fowles 1977, 295). This hoax is therefore a bolder form of the depiction of characters' virtual futures already practiced in realist fiction by writers like Jane Austen and George Eliot.

The second bifurcation is more radical because it presents the novel's denouement as two equally actual contradictory versions. The bifurcation centers on the moment when Charles has found Sarah again in London: in the first version their meeting ends in reconciliation; in the second they part forever because Sarah does not prevent Charles from leaving, as she does in the first version (388, 395). The first ending therefore presents a traditionally convergent love plot closure, while the second empowers the female character to escape the conventional ending. Fowles's text therefore continues in the tradition of real nineteenth-century novels that, from Brontë's *Villette* onward, use alternate or counterfactual plotting to undermine romantic convergence.

Moreover, in contrast to other radical metafictions, a degree of *transworld differentiation* can also be perceived between the two versions of Sarah created in these scenes. Two lines describing Sarah's behavior are inserted into the first version that are absent in the second: "For a long moment she continued to stare at him; something of the terrible outrage in his soul was reflected in her eyes. With an acute abruptness she lowered her head" (388). The lowering of the head indicates a different version of Sarah in contrast to the more defiant one of the second version and prepares the way for an increasingly submissive Sarah, "her eyes ... full of tears, and her look unbearably naked" (393). The first version therefore tames Sarah's behavior and character to facilitate the traditionally convergent romantic ending. In the second version Fowles creates a less compliant Sarah who shows no emotion; Charles can only interpret "a suggestion of a smile" "in her eyes" as a "last gloating over his misery" (396). Fowles's text therefore fleshes out his alternate narratives by describing the different facial and emotional responses in the two distinct versions of Sarah as part of his emancipation of the heroine from the conventions of the nineteenth-century love plot in the second ending.

Whereas coincidence features widely in Julian Barnes's *Flaubert's Parrot* (1984) (see chapter 6), multiple story versions are dispatched to the level of metanarrative. Indeed, Geoffrey Braithwaite's polemic on the contemporary art of novel writing seems to refer to *The French Lieutenant's Woman*: "When the writer provides two different endings to his novel (why two? why not a hundred?), does the reader seriously imagine he is being 'offered a choice' and that the work is reflecting life's variable outcomes? Such a 'choice' is never real, because the reader is obliged to consume both endings. In life, we make a decision . . . and we go one way; had we made a different decision . . . we would have been elsewhere" (Barnes 1985, 89). Braithwaite is essentially arguing the same point as Turner (1991, 273)—that the metaphorical conceptualization of "choice" as a fork in the road is a deceptive one, since in the real world the fork ceases to exist as soon as a decision has been made. Braithwaite is thus used to pour cold water on radical metafiction and provides his own more practical suggestions of how novelists could "simulate the delta of life's possibilities": "At the back of the book would be a set of sealed envelopes in various colours. Each would be clearly marked on the outside: Traditional Happy Ending; Traditional Unhappy Ending; Traditional Half-and-Half Ending; Deus ex Machina; Modernist Arbitrary Ending; End of the World Ending; Cliffhanger Ending; Dream Ending; Opaque Ending; Surrealist Ending; and so on" (Barnes 1985, 89).

Alternate History and Historiographic Metafiction

Geoffrey Braithwaite's criticism of the experiments of radical metafiction is symptomatic of the conceptual thrust of historiographically metafictional texts like *Flaubert's Parrot* that moved out of the self-referential narrative ghetto of radical experimentation toward a renewed historical and cultural engagement. Historiographic metafiction (Hutcheon 1988) is concerned with the question of historiographic referentiality and foregrounds the fact that, seen from the present, the past is "a distant, receding coastline, and we are all in the same boat" (Barnes 1985, 101). As part of this agenda, some historiographic metafictions embed multiple alternate historical narratives or counterfactual biographies of real-world historical figures within the text. The alternate histories of science fiction and of historiographic metafiction are therefore generically interrelated. In the conventional history-alteration narrative of science fiction, history is interfered with (i.e., causally manipulated) by a single agent who changes the causal-progenerative flow of history by creating a new counterfactual antecedent. By contrast, the crucial point made by historiographic metafiction is that no single agent—and no single authority—can be attributed with responsibility for the multiple versions of history that constitute human culture and are the result of human cultural production across time.

Peter Ackroyd's *Chatterton* (1987), already discussed for its use of the postmodernist coincidence plot in chapter 6, is a key example of such a multiplication of histories and biographies; the novel contains a multiplicity of contrasting, and often contradictory, narrative and ekphrastic texts concerning the real-world eighteenth-century poet Chatterton. The key conundrum under investigation by characters on the twentieth-century time level is whether Chatterton died by suicide as a young man or whether he faked his death and secretly lived on. The narrative fabric of *Chatterton* is made up of multiple factual and counterfactual versions of his biography.

These narratives can be organized into three groups. The novel's (seemingly) official historical narratives of Chatterton's life include (1) a summary of Chatterton's life (without source), which prefaces the novel (Ackroyd 1993, 1); (2) a summary of Chatterton's life from an unspecified reference work at Charles Wychwood's home (21); (3) a pamphlet entitled *Thomas Chatterton: Son of Bristol* (55, 57–58); (4) "Meyerstein's *Life of Chatterton*" (125); (5) unspecified references to other biographies that (according to Charles Wychwood) "each ... described a different poet" (127).

Further embedded narratives have a less factual or a creatively ambivalent nature: (6) a book of "literary reminiscences" in which the ghost of Chatterton appears to the nineteenth-century poet Meredith (70–71); (7) a book entitled *Thou Marvellous Boy: the Influence of Thomas Chatterton on the Writings of William Blake* by an American professor (72); (8) Charles Wychwood's narrative of Chatterton's life, which he begins writing under the belief that Chatterton's early death was faked (126–27); (9) Henry Wallis's (real-world) painting of the death of Chatterton, which, on the twentieth-century time level, is located in the Tate Gallery in London (132, 169) and, on the nineteenth-century time level, is being painted by Wallis with the poet Meredith as the model for Chatterton (132–44, 152–64, 170–75); (10) the novel's own concluding narrative of Chatterton's death, which represents it not as suicide (the traditional historical narrative) but as accidentally caused by Chatterton in an attempt to cure his venereal disease with arsenic (191–234); (11) a projected counterfactual novel by Philip Slack, who decides to write "how Chatterton might have lived on" (232).

In addition, the novel contains several texts that are exposed as forgeries in the course of the narrative, even though they temporarily stimulate genuine belief: (12) a nineteenth-century painting of a middle-aged man, which is seen by Charles Wychwood as proof that Chatterton did not die as a young man in 1770 (11–12, 21–23); (13) an old manuscript written in the first person, supposedly by Chatterton, obtained by Charles Wychwood (59–60), indicating that Chatterton faked his own death and lived on as a master forger of literary works (81–93, 221).

Therefore, within the historiographic-metafictional framework of Ackroyd's text, *belief* becomes the crucial criterion for the distinction of historical versions: counterfactual history is only counterfactual by virtue of its being identified as such. The fact that many characters are portrayed as accepting the "truth" of both apparently genuine and forged texts underlines the random manner in which historical narratives are given authoritative status. Thus, while Wychwood and Slack both plan to write a counterfactual narrative of Chatterton's extended life, only the latter will write a *consciously counterfactual* narrative, whereas Wychwood believes he is writing a true narrative on the basis of his belief in the authenticity of forged texts (numbers 12 and 13 above). The novel therefore emphasizes that the circumstances of representation and reception determine narrative authority.

These key themes of historiographic metafiction—belief, authenticity, and forgery—are also central in Barnes's *Flaubert's Parrot*. While the novel also contains representations of multiple alternate biographies (three different biographical chronologies of Flaubert highlight how different narratives can be made out of one life [Barnes 1985, 23–37]), it is Geoffrey Braithwaite's quest to identify the original parrot that inspired Flaubert that forms the novel's ultimate game with versions, originals, and forgeries. The authentic parrot, if it exists, cannot be distinguished from the number of stuffed parrots Braithwaite is shown on his visit to Rouen: "After I got home the duplicate parrots continued to flutter in my mind. . . . I wrote letters to various academics who might know if either of the parrots had been authenticated. I wrote to the French Embassy and to the editor of the Michelin guide-books" (Barnes 1985, 22). In *Flaubert's Parrot* transhistorical discontinuity sabotages the ability to construct a causal-progenerative narrative line; Braithwaite seeks the authoritative parrot in vain. Collectively, the parrots become an indistinct *blend* that makes the recognition of individuality, cognitive differentiation, and the erection of world boundaries impossible. Like Charles Wychwood's quest for the truth about Chatterton's life in Ackroyd's novel, Braithwaite's quest to identify the authentic parrot of Flaubert's narrative documents the deep human desire for the *cognitive security* provided by a sense of authenticity created by a knowledge of origins and causal-progenerative narrative sequences—but at the very same time it exposes the illusory nature of such a desire.

The questioning of the concept of the "real" and the foregrounding of the fuzzy border between historical authenticity and forgery are shared by Ackroyd's and Barnes's novels as representatives of the late-twentieth-century genre of historiographic metafiction. However, these key concerns are already anticipated by Dick's *The Man in the High Castle* (already discussed above), which reveals how mid-twentieth-century alternate history sets important precedents on the way to the later development of historiographic metafiction. The themes of authenticity and forgery are prominent in Dick's novel. In the novel's counterfactual postwar world, genuine prewar American antiques are sought-after items by the ruling Japanese elite. In order to capitalize on this demand, a factory owned by a character called Wyndam-Matson turns out "a constant flow of forgeries of pre-war American artifacts [that are] fed into the wholesale art object market, to join the genuine objects" (Dick 1965, 51). In a passage reminiscent of *Flaubert's Parrot* but written twenty years before it, Wyndam-Matson enlightens a lady friend on the subject of "historicity" (i.e., historical authenticity) by presenting her with two identical cigarette lighters:

> Getting up, he hurried to his study, returned at once with two cigarette lighters which he set down on the coffee table. "Look at these. Look the same, don't they? Well, listen. One has historicity in it." He grinned at her. "Pick them up. Go ahead. One's worth, oh, maybe forty or fifty dollars on the collector's market."
> The girl gingerly picked up the two lighters and examined them. (65)

As Jon-K Adams comments, the passage shows that "historicity is in the mind, not in the object" (1994, 155):

> "Don't you feel it?" he kidded her. "The historicity?"
> She said, "What is historicity?"
> "When a thing has history in it. Listen. One of those two Zippo lighters was in Franklin D. Roosevelt's pocket when he was assassinated. And one wasn't. One has historicity, a hell of a lot of it.... And one has nothing. Can you feel it?" He nudged her. "You can't. You can't tell which is which." (Dick 1965, 65–66)

In Dick's text the question of the authentic and the false is further complicated by the fact that the reader knows that Roosevelt's assassination—the basis for the concept of "historicity" postulated within the text—is itself a *counterfactual* historical event. Thus, all the characters in the novel's main counterfactual world are depicted believing in the historical circumstances that have created the world they inhabit, even though at the end of the novel another book—the *I Ching*—pronounces that this history is not true and that a further counter-counterfactual version of history has "Inner Truth" (247). The historically divergent worlds of Dick's novel are thus represented not as objectively verifiable realities but either as embedded narratives or as subjective or collective hallucinations.

The impulse of the counterfactual continues to invigorate contemporary fiction. A glance at the list of new publications on www.uchronia.net shows the alternate history to be an indefatigable genre of popular fiction. Counterfactual history and biography continue to feature in new writing. Peter Ackroyd's *Milton in America* (1996) narrates the counterfactual biography of the seventeenth-century poet John Milton, who in this narrative world decides to seek his fortune in New England rather than stay in Britain after the Restoration. Philip Roth's *The Plot against America* (2004) is an alternate history of 1940s American politics and the Second World War in which the historical antecedent is the altered biography of American aviator Charles Lindbergh, who here becomes president of the United States in 1940 instead of Roosevelt. This change has disastrous consequences for American democracy and the Jewish American population when growing anti-Semitic activity in the United States is inspired by and parallels events in Germany, beginning with the "first large-scale pogrom ... Detroit's *Kristallnacht*" (Roth 2005, 266). The novel's historical plotting ultimately bends history back to the real-world course of events in the 1940s; however, its final chapter, entitled "Perpetual Fear," works to counteract this optimistic ending by continuing to evoke the experience of the novel's protagonist, young Philip Roth (the author's counterfactual self), as "a nightmarish vision of America's anti-Semitic fury" (Roth 2005, 343). The reader is thus left with a sense of the continuing volatility of race relations in American society, potentially also in the post-9/11 context in which Roth's novel has been interpreted (see Rosenfeld 2005, 156). As Rosenfeld also comments: "The fact that Roth, one of America's most celebrated and accomplished writers, chose to write a work of alternate history ... affirms the genre's arrival into the American cultural mainstream" (2005, 152).

As the two previous sections have illustrated, the counterfactual impulse has pervaded twentieth-century fiction in many forms and across many genres. This study's scope has not been able to consider the divergent narrative structures of hypertext fictions (see, e.g., Bolter 1991; Ryan 2001; Dannenberg 1998b). Neither has it been able to devote attention to the history of counterfactuals in film narrative. However, it should be noted that, in comparison to the long history of innovations in twentieth-century print narrative, the film genre has been slow to adopt the counterfactual world motif. In terms of the overall historical development of counterfactuals in cinematic narrative, a key starting point, in the form of counterfactual biographical fantasy, is Frank Capra's perennially popular movie, *It's a Wonderful Life* (1946). Here an angel temporarily transports the protagonist, George Bailey, to a downward counterfactual world in which he was never born so that he can understand the profoundly positive effect his existence has had on his community and fellow citizens (see Roese and Olson 1995b, 191–92; Dannenberg 2004a). A relatively early cinematic alternate history is the British film *It Happened Here* (1964), which explores the consequences of a Nazi invasion of Britain in 1940. (For discussion of this text and others like it see Rosenfeld 2005, 50–70.) In the field of science fiction television narrative, the two longest running American and British science fiction television series both use the transworld journey motif in early episodes: the *Star Trek* episode "Mirror Mirror" (1967) features a transfer to a downward parallel world with negative alternate versions of the show's protagonists; similarly, the seven-episode *Doctor Who* story "Inferno" (1970) features a transworld journey to a counterfactual historical world in which the Nazis conquered Britain and uses counterfactual characterization by transforming several of the regular characters into British fascists. It is, however, only a good decade later that counterfactuals and related forms of alternate world begin to become and then remain recognizable narrative motifs in box-office cinema. Multiple counterfactual biographies are created in time travel narratives in *Back to the Future* (1985), *Back to the Future II* (1989), *Donnie Darko* (2001), and *The Butterfly Effect* (2004). The films *The Terminator* (1984) *Terminator 2: Judgment Day* (1991), and *Terminator 3: Rise of the Machines* (2003) all feature attempts to alter history through time travel from the future into the present. Transworld journeys are combined with alternate history in *The Philadelphia Experiment 2* (1993) and with counterfactual biographical fantasy in *The Family Man* (2000). More loosely or enigmatically structured juxtapositions or repetitions of multiple versions of characters' lives feature in the movies *Groundhog Day* (1993) and *Sliding Doors* (1998).

If we survey the evolutionary map charted in this chapter, we can see how, following the groundbreaking use of counterfactuals by Defoe and Richardson to simulate an autobiographical consciousness in the eighteenth century, nineteenth-century texts by Jane Austen and George Eliot initiated conceptual breakthroughs that paved the way for rampant ontological pluralization in twentieth-century fictions of alternate and counterfactual worlds. The two alternative counterfactual versions embedded in the denouemental discourse of *Mansfield Park* move Austen's novel beyond the simple binary counterfactual constellation of actual narrative world versus hypothetical counterfact. In George Eliot's novels, counterfactual biographies and alternate future worlds compete chaotically with each other in the different visions, plans, and disappointments that are a crucial part of the representation of the mental worlds of Eliot's characters. In early-twentieth-century science fiction, radical ontological innovations are introduced with the idea of competing counterfactual historical worlds engaging in battle with each other (Williamson's *The Legion of Time*), while De Camp's time travel narrative depicting Padway's alteration of the official history of the Dark Ages in *Lest Darkness Fall* and the multiple transworld journeys and selves of Allister Park in "The Wheels of If" are key innovations in the narrative configuration of counterfactual history. In experimental metafiction, the battle between the virtual and the actual takes place less in the story on the page than in the mind of the reader, who must fight to create any kind of ontological hierarchy in a disorienting chaos of story fragments. By contrast, in historiographic metafiction and in the postmodernist science fiction of writers like Dick and Le Guin, the virtual is everywhere because it is part of culture itself—and so the battle between the virtual and the actual, and between the factual and the counterfactual, cannot ever be truly fought and won because it has already been permanently lost. Seen in terms of the counterfactual, the historical development of fiction therefore centers on the gradual evolution of increasingly ontologically pluralistic and ambivalent forms of narrative discourse.

Conclusion

The following sections highlight the results of part 3 in terms of three of the key aspects that were traced through the developmental stages of the plots of coincidence and counterfactuality: the evolution of plot and narrative fiction; key developments in the representation of plots of love, marriage, and gender within patterns of convergence and divergence; the historical development of cognitive plotting.

Plot and the Historical Development of Narrative Fiction

The study's results for the development of narrative fiction and plot reveal several significant features. The overall tendency, observed in both counterfactuality and coincidence, is the development of an increasingly more complex emplotment of events in time, space, and the reader's mind. These developments are part of the overall increase in *qualitative narrativity* that accompanies key steps in the development of the modern novel. As the novel and its subgenres grow, counterfactuals gradually expand from single sentences to engender whole narrative worlds; the plotting of coincidence is stretched in many ways, both through the protraction of the recognition phase in its traditional form and through the proliferation of old and new forms, particularly in the postmodernist era.

The development of the counterfactual from a brief rhetorical construct in Renaissance fiction to the extensive counterfactual imaginings of characters in the eighteenth-and nineteenth-century novel represents the initial phase of a more complex emplotment of counterfactuals. A further new stage in this expansion comes with the late-nineteenth-century use of historical counterfactuals to create whole narrative worlds in the genre of alternate history. Likewise, the development of the coincidence plot in the novel is marked by the expansion of the ad hoc presentation of the coincidental encounter (which is often used in romance and simple forms of the picaresque) into an extended representation involving more complex cognitive, ontological, and spatial configurations. The use of temporal orchestration and staggered recognition to generate suspense, the expansion of character-cognitive depiction in the extended recognition phase, and the increasingly detailed depiction of narrative space in the actual recognition scene using the schemata of the *container* and the *portal* all constitute key aspects of this process.

The technical developments in the representation of character consciousness in both plots are a further notable feature. The rise in the work of Defoe and Richardson of the autobiographical counterfactual, which simulates the responses of a real-world autobiographical subject to life's experience, and the representation of multiple futures and complex counterfactual thought experiments in the mental worlds of the protagonists of George Eliot's novels are notable landmarks in this process. Equally, the growing complexity in the representation of character-cognitive detail in the recognition scene of the coincidence plot, as observed in the work of Aphra Behn and Jane Austen, is a manifestation of a new depth in consciousness representation. The evolution of these more complex narrative features in the representation of narrative space, time, and mind goes hand in hand with the creation of a state of immersion in the reader that is central to the construction of narrative "realism."

Convergence and Divergence in Love, Marriage, and Gender Plots

This study began by positing a basic distinction between coincidence and counterfactuality in spatiometaphorical terms. The *convergent* meeting of paths and the closing network of characters in the coincidence plot were opposed to the *divergent* branching structure of counterfactuals. Convergence can be seen both as a strategy to achieve conventional artistic unity and also sometimes as the articulation of a Romantic sense of interconnection; accordingly, both of these tendencies are often expressed at closure in the euphoric marriage plot. In the course of the nineteenth century, this harmonious sense of convergence came under pressure in many different ways, including the menacing criminal convergence of Dickens's *Great Expectations* and the tragically negative coincidences of Hardy's novels, whose narrative effect is intensified by the use of contrasting counterfactuals.

Convergence, however, can also be seen as the reflection of certain cultural norms with regard to a character's gender and role within the plots of narrative fiction. Plots using coincidence as part of a convergent love plot often force the heroine into a subordinate position in which she must conform to the cultural pressures of marriage and thus become the subject of an unrealistic fairy-tale narrative of blissful wedlock. As Miller (1980) and DuPlessis (1985) have observed, in eighteenth-and nineteenth-century fiction, the alternative road to the convergent pathway into marriage is usually death for the heroine. In the nineteenth-century novel, however, counterfactuality can already be seen to be instigating a revolt against these two stark alternatives. Whereas Richardson's eighteenth-century heroine Clarissa Harlowe uses counterfactuals to express a quietist, resigned position to her fate, counterfactuals in the nineteenth century undermine the traditional binary alternatives of death or marriage for the heroine.

This nineteenth-century trend and its extension in the twentieth century are confirmed by the various uses of the convergent and divergent plot forms in the fiction of four women writers: Charlotte Brontë, George Eliot, Joanna Russ, and Jeanette Winterson. In its double ending, *Villette* stages a twofold rebellion, both against the conventional authority of narrative closure by destroying the single-world coherence of the definitive ending, and against the convergent tying of marriage knots and social integration that characterized the ending of Brontë's earlier novel, *Jane Eyre*. Eliot's *Daniel Deronda* stages a more radical formulation of the inequalities of gender by giving the positive convergent plot of identity finding, social integration, and concluding happy wedlock to the male character, Daniel Deronda, while it places the female protagonist, Gwendolen Harleth, in a plot of unhappy marriage and thwarted plans; a positive plot for the heroine is only represented in terms of her imaginings of virtual futures and counterfactual visions of what might have been. This process is radicalized in the twentieth century. In *The Female Man* Russ uses the science fiction plot of alternate worlds to explore the female position in a male-dominated society by framing different alternate or counterfactual variations of the gender conflict, one in which a worldwide gender war has literally been waged on Earth. Winterson's approach in *The Passion* is similar to Eliot's in *Daniel Deronda* in that it frames the gender fault line in terms of contrasting plot patterns, but in this late twentieth-century text the distinction is between heterosexual and lesbian love plots. Much more deviously than Eliot, Winterson uses a plot of coincidental relations to bring the heterosexual love plot to a climax but in the actual working out of this plot kills or imprisons the two male characters. Having thus ultimately sabotaged the convergent heterosexual love plot, *The Passion* then instates the supremacy of the lesbian love plot by framing it in terms of a wistful counterfactual, but in doing so the narrative also constructs an open ending for the heroine, Villanelle, leaving her free to go her own way and retain her own independent identity by remaining *outside any romantic plot of convergence*, whether lesbian or heterosexual. As the text emphasizes, romantic convergence—and passion—threatens to consume an individual's identity and "real life" (Winterson 1996, 146).

In their use of coincidence and counterfactuality, these four texts are thus all manifestations of a correlated principle: men's plots are goal oriented and are idealistically represented as reaching a final point of closure and telos; women's plots are located within a system of divergent or alternate worlds in which closure, convergence, and happiness are eternally deferred. The alternate worlds of these female characters are thus first framed as a formulation of the dilemma and isolation of women and their role in a world dominated by the idealized patriarchal teleology of marriage and romantic convergence (Brontë, Eliot); later, however, in the twentieth century, alternate worlds and counterfactuality are used to provide a fictional escape route that leads the female protagonist into new worlds and away from entrapment in the romance of the love plot. In these plots counterfactuality thus provides a countermovement to the traditional pressure for plot convergence powered both by intertextual traditions and other patriarchal cultural pressures. In the nineteenth and twentieth centuries, therefore, counterfactuality and coincidence are clearly not independent narrative phenomena but plots between which significant developmental and cultural tensions exist.

Cognitive Plotting and the Development of Narrative Fiction

As was stressed in chapter 4, each epoch has its own complex cultural landscape of worldviews and mentalities. Nevertheless, the development of the plotting principle in the historical phases of realism, modernism, and postmodernism reveals key stages in the coordination of sense-making patterns. In realism, both coincidence and counterfactuality are presented in terms of linear patterns of causation. As well as creating a reality effect through the simulation of a dominant real-world thought pattern, the basic causal-progenerative structure of counterfactuals (constituted by the *link* created between the counterfactual antecedent and its consequent) generates causal-linear connections across time. A similar effect is created within the kinship reunion plot in coincidence: the discovery of biological identity and genealogy leads to the construction of causal-progenerative links between generations that can be traced back to a point of origin or source. As we have seen, in the kinship coincidence plot these patterns often function to override the reader's consciousness of the constructedness of the coincidence itself (i.e., the ultimate causal manipulation of the story and discourse by the author).

Historically, the coincidence plot starts out as the simulation of an *externally* influenced process in which the intersection of characters in the narrative world is orchestrated by causal-manipulative forces from a divine and providential metaworld. In the course of the nineteenth century coincidence then begins to be framed as a plot without a causal-manipulative deity acting behind events. A shift to causal-manipulative explanations centering on human beings and not God is one stage in this development, as is the increasing thematization of explanatory systems themselves (George Eliot, E. M. Forster, Ford Madox Ford). This leads to the growing modernist sense of randomness at work in the universe, sometimes in conjunction with causal-progenerative chains (Conrad), and to the representation of coincidence as an internal and subjective cognitive process in which the human act of perception is foregrounded, particularly in plots of analogical coincidence (Joyce). Subsequently, in postmodernism, analogical patterning is extended to refer to the overall sense of the constructedness of all sense-making patterns, both in individual acts of perception and in the narration of history and former epochs, and the construction of causal-progenerative links across time is also undermined.

The less realistic genres using counterfactuality and coincidence in the twentieth century all to a lesser or greater extent background or undermine the causal patterns by which realist texts create linear *links* across single paths of time. This development goes hand in hand with the erosion of the ontological hierarchy of realism in which only one single world is allowed to have actual status. Realist narrative systems, in which virtual worlds are always given a subordinate status to a single actual world, are gradually challenged and replaced by systems of multiple, often *competing* worlds, where multiple alternate worlds exist side by side in ontological plurality. While the breakdown of this realist ontology does not fully occur until the twentieth century, key stages in its gradual erosion can be pinpointed well beforehand, for example, in the multiple counterfactual endings of Austen's *Mansfield Park*, in the double ending of Brontë's *Villette*, and in the multiple antagonistic virtual futures of characters in Eliot's *Middlemarch*. These narratives, however, still enable the reader to construct a coherently multilinear system of worlds. By contrast, in the twentieth century the alternate worlds of experimental postmodernist writing and historiographic metafiction radically subvert the reader's desire to construct intradiegetic causal links; instead, they foreground the causal-manipulative or causal-progenerative role of the author in producing texts that pass as authoritative narratives for subsequent generations or they emphasize the fragmentary nature and constructedness of alternate historical narratives within human culture. The undermining of clear ontological relations to official versions of history in the counterfactual plotting of key texts such as De Camp's *Lest Darkness Fall*, Dick's *The Man in the High Castle*, and Ackroyd's *Chatterton* reveals a conceptual and ontological liberation from the master narrative path of real-world history that commences in twentieth-century science fiction texts and then later fully develops in historiographic metafiction.

Moreover, in the twentieth century analogical plotting—the creation of lateral links of similarity between worlds and their constituent parts—competes with causation as a key sense-making operation. Analogical patterning increases in the plotting of both coincidence and counterfactuality. In counterfactuality the demise of the ontological hierarchy of realism means that looser patterns of multiple alternate worlds take the place of a sharp distinction between the factual and the *counter*factual based on causal premises. The modernist form of analogical coincidence is one key point of departure within this shift in sense-making operations; it replaces the kinship reunion plots of traditional coincidence in realist narrative in which genealogical, causal-progenerative *links* establishing a character's identity and origins crowned the unraveling of the recognition process within the coincidence plot. The advent of pluralistic multiple-world ontologies in science fiction from the 1930s onward can be seen as another manifestation of the analogical principle that actually anticipates later "mainstream" postmodernist developments: worlds exist side by side as analogues and variants of each other and not as points in a single-world linear sequence. However, the alternate worlds of science fiction still generally possess sufficient coherence by virtue of the construction of additional causal links, within or across their multiple worlds, to remain semirealistic narrative systems. The analogous aspect does not become sufficiently rampant to fully fragment their structure because the causal reasoning of counterfactuality traces the evolution of these worlds back to a *single originary point* of historical bifurcation (the counterfactual antecedent) in the past.

By contrast, in the alternate worlds of postmodernist fiction (both the radically experimental and historiographically metafictional forms) analogical connections override the construction of causal-linear *links*. The alternate stories of radical postmodernist fiction diverge from each other in the form of multiple story fragments. Here the only form of causal plotting that offers itself is the causal-manipulative connection which can be traced from the textual fragments back to the real-world author. In historiographic metafiction rampantly analogical relationships and the frustration of causal-progenerative patterning across multiple historical levels occur within the plots of both coincidence and alternate history. Incomprehensible or irreconcilable analogical relationships are created between fictional texts and the novel's (purported) real-world level, between the artifacts of history itself and their imitations (Barnes's *Flaubert's Parrot*, Dick's *The Man in the High Castle*), and between characters on different time levels (Prawer Jhabvala's *Heat and Dust*, Ackroyd's *Chatterton*). The dominance of patterns of similarity within these analogous constellations is such that no *original* or *authentic* version can be distinguished. Moreover, the alternate versions and interpretations of history in texts like Ackroyd's *Chatterton* and DeLillo's *Libra* are construed as analogous because their mutual status as fictions or texts means that no overriding and authoritative version can be isolated amongst them. In contrast to traditional realism, no *source* or true causal-pro-generative point of departure in the generation of history can be constructed by the reader out of this array. This conflation of reality and fiction, of authenticity and falsification, and of historiography and fiction creates a complex *blend* that makes the recognition of individuality, originality, and the erection of world boundaries impossible. The complex interaction of analogical relationships and the frustration of causal plotting within historiographic metafiction thus constitute the final point in the history of narrative fiction charted in this study where coincidence and counterfactuality meet and interact.

Source Acknowledgments

Parts of this volume previously appeared in the following publications:

"Ontological Plotting: Narrative as a Multiplicity of Temporal Dimensions." In *The Dynamics of Narrative Form*, edited by John Pier, 159–89. *Narratologia*, vol. 4. Berlin: de Gruyter, 2005.

"A Poetics of Coincidence in Narrative Fiction." *Poetics Today* 25.3 (2004): 399–436.

"The Coincidence Plot in Narrative Fiction." *Anglistentag 2002 Bayreuth: Proceedings*, edited by Ewald Mengel, Hans-Jörg Schmid, and Michael Steppat, 509–20. Trier: WVT, 2003.

"Divergent Plot Patterns in Narrative Fiction from Sir Philip Sidney to Peter Ackroyd." *Anglistentag 1999 Mainz: Proceedings*, edited by Bernhard Reitz and Sigrid Rieuwerts, 415–27. Trier: WVT, 2000.

"Hypertextuality and Multiple World Construction in English and American Narrative Fiction." *Bildschirmfiktionen: Interferenzen zwischen Literatur und neuen Medien*, edited by Julika Griem, 265–94. Tübingen: Narr, 1998.

"Story and Character Patterning in Jane Austen's Plots." *Sprachkunst* 26 (1995): 75–104.

Notes

Introduction

1. In fact, as Genette (1980, 36–37) demonstrates with reference to Homer's *Iliad* and as Richardson highlights in an analysis of Shakespeare's *Macbeth*, nonlinearity and "deformations of chronology" (1989, 283) are very widespread literary phenomena.

2. Plot and the temporal dimension of narrative have frequently been isolated as a key constituent of narrativity (i.e., in Prince's generic sense of "narrativeness" [1999, 44]), for example, by Scholes and Kellogg (1966), Labov (1972), Prince (1973, 1982), Culler (1975), and Todorov (1980). By contrast, Fludernik (1996a) backgrounds the role of plot in narrativity in favor of consciousness and experientiality.

3. See, for example, Culler (1975, 205–24), Boheemen (1982), Korte (1985b), Brooks (1992, 10–36), Ricoeur (1985, 7–28), Godzich (1994, 106–22), Ronen (1990, 1994, 144–74), Dannenberg (1995a), Richardson (2002b), and Page (2006, 49–70).

4. For Todorov story is "a convention; it does not exist at the level of events themselves. . . . [It] is an abstraction because it is always perceived and recounted by someone" (1980, 6); likewise, Brooks observes that "the *fabula*—'what really happened'—is in fact a mental construction that the reader derives from the *sjuzet*, which is all that he ever directly knows" (1992, 13). Seen this way, story is thus an unreachable signified; for practical analytical purposes, however, this theoretical difficulty is generally disregarded; see Genette: "[We] implicitly assume the existence of a kind of zero degree that would be a condition of perfect temporal correspondence between narrative and story" (1980, 36).

5. It can, of course, also be argued that "for English speakers 'plot' is pretty well disabled" (Abbott 2002, 16) because it is often used interchangeably with story. However, this has certainly not prevented narrative theorists from developing a multitude of plot models that move well beyond the concept of story. By contrast, Caserio (1979, 4) uses plot and story interchangeably, taking his lead from the use of the term by the authors focused on in his study—nineteenth-century and modernist novelists.

6. When referring to a theoretical reader in this study, I alternate between female and male pronouns, since I do not wish to implicitly exclude either group by the consistent use of one gender designation.

7. Important contributions in the fields of postclassical and feminist narratology that cannot be individually discussed here include Prince (1992), Lanser (1992), Fludernik (1993, 1996a) Herman (1995, 1999, 2002, 2003), Phelan (1996, 2005), Aczel (1998), Grünzweig and Solbach (1999), Palmer (2004), and Page (2006).

8. Beer implies an understanding of "plot" as referring to the "organizing principles of . . . thinking" (1983, 47).

9. For a review of theories of desire in narrative see Clayton (1989); see also Chambers (1984) for a further erotically oriented angle on "narrative seduction."

10. Introductions and theoretical outlines of possible-worlds theory and literature are contained in Ryan (1991, 1992) and Ronen (1994). Eco (notably 1981) also integrates possible-worlds theory into his analytical models.

11. Textually oriented studies of plot and narrative have often limited themselves to one epoch (e.g., Goetsch 1967; Caserio 1999; DuPlessis 1985; Watt 1987; Bell 1993; Monk 1993; Richardson 1997) or, while having a broader diachronic focus, have subordinated the diachronic textual perspective to the model itself (Stanzel 1984). The present study follows a more recent trend toward a balance between theory and literary history (e.g., Wicks 1989; Wolf 1993; Fludernik 1993, 1996a; Gutenberg 2000; Bueler 2001; Ryan 2001).

1. Cognitive Plotting

1. The concept of expulsion is not foregrounded in Ryan's model; however, she does use the term once in talking about Italo Calvino's novel *If on a Winter's Night a Traveler*, which is "a tale of frustrated immersion: as soon as a fictional world begins to solidify around the reader, he is expelled from it and must start all over again" (2001, 168).

2. For a thorough interrogation of the concept of narrative levels see Sternberg (1992).

3. The conjoinment of episodes formulated as part of the structuralist definition of narrative (e.g., Prince 1973) implied a basic level of causality in the sense of sequentiality, but it did not consider causation in the higher sense-making function.

4. See Turner (1987, 151–54) for a review of major philosophical and scientific conceptions of causation in which the tendency is to argue that "we have a single commonsense conception of causation" (1987, 151). See Richardson (1997, 13–107) for a wide-ranging overview of conceptualizations of both causality and chance.

5. For this reason, the causal pattern indicated here does not fit well into Richardson's (1997) category of supernatural agency, but neither can it be embraced by the term "naturalistic."

6. Bell (1993) presents chance and causality as opposing forces in the nineteenth-century French novel. Monk (1993) focuses more centrally on chance. Richardson uses "the admittedly limited term 'chance' to cover the range of modern subversions of the naturalistic causal system" (1997, 73).

2. Ontological Plotting

1. The use of possible-worlds theory in this chapter is selective and applications oriented. The initial sections draw in particular from Ryan's work and also from that of Doležel, Eco, Pavel, and Prince. The later sections on counterfactuals are indebted to the work of Lewis, Rescher, and Margolin. For comprehensive accounts of possible-worlds theory see Ryan (1991, 1992, 1995a), Ronen (1994), and Doležel (1998, 12–28).

2. The modern philosophical proposal that possible worlds are constructs of the human mind differs fundamentally from Leibniz's (1996) conception of God as the omnipotent knower of all possible worlds. For a discussion of Leibniz in contrast to modern possible-worlds theory see Adams (1979).

3. Ryan (1991, 110–23) distinguishes between four major modal types in her definition of the character's "private world": "K[nowledge]-world," "W[ish]-world," "O[bligation]-world," and "I[ntention]-world." Ryan is here building on modal categories suggested by Todorov (1969, 1977) and Doležel (1976a).

4. Focalization here refers not only to a character's visual perception of the narrative world, as implied in Genette's (1980) original definition of focalization as "who sees?" but to the granting of access to the sum total of the character's mental operations, "includ[ing] nonvisual perception, thinking, remembering, dream visions, and so on, all of which are central to focalization" (Jahn 1996, 254); see Herman (2002, 301–30) for a recent comprehensive discussion of focalization.

5. Genette's discussion of the "repeating analepsis," that is, when the narrative "retraces its own path" and "confers on the past episode a meaning that in its own time it did not yet have" (1980, 54–56), does not deal with alternate versions of the past but with differing interpretations of single events. He comes closest to addressing ontological multiplicity in the discussion of proleptic "false advance mentions, or *snares*," which form part of a "complex system of frustrated expectations, disappointed suspicions, surprises looked forward to" (Genette 1980, 77).

6. See Aristotle's *Poetics* (52a30–52b6, 1996, 18–19); Aristotle's concept of anagnorisis is discussed in detail in chapter 4.

7. I have quoted Doležel (1988) because here he states the possible-worlds argument in the most radically world-separatist terms. However, Doležel does later mellow the separatist stance on the ontological homogeneity of fictional entities by conceding that "persons with actual-world 'prototypes' constitute a distinct semantic class" (1998, 16). In dealing with boundary crossing between historical and fictional worlds, including the counterfactual, Doležel then also writes that "possible-worlds semantics has no quarrel with the idea of open boundary" (1999, 264).

8. Indeed, as Fauconnier and Turner (2003, 255–58) illustrate, key articulations of a person's identity and character are made in the form of counterfactual blends such as "if I were you, I would . . ." (2003, 255).

9. In focusing on the intertextual as opposed to the counterfactual multiplication of characters, Margolin (1996) has already proposed a comparative analysis of characters in terms of the difference between original and subsequent versions.

10. I have appropriated this term from Shea's (1989) report on possible worlds in philosophy.

11. Modernist narrative differs from conventional realist narrative because it often leaves various alternatives open (e.g., Henry James's *The Turn of the Screw* [1898]) instead of instating one version as actual.

12. There is one paragraph at the end of *Pavane* in which the heterodiegetic narrator destabilizes the novel's otherwise single-world framework by referring to the Holocaust. References to "Belsen" and "Buchenwald" (Roberts 1995, 275) underline the point that the technological progress of the real-world twentieth century did not serve human civilization; this late addition makes *Pavane* a slightly deviant single-world alternate history.

13. In the field of counterfactuals in political science, Weber advances the (self-confessedly "controversial") claim that it is also possible to talk of the future as counterfactual, since "most people ... carry around with them an 'official future,' a set of assumptions about what probably will be" (1996, 276, 279).

14. Ryan calls this the "factual domain" or "textual actual world" (1991, 113).

3. Spatial Plotting

1. Stewart (1987) and Ryan (1991, 201–32) are notable examples of the use of spatial diagrams to map narrative time and other more abstract analytical concepts. See Herman (2002, 265–99) for a recent comprehensive account of approaches to the question of space in narrative. The interconnectedness of time and space in plot has repeatedly been explored by twentieth-century criticism in a variety of ways (see, e.g., Frank 1945, 63; Rabkin 1977; Mitchell 1980a). In the field of narrative fiction itself, Laurence Sterne's *Tristram Shandy* (1759–67) was probably the first novel to graphically map plot as space. For a range of approaches to the topic of space in fiction, see, for example, Spencer (1971), Hoffmann (1978), Ibsch (1982), Malmgren (1985), and Yacobi (1991).

2. Bremond's (1980) mapping of plot as the actualization versus nonactualization of two possible futures marks the beginnings of such bifurcating spatial representations of plot. Ryan's (1991, 156–61) mapping of virtual and actual plotlines represents an important new departure in the spatial mapping of plot. In drama studies in particular the concept of character constellation (Pfister 2000) as a map of essential character relationships in the plot has long been current; see also Dannenberg (1995b) for maps of virtual and actual constellations in the love plots of Austen's novels.

3. The existence of a diverse range of opinions on Dickens is further substantiated in chapter 4's summary of the varying interpretations of the narrative explanation of coincidence in his works.

4. See Bordwell (1985, 99–146) for an in-depth consideration of narration and space in the medium of film itself and Kern (1983, 131–80) for a more general discussion of the culture of space in the modernist period.

5. Two further main schemata foregrounded by Johnson, the concepts of compulsive force and of cycles, have not been discussed here because they are not so significant for the representation of fictional space. For a list of basic schemata see Johnson (1987, 126).

6. For an account of the widespread use and key role of "portals" between worlds in fantasy literature see Clute and Grant (1997, 776); see also Dannenberg (1998a) for a study of portals, doorways, and relationships between worlds in the Narnia Chronicles

of C. S. Lewis. Fludernik (1999) uses the schemata of the container, the door, and the window to explore representations of imprisonment. On the literary use of windows see also Eitner (1955), Sebeok and Margolis (1982), and Dannenberg (2000b).

7. I have opted to use Genette's (1980) terms for classifying narrators (homodiegetic versus heterodiegetic) because of their wide currency. However, there is much to be said for the use of the term *character narration* (Phelan 2005) in preference to "homodiegetic"; the drawback is that its opposing term, *noncharacter narration* (Phelan 2005, 215), is not as evocative.

4. The Coincidence Plot

1. Dessner's definition covers any intersection of characters within a narrative world and thus, like most definitions, neglects the key aspect of the *previous relationship*, which elevates a random intersection into a coincidental encounter. Such one-off "chance encounters" are dealt with by Biard (1988), Bell (1993), and Wolf (1993). Wolf highlights the key difference between the different forms by noting that "anaphorischer Zufall" ("anaphoric chance," which is his term for the coincidental encounter) refers backward in the narrative, while "kataphorischer Zufall" (the single chance encounter) only refers forward (1993, 162). Martínez (1996, 109–50) discusses various categories, including the comic and the fatal, in the narrative representation of chance ("Zufall").

2. The phrase "coincidental connections" is also used by McDonald (1968, 373) and Harvey (1965, 140) (cf. also Caserio 1979, 105). Forsyth (1985) uses "Wonderful Chains," a quotation from Dickens, to express the essential connecting nature of coincidence. Elliott defines coincidence (in Hardy) as "noticeable or surprising concurrences of events . . . [that] have usually proved links in a concatenation of incidents tending toward evil" (1966, 58). Examining coincidence in Isak Dinesen's "plots of space," Yacobi (1991, 465) foregrounds the spatial element of "multiple convergence."

3. Articles that might seem relevant from their titles in fact reveal the wide range of "semantic plots" that the term "coincidence" can be given (see White 1965; Shaw 1974; Pinion 1979; Lindskoog 1989; Nakano 1991; Helms 1995). Some discussions focus on the influence of coincidences on authors, tracing literary-biographical connections in the manner of the fictional genre of historiographic metafiction.

4. Of course, coincidence also occurs in drama, such as in Shakespeare's romantic comedies *A Midsummer Night's Dream*, *Twelfth Night*, and *As You Like It* (a reworking of Lodge's *Rosalynde*) and in Oscar Wilde's *The Importance of Being Earnest*. However, a comparative analysis falls outside the scope of the present study.

5. Reed's (1975) many examples from numerous Victorian novels underline its ubiquity in that period. For discussions or briefer references to nineteenth-century coincidence (above all in Dickens and Hardy) see Van Ghent (1961, 222–23), Harvey (1965, 139–43), Beyer (1976), Caserio (1979, 105–22), Brown (1982, 57), Forsyth (1985), Frazee (1985, 235), Vargish (1985, 7–10, 209–11, 230–33), Jones (1970, 46–47), Elliott (1966, 57–70), Hornback (1971), Dessner (1992), Wolf (1993, 163–64), and Nakano (1991). McDonald (1968) offers a broader perspective (due in part to his broader definition of coincidence as all chance events) using examples from Faulkner, Dostoevsky, Hardy, and Forster.

6. Goldknopf exclaims of Charlotte Brontë's *Jane Eyre*: "One almost expects Miss Brontë to be ashamed of her handiwork. . . . Far from being ashamed, the author is proud!" (1969, 41–42). Reed speaks of coincidence being used "unashamedly in what were supposedly matter-of-fact tales" (1975, 130).

7. On Joyce's *Ulysses* see Hannay (1983, 1988) and Ackerley (1997); on Pasternak see Harvey (1965, 138–39); on Dinesen see Yacobi (1991, 463–66); on DeLillo see Ickstadt (1994). Ackerley (1997) focuses extensively on analogical relationships with reference to Kammerer (1919) and Jung (1960). Lodge (1992) focuses on the parodistic use of coincidence in the postmodern novel, using his own novels as examples; Wolf (1993, 288–89) comments on the metafictional purpose of multiple "anaphoric chance" (coincidental encounters) in Barth's *The Sot-Weed Factor*.

8. Coincidence or chance is often briefly mentioned in lists of the generic attributes of romance or the picaresque; see Watt (1987, 22), Bonheim (1993, 172), Fludernik (1996a, 162, 1996b, 62), and Wicks (1989, 55).

9. Inglis (1990, 1–12) constructs a fascinating narrative of connections in the study of coincidence itself, tracing a line of influence from Émile Deschamp's narration of a particularly striking serial coincidence (involving the eating of plum pudding and the recurrent appearance of a Monsieur de Fontgibu) that was mentioned in Camille Flammarion's *L'inconnu* (1900). This book in turn "impressed . . . the Austrian biologist Paul Kammerer" (Inglis 1990, 3), who then wrote *Das Gesetz der Serie*. Kammerer's work influenced Jung and the quantum physicist Wolfgang Pauli, who attracted the attention of Arthur Koestler, who wrote a biography of Kammerer and *The Roots of Coincidence* (1972).

10. Inglis (1990, 209) lists seven categories of coincidence. His fourth type, "'small-world' (encounters with people in improbable circumstances)," is the real-world equivalent of the traditional coincidence plot. His list of possible explanations of coincidence comprises "Chance," "Human Fallibility," "Embroidery," "Concurrence," "Cumberlandism," "Intuition," "Serendipity," "Destiny," "The Stars," "Numerology," "Prayer," "Psi," "Precognition," "Identifying Paramnesia," "Apparitions," and "Psychokinesis" (Inglis 1990, 96–177).

11. Sophocles' drama, of course, falls outside the generic and historical focus of this study. However, it is cited because of its status as a master narrative of Western culture, which is also manifested in its textual progeny (e.g., Freud 1972; Gide 1947).

12. I follow Wicks (1989) in treating the picaresque not as a limited canon of texts but as a narrative tradition or "mode" that can be seen embodied in its different and changing aspects across a large corpus of texts.

13. Kinship and romantic relationships are occasionally mixed when coinciding cousins discover a mutual romantic interest, as in Austen's *Persuasion* and Brontë's *Jane Eyre*. However, both these texts ultimately reject the cousin (William Elliot and St. John Rivers, respectively) as suitor over the outsider (Captain Wentworth and Rochester).

14. The term "small world" effect recurs in the discussion of coincidence; see, for example, Inglis (1991), McDonald (1968), and of course Lodge's (1985) novel of the same name.

15. Cave's thesis that "recognition scenes in literary works are by their nature 'problem' moments rather than moments of satisfaction and completion" (1988, 489) does not hold true for this type of recognition.

16. See Frye (1971, notably 170, 212–14) on anagnorisis in comedy and tragedy. In coincidence research, only Forsyth (1985) and Wolf (1993) discuss recognition. Forsyth shows how progressively in Dickens's novels the "recognition scenes become the discovery of the plot by the central character" (1985, 159). Wolf (1993, 162) draws the link to Aristotelian anagnorisis in discussing the coincidental encounter, which he calls "anaphoric chance."

17. Harvey (1965, 139) highlights one opposing pair of explanations in the narrative justification of coincidence—causality versus absolute randomness. Goldknopf, by contrast, makes a fundamental distinction between coincidence as "a 'quick-and-dirty' way of getting on with the narrative," in which case it is simply "a convenience of plot" and a different type that is given greater significance and thus has "supernal import" (1969, 43, 50).

18. McDonald discusses the techniques used by Faulkner and Dostoevsky to camouflage coincidence and make it seem "natural" rather than explain it metaphysically, tracing the minor causal chains of human action constructed in plots and thus "letting us believe that . . . events are growing out of the given story" (1968, 374).

19. Compare, for example, Brown (1982) on the social message of coincidence in *Bleak House* with Vargish's (1985) and Frazee's (1985) examination of Dickens in terms of its providential significance. Harvey gives a more complex account, highlighting how in the use of chance in Dickens's novels "explanations are carefully broken-up, placed, and distributed" (1965, 141). Forsyth's (1985) approach is more flexible and pluralistic and highlights Dickens's variety of approaches (seriously tragic or providential versus comic or self-conscious). Goldknopf contrasts Dickens's questioning attitude to the idea that life is "divinely sponsored" (1969, 46) with Charlotte Brontë's sense of divine Providence.

20. Another key example from drama is the nondelivery of the letter to Romeo in Shakespeare's *Romeo and Juliet*, which ultimately leads to the lovers' deaths.

21. Rhetorical analogies in literature, such as those in metaphor and rhyme, are of course a much wider phenomenon. The use of rhyme as the organization of analogous phonemes is drawn attention to in Barnes's *Flaubert's Parrot* in the phrase "the coincidence of rhyme" (1985, 67). Ackerley discusses the affinities between words perceived by Bloom in *Ulysses*: "An 'acoustic knot' implies a coincidence, one born from the necessary double articulation of language" (1997, 44).

22. The most extreme form of postmodernist duplication across narrative levels is the infinite recursive structure of the *mise-en-abyme*; see, for example, Wolf (1993, 295–305) and McHale (1987, 124–28).

5. Counterfactuals and Other Alternate Narrative Worlds

1. Other brief allusions to counterfactuals in literature are made by Roese and Olson (1995a, 1) and Seelau et al. (1995, 57).

2. Earlier important work that paved the way for Roese and Olson 1995c includes Tversky and Kahneman (1982) and Kahneman and Miller (1986).

3. The relativism of Fauconnier and Turner's definition of the counterfactual is in fact in some ways closer to the decentered relativism of the "virtual" and "actual" formulated by Ryan (1991, 1995b).

4. I omit reference to further formal distinctions, such as that between additive counterfactuals, which "add a new antecedent, in order to create a new alternative," and subtractive counterfactuals, which "remove some factual antecedent in order to reconstruct reality" (Roese and Olson 1995b, 174–75).

5. A "study of Olympic medalists revealed that imagined alternatives to reality are sufficiently powerful to cause those who are objectively worse off [bronze medal winners] to nonetheless feel better about their standing than those in a superior position [silver medal winners]" (Gilovich and Medvec 1995, 278).

6. See also Kahneman: "Event X will not be considered a cause of anything unless one can readily conceive of an alternative to it" (1995, 384). In the psychological literature, the purpose of counterfactual constructions is also seen as the desire to attribute *fault* (Seelau et al. 1995, 62), a concept allied to causality.

7. Using the term "alternative story," Stanzel (1977, 244–45) briefly refers to counterfactual narratives within a discussion of a different phenomenon, "the complementary story," by which he means (leading on from the work of Ingarden and Iser) the reader's filling in of indeterminate points in the text; this is similar to what Eco (1981, 206–17) calls the reader's "inferential walks" (cf. also Goetsch 1980).

8. The category "counterfactual thought" used sporadically in Palmer (2004, 120–21) refers to a variety of nonactual thoughts, including the future.

9. Other studies use the terms "alternate world" (Pfister 1982; Kuehl 1989) as a general term for the fictional depiction of worlds set in times and spaces beyond quotidian reality.

10. Harrison proposes a typology of forms based on ontological criteria: (1) "the parallel worlds in the present"; (2) "the parallel world in the present"; and (3) a subform of (2), "changing this world in the past to alter the present" (1976, 108). Adams's typology depends on the temporal focus with reference to the reader: "Alternative history is about what happened in a past that is different from our past; parallel history is about what is happening in a present that is occurring simultaneous with our present[;] . . . future history is about what happens in a future that may—or may not—happen in our future" (1994, 149–50).

11. Additional confusion is caused by the imprecise use of "alternative history" to refer to *future* history (Suvin 1983); such works, however, are not "alternative," since they map an uncontrastable area of time (the future).

12. For examples of the discursive form of alternate history see Squire (1932) and Cowley (2001).

13. See also Korte (1985a, 199–205), Moosmüller (1993, 160–66), and Ashline (1995).

14. The distinctions between self-focused versus externally focused and characterological versus behavioral counterfactuals are adapted from McMullen, Markman, and Gavanski (1995, 149–50).

15. Riffaterre cites this passage as an example of "[f]ictionality [d]eclared" (1990, 32).

16. See also Prince: "When the disnarrated relates to a narrator's vision, it foregrounds ways of creating a world" (1992, 36).

17. This competition between different characters' private wishes and intention worlds is a key part of the "principle of diversification" that creates "tellability," as defined by Ryan (1991).

6. The Metamorphoses of the Coincidence Plot

1. *The New Arcadia* also uses ad hoc coincidence and coincidental relationships, like those between Clitophon, Ismenus, and Amphialus (Sidney 1987, 242, 259, 66).

2. *Rosalynde* also provided the source for Shakespeare's *As You Like It* (1599). The Rosalynde part of the coincidence plot is Lodge's creation, while the fourteenth-century *Tale of Gamelyn* provided the Rosader/Saladyne constellation (see Salzman 1985, 73).

3. For research into the developmental history of the novel before the eighteenth century see, for example, Davis (1983), Salzman (1985), McKeon (1987), Hunter (1990), and Fludernik (1996b).

4. Helbig (1990, 53–56) also reads the incestuous marriage as signifying providential punishment.

5. Compare the scenes depicting Roderick's coincidental encounter with his uncle and with his long-lost father (Smollett 1979, 232–33, 412–13). As Damrosch observes: "*Roderick Random* puts its unlovable hero through a series of disasters and recoveries that are as random as the title suggests" (1985, 286).

6. Crane's (1952) analysis of the novel's "plot" in fact focuses more on the intricate story as established at closure rather than on the narrator's manipulative plotting. More insightful in this respect is Füger (1978).

7. Dowling and the would-be highwayman are two significant minor characters who cross and recross Tom's path. The failed highwayman's coincidental coidentity as the husband of Mrs. Miller's cousin secures her goodwill toward Tom by his revelation of Tom's generosity, paving the way for her role in Allworthy's final reevaluation of Tom. Dowling is central to Blifil's conspiracy against Tom and its revelation to Allworthy. In addition, the tale told to Tom by "the man of the hill" (Fielding 1966, 404–29) is an intense microcosm of coincidence.

8. Significantly, in terms of the history of the explanation of coincidence there is here a shift away from the idea of a metaworld influencing events toward a focus on the individual character's actions in the fictional world: in his further response to the revelation, Tom Jones rejects "Fortune," conceding his own responsibility for events (Fielding 1966, 815).

9. By contrast, in its parodistic treatment of romance, Charlotte Lennox's *The Female Quixote* (1752) contains an ironic representation of female coincidental encounters with threatening male figures (1970, 19).

10. In claiming that "'paternal' affection offers [Adeline] nothing but alienation and despair" (1998, 164), Haggerty neglects the positive role played by M. La Luc as her ersatz father.

11. Likewise, *Pride and Prejudice* uses successive triangles of coincidental relationships to advance the plot; these concern links between (1) Darcy, Wickham, and the Bennets; (2) the Bennets, Mr. Collins, Lady de Bourgh, and Darcy; and (3) the Bennets, Mrs. Gardiner, and her connections with the Derbyshire area, including Darcy's Pemberley estate (Austen 1972, 116, 126, 180).

12. Similarly, in *Sense and Sensibility* a coincidental network of relationships reveals the truth of Willoughby's attempts on the virtue of Colonel Brandon's niece (Austen 1969, 218).

13. See Weinsheimer on the wider use of "chance" in *Pride and Prejudice* "as a realistic technique of plot development . . . without apology for mystery or legerdemain" (1972, 407).

14. Even before this, as Kiely suggests, the "romantic novel" stages a "wild and flamboyant, grotesque and luxuriously artificial" (1972, vii) reaction against eighteenth-century realism. See also Warhol (1996a) on the productive relationship between realism and gothic romance in Charlotte Brontë's novels.

15. As Würzbach shows, the "mother image . . . based on sympathy, self-sacrifice [and] the domestic sphere" can be traced back to the Romantic period with its "increased interest in the child" (1996, 371).

16. A plot of coincidental relationships is also used to expose Rochester's bigamous marriage attempt. When the wedding is stopped, it is revealed that Rochester's brother-in-law, Richard Mason, "happened to be with" (Brontë 1966, 322) Jane's uncle in Madeira when the latter read Jane's letter informing him of her intended marriage.

17. Dickens's reluctance to impose a happy ending on the novel is understandable in view of its nightmarish network of menace and disappointed dreams and illusions. The convergent ending, in which Pip and Estella meet again coincidentally, was only adopted in response to reader demand.

18. See in particular the passage in which the narrator comments on how a candle placed against a "surface of polished steel" that is "multitudinously scratched in all directions" will create the illusion of "a fine series of concentric circles round that little sun" (Eliot 1965, 297).

19. On the search for or perception of familiar facial characteristics see also Eliot (1967, 205, 226, 438, 451, 528).

20. Compare the repeated use of facial description within recognition in *Villette* (Brontë 1979, 247–48, 361) and a passage from Radcliffe's *The Romance of the Forest* in which Clara perceives "something in [Adeline's] features" that awakens her sympathy, to which her aunt replies: "'Shall I never persuade you to give up that romantic notion of judging people by their faces'" (1986, 256).

21. Compare, for example, Dickens's narration of the reunion of Esther with her mother (Lady Dedlock) in *Bleak House*: "She caught me to her breast, kissed me, wept over me. . . . [S]he fell on her knees and cried to me, 'O my child, my child, I am your wicked and unhappy mother! O try to forgive me!'" (1971, 565).

22. Chase performs a "double-reading" of the dual causal directions of plot in Eliot's novel that "involves a revelation of origin . . . , cause, and identity" on one level, while

"the progression of the story ... positively requires a revelation that [Daniel] is of Jewish birth" (1978, 217, 218). However, Chase does not acknowledge the deconstructional forces that are created by the novel's own multiple explanatory modes.

23. Similarly, coincidental encounters in *Tess of the d'Urbervilles* contain extended spatialized descriptions of Tess's unilateral recognition of other characters, notably, Tess's first reencounters with Angel and with Alec d'Urberville (Hardy 1978, 164–67, 379–84). The sense that Tess cannot escape being the victim of male characters is intensified by the many coincidental encounters with Farmer Groby and the coincidental relationship linking Angel's father and Alec d'Urberville (Hardy 1978, 273, 350, 366 and 228, 235).

24. On the techniques of postmodernist fiction see Scholes (1967), Waugh (1984), McHale (1987, 1992), Wolf (1993), Hutcheon (1988), and Fludernik (1996a, 267–310). On the distinction between "soft" and "hard" metafiction see Wolf (1993) and Fludernik (1996a).

25. Cf. Nünning (1995b, 233), who comments that in *Chatterton* Ackroyd uses an innovative narrative structure and a dense intertextual network of references to cast doubt on conventional conceptions of time and history.

26. A similar strategy is employed in Prawer Jhabvala's *Heat and Dust* when the narrator from the 1970s level seems to appear in the Nawab's dream on the 1923 time level (1994, 123).

27. The novel has at least five narrative levels: the retrospective of the narrator's own private life centering on his wife's suicide, his account of his visit to France researching Flaubert's life, his discussion of Flaubert's life, his discussion of Flaubert's works, and his metanarrative commentaries on literature in general.

28. Cf. Scott: "And just as a stuffed parrot is only a facsimile of 'parrot-ness,' so too is a word only a facsimile of meaning. Thus, each museum's parrot ... is actually an arbitrarily selected facsimile that signifies only the conventions attributed to it" (1990, 68).

29. Cf. Brooks: "*Flaubert's Parrot* ... provides insight into a postmodern world where a stable version neither of history nor of books can be conceded" (1999, 45). Interestingly, Brooks also points to parallels between Barnes's novel and Ford's *The Good Soldier*.

30. Maiden's abandonment of the babies in a Gladstone bag is a further intertextual reference to the coincidence plot of Oscar Wilde's *The Importance of Being Earnest* (1895).

31. As Lodge himself comments, *Small World* "consciously imitates the interlacing plots of chivalric romance, so there is an intertextual justification ... for the multiplicity of coincidences in the story" (1992, 152).

32. Nünning (1995b, 131–42) reads *The Passion* as historiographic metafiction for its feminist rewriting of history. However, the novel's fantastic elements (see Kutzer 1994, 139; Seaboyer 1997, 506) also qualify it for McHale's definition of the "postmodernist historical novel" as the "illicit mergings of history and the fantastic" (1987, 89); for example, Villanelle, the daughter of a Venetian boatman, has webbed feet.

33. See, for example, Ickstadt (1994). By contrast, Reeve objects to this designation because he sees the novel's thrust as being at variance with Hutcheon's (1988) definition: "To write a novel about so slippery a subject as Oswald is not quite to challenge or subvert an authorized version of history" (1999, 138).

34. Cf. Ickstadt: "The stories of these various plotters are in turn told by a narrator-figure whose plotting imagination despairingly tries to create sense and order out of a meaningless mass of information" (1994, 306).

35. This is a new variant of Eliot's polished steel surface metaphor in *Middlemarch* (see note 18 above).

36. A further passage continues in the same tradition of perceptional relativism as Eliot's *Middlemarch* and DeLillo's *Libra* (see notes 18 and 35 above): the bizarre, randomly formed shapes in a canyon landscape can be shaped by human perception into meaningful patterns: "You couldn't help seeing familiar shapes when you looked at them, even though you knew it was all chance . . . a million years of wind and weather. . . . It was like making pictures out of clouds" (Auster 1990, 156–57).

7. The Narrative Evolution of Counterfactuals

1. *Jack of Newbury* contains an exchange of historical counterfactuals between Henry VIII and his jester concerning the fates of the two traitors Empson and Dudley; a brief, linguistically half-formed counterfactual is also expressed by an Italian character, Benedick (Deloney 1987, 347, 374).

2. Cf. Fowler: "We may coin the term 'mind-style' to refer to any distinctive linguistic presentation of an individual mental self" (1977, 103). Schneider classes Philanax's words as an example of "persuasive speech" (1999, 104–13) in Sydney's *Arcadia* versions.

3. In *The New Arcadia* Philanax's speech is embedded in a letter to Basilius (Sidney 1987, 20–21). See also Sidney (1987, 247, 416, 1994, 248–49) for further minor examples of counterfactuals.

4. A further counterfactual is used in an observation made by Oroonoko that is reported to the reader by the narrator (Behn 1994, 32).

5. In addition, the briefly narrated story of Miss Sally Godfrey, who had a child after being seduced by Mr. B., functions as a counterfactual personification of Pamela; as Pamela herself observes: "I have had the grace to escape the misfortune of this poor lady" (Richardson 1980, 495–98, 497). *Pamela* also occasionally constructs alternate future worlds, such as those Pamela constructs while she contemplates suicide as a means of escaping from Mr. B. (Richardson 1980, 212).

6. Critics such as Miller (1981, 86) and Rowen (1995, 33–34) have expressed dissatisfaction with the ending of *Mansfield Park* (see also Dannenberg 1995b). Müller (1977, 98), however, parallels the reserved portrayal of the love plot in *Mansfield Park* with a passage in chapter 58 of *Pride and Prejudice* and attributes both to Austen's critical stance toward the sentimental romance.

7. *Villette* also uses autobiographical counterfactuals, as in the following grimly ironic downward counterfactual, in which Lucy imagines herself as having, in her loneliness and isolation, become a Catholic convert: "I might just now, instead of writing this heretic narrative, be counting my beads in the cell of a certain Carmelite convent on the Boulevard of Crécy in Villette" (Brontë 1979, 235).

8. Critics from Gilbert and Gubar (1984, 438) to Cervetti (1998) have seen the end as empowering the heroine: the removal of the rather stern M. Paul liberates Lucy from

"the stress, subordination and confinement that would come with marriage" (Cervetti 1998, 80); see Preston (1996, 398) for a contradictory argument.

9. The sense of characters' lives as part of an infinitely complex matrix of influences and possibilities is also reflected in the recurrence of images of pathways and networks: Lydgate feels a "hampering threadlike pressure" (Eliot 1965, 210), while Mordecai tells Deronda, "We know not all the pathways" (Eliot 1967, 818).

10. For further counterfactuals in *Daniel Deronda* see, for example, Eliot (1967, 99, 274).

11. Even Grandcourt's death is presented using the kind of counterfactual identified in the psychological literature as typically produced in dramatic, unforeseen events: Gwendolen wonders if she "had thrown the rope [to the drowning Grandcourt] on the instant—perhaps it would have hindered death?" (Eliot 1967, 763).

12. See Rodiek (1997, 63–89) for an account of the French counterfactual tradition—Louis Geoffroy's *Napoléon et la conquête du monde 1812–1832* (1836) and Charles Renouvier's *Uchronie (l'utopie dans l'histoire)* (1857).

13. Cf. Beer (1983), who stresses the key roles of growth, transformation, and variability in Darwin's work but not in the context of counterfactuality.

14. According to Pinkerton, "Hands Off" is "one of the early examples of backward time travel" (1979, 168). However, rather than traveling in time, the two godlike protagonists seem to be free of the normal constraints of time and space, surveying the universe as it is, was, and could have been.

15. H. G. Wells's story "The Man Who Could Work Miracles" (1898) does not strictly involve historical counterfactuals, but it also deserves mention as a significant text because it narrates two contradictory versions of events: the first one is at the beginning, when the miracle worker receives his miraculous powers and ultimately causes the destruction of the world (the events that constitute the main story), while a new version of this initial scene is narrated at the end after his miraculous powers and their effects have been canceled.

16. Collins's (1986) claim that *A Connecticut Yankee* represents an early form of "alternative history" is not correct precisely because no deviating counterfactual historical sequence is created.

17. Everett's (1957) interpretation of quantum theory formulated a theory of multiple parallel worlds (see also DeWitt and Graham 1973). For nonphysicists, John Gribbin's paraphrase is easier to follow than Everett's equations: "The basic idea of the many-worlds theory is that every time the Universe is faced with a choice at the quantum level, the entire Universe splits into as many copies of itself as it takes to carry out every possible option" (1996, 161, see also 1991, 235–54).

18. The premise of an earlier text, Guy Dent's *Emperor of the If* (1926), is less coherent, and the text does not use multiple counterfactuals: evolutionary history is retrospectively altered by a mad scientist, so that overnight London is transformed into a prehistoric landscape, and "human beings bec[o]me impossible" (1926, 51).

19. "Throughout his work Dick pays obsessive attention to imitations" (Huntington 1988, 156); see, for example, Dick (1965, 66) on historical authenticity and Dick (1996b, 25–26) on the power of recordings to create the illusion of reality.

20. The counterfactual antecedent is revealed in a number of character conversations: it centers on the collapse of Russia in 1941 and the assassination of Franklin D. Roosevelt (Dick 1965, 15, 66–68).

21. Cf. Adams: "Instead of using a mechanical or scientific device like a time machine, Dick uses a literary device, a novel-within-a-novel" (1994, 153).

22. The textual recursiveness of *The Man in the High Castle* is not only internal; its canonical status has led to its intertextual reverberations occurring in subsequent texts (cf. Benford 1982, 213; Amis 1976, 26–27).

23. Cf. Rieder: "*High Castle* undermines any interpretative attempt to posit 'Inner Truth'" (1988, 215); see also Hayles (1983, 66). For a more solipsistic interpretation of "Inner Truth" see Hellekson (2001, 70).

24. The novel's catastrophic denouement of human "miracle working" gone out of control echoes Wells's "The Man Who Could Work Miracles," which may have served as an inspiration; see also Schenkel (1994, 244).

25. Cf. Sussmann: "*The Difference Engine* vividly presents [a] deterministic historical narrative of information technology as the necessary instrument of panoptical discipline and surveillance" (1994, 6).

26. Cf. Doležel: "Since all the conflicting versions ... are constructed by the authoritative narrator, they are all fully authentic"; however, "the authenticity of fictional existence is denied by the logico-semantic structure of the world itself" (1989, 239).

27. In texts from Joyce's *Afternoon* (1987) onward, the radical techniques of print metafictions were extended in interactive hyperfiction (see, e.g., Bolter 1991; Ryan 2001, 204–80).

28. Critics have been unanimous in concluding that in this story "no reader will ever apprehend the 'whole' situation. Coover forces the reader to provide whatever order he or she can" (Petitjean 1995, 50; see also Weinstock 1975, 386; Waugh 1984, 138–39).

29. A more coherent case of plot profusion which is also completely at the expense of character comes at the end of B. S. Johnson's story "Broad Thoughts from a Home" (1973, 110). Malcolm Bradbury's story "Composition" (1976) concludes with three alternate endings (1987, 143–46). See Moosmüller (1993, 160–66) for a discussion of these texts.

Glossary of Key Terms

alternate possible future worlds: These can be contrasted with *counterfactuals* in terms of their *ontological hierarchy*. Here there is a less rigid hierarchy of relations between worlds because no definitive factual world yet exists.

analogical coincidence: A striking correspondence between characters, fictional objects, or events.

autobiographical counterfactuals: In narrative fiction autobiographical counterfactuals in particular imitate the psychological patterns observed in real-world, self-focused counterfactualizing; according to the context, individuals construct short-term or long-term retrospective counterfactual narratives in response to events in their lives. Autobiographical counterfactualizing in particular can generate strong *counterfactual emotions*.

biographical counterfactuals: These can be distinguished from *historical counterfactuals* in that they involve counterfactuals about individual characters' lives. Biographical counterfactuals can, however, be used to initiate larger historical counterfactual scenarios if the character concerned is given a pivotal role in a historical narrative or is a real-world historical figure.

causation: Causal-manipulative plotting involves an active agent purposefully influencing events. Causal-progenerative plotting involves a randomly initiated but causally linked temporal sequence, including the lineage of genealogical relations between characters.

cognitive stratification: This involves various combinations of knowledge imbalance on the part of characters and the reader. *Suspense* can be intensified if the reader is privy to the knowledge world of one character while another character remains ignorant of that knowledge.

coincidence: As an overall phenomenon both in life and in fiction, this can be defined as a constellation of two or more apparently random events in space and time with an uncanny or striking connection.

coincidence plot: This plot occurs in various forms. The *traditional coincidence plot* has been widely used in narrative fiction from the Renaissance romance to postmodernist fiction and occurs particularly in the form of the *coincidental encounter* or *coincidental relationships*. *Modernist coincidence* and the *postmodernist coincidence plot* (the latter occurs predominantly in historiographic metafiction) differ from the traditional coincidence plot and involve *analogical coincidence*.

coincidental encounter: In the traditional coincidence plot this is the moment of intersection between two characters with a previous relationship. In complex forms of the coincidence plot the *recognition* of the previous relationship and the characters' true identities does not take place instantaneously, resulting in an extended narrative of suspense and/or discovery.

coincidental relationships: An uncanny network of double relationships between three or more characters in which one character has a dual identity that is the subject of a discovery plot.

counterfactual: A hypothetical alteration to a sequence of events in the past. A counterfactual constructs a new antecedent in the past that alters or "undoes" the events of a factual world and creates a new counterfactual consequent. Counterfactuals can be applied in many contexts, ranging from externally focused *historical counterfactuals* to self-focused *autobiographical counterfactuals*. Behavioral counterfactuals alter events and actions but not character. Characterological counterfactuals alter character, thereby creating a more complex constellation of *transworld identity*, which results from differences in the factual and counterfactual versions of a character. In its basic form, a counterfactual constructs a binary hierarchy of events in which fact is contrasted with a hypothetical counterfact. More complex counterfactual narratives can involve additional propositions, or counter-counterfactuals, creating a more intricate and pluralistic *ontological hierarchy*.

counterfactual emotions: Emotions generated as a result of counterfactual narratives; these can be particularly intense in self-focused counterfactuals. *Satisfaction* is often created through imagining *downward counterfactuals*. *Regret* is generated by *upward counterfactuals*. In *autobiographical counterfactuals*, hot regret is a transient response to a negative event, while wistful regret occurs in long-term retrospectives about what might have been.

downward counterfactual: The postulation of a world that is worse than the factual world.

expulsion: This is the opposite of *immersion* and is generally triggered by metafiction. The reader is mentally expelled from his cognitive sojourn in the fictional world when a metafictional strategy destroys immersion by reminding him of his true ontological location.

historical counterfactual: A historical counterfactual is a proposition that hypothetically alters real-world history. Counterfactual versions of history can be plausible or implausible, depending, for example, on whether they occur in academic historical analysis or in narrative fiction. In the fictional genre of alternate history, *downward counterfactuals* (e.g., in which the Axis powers win the Second World War) play a key role because they allow the reader to vicariously experience a dysphoric world but also to experience the *counterfactual emotion* of satisfaction that she does not live in such a world.

immersion: The reader's mental journey into the world created in the reading of the text; immersion can only take place if the text offers sufficient information for the construction of a narrative destination for the reader's mental journey. The reader's enjoyment of the world created by the text can therefore be understood as the cognitive simulation of ontological liberation. Immersion is fueled by narrative strategies such as suspense, character-cognitive detail, and spatialization.

kinship: Used in narrative fiction, plots of kinship activate the reader's inherent knowledge of family connections; cognitively, kinship activates ideas of causal-progenerative family lineage and the perception of genetic similarity. In the traditional coincidence plot, plots of kinship constitute the most powerful narratives because of their ability to evoke the deep-seated experience of parent-child or sibling *recognition* and reunion in the mind of the reader.

liminal plotting: The reader's semiconscious mental images of possible future events in the fictional world while in the grips of suspense.

modernist coincidence: Analogous relationships link characters and objects on the same spatial and temporal level.

negative coincidence: This involves a situation of thwarted convergence when the intended intersection of objects in the narrative world (frequently a letter from one character to another or a meeting between characters) miscarries; negative coincidence is frequently used in tragedies of circumstance.

ontological hierarchy: The hierarchy of relations between the different alternate worlds generated by the text. In realist texts only one world can be truly actual; ultimately, all other world versions are revealed to be constructs. Semi- and antirealist texts rebel against these realist constraints and often have a multiple-world ontological hierarchy in which more than one world is actual or the relations between worlds remain unclear. Counterfactuals have a clearer binary hierarchy of fact versus counterfact in contrast with other forms, for example, *alternate possible future worlds*.

plotting principle: The creation of key forms of cognitive connection, in particular, those based on causation, kinship, and similarity. Traditional realist texts rely in particular on the plotting principle of causation, whereas many postmodernist texts sabotage causal connections and create predominantly analogical systems of connection.

postmodernist coincidence: A form of the coincidence plot that occurs particularly in the genre of historiographic metafiction. It creates networks of analogical relationships between characters across different narrative levels that are generally only recognizable by the reader.

recognition: This is the central feature of the traditional coincidence plot and is used to create key effects involving *suspense, temporal orchestration*, and *spatialization*. Suspense can be created by deferred recognition, in which only the reader is aware of the characters' true identity, or by unilateral (staggered) recognition, in which only one of the characters involved is initially aware of the other's true identity. In plots of kinship reunion, recognition can involve dysphoric (Oedipus) or euphoric (Jane Eyre) discoveries by characters; because of their activation of the real-world experience of sibling and parent recognition in the reader's imagination, plots of kinship reunion in fiction are widespread and often emotionally charged.

similarity: The perception or creation of correspondences or analogies between characters or events.

spatialization: The detailed and immersive representation of fictional space that reproduces the cognitive schemata of the real-world human negotiation of space, notably, in this study, the path, the link, the container, and the portal or window.

spatial metaphor: Nonspatial concepts are often mapped using spatial metaphors. The more abstract phenomenon of time is often conceptualized in spatial terms; time is conceived of as a path; decisions and turning points in (auto)biography and history are conceptualized as diverging paths or forks in a road.

suspense: The narrative's suggestion of *alternate possible future worlds* that create a state of emotional tension and anticipation in the reader. Suspense can be a highly immersive narrative strategy because it strongly preoccupies the reader's mind about events occurring in the narrative present and their possible developments; see also *liminal plotting* and *cognitive stratification*.

temporal orchestration: A strategy used by realist narratives in which more than one version of the past or future is suggested by the text, but where ultimately, due to the *ontological hierarchy* of realism, only one version is actual. Temporal orchestration in the coincidence plot involves the mystification of past-world relationships (particularly in the mystery genealogy plot), the transformation of character identity in terms of origins and family lineage, or the suspenseful suggestion of possible future recognition scenarios.

traditional coincidence plot: The paths of characters with a previous connection intersect in the space and time of the narrative world in apparently random and remarkable circumstances and through no causal intent of the characters involved. The prerequisite of this plot consists of characters with a previous relationship and the intersection (the *coincidental encounter*) between those characters in the fictional world. However, the narrative center of the coincidence plot is the characters' *recognition* of each other's identity.

transworld identity: Readers perform complex acts of *identification* and *differentiation* between characters and their counterparts or different versions in alternate worlds using input spaces either from real-world history or, in the case of intertextual character recycling, from other fictional worlds.

upward counterfactual: The postulation of a world that is an improvement on the factual world.

Works Cited

Primary Sources

Ackroyd, Peter. 1993 [1987]. *Chatterton*. Harmondsworth: Penguin.
———. 1997 [1996]. *Milton in America*. London: Vintage.
Aldiss, Brian G. 1976. *The Malacia Tapestry*. London: Jonathan Cape.
Allen, Woody. 1980 [1977]. "The Kugelmass Episode." In *Side Effects*, 41–55. New York: Random House.
Amis, Kingsley. 1976. *The Alteration*. London: Jonathan Cape.
Annals of the Twenty-ninth Century; or, The Autobiography of the Tenth President of the World-Republic. 1874. 3 vols. London: Samuel Tinsley.
Asimov, Isaac. 1959 [1955]. *The End of Eternity*. St. Albans: Panther.
Austen, Jane. 1966 [1814]. *Mansfield Park*. Harmondsworth: Penguin.
———. 1965 [1818]. *Persuasion*. Harmondsworth: Penguin.
———. 1969 [1811]. *Sense and Sensibility*. Harmondsworth: Penguin.
———. 1972 [1813]. *Pride and Prejudice*. Harmondsworth: Penguin.
———. 2005. *Emma*. Cambridge: Cambridge University Press.
Auster, Paul. 1990 [1989]. *Moon Palace*. London: Faber and Faber.
Back to the Future. 1985. Directed by Robert Zemeckis. Universal.
Back to the Future II. 1989. Directed by Robert Zemeckis. Universal.
Barnes, Julian. 1985 [1984]. *Flaubert's Parrot*. London: Picador.
———. 1992 [1991]. *Talking It Over*. London: Picador.
Barth, John. 1967 [1960]. *The Sot-Weed Factor*. Rev. ed. Garden City: Doubleday.
Bayley, Barrington J. 1989 [1974]. *The Fall of Chronopolis*. In *The Fall of Chronopolis* and *Collision with Chronos*, 7–204. London: Pan.
Behn, Aphra. 1998 [1688]. *Oroonoko, or, The Royal Slave: A True History*. In *Oroonoko and Other Writings*, 3–73. Oxford: Oxford University Press.

Bellamy, Edward. 1966 [1888]. *Looking Backward, 2000–1887*. Boston: Houghton Mifflin.
Benford, Gregory. 1982 [1980]. *Timescape*. London: Sphere.
Borges, Jorge Luis. 1970 [1941, in Spanish as "El jardín de senderos que se bifurcan"]. "The Garden of Forking Paths." In *Labyrinths*, 44–54. Harmondsworth: Penguin.
Boyd, John. 1972 [1968]. *The Last Starship from Earth*. London: Pan.
Bradbury, Malcolm. 1987 [1976]. "Composition." In *Who Do You Think You Are?* 121–46. London: Secker & Warburg.
Bradbury, Ray. 1953. "A Sound of Thunder." In *The Golden Apples of the Sun*, 100–113. London: Rupert Hart-Davis.
Brontë, Charlotte. 1966 [1847]. *Jane Eyre*. Harmondsworth: Penguin.
———. 1979 [1853]. *Villette*. Harmondsworth: Penguin.
Brunner, John. 1974 [1962, 1969, revised and expanded ed.]. *Times without Number*. Leeds: Elmfield Press.
The Butterfly Effect. 2004. Directed by Eric Bress and J. Mackye Gruber. Benderspink.
Byatt, A. S. 1990. *Possession*. New York: Vintage.
Chesney, George. 1871. *The Battle of Dorking: Reminiscences of a Volunteer*. Edinburgh: Blackwood.
Chesnoff, Richard Z., Edward Klein, and Robert Littel. 1969 [1968]. *If Israel Lost the War*. New York: Coward-McCann.
Collins, Wilkie. 1982 [1859–60]. *The Woman in White*. Harmondsworth: Penguin.
Congreve, William. 1991 [1692]. *Incognita*. In *An Anthology of Seventeenth-Century Fiction*, edited by Paul Salzman, 471–525. Oxford: Oxford University Press.
Conrad, Joseph. 1974 [1913]. *Chance*. Harmondsworth: Penguin.
Coover, Robert. 1970. "The Babysitter." *Pricksongs and Descants*, 206–39. New York: New American Library.
De Camp, L. Sprague. 1955 [1939]. *Lest Darkness Fall*. Melbourne: William Heinemann.
———. 1970 [1940]. "The Wheels of If." In *The Wheels of If*, 5–86. New York: Berkley.
Defoe, Daniel. 1965 [1719]. *Robinson Crusoe*. Harmondsworth: Penguin.
———. 1978 [1722]. *Moll Flanders*. Harmondsworth: Penguin.
DeLillo, Don. 1991 [1988]. *Libra*. Harmondsworth: Penguin.
Deloney, Thomas. 1987 [ca. 1597]. *Jack of Newbury*. In Salzman 1987, 311–92.
Dent, Guy. 1926. *Emperor of the If*. London: Heinemann.
Dick, Philip K. 1965 [1962]. *The Man in the High Castle*. Harmondsworth: Penguin.

———. 1989 [1957]. *Eye in the Sky*. New York: Collier.
———. 1996a [1974]. *Flow My Tears, the Policeman Said*. London: HarperCollins.
———. 1996b [1975]. *Now Wait for Last Year*. London: HarperCollins.
Dickens, Charles. 1964 [1843]. *A Christmas Carol*. In *A Christmas Carol and Other Christmas Books*, 5–82. London: Dent.
———. 1965 [1861]. *Great Expectations*. Harmondsworth: Penguin.
———. 1968 [1843–44]. *Martin Chuzzlewit*. Harmondsworth: Penguin.
———. 1970 [1837–38]. *Oliver Twist*. London: Oxford University Press.
———. 1971 [1853]. *Bleak House*. Harmondsworth: Penguin.
Disraeli, Benjamin. 1980 [1845]. *Sybil*. Harmondsworth: Penguin.
Donnie Darko. 2001. Directed by Richard Kelly. Metrodome.
Drabble, Margaret. 1977 [1975]. *The Realms of Gold*. Harmondsworth: Penguin.
Eliot, George. 1965 [1871–72]. *Middlemarch*. Harmondsworth: Penguin.
———. 1967 [1876]. *Daniel Deronda*. Harmondsworth: Penguin.
Evans, Christopher. 1994 [1993]. *Aztec Century*. London: Gollancz.
The Family Man. 2000. Directed by Brett Ratner. Universal.
Fielding, Henry. 1966 [1749]. *The History of Tom Jones*. Harmondsworth: Penguin.
———. 1977 [1742]. *Joseph Andrews*. Harmondsworth: Penguin.
Flaubert, Gustave. 1979 [1857]. *Madame Bovary*. Paris: Flammarion.
Ford, Ford Madox. 1946 [1915]. *The Good Soldier: A Tale of Passion*. Harmondsworth: Penguin.
Forster, E. M. 1978 [1908]. *A Room with a View*. Harmondsworth: Penguin.
Fowles, John. 1977 [1969]. *The French Lieutenant's Woman*. N.p.: Triad/Granada.
Frost, Robert. 1969 [1916]. "The Road Not Taken." In *The Poetry of Robert Frost*, edited by Edward Connery Lathem, 105. New York: Holt, Rinehart and Winston.
Fry, Stephen. 1997 [1996]. *Making History*. London: Arrow.
Fuentes, Carlos. 1975. *Terra Nostra*. Barcelona: Editorial Seix Barral.
Geoffroy, Louis. 1983 [1836]. *Napoléon et la conquête du monde 1812–1832: Histoire de la monarchie universelle (Napoléon apocryphe)*. Paris: Tallandier.
Gibson, William, and Bruce Sterling. 1992 [1990]. *The Difference Engine*. London: Gollancz.
Gide, André. 1947 [1932]. *Oedipe*. In *Le théâtre complet de André Gide*, 57–111. Neuchâtel: Ides et Calendes.
Greene, Robert. 1987 [1588]. *Pandosto: The Triumph of Time*. In Salzman 1987, 151–204.

Groundhog Day. 1993. Directed by Harold Ramis. Columbia Tristar.
Hale, Edward Everett. 1910 [1881]. "Hands Off!" In *In His Name and Christmas Stories*, 317–37. Vol. 2 of *The Works of Edmund Everett Hale*. Boston: Little, Brown and Co.
Hardy, Thomas. 1974a [1886]. *The Mayor of Casterbridge*. London: Macmillan.
———. 1974b [1878]. *The Return of the Native*. London: Macmillan.
———. 1978 [1891]. *Tess of the d'Urbervilles*. Harmondsworth: Penguin.
Harris, Robert. 1993 [1992]. *Fatherland*. London: Arrow.
Harrison, Harry. 1984. *West of Eden*. London: Granada.
Hawthorne, Nathaniel. 1903 [1845]. "P.'s Correspondence." In *Mosses from an Old Manse*, vol. 2, 166–94. Boston: Houghton Mifflin.
Henry, O. 1922 [1903]. "Roads of Destiny." In *Roads of Destiny*, 3–28. N.p.: Doubleday, Page and Co.
"Inferno." *Doctor Who*. 1970. Directed by Douglas Camfield. BBC Television, seven episodes.
It Happened Here. 1964. Directed by Kevin Brownlow and Andrew Mollo. United Artists.
It's a Wonderful Life. 1946. Directed by Frank Capra. RKO.
James, Henry. 1969. *The Turn of the Screw and Other Stories*. Harmondsworth: Penguin.
———. 1984 [1908]. "The Jolly Corner." In *Tales of Henry James*, edited by Christof Wegelin, 313–40. New York: Norton.
Johnson, B. S. 1973. "Broad Thoughts from a Home." In *Aren't You Rather Young to Be Writing Your Memoirs?* 91–110. London: Hutchinson.
Joyce, James. 1960 [1914–15]. *A Portrait of the Artist as a Young Man*. Harmondsworth: Penguin.
———. 1986 [1922]. *Ulysses*. London: Bodley Head.
Joyce, Michael. 2001 [1987]. *Afternoon, a Story*. Watertown MA: Eastgate Systems.
Lawrence, Edmund. 1899. *It May Happen Yet: A Tale of Bonaparte's Invasion of England*. London: Published by the author.
Le Guin, Ursula K. 1974 [1971]. *The Lathe of Heaven*. London: Panther/Granada.
Leiber, Fritz. 1976 [1958]. *The Big Time*. Boston: Gregg Press.
Leinster, Murray. 1974 [1934]. "Sidewise in Time." In *Before the Golden Age: A Science Fiction Anthology of the 1930s*, edited by Isaac Asimov, 537–83. London: Robson Books.
Lennox, Charlotte. 1970 [1752]. *The Female Quixote*. London: Oxford University Press.
Lewis, Matthew G. 1959 [1796]. *The Monk*. New York: Grove Press.

Lodge, David. 1985 [1984]. *Small World: An Academic Romance.* Harmondsworth: Penguin.
Lodge, Thomas. 1971 [1590]. *Rosalynde, or Euphues' Golden Legacy.* New York: Duffield.
McAuley, Paul J. 1995 [1994]. *Pasquale's Angel.* London: Gollancz.
Mann, Phillip. 1994 [1993]. *Escape to the Wild Wood.* Vol. 1 of *A Land Fit for Heroes.* London: Gollancz.
"Mirror Mirror." *Star Trek.* 1967. Directed by Marc Daniels. CBS.
Moore, Ward. 1953. *Bring the Jubilee.* New York: Farrar, Straus and Young.
Nabokov, Vladimir. 1971 [1969]. *Ada or Ardor: A Family Chronicle.* Harmondsworth: Penguin.
Nashe, Thomas. 1987 [1594]. *The Unfortunate Traveller.* In Salzman 1987, 205–309.
Orwell, George. 1954 [1949]. *Nineteen Eighty-Four.* Harmondsworth: Penguin.
The Philadelphia Experiment 2. 1993. Directed by Stephen Cornwell. Trimark.
Prawer Jhabvala, Ruth. 1994 [1975]. *Heat and Dust.* Harmondsworth: Penguin.
Radcliffe, Ann. 1986 [1791]. *The Romance of the Forest.* Oxford: Oxford University Press.
Renouvier, Charles. 1988 [1857, 1876]. *Uchronie (l'utopie dans l'histoire): Esquisse historique apocryphe du développement de la civilisation européenne tel qu'il n'a pas été, tel qu'il aurait pu être.* N.p.: Fayard.
Richardson, Samuel. 1980 [1740]. *Pamela, or Virtue Rewarded.* Harmondsworth: Penguin.
———. 1985 [1747–48]. *Clarissa, or the History of a Young Lady.* Harmondsworth: Penguin.
Robbe-Grillet, Alain. 1965. *La maison de rendez-vous.* Paris: Éditions de Minuit.
Roberts, Keith. 1995 [1966]. *Pavane.* London: Gollancz.
Roth, Philip. 1989 [1986]. *The Counterlife.* Harmondsworth: Penguin.
———. 2005 [2004]. *The Plot against America.* New York: Vintage.
Rushdie, Salman. 1982 [1981]. *Midnight's Children.* London: Picador.
———. 1984 [1983]. *Shame.* London: Picador.
Russ, Joanna. 1985 [1975]. *The Female Man.* London: Women's Press.
Sachar, Louis. 2000 [1998]. *Holes.* London: Bloomsbury.
Salzman, Paul, ed. 1987. *An Anthology of Elizabethan Prose Fiction.* Oxford: Oxford University Press.
Scott, Sir Walter. 1991 [1819]. *The Bride of Lammermoor.* Oxford: Oxford University Press.

Shakespeare, William. 1963 [1611]. *The Winter's Tale*. London: Methuen.
———. 1975a [1599]. *As You Like It*. London: Methuen.
———. 1975b [ca. 1601]. *Twelfth Night*. London: Methuen.
———. 1979 [ca. 1595]. *A Midsummer Night's Dream*. London: Methuen.
———. 1980 [ca. 1595]. *Romeo and Juliet*. London: Methuen.
Sidney, Sir Philip. 1987 [1590]. *The Countess of Pembroke's Arcadia (The New Arcadia)*. Oxford: Clarendon Press.
———. 1994 [ca. 1580]. *The Countess of Pembroke's Arcadia (The Old Arcadia)*. Oxford: Oxford University Press.
Sliding Doors. 1998. Directed by Peter Howitt. Paramount.
Smollett, Tobias. 1981 [1748]. *Roderick Random*. Oxford: Clarendon Press.
Sophocles. 1984. *The Three Theban Plays: Antigone, Oedipus the King, Oedipus at Colonus*, translated by Robert Fagles. Harmondsworth: Penguin.
Sterne, Laurence. 1967 [1759–67]. *The Life and Opinions of Tristram Shandy*. Harmondsworth: Penguin.
The Tale of Gamelyn. 1884 [ca. 1370]. Oxford: Clarendon Press.
The Terminator. 1984. Directed by James Cameron. Orion.
Terminator 2: Judgment Day. 1991. Directed by James Cameron. Guild/Carolco.
Terminator 3: Rise of the Machines. 2003. Directed by Jonathan Mostow. Warner.
Thackeray, William Makepeace. 1968 [1848]. *Vanity Fair*. Harmondsworth: Penguin.
Trollope, Anthony. 1995 [1857]. *Barchester Towers*. London: Trollope Society.
Twain, Mark. 1971 [1889]. *A Connecticut Yankee at King Arthur's Court*. Harmondsworth, Penguin.
Wells, H. G. 1958. "The Time Machine" [1894–95], "The Man Who Could Work Miracles" [1898]. In *Selected Short Stories*, 7–83, 299–315. Harmondsworth: Penguin.
Whitbourn, John. 1993 [1992]. *A Dangerous Energy*. London: Victor Gollancz.
Wilde, Oscar. 1954 [1895]. *The Importance of Being Earnest*. In *Plays*, 247–313. Harmondsworth: Penguin.
Williamson, Jack. 1952 [1938]. *The Legion of Time*. Reading, Pennsylvania: Fantasy Press.
Winterson, Jeanette. 1996 [1987]. *The Passion*. London: Vintage.
Woolf, Virginia. 1992 [1925]. *Mrs Dalloway*. Harmondsworth: Penguin.
Wyndham, John. 1959 [1956]. "Opposite Number." In *The Seeds of Time*, 121–39. Harmondsworth: Penguin.
———. 1965 [1961]. "Random Quest." In *Consider Her Ways and Others*, 131–73. Harmondsworth: Penguin.

Secondary Sources

Abbott, H. Porter. 2000. "The Evolutionary Origins of the Storied Mind: Modeling the Prehistory of Narrative Consciousness and Its Discontents." *Narrative* 8 (3): 247–56.

———. 2002. *The Cambridge Introduction to Narrative*. Cambridge: Cambridge University Press.

Abel, Elizabeth. 1983. "Narrative Structure(s) and Female Development: The Case of *Mrs Dalloway*." In *The Voyage In: Fictions of Female Development*, edited by Elizabeth Abel, Marianne Hirsch, and Elizabeth Langland, 161–85. Hanover: University Press of New England.

Ackerley, Chris. 1997. "'Well, of course, if we knew all the things': Coincidence and Design in *Ulysses* and *Under the Volcano*." In *Joyce/Lowry: Critical Perspectives*, edited by Patrick A. McCarthy and Paul Tiessen, 41–62. Lexington: University Press of Kentucky.

Aczel, Richard. 1998. "Hearing Voices in Narrative Texts." *New Literary History* 29:467–500.

Adams, Jon-K. 1994. "Science Fiction in Pursuit of History." In Engler and Müller 1994, 147–61.

———. 1996. *Narrative Explanation: A Pragmatic Theory of Discourse*. Frankfurt: Lang.

Adams, Robert Merrihew. 1979. "Theories of Actuality." In Loux 1979, 190–209.

Alkon, Paul. 1994. "Alternate History and Postmodern Temporality." In *Time, Literature and the Arts. Essays in Honor of Samuel L. Macey*, edited by Thomas R. Cleary, 65–85. Victoria BC: University of Victoria.

Allén, Sture, ed. 1989. *Possible Worlds in Humanities, Arts and Sciences: Proceedings of Nobel Symposium 65*. Berlin: de Gruyter.

Aristotle. 1987. *"Poetics" I with the "Tractatus Coislinianus": A Hypothetical Reconstruction of "Poetics" II; the Fragments of the "On Poets,"* translated by Richard Janko. Indianapolis: Hackett Publishing.

———. 1996. *Poetics,* translated by Malcolm Heath. Harmondsworth: Penguin.

Ashline, William L. 1995. "The Problem of Impossible Fictions." *Style* 29 (2): 215–34.

Bakhtin, Mikhail. 1981. *The Dialogic Imagination*, edited by Michael Holquist. Austin: University of Texas Press.

Barth, John. 1977 [1967]. "The Literature of Exhaustion." In *The Novel Today: Contemporary Writers on Modern Fiction*, edited by Malcolm Bradbury, 70–83. Manchester: Manchester University Press.

———. 1996 [1980]. "The Literature of Replenishment: Postmodernist Fiction." In *Essentials of the Theory of Fiction*, edited by Michael J. Hoffman and Patrick D. Murphy, 273–86. London: Leicester University Press.

Barthes, Roland. 1966. "Introduction à l'analyse structurale des récits." *Communications* 8:1–27.

———. 1968. "L'effet de réel." *Communications* 11:84–89.

Baudrillard, Jean. 1988 [1981]. "Simulacra and Simulations," translated by Paul Foss, Paul Patton, and Philip Beitchman. In *Selected Writings*, edited by Mark Poster, 166–84. Cambridge: Polity Press.

Beer, Gillian. 1983. *Darwin's Plots: Evolutionary Narrative in Darwin, George Eliot and Nineteenth-Century Fiction*. London: Routledge & Kegan Paul.

Bell, David F. 1993. *Circumstances: Chance in the Literary Text*. Lincoln: University of Nebraska Press.

Beyer, Manfred. 1976. "Zufall und Fügung im Romanwerk von Charles Dickens." Dissertation, University of Düsseldorf.

Bhabha, Homi K. 1994. *The Location of Culture*. London: Routledge.

Biard, J.-D. 1988. "Chance Encounters as a Novelistic Device." *Journal of European Studies* 18:21–35.

Boheemen, Christine van. 1982. "The Semiotics of Plot: Toward a Typology of Fictions." *Poetics Today* 3 (4): 89–96.

Bolter, Jay David. 1991. *Writing Space: The Computer, Hypertext and the History of Writing*. Hillsdale NJ: Erlbaum.

Bonheim, Helmut. 1993. "Defining the Novel: Congreve's *Incognita*." In *Tales and "their telling difference": Zur Theorie und Geschichte der Narrativik. Festschrift zum 70. Geburtstag von Franz K. Stanzel*, edited by Herbert Foltinek, Wolfgang Riehle, and Waldemar Zacharasiewicz, 165–82. Heidelberg: Winter.

Booth, Wayne. 1991 [1961]. *The Rhetoric of Fiction*. 2nd ed. Harmondsworth: Penguin.

Bordwell, David. 1985. *Narration in the Fiction Film*. Madison: University of Wisconsin Press.

Bremond, Claude. 1970. "Morphology of the French Folktale." *Semiotica* 2:247–76.

———. 1980 [1966]. "The Logic of Narrative Possibilities." *New Literary History* 11:387–411.

Breslauer, George W. 1996. "Counterfactual Reasoning in Western Studies of Soviet Politics and Foreign Relations." In Tetlock and Belkin 1996a, 71–94.

Brewer, William F. 1996. "The Nature of Narrative Suspense and the Problem of Rereading." In Vorderer, Wulff, and Friedrichsen 1996, 107–27.
Brooks, Neil. 1999. "Interred Textuality: *The Good Soldier* and *Flaubert's Parrot.*" *Critique* 41 (1): 45–51.
Brooks, Peter. 1992 [1984]. *Reading for the Plot: Design and Intention in Narrative*. Cambridge MA: Harvard University Press.
Brown, James M. 1982. *Dickens: Novelist in the Market-Place*. London: Macmillan.
Brown, Laura. 1987. "The Romance of Empire: *Oroonoko* and the Trade in Slaves." In *The New Eighteenth Century: Theory, Politics, English Literature*, edited by Felicity Nussbaum and Laura Brown, 41–61. New York: Methuen.
Bueler, Lois E. 2001. *The Tested Woman Plot: Women's Choices, Men's Judgments, and the Shaping of Stories*. Columbus: Ohio State University Press.
Burkhardt, Charles. 1983 [1963]. "Conrad the Victorian." In *Englische Literatur zwischen Viktorianismus und Moderne*, edited by Paul Goetsch, 281–92. Darmstadt: Wissenschaftliche Buchgesellschaft.
Carroll, Noël. 1996. "The Paradox of Suspense." In Vorderer, Wulff, and Friedrichsen 1996, 71–91.
Caserio, Robert L. 1979. *Plot, Story, and the Novel: From Dickens and Poe to the Modern Period*. Princeton NJ: Princeton University Press.
———. 1999. *The Novel in England, 1900–1950: History and Theory*. New York: Twayne.
Cave, Terence. 1988. *Recognition: A Study in Poetics*. Oxford: Clarendon Press.
Cervetti, Nancy. 1998. *Scenes of Reading: Transforming Romance in Brontë, Eliot, and Woolf*. New York: Lang.
Chambers, Ross. 1984. *Story and Situation: Narrative Seduction and the Power of Fiction*. Minneapolis: University of Minnesota Press.
Chase, Cynthia. 1978. "The Decomposition of the Elephants: Double-Reading *Daniel Deronda.*" PMLA 93 (2): 215–27.
Chatman, Seymour. 1978. *Story and Discourse: Narrative Structure in Fiction and Film*. Ithaca NY: Cornell University Press.
Churchill, Winston S. 1932 [1931]. "If Lee Had Not Won the Battle of Gettysburg." In Squire 1932, 173–96.
Clayton, Jay. 1989. "Narrative and Theories of Desire." *Critical Inquiry* 16 (1): 33–53.
Clute, John, and John Grant, eds. 1997. *The Encyclopedia of Fantasy*. London: Orbit.
Clute, John, and Peter Nicholls, eds. 1993. *The Encyclopedia of Science Fiction*. London: Orbit.

Cohn, Dorrit. 1978. *Transparent Minds: Narrative Modes for Presenting Consciousness in Fiction.* Princeton NJ: Princeton University Press.
Coleridge, Samuel Taylor. 1975 [1817]. *Biographia Literaria.* London: Dent.
Collins, William J. 1986. "Hank Morgan in the Garden of Forking Paths: *A Connecticut Yankee in King Arthur's Court* as Alternative History." *Modern Fiction Studies* 32 (1): 109–14.
Cowley, Robert, ed. 2001 [1999]. *What If? Military Historians Imagine What Might Have Been.* London: Pan.
Craik, W. A. 1968. *The Brontë Novels.* London: Methuen.
Crane, R. S. 1952. "The Concept of Plot and the Plot of *Tom Jones*." In *Critics and Criticism*, edited by R. S. Crane, 616–47. Chicago: University of Chicago Press.
Crowder, Diane Griffin. 1993. "Separatism and Feminist Utopian Fiction." In *Sexual Practice/Textual Theory: Lesbian Cultural Criticism*, edited by Susan J. Wolfe and Julia Penelope, 237–50. Cambridge MA: Blackwell.
Culler, Jonathan. 1975. *Structuralist Poetics: Structuralism, Linguistics and the Study of Literature.* London: Routledge & Kegan Paul.
———. 1981. *The Pursuit of Signs: Semiotics, Literature, Deconstruction.* Ithaca NY: Cornell University Press.
Damrosch, Jr., Leopold. 1985. *God's Plot and Man's Stories: Studies in the Fictional Imagination from Milton to Fielding.* Chicago: University of Chicago Press.
Dannenberg, Hilary P. 1995a. "Die Entwicklung von Theorien der Erzählstruktur und des Plot-Begriffs." In *Literaturwissenschaftliche Theorien, Modelle und Methoden: Eine Einführung*, edited by Ansgar Nünning, 51–68. Trier: WVT.
———. 1995b. "Story and Character Patterning in Jane Austen's Plots." *Sprachkunst* 26:75–104.
———. 1998a. "Doorways to Anywhere vs. Repetitive Hierarchy: The Multiple-World Structure of C. S. Lewis's Narnian Universe." *Inklings—Jahrbuch für Literatur und Ästhetik* 16:138–63.
———. 1998b. "Hypertextuality and Multiple World Construction in English and American Narrative Fiction." In *Bildschirmfiktionen: Interferenzen zwischen Literatur und neuen Medien*, edited by Julika Griem, 265–94. Tübingen: Narr.
———. 1998c. "Virtuality in Narrative Fiction." *diss.sense*, http://www.diss.sense.uni-konstanz.de/virtualitaet/dannenberg.htm. Accessed October 7, 2007.
———. 2000a. "Divergent Plot Patterns in Narrative Fiction from Sir Philip Sidney to Peter Ackroyd." In Reitz and Rieuwerts 2000, 415–27.

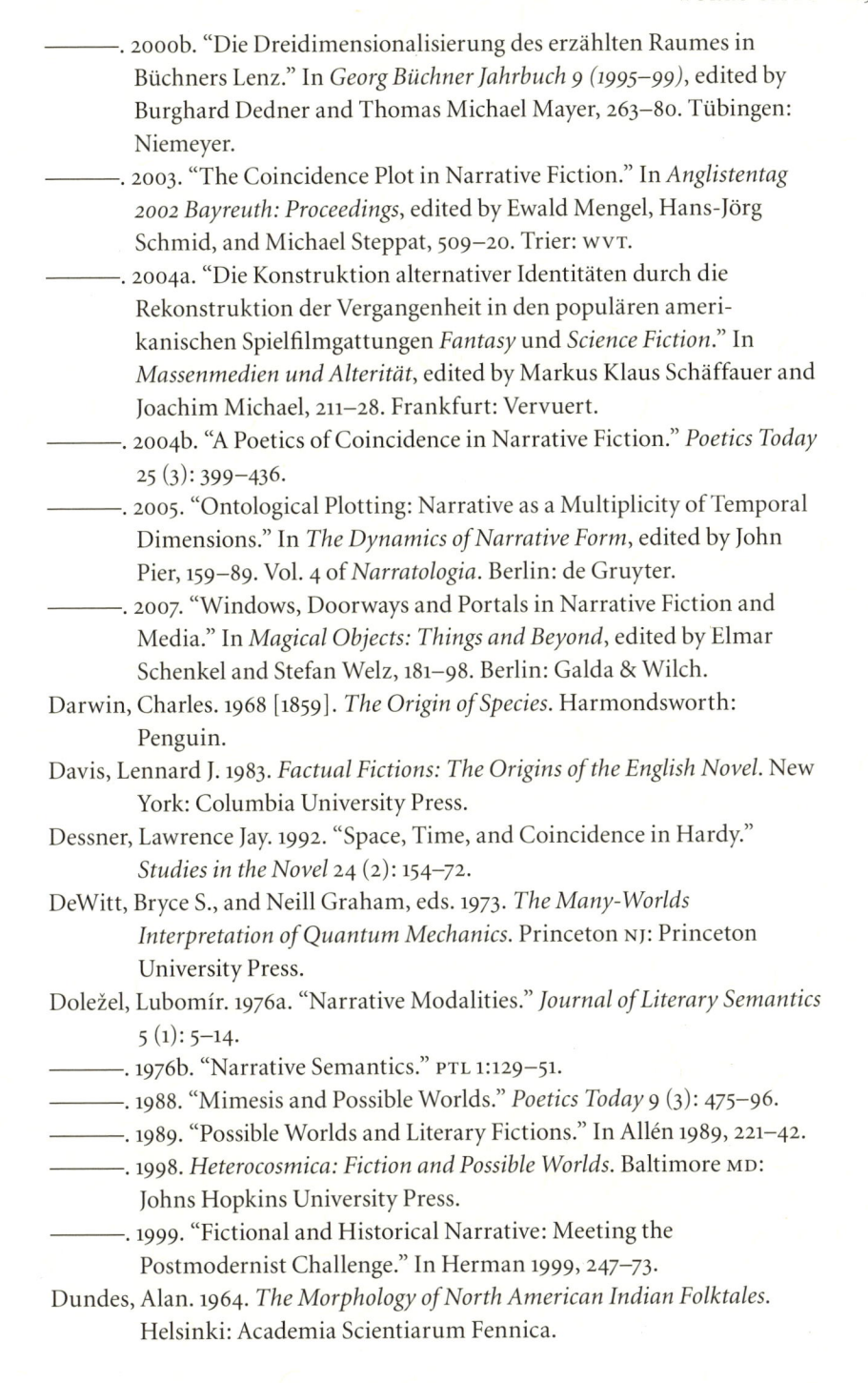

———. 2000b. "Die Dreidimensionalisierung des erzählten Raumes in Büchners Lenz." In *Georg Büchner Jahrbuch 9 (1995–99)*, edited by Burghard Dedner and Thomas Michael Mayer, 263–80. Tübingen: Niemeyer.

———. 2003. "The Coincidence Plot in Narrative Fiction." In *Anglistentag 2002 Bayreuth: Proceedings*, edited by Ewald Mengel, Hans-Jörg Schmid, and Michael Steppat, 509–20. Trier: WVT.

———. 2004a. "Die Konstruktion alternativer Identitäten durch die Rekonstruktion der Vergangenheit in den populären amerikanischen Spielfilmgattungen *Fantasy* und *Science Fiction*." In *Massenmedien und Alterität*, edited by Markus Klaus Schäffauer and Joachim Michael, 211–28. Frankfurt: Vervuert.

———. 2004b. "A Poetics of Coincidence in Narrative Fiction." *Poetics Today* 25 (3): 399–436.

———. 2005. "Ontological Plotting: Narrative as a Multiplicity of Temporal Dimensions." In *The Dynamics of Narrative Form*, edited by John Pier, 159–89. Vol. 4 of *Narratologia*. Berlin: de Gruyter.

———. 2007. "Windows, Doorways and Portals in Narrative Fiction and Media." In *Magical Objects: Things and Beyond*, edited by Elmar Schenkel and Stefan Welz, 181–98. Berlin: Galda & Wilch.

Darwin, Charles. 1968 [1859]. *The Origin of Species*. Harmondsworth: Penguin.

Davis, Lennard J. 1983. *Factual Fictions: The Origins of the English Novel*. New York: Columbia University Press.

Dessner, Lawrence Jay. 1992. "Space, Time, and Coincidence in Hardy." *Studies in the Novel* 24 (2): 154–72.

DeWitt, Bryce S., and Neill Graham, eds. 1973. *The Many-Worlds Interpretation of Quantum Mechanics*. Princeton NJ: Princeton University Press.

Doležel, Lubomír. 1976a. "Narrative Modalities." *Journal of Literary Semantics* 5 (1): 5–14.

———. 1976b. "Narrative Semantics." PTL 1:129–51.

———. 1988. "Mimesis and Possible Worlds." *Poetics Today* 9 (3): 475–96.

———. 1989. "Possible Worlds and Literary Fictions." In Allén 1989, 221–42.

———. 1998. *Heterocosmica: Fiction and Possible Worlds*. Baltimore MD: Johns Hopkins University Press.

———. 1999. "Fictional and Historical Narrative: Meeting the Postmodernist Challenge." In Herman 1999, 247–73.

Dundes, Alan. 1964. *The Morphology of North American Indian Folktales*. Helsinki: Academia Scientiarum Fennica.

Dunning, David, and Scott F. Madey. 1995. "Comparison Processes in Counterfactual Thought." In Roese and Olson 1995c, 103–31.
DuPlessis, Rachel Blau. 1985. *Writing beyond the Ending: Narrative Strategies of Twentieth-Century Women Writers.* Bloomington: Indiana University Press.
Eco, Umberto. 1976. *A Theory of Semiotics.* Bloomington: Indiana University Press.
———. 1981 [1979]. *The Role of the Reader: Explorations in the Semiotics of Texts.* London: Hutchinson.
———. 1989. "Report on Session 3: Literature and Arts." In Allén 1989, 343–55.
Eitner, Lorenz. 1955. "The Open Window and the Storm-Tossed Boat, an Essay in the Iconography of Romanticism." *Art Bulletin* 37:281–90.
Elliott, Albert Pettigrew. 1966. *Fatalism in the Works of Thomas Hardy.* New York: Russell & Russell.
Engler, Bernd, and Kurt Müller, eds. 1994. *Historiographic Metafiction in Modern American and Canadian Literature.* Paderborn: Schöningh.
Everett, Hugh. 1957. "'Relative State' Formulation of Quantum Mechanics." *Reviews of Modern Physics* 29 (3): 454–62.
Fauconnier, Gilles, and Mark Turner. 1998a. "Conceptual Integration in Counterfactuals." In Koenig 1998, 285–96.
———. 1998b. "Principles of Conceptual Integration." In Koenig 1998, 269–83.
———. 2003 [2002]. *The Way We Think: Conceptual Blending and the Mind's Hidden Complexities.* New York: Basic Books.
Fearon, James D. 1996. "Causes and Counterfactuals in Social Science: Exploring an Analogy between Cellular Automata and Historical Processes." In Tetlock and Belkin 1996a, 39–67.
Ferguson, Niall, ed. 1997. *Virtual History: Alternatives and Counterfactuals.* London: Picador.
Fischer, David Hackett. 1970. *Historians' Fallacies: Toward a Logic of Historical Thought.* New York: Harper & Row.
Flammarion, Camille. 1905 [1900, in French as *L'inconnu*]. *The Unknown.* New York: Harper.
Fludernik, Monika. 1993. *The Fictions of Language and the Languages of Fiction: The Linguistic Representation of Speech and Consciousness.* London: Routledge.
———. 1994. "History and Metafiction: Experientiality, Causality and Myth." In Engler and Müller 1994, 81–101.
———. 1996a. *Towards a "Natural" Narratology.* London: Routledge.

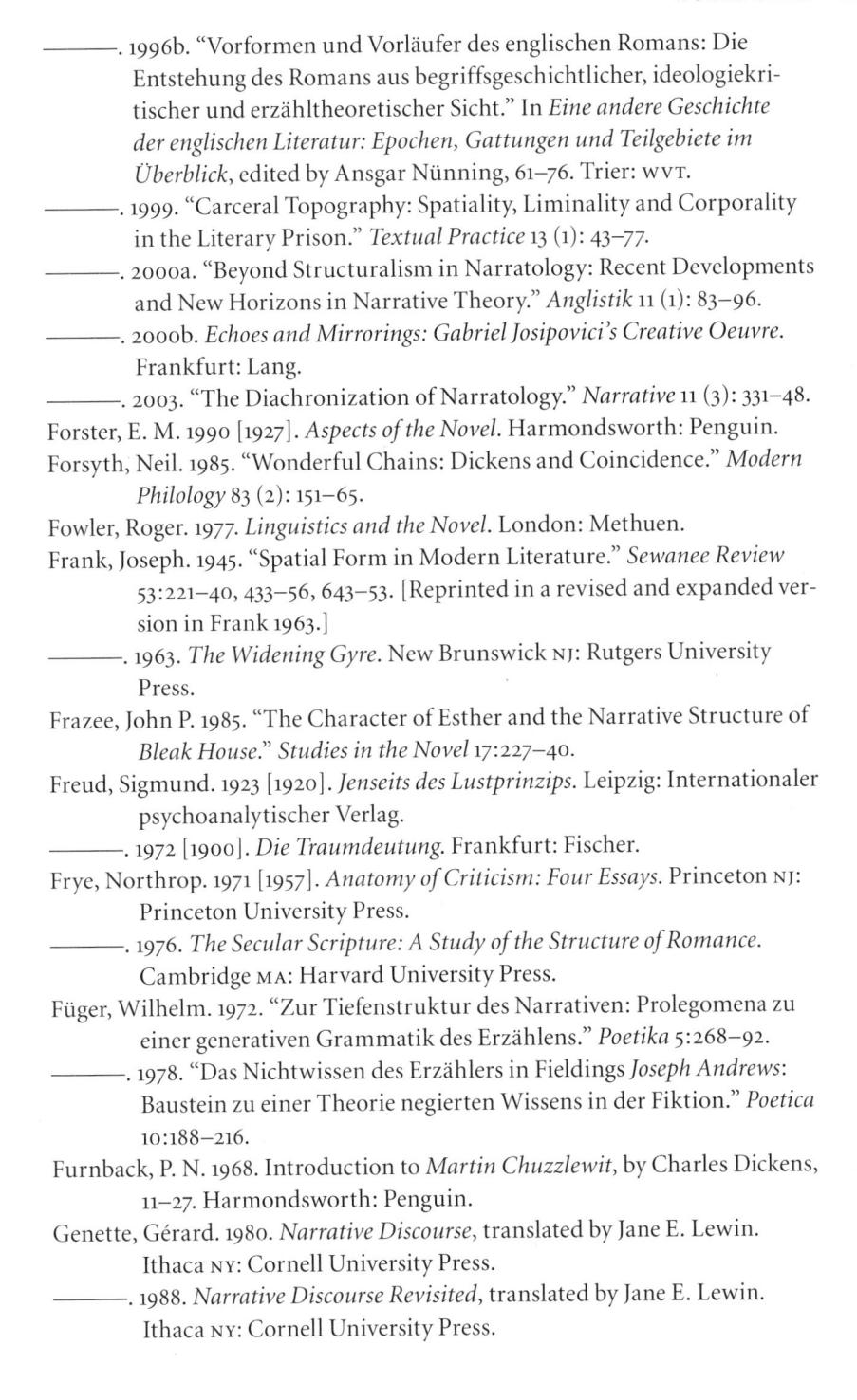

———. 1996b. "Vorformen und Vorläufer des englischen Romans: Die Entstehung des Romans aus begriffsgeschichtlicher, ideologiekritischer und erzähltheoretischer Sicht." In *Eine andere Geschichte der englischen Literatur: Epochen, Gattungen und Teilgebiete im Überblick*, edited by Ansgar Nünning, 61–76. Trier: WVT.

———. 1999. "Carceral Topography: Spatiality, Liminality and Corporality in the Literary Prison." *Textual Practice* 13 (1): 43–77.

———. 2000a. "Beyond Structuralism in Narratology: Recent Developments and New Horizons in Narrative Theory." *Anglistik* 11 (1): 83–96.

———. 2000b. *Echoes and Mirrorings: Gabriel Josipovici's Creative Oeuvre*. Frankfurt: Lang.

———. 2003. "The Diachronization of Narratology." *Narrative* 11 (3): 331–48.

Forster, E. M. 1990 [1927]. *Aspects of the Novel*. Harmondsworth: Penguin.

Forsyth, Neil. 1985. "Wonderful Chains: Dickens and Coincidence." *Modern Philology* 83 (2): 151–65.

Fowler, Roger. 1977. *Linguistics and the Novel*. London: Methuen.

Frank, Joseph. 1945. "Spatial Form in Modern Literature." *Sewanee Review* 53:221–40, 433–56, 643–53. [Reprinted in a revised and expanded version in Frank 1963.]

———. 1963. *The Widening Gyre*. New Brunswick NJ: Rutgers University Press.

Frazee, John P. 1985. "The Character of Esther and the Narrative Structure of *Bleak House*." *Studies in the Novel* 17:227–40.

Freud, Sigmund. 1923 [1920]. *Jenseits des Lustprinzips*. Leipzig: Internationaler psychoanalytischer Verlag.

———. 1972 [1900]. *Die Traumdeutung*. Frankfurt: Fischer.

Frye, Northrop. 1971 [1957]. *Anatomy of Criticism: Four Essays*. Princeton NJ: Princeton University Press.

———. 1976. *The Secular Scripture: A Study of the Structure of Romance*. Cambridge MA: Harvard University Press.

Füger, Wilhelm. 1972. "Zur Tiefenstruktur des Narrativen: Prolegomena zu einer generativen Grammatik des Erzählens." *Poetika* 5:268–92.

———. 1978. "Das Nichtwissen des Erzählers in Fieldings *Joseph Andrews*: Baustein zu einer Theorie negierten Wissens in der Fiktion." *Poetica* 10:188–216.

Furnback, P. N. 1968. Introduction to *Martin Chuzzlewit*, by Charles Dickens, 11–27. Harmondsworth: Penguin.

Genette, Gérard. 1980. *Narrative Discourse*, translated by Jane E. Lewin. Ithaca NY: Cornell University Press.

———. 1988. *Narrative Discourse Revisited*, translated by Jane E. Lewin. Ithaca NY: Cornell University Press.

Gerrig, Richard J. 1993. *Experiencing Narrative Worlds: On the Psychological Activities of Reading.* New Haven CT: Yale University Press.

———. 1996. "The Resiliency of Suspense." In Vorderer, Wulff, and Friedrichsen 1996, 93–105.

Gilbert, Sandra M., and Susan Gubar. 1984. *The Madwoman in the Attic: The Woman Writer and the Nineteenth-Century Imagination.* New Haven CT: Yale University Press.

Gilovich, Thomas, and Victoria Husted Medvec. 1994. "The Temporal Pattern to the Experience of Regret." *Journal of Personality and Social Psychology* 67 (3): 357–65.

———. 1995. "Some Counterfactual Determinants of Satisfaction and Regret." In Roese and Olson 1995c, 259–82.

Gleick, James. 1996 [1987]. *Chaos: Making a New Science.* London: Minerva.

Godzich, Wlad. 1994. *The Culture of Literacy.* Cambridge MA: Harvard University Press.

Goetsch, Paul. 1967. *Die Romankonzeption in England 1880–1910.* Heidelberg: Winter.

———. 1980. "Defoes *Moll Flanders* und der Leser." *Germanisch-romanische Monatsschrift* 30:271–88.

———. 1998. "Virtual History in Donald Barthelme's 'Cortés and Montezuma.'" In *Re-Visioning the Past: Historical Self-Reflexivity in American Short Fiction*, edited by Bernd Engler and Oliver Scheiding, 297–312. Trier: WVT.

Goldknopf, David. 1969. "Coincidence in the Victorian Novel: The Trajectory of a Narrative-Device." *College English* 31:41–50. [Reprinted with minor alterations in Goldknopf 1972, 159–76.]

———. 1972. *The Life of the Novel.* Chicago: University of Chicago Press.

Goodman, Nelson. 1947. "The Problem of Counterfactual Conditionals." *Journal of Philosophy* 44 (5): 113–28.

Greenblatt, Stephen J. 1990. *Learning to Curse: Essays in Early Modern Culture.* New York: Routledge.

Greimas, A. J. 1966. *Sémantique structurale.* Paris: Larousse.

Gribbin, John. 1991 [1984]. *In Search of Schrödinger's Cat: Quantum Physics and Reality.* London: Black Swan.

———. 1996 [1995]. *Schrödinger's Kittens and the Search for Reality.* London: Phoenix.

Grünzweig, Walter, and Andreas Solbach, eds. 1999. *Grenzüberschreitungen: Narratologie im Kontext/Transcending Boundaries: Narratology in Context.* Tübingen: Narr.

Gutenberg, Andrea. 2000. *Mögliche Welten: Plot und Sinnstiftung im englischen Frauenroman.* Heidelberg: Winter.

Haggerty, George E. 1998. *Unnatural Affections: Women and Fiction in the Later 18th Century*. Bloomington: Indiana University Press.

Hannay, John. 1983. "Coincidence and Analytic Reduction in the 'Ithaca' Episode in *Ulysses*." *Journal of Narrative Technique* 13 (3): 141–53.

———. 1988. "What Joyce's Ulysses Can Teach Us about Coincidence." *University of Dayton Review* 19 (2): 89–97.

Hardy, Alister, Robert Harvie, and Arthur Koestler. 1973. *The Challenge of Chance: Experiments and Speculations*. London: Hutchinson.

Hardy, Barbara. 1964. *The Appropriate Form: An Essay on the Novel*. London: Athlone Press/University of London.

Harrison, Harry. 1976. "Worlds beside Worlds." In *Science Fiction at Large*, edited by Peter Nicholls, 105–14. London: Gollancz.

Harvey, W. J. 1965. *Character and the Novel*. Ithaca NY: Cornell University Press.

Hayles, N. B. 1983. "Metaphysics and Metafiction in *The Man in the High Castle*." In *Philip K. Dick*, edited by Martin Harry Greenberg and Joseph D. Olander, 53–71. New York: Taplinger.

Hayles, N. Katherine, ed. 1991. *Chaos and Order: Complex Dynamics in Literature and Science*. Chicago: University of Chicago Press.

Heintz, John. 1979. "Reference and Inference in Fiction." *Poetics* 8:85–99.

Heise, Ursula K. 1997. *Chronoschisms: Time, Narrative and Postmodernism*. Cambridge: Cambridge University Press.

Helbig, Jörg. 1988. *Der parahistorische Roman: Ein literaturhistorischer und gattungstypologischer Beitrag zur Allotopieforschung*. Frankfurt: Lang.

———. 1990. *Moll Flanders als Allegorie*. Berlin: Profil.

———. 2000. "Was wäre wenn . . . : 150 Jahre parahistorische Literatur in Großbritannien und den USA." *Quarber Merkur* 91–92:95–168.

Hellekson, Karen. 2001. *The Alternate History: Refiguring Historical Time*. Kent OH: Kent State University Press.

Helms, Gabriele. 1995. "The Coincidence of Biography and Autobiography: Elizabeth Gaskell's *The Life of Charlotte Brontë*." *Biography* 18 (4): 339–59.

Herman, David. 1994. "Hypothetical Focalization." *Narrative* 2 (3): 230–53.

———. 1995. *Universal Grammar and Narrative Form*. Durham NC: Duke University Press.

———, ed. 1999. *Narratologies: New Perspectives on Narrative Analysis*. Columbus: Ohio State University Press.

———. 2002. *Story Logic: Problems and Possibilities of Narrative*. Lincoln: University of Nebraska Press.

———, ed. 2003. *Narrative Theory and the Cognitive Sciences*. Stanford CA: CSLI Publications.

Higgins, Dick. 1978. *A Dialectic of Centuries: Notes towards a Theory of the New Arts*. New York: Printed Editions.

Hirsch, Marianne. 1989. *The Mother/Daughter Plot: Narrative, Psychoanalysis, Feminism*. Bloomington: Indiana University Press.

Hoffmann, Gerhard. 1978. *Raum, Situation, erzählte Wirklichkeit: Poetologische und historische Studien zum englischen und amerikanischen Roman*. Stuttgart: Metzler.

Hogan, Patrick Colm. 2003. *The Mind and Its Stories: Narrative Universals and Human Emotion*. Cambridge: Cambridge University Press.

Homans, Margaret. 1983. "'Her Very Own Howl': The Ambiguities of Representation in Recent Women's Fiction." *Signs* 9 (1): 186–205.

Hornback, Bert G. 1971. *The Metaphor of Chance: Vision and Technique in the Works of Thomas Hardy*. Athens: Ohio University Press.

Horne, Alistair. 2001. "Ruler of the World: Napoleon's Missed Opportunities." In Cowley 2001, 201–19.

Hughes, Linda K., and Michael Lund. 1991. "Linear Stories and Circular Visions: The Decline of the Victorian Serial." In Hayles 1991, 167–94.

Hulme, Peter. 1986. *Colonial Encounters: Europe and the Native Caribbean, 1492–1797*. London: Methuen.

Hunter, J. Paul. 1990. *Before Novels: The Cultural Contexts of Eighteenth-Century English Fiction*. New York: Norton.

Huntingdon, John. 1988. "Philip K. Dick: Authenticity and Insincerity." *Science Fiction Studies* 15: 152–160.

Hutcheon, Linda. 1988. *A Poetics of Postmodernism: History, Theory, Fiction*. London: Routledge.

Ibsch, Elrud. 1982. "Historical Changes of the Function of Spatial Description in Literary Texts." *Poetics Today* 3 (4): 97–113.

Ickstadt, Heinz. 1994. "Loose Ends and Patterns of Coincidence in Don DeLillo's *Libra*." In Engler and Müller 1994, 299–312.

Inglis, Brian. 1990. *Coincidence: A Matter of Chance—or Synchronicity?* London: Hutchinson.

Iser, Wolfgang. 1972. "The Reading Process: A Phenomenological Approach." *New Literary History* 3:279–99.

Jahn, Manfred. 1996. "Windows of Focalisation: Deconstructing and Reconstructing a Narratological Concept." *Style* 30 (2): 241–67.

———. 1997. "Frames, Preferences, and the Reading of Third-Person Narratives: Towards a Cognitive Narratology." *Poetics Today* 18:441–68.

———. 1999. "'Speak, friend, and enter': Garden Paths, Artificial Intelligence, and Cognitive Narratology." In Herman 1999, 167–94.

Jahn, Manfred, and Ansgar Nünning. 1994. "A Survey of Narratological Models." *Literatur in Wissenschaft und Unterricht* 27 (4): 283–303.
Janoff-Bulman, Ronnie. 1979. "Characterological versus Behavioural Self-Blame: Inquiries into Depression and Rape." *Journal of Personality and Social Psychology* 37 (10): 1798–1809.
Jencks, Charles. 1991 [1989]. "Postmodern vs. Late-Modern." In *Zeitgeist in Babel: The Postmodernist Controversy*, edited by Ingeborg Hoesterey, 4–21. Bloomington: Indiana University Press.
Johnson, Alice. 1899. "Coincidence." In *Proceedings of the Society for Psychical Research*, vol. 14, 158–330. London: Kegan Paul, Trench, Trübner and Co.
Johnson, Mark. 1987. *The Body in the Mind: The Bodily Basis of Meaning, Imagination, and Reason*. Chicago: University of Chicago Press.
Johnson, Mark H., and John Morton. 1991. *Biology and Cognitive Development: The Case of Face Recognition*. Oxford: Blackwell.
Jones, R. T. 1970. *George Eliot*. Cambridge: Cambridge University Press.
Jung, C. G. 1967 [1952]. "Synchronizität als ein Prinzip akausaler Zusammenhänge." In *Die Dynamik des Unbewussten*, 475–591. Zurich: Rascher.
———. 1985 [1952]. *Synchronicity: An Acausal Connecting Principle*, translated by R. F. C. Hull. London: Ark.
Kafalenos, Emma. 1999. "Not (Yet) Knowing: Epistemological Effects of Deferred and Suppressed Information in Narrative." In Herman 1999, 33–65.
———. 2001. "Reading Visual Art, Making—and Forgetting—Fabulas." *Narrative* 9 (2): 138–45.
———. 2006. *Narrative Causalities*. Columbus: Ohio State University Press.
Kahneman, Daniel. 1995. "Varieties of Counterfactual Thinking." In Roese and Olson 1995c, 375–96.
Kahneman, Daniel, and Dale T. Miller. 1986. "Norm Theory: Comparing Reality to Its Alternatives." *Psychological Review* 93 (2): 136–53.
Kammerer, Paul. 1919. *Das Gesetz der Serie: Eine Lehre von den Wiederholungen im Lebens- und im Weltgeschehen*. Stuttgart: Deutsche Verlags-Anstalt.
Keen, Suzanne. 2001. *Romances of the Archive in Contemporary British Fiction*. Toronto: University of Toronto Press.
Keitel, Evelyne. 1996. *Von den Gefühlen beim Lesen: Zur Lektüre amerikanischer Gegenwartsliteratur*. Munich: Fink.
Kennard, Jean E. 1978. *Victims of Convention*. Hamden CT: Archon.
Kermode, Frank. 1967. *The Sense of an Ending: Studies in the Theory of Fiction*. London: Oxford University Press.

Kern, Stephen. 1983. *The Culture of Time and Space 1880–1918*. London: Weidenfeld and Nicolson.

Kiely, Robert. 1972. *The Romantic Novel in England*. Cambridge MA: Harvard University Press.

Kiser, Edgar, and Margaret Levi. 1996. "Using Counterfactuals in Historical Analysis: Theories of Revolution." In Tetlock and Belkin 1996a, 187–207.

Klass, Philip. 1974. "An Innocent in Time: Mark Twain in King Arthur's Court." *Extrapolation* 16:17–32.

Koenig, Jean-Pierre, ed. 1998. *Discourse and Cognition: Bridging the Gap*. Stanford CA: CSLI.

Koestler, Arthur. 1972. *The Roots of Coincidence*. London: Hutchinson.

Köhler, Erich. 1973. *Der literarische Zufall, das Mögliche und die Notwendigkeit*. Munich: Fink.

Korte, Barbara. 1985a. *Techniken der Schlußgebung im Roman: Eine Untersuchung englisch-und deutschsprachiger Romane*. Frankfurt: Lang.

———. 1985b. "Tiefen-und Oberflächenstrukturen in der Narrativik." *Literatur in Wissenschaft und Unterricht* 18 (4): 331–52.

Krämer, Walter. 1996 [1995]. *Denkste! Trugschlüsse aus der Welt des Zufalls und der Zahlen*. 2nd rev. ed. Frankfurt: Campus.

Kuehl, John. 1989. *Alternate Worlds: A Study of Postmodern Antirealistic American Fiction*. New York: New York University Press.

Kutzer, M. Daphne. 1994. "The Cartography of Passion: Cixous, Wittig and Winterson." In *Renaming the Landscape*, edited by Jürgen Kleist and Bruce A. Butterfield, 133–145. New York: Lang.

Labov, William. 1972. *Language in the Inner City: Studies in the Black English Vernacular*. Philadelphia: University of Pennsylvania Press.

Lakoff, George. 1987. *Women, Fire, and Dangerous Things: What Categories Reveal about the Mind*. Chicago: University of Chicago Press.

Lakoff, George, and Mark Johnson. 1980. *Metaphors We Live By*. Chicago: University of Chicago Press.

Lakoff, George, and Mark Turner. 1989. *More than Cool Reason: A Field Guide to Poetic Metaphor*. Chicago: University of Chicago Press.

Lämmert, Eberhard. 1991 [1955]. *Bauformen des Erzählens*. 8th ed. Stuttgart: Metzlersche Verlagsbuchhandlung.

Lanser, Susan Sniader. 1981. *The Narrative Act: Point of View in Prose and Fiction*. Princeton NJ: Princeton University Press.

———. 1992. *Fictions of Authority: Women Writers and Narrative Voice*. Ithaca NY: Cornell University Press.

Lebow, Richard Ned, and Janice Gross Stein. 1996. "Back to the Past:

Counterfactuals and the Cuban Missile Crisis." In Tetlock and Belkin 1996a, 119–48.

Le Guin, Ursula K. 1979 [1977]. "Introduction to *The Word for World Is Forest*." In *The Language of the Night: Essays on Fantasy and Science Fiction*, 149–54. New York: G. P. Putnam's Sons.

Leibniz, Gottfried Wilhelm. 1996 [1720]. *Monadologie*, edited by Dietmar Till, translated by Heinrich Köhler. Frankfurt: Insel.

Lemon, Lee T., and Marion J. Reis, eds. 1965. *Russian Formalist Criticism: Four Essays*. Lincoln: University of Nebraska Press.

Lévi-Strauss, Claude. 1963. *Structural Anthropology*, translated by Claire Jacobson. Harmondsworth: Penguin.

Lewis, David. 1973. *Counterfactuals*. Oxford: Blackwell.

———. 1979. "Possible Worlds." In Loux 1979, 182–89.

———. 1983. *Philosophical Papers*, vol. 1. New York: Oxford University Press.

———. 1986. *On the Plurality of Worlds*. Oxford: Blackwell.

Lindskoog, Kathryn. 1989. "Golden Chains of Coincidence: A C. S. Lewis Puzzle Solved and Mystery to Ponder." *Mythlore* 58:21–25.

Lodge, David. 1981. "Thomas Hardy as a Cinematic Novelist." In *Working with Structuralism: Essays and Reviews on Nineteenth-and Twentieth-Century Literature*, 95–105. London: Routledge and Kegan Paul.

———. 1992. *The Art of Fiction*. Harmondsworth: Penguin.

Loux, Michael J., ed. 1979. *The Possible and the Actual: Readings in the Metaphysics of Modality*. Ithaca NY: Cornell University Press.

Malmgren, Carl D. 1985. *Fictional Space in the Modernist and Postmodernist Novel*. Lewisburg: Bucknell University Press.

———. 1991. *Worlds Apart: Narratology of Science Fiction*. Bloomington: Indiana University Press.

Mardorf, Elisabeth. 1997. *Das kann doch kein Zufall sein: Verblüffende Ereignisse und geheimnisvolle Fügungen in unserem Leben*. Munich: Kösel.

Margolin, Uri. 1996. "Characters and Their Versions." In *Fiction Updated: Theories of Fictionality, Narratology and Poetics*, edited by Calin-Andrei Mihailescu and Walid Hamarneh, 113–32. Toronto: University of Toronto Press.

Martínez, Matías. 1996. *Doppelte Welten: Struktur und Sinn zweideutigen Erzählens*. Göttingen: Vandenhoeck & Ruprecht.

McAlindon, T. 1991. *Shakespeare's Tragic Cosmos*. Cambridge: Cambridge University Press.

McDonald, Walter R. 1968. "Coincidence in the Novel: A Necessary Technique." *College English* 29:373–88.

McHale, Brian. 1987. *Postmodernist Fiction*. New York: Methuen.
———. 1992. *Constructing Postmodernism*. London: Routledge.
McKeon, Michael. 1987. *The Origins of the English Novel, 1600–1740*. Baltimore MD: Johns Hopkins University Press.
McMullen, Matthew N., Keith D. Markman, and Igor Gavanski. 1995. "Living in neither the Best nor Worst of All Possible Worlds: Antecedents and Consequences of Upward and Downward Counterfactual Thinking." In Roese and Olson 1995c, 133–67.
Michael, Magali Cornier. 1994. "The Political Paradox within Don DeLillo's *Libra*." *Critique* 35 (3): 146–56.
Miller, D. A. 1981. *Narrative and Its Discontents: Problems of Closure in the Traditional Novel*. Princeton NJ: Princeton University Press.
Miller, Nancy K. 1980. *The Heroine's Text: Readings in the French and English Novel, 1722–1782*. New York: Columbia University Press.
———. 1985. "Emphasis Added: Plots and Plausibilities in Women's Fiction." In *The New Feminist Criticism: Essays on Women, Literature and Theory*, edited by Elaine Showalter, 339–60. New York: Pantheon Books.
Mitchell, W. J. T., ed. 1980a. *On Narrative*. Chicago: University of Chicago Press.
———. 1980b. "Spatial Form in Literature: Toward a General Theory." *Critical Inquiry* 6 (3): 539–67.
Monk, Leland. 1993. *Standard Deviations: Chance and the Modern British Novel*. Stanford CA: Stanford University Press.
Moosmüller, Birgit. 1993. *Die experimentelle englische Kurzgeschichte der Gegenwart*. Munich: Fink.
Müller, Günther. 1968 [1948]. "Erzählzeit und erzählte Zeit." In *Morphologische Poetik: Gesammelte Aufsätze*, edited by Elena Müller, 269–86. Darmstadt: Wissenschaftliche Buchgesellschaft.
Müller, Wolfgang G. 1977. "Gefühlsdarstellung bei Jane Austen." *Sprachkunst* 8:87–103.
———. 1991. "Interfigurality: A Study on the Interdependence of Literary Figures." In *Intertextuality*, edited by Heinrich F. Plett, 100–121. Berlin: de Gruyter.
Nakano, Kii. 1991. "Poe's Coincidences: An Intersection of Literature and History." *Journal of American and Canadian Studies* 7:1–21. [In Japanese with an English summary.]
Nell, Victor. 1988. *Lost in a Book: The Psychology of Reading for Pleasure*. New Haven CT: Yale University Press.
Newsom, Robert. 1988. *A Likely Story: Probability and Play in Fiction*. New Brunswick NJ: Rutgers University Press.

Nischik, Reingard M. 1981. *Einsträngigkeit und Mehrsträngigkeit der Handlungsführung in literarischen Texten*. Tübingen: Narr.

Nünning, Ansgar. 1995a. *Erscheinungsformen und Entwicklungstendenzen des historischen Romans in England seit 1950*. Vol. 2 of *Von historischer Fiktion zu historiographischer Metafiktion*. Trier: WVT.

———. 1995b. *Theorie, Typologie und Poetik des historischen Romans*. Vol. 1 of *Von historischer Fiktion zu historiographischer Metafiktion*. Trier: WVT.

———. 2000. "Towards a Cultural and Historical Narratology: A Survey of Diachronic Approaches, Concepts, and Research Projects." In Reitz and Rieuwerts 2000, 345–73.

Nussbaum, Felicity A. 1989. *The Autobiographical Subject: Gender and Ideology in Eighteenth-Century England*. Baltimore MD: Johns Hopkins University Press.

Olson, James M., Neal J. Roese, and Ronald J. Deibert. 1996. "Psychological Biases in Counterfactual Thought Experiments." In Tetlock and Belkin 1996a, 296–300.

Page, Ruth E. 2006. *Literary and Linguistic Approaches to Feminist Narratology*. Houndmills: Palgrave Macmillan.

Palmer, Alan. 2004. *Fictional Minds*. Lincoln: University of Nebraska Press.

Pascal, Blaise. 1960. *Pensées*. Paris: Garnier.

Pavel, Thomas G. 1985. *The Poetics of Plot: The Case of English Renaissance Drama*. Minneapolis: University of Minnesota Press.

Perry, Menakhem. 1979. "Literary Dynamics: How the Order of a Text Creates Its Meanings." *Poetics Today* 1 (1–2): 35–64, 311–61.

Petitjean, Tom. 1995. "Coover's 'The Babysitter.'" *Explicator* 54 (1): 49–51.

Pfister, Manfred, ed. 1982. *Alternative Welten*. Munich: Fink.

———. 2000 [1977]. *Das Drama: Theorie und Analyse*. 10th ed. Munich: Fink.

Phelan, James. 1989. *Reading People, Reading Plots: Character, Progression, and the Interpretation of Narrative*. Chicago: University of Chicago Press.

———. 1996. *Narrative as Rhetoric: Technique, Audiences, Ethics, Ideology*. Columbus: Ohio State University Press.

———. 2005. *Living to Tell about It: A Rhetoric and Ethics of Character Narration*. Ithaca NY: Cornell University Press.

Piaget, Jean. 1974. *Understanding Causality*. New York: Norton.

Pinion, F. B. 1979. "Coincidence and Consequence Relative to a Scene in *Felix Holt*." *George Eliot Fellowship Review* 10:7–9.

Pinkerton, Jan. 1979. "Backward Time Travel, Alternate Universes, and Edward Everett Hale." *Extrapolation* 20 (2): 168–75.

Preston, Elizabeth. 1996. "Relational Reconsiderations: Reliability, Heterosexuality and Narrative Authority in *Villette*." *Style* 30 (3): 386–408.
Prince, Gerald. 1973. *A Grammar of Stories*. The Hague: Mouton.
———. 1982. *Narratology*. Berlin: Mouton.
———. 1988. "The Disnarrated." *Style* 22:1–8.
———. 1992. *Narrative as Theme: Studies in French Fiction*. Lincoln: University of Nebraska Press.
———. 1999. "Revisiting Narrativity." In Grünzweig and Solbach 1999, 43–51.
Propp, Vladimir. 1968 [1928]. *Morphology of the Folktale*, translated by Laurence Scott. Austin: University of Texas Press.
Rabinowitz, Peter J. 1987. *Before Reading: Narrative Conventions and the Politics of Interpretation*. Ithaca NY: Cornell University Press.
Rabkin, Eric S. 1977. "Spatial Form and Plot." *Critical Inquiry* 4:253–70.
Reed, John R. 1975. *Victorian Conventions*. Athens: Ohio University Press.
Reeve, Clara. 1930 [1785]. *The Progress of Romance and the History of Charoba, Queen of Aegypt*. New York: Facsimile Text Society.
Reeve, N. H. 1999. "Oswald Our Contemporary: Don DeLillo's *Libra*." In *An Introduction to Contemporary Fiction: International Writing in English since 1970*, edited by Rod Mengham, 135–48. Cambridge: Polity Press.
Reitz, Bernhard, and Sigrid Rieuwerts, eds. 2000. *Anglistentag 1999 Mainz: Proceedings*. Trier: WVT.
Rescher, Nicholas. 1975. *A Theory of Possibility: A Constructivistic and Conceptualistic Account of Possible Individuals and Possible Worlds*. Oxford: Blackwell.
Richardson, Brian. 1989. "'Hours Dreadful and Things Strange': Inversions of Chronology and Causality in *Macbeth*." *Philological Quarterly* 68:283–94.
———. 1997. *Unlikely Stories: Causality and the Nature of Modern Narrative*. Newark: University of Delaware Press.
———. 2002a. "Beyond Story and Discourse: Narrative Time in Postmodern and Nonmimetic Fiction." In Richardson 2002b, 47–63.
———, ed. 2002b. *Narrative Dynamics: Essays on Time, Plot, Closure, and Frames*. Columbus: Ohio State University Press.
Ricoeur, Paul. 1980. "Narrative Time." In Mitchell 1980a, 165–86.
———. 1984. *Time and Narrative*, vol. 1, translated by Kathleen McLaughlin and David Pellauer. Chicago: University of Chicago Press.
———. 1985. *Time and Narrative*, vol. 2, translated by Kathleen McLaughlin and David Pellauer. Chicago: University of Chicago Press.

———. 1988. *Time and Narrative*, vol. 3, translated by Kathleen McLaughlin and David Pellauer. Chicago: University of Chicago Press.
Rieder, John. 1988. "The Metafictive World of *The Man in the High Castle*: Hermeneutics, Ethics, and Political Ideology." *Science-Fiction Studies* 15:214–25.
Riffaterre, Michael. 1990. *Fictional Truth*. Baltimore MD: Johns Hopkins University Press.
Rodiek, Christoph. 1993. "Prolegomena zu einer Poetik des Kontrafaktischen." *Poetica* 25:262–81.
———. 1997. *Erfundene Vergangenheit: Kontrafaktische Geschichtsdarstellung (Uchronie) in der Literatur*. Frankfurt: Klostermann.
Roese, Neal J., and James M. Olson. 1995a. "Counterfactual Thinking: A Critical Overview." In Roese and Olson 1995c, 1–55.
———. 1995b. "Functions of Counterfactual Thinking." In Roese and Olson 1995c, 169–97.
———, eds. 1995c. *What Might Have Been: The Social Psychology of Counterfactual Thinking*. Mahwah NJ: Lawrence Erlbaum.
Ronen, Ruth. 1990. "Paradigm Shift in Plot Models: An Outline of the History of Narratology." *Poetics Today* 11 (4): 817–42.
———. 1994. *Possible Worlds in Literary Theory*. Cambridge: Cambridge University Press.
Rosenfeld, Gavriel D. 2005. *The World Hitler Never Made: Alternate History and the Memory of Nazism*. Cambridge: Cambridge University Press.
Rowen, Norma. 1995. "Reinscribing Cinderella: Jane Austen and the Fairy Tale." In *Functions of the Fantastic*, edited by Joe Sanders, 29–36. Westport CT: Greenwood Press.
Russ, Joanna. 1973. "What Can a Heroine Do? Or Why Women Can't Write." In *Images of Women in Fiction: Feminist Perspectives*, edited by Susan Koppelman Cornillon, 3–20. Bowling Green OH: Bowling Green University Popular Press.
Ryan, Marie-Laure. 1987. "On the Window Structure of Narrative Discourse." *Semiotica* 64 (1–2): 59–81.
———. 1991. *Possible Worlds, Artificial Intelligence and Narrative Theory*. Bloomington: Indiana University Press.
———. 1992. "Possible Worlds in Recent Literary Theory." *Style* 26 (4): 528–53.
———. 1993. "Narrative in Real Time: Chronicle, Mimesis and Plot in the Baseball Broadcast." *Narrative* 1 (2): 138–55.
———. 1995a. "Allegories of Immersion: Virtual Narration in Postmodern Fiction." *Style* 29:262–86.

———. 1995b. "Introduction: From Possible Worlds to Virtual Reality." *Style* 29:173–83.

———. 2001. *Narrative as Virtual Reality: Immersion and Interactivity in Literature and Electronic Media*. Baltimore MD: Johns Hopkins University Press.

———. 2003. "Cognitive Maps and the Construction of Narrative Space." In Herman 2003, 214–42.

Salzman, Paul. 1985. *English Prose Fiction 1558–1700: A Critical History*. Oxford: Clarendon Press.

Schenkel, Elmar. 1994. "Dreaming History: Fantasy and Historiography in Ursula K. Le Guin's *The Lathe of Heaven*." In Engler and Müller 1994, 241–51.

———. 1996. "Die Macht des Ungeschehenen: Phantastische Geschichtsschreibung in *alternative histories*." In *Fantasy in Film and Literature*, edited by Dieter Petzold, 127–42. Heidelberg: Winter.

Schneider, Regina. 1999. "Sidney's 'Arcadias': Prose Romance or Proto-Novel?" Dissertation, University of Oxford.

Scholes, Robert. 1967. *The Fabulators*. New York: Oxford University Press.

———. 1975. *Structural Fabulation: An Essay on Fiction of the Future*. Notre Dame IN: University of Notre Dame Press.

Scholes, Robert, and Robert Kellogg. 1966. *The Nature of Narrative*. New York: Oxford University Press.

Scholes, Robert, and Eric S. Rabkin. 1977. *Science Fiction: History, Science, Vision*. New York: Oxford University Press.

Schwartz, Peter. 1998 [1991]. *The Art of the Long View: Planning for the Future in an Uncertain World*. Chichester: Wiley.

Scott, James B. 1993. "Coincidence or Irony? Ford's Use of August 4th in *The Good Soldier*." *English Language Notes* 30 (4): 53–58.

Seaboyer, Judith. 1997. "Second Death in Venice: Romanticism and the Compulsion to Repeat in Jeanette Winterson's *The Passion*." *Contemporary Literature* 38 (3): 483–509.

Sebeok, Thomas A., and Harriet Margolis. 1982. "Captain Nemo's Porthole: Semiotics of Windows in Sherlock Holmes." *Poetics Today* 3 (1): 110–39.

Seelau, Eric P., Sheila M. Seelau, Gary L. Wells, and Paul D. Windschitl. 1995. "Counterfactual Constraints." In Roese and Olson 1995c, 57–79.

Shaw, Sharon. 1974. "Gertrude Stein and Henry James: The Difference between Accidence and Coincidence." *Pembroke Magazine* 5:95–101.

Shea, William R. 1989. "Transworld Journeys: Report on Session 1: Philosophy." In Allén 1989, 82–89.

Shklovsky, Viktor. 1990 [1929]. *Theory of Prose*, translated by Benjamin Sher. Elmwood Park IL: Dalkey Archive Press.
Spencer, Sharon. 1971. *Space, Time and Structure in the Modern Novel*. New York: New York University Press.
Squire, J. C., ed. 1932 [1931]. *If It Had Happened Otherwise: Lapses into Imaginary History*. London: Longmans, Green and Co.
Stanzel, Franz K. 1977. "Die Komplementärgeschichte: Entwurf einer leserorientierten Romantheorie." In *Erzählforschung 2*, edited by Wolfgang Haubrichs, 240–59. Göttingen: Vandenhoeck & Ruprecht.
———. 1984 [1979]. *A Theory of Narrative*, translated by Charlotte Goedsche. Cambridge: Cambridge University Press.
———. 1989 [1979]. *Theorie des Erzählens*. 4th ed. Göttingen: Vandenhoeck & Ruprecht.
———. 1995. "Historie, historischer Roman, historiographische Metafiktion." *Sprachkunst* 26:113–23.
Stemmler, Theo. 1992. "The Rise of a New Literary Genre: Thomas Deloney's Bourgeois Novel *Jack of Newbury*." In *Telling Stories: Studies in Honour of Ulrich Broich on the Occasion of His 60th Birthday*, edited by Elmar Lehmann and Bernd Lenz, 47–55. Amsterdam: B. R. Grüner.
Sternberg, Meir. 1978. *Expositional Modes and Temporal Ordering in Fiction*. Baltimore MD: Johns Hopkins University Press.
———. 1985. *The Poetics of Biblical Narrative: Ideological Literature and the Drama of Reading*. Bloomington: Indiana University Press.
———. 1992. "Telling in Time (II): Chronology, Teleology, Narrativity." *Poetics Today* 13 (3): 463–541.
Stewart, Ann Harleman. 1987. "Models of Narrative Structure." *Semiotica* 64:83–97.
Stone, Donald D. 1980. *The Romantic Impulse in Victorian Fiction*. Cambridge MA: Harvard University Press.
Sussmann, Herbert. 1994. "Cyberpunk Meets Charles Babbage: *The Difference Engine* as Alternative Victorian History." *Victorian Studies* 38 (1): 1–23.
Suvin, Darko. 1983. "Victorian Science-Fiction, 1871–85: The Rise of the Alternative History Sub-Genre." *Science-Fiction Studies* 10:148–69.
Tanner, Tony. 1986. *Jane Austen*. Basingstoke: Macmillan.
Tanous, Alex, with Harvey Ardman. 1976. *Beyond Coincidence: One Man's Experiences with Psychic Phenomena*. Garden City NY: Doubleday.
Tetlock, Philip E., and Aaron Belkin, eds. 1996a. *Counterfactual Thought Experiments in World Politics: Logical, Methodological, and Psychological Perspectives*. Princeton NJ: Princeton University Press.

———. 1996b. "Counterfactual Thought Experiments in World Politics: Logical, Methodological, and Psychological Perspectives." In Tetlock and Belkin 1996a, 1–38.
Todorov, Tzvetan. 1969. *Grammaire du Décaméron*. The Hague: Mouton.
———. 1977. *The Poetics of Prose*, translated by Richard Howard. Ithaca NY: Cornell University Press.
———. 1980. "The Categories of Literary Narrative." *Papers on Language and Literature* 16:3–36.
Tolkien, J. R. R. 1988 [1940, revised 1964]. "On Fairy-Stories." In *Tree and Leaf*, 9–73. London: Unwin Hyman.
Tomashevsky, Boris. 1965. "Thematics." In Lemon and Reis 1965, 61–95.
Truffaut, François, with the collaboration of Helen G. Scott. 1967. *Hitchcock*. New York: Simon & Schuster.
Turner, Mark. 1987. *Death Is the Mother of Beauty: Mind, Metaphor, Criticism*. Chicago: University of Chicago Press.
———. 1991. *Reading Minds: The Study of English in the Age of Cognitive Science*. Princeton NJ: Princeton University Press.
———. 1992. "Language Is a Virus." *Poetics Today* 13 (4): 725–36.
———. 1996. "Conceptual Blending and Counterfactual Argument in the Social and Behavioural Sciences." In Tetlock and Belkin 1996a, 291–95.
Tversky, Amos, and Daniel Kahneman. 1982. "The Simulation Heuristic." In *Judgment under Uncertainty: Heuristics and Biases*, edited by Daniel Kahneman, Paul Slovic, and Amos Tversky, 201–8. Cambridge: Cambridge University Press.
Uchronia: The Alternate History List. http://www.uchronia.net. Accessed October 7, 2007.
Van Ghent, Dorothy. 1961 [1950]. "The Dickens World: A View from Todgers's." In *The Dickens Critics*, edited by George H. Ford and Lauriat Lane, Jr., 213–32. Ithaca NY: Cornell University Press.
Vargish, Thomas. 1985. *The Providential Aesthetic in Victorian Fiction*. Charlottesville: University Press of Virginia.
Vescovi, Alessandro. 1997. "*Moll Flanders*: The Cohesion of the Picaresque." In *Wrestling with Defoe*, edited by Marialuisa Bignami, 131–43. Bologna: Cisalpino.
Vorderer, Peter, Hans J. Wulff, and Mike Friedrichsen, eds. 1996. *Suspense: Conceptualisations, Theoretical Analyses, and Empirical Explorations*. Mahwah NJ: Lawrence Erlbaum.
Walsh, Sister Mary Brian. 1966. "'Swift Eyesight like a Flame': A Study of Anagnorisis in Shakespearean Tragedy." *Thoth: Syracuse University Graduate Studies in English* 7:35–52.

Walton, Kendall L. 1990. *Mimesis as Make-Believe: On the Foundations of the Representational Arts.* Cambridge MA: Harvard University Press.

Warhol, Robin. 1996a. "Double Gender, Double Genre in *Jane Eyre* and *Villette.*" *Studies in English Literature* 36:857–75.

———. 1996b. "The Look, the Body, and the Heroine of *Persuasion*: A Feminist-Narratological View of Jane Austen." In *Ambiguous Discourse: Feminist Narratology and British Women Writers,* edited by Kathy Mezei, 21–39. Chapel Hill: University of North Carolina Press.

———. 2003. *Having a Good Cry: Effeminate Feelings and Pop-Culture Forms.* Columbus: Ohio State University Press.

Watt, Ian. 1987 [1957]. *The Rise of the Novel: Studies in Defoe, Richardson and Fielding.* London: Hogarth Press.

Waugh, Patricia. 1984. *Metafiction: The Theory and Practice of Self-Conscious Fiction.* London: Methuen.

Weber, Steven. 1996. "Counterfactuals, Past and Future." In Tetlock and Belkin 1996a, 268–88.

Weinsheimer, Joel. 1972. "Chance and the Hierarchy of Marriages in *Pride and Prejudice.*" ELH 39:404–19.

Weinstock, E. B. 1975. "Robert Coover—'The Babysitter': An Observation on Experimental Writing." *Style* 9 (1): 378–87.

Weissert, Thomas P. 1991. "Representation and Bifurcation: Borges's Garden of Chaos Dynamics." In Hayles 1991, 223–43.

Wells, Gary L., and Igor Gavanski. 1989. "Mental Simulation of Causality." *Journal of Personality and Social Psychology* 56 (2): 161–69.

White, Hayden. 1980. "The Value of Narrativity in the Representation of Reality." In Mitchell 1980a, 1–23.

White, William. 1965. "A 'Strange Coincidence' in Walt Whitman." *Walt Whitman Review* 11 (4): 100–102.

Wicks, Ulrich. 1989. *Picaresque Narrative, Picaresque Fictions: A Theory and Research Guide.* New York: Greenwood Press.

Wittgenstein, Ludwig. 1977 [1953]. *Philosophische Untersuchungen.* Frankfurt am Main: Suhrkamp.

Wolf, Werner. 1993. *Ästhetische Illusion und Illusionsdurchbrechung in der Erzählkunst: Theorie und Geschichte mit Schwerpunkt auf englischem illusionsstörenden Erzählen.* Tübingen: Niemeyer.

Wolfe, Gary K. 1986. *Critical Terms for Science Fiction and Fantasy: A Glossary and Guide to Scholarship.* New York: Greenwood Press.

Würzbach, Natascha. 1996. "The Mother Image as Cultural Concept and Literary Theme in the Nineteenth- and Twentieth-Century English Novel: A Feminist Reading within the Context of New Historicism and the History of Mentalities." In *Why Literature Matters: Theories and Functions of Literature*, edited by Rüdiger Ahrens and Laurenz Volkmann, 367–91. Heidelberg: Winter.

Yacobi, Tamar. 1991. "Plots of Space: World and Story in Isak Dinesen." *Poetics Today* 12 (3): 447–93.

Young, Robert J. C. 1995. *Colonial Desire: Hybridity in Theory, Culture and Race*. London: Routledge.

Zunshine, Lisa. 2006. *Why We Read Fiction: Theory of Mind and the Novel*. Columbus: Ohio State University Press.

Index

Page numbers in italic refer to figures

Ackroyd, Peter: *Chatterton*, 107, 130, 168–70, 218–20; *Milton in America*, 126, 221
Allen, Woody, "The Kugelmass Episode," 67
alternate history, 53–54, 58–61, 62, 70, 73, 117–18, 126–29, 199–211, 242n10; and the conceptualization of historical time, 199–200; ontological pluralization in, 70, 202–11; reader's cognitive processing of, 55, 58–61, 62; ontological conservatism in, 200–202; and time travel plots, 128, 200–202, 204–7; and transworld journey plots, 32, 58–61, 70, 205, 223. *See also* counterfactuals, historical; historiographic metafiction; science fiction
alternate story plotting: in experimental postmodernist fiction, 34–36, 61–62, 63, 117–18, 131–32, 215–18; in realist narrative, 131, 193–94
alternate worlds in fiction. *See* alternate story plotting; counterfactuals; multiple futures, ontological pluralization; temporal orchestration
Amis, Kingsley, *The Alteration*, 206
anachrony, 8, 50, 237n5
analogy, 3, 34, 35, 104–8, 164, 168–69, 176–77, 229–31. *See also* coincidence, analogical; similarity
antecedent. *See* counterfactuals, and the point of divergence
Asimov, Isaac, *The End of Eternity*, 31, 73
Austen, Jane, 4, 13, 150, 223; *Emma*, 152; *Mansfield Park*, 55, 56, 57–58, 68–69, 69, 123–24, 191–93, 246n6; *Persuasion*, 68, 79, 84, 85, 97, 97–98, 101–2, 151–52; *Pride and Prejudice*, 244n11; *Sense and Sensibility*, 45, 49–51, 154, 244n12
Auster, Paul, *Moon Palace*, 3, 33–34, 41, 82–83, 84, 97, 125, 177–79, 246n36
autobiographical counterfactual. *See* counterfactuals, autobiographical

Back to the Future, 223
Barnes, Julian, *Flaubert's Parrot*, 1, 106–7, 170–72, 217–18, 220
Behn, Aphra, 144; *Oroonoko*, 145–46, 183–84
Benford, Gregory, *Timescape*, 207
biographical counterfactual. *See* counterfactuals, biographical
Borges, Jorge Luis, "The Garden of Forking Paths," 73, 118
Boyd, John, *The Last Starship from Earth*, 206–7
Bradbury, Ray, "A Sound of Thunder," 206
Brontë, Charlotte, 4; *Jane Eyre*, 27–28, 32–33, 138, 153–55, 194, 244n16; *Villette*, 16, 80–82, 84, 131, 138, 154–55, 193–94, 244n20, 246n7, 246–47n8
Brunner, John, *Times without Number*, 31
The Butterfly Effect, 223

causation, 25–31, 131–32, 228–29, 249; as authorial manipulation, 26, 27, 29, 107, 191; in the coincidence plot, 27–29, 92–93, 108; in counterfactuals, 29–31, 113–14, 122, 127, 129, 182, 185, 192, 201, 206; as divine manipulation, 26–28, 30, 147, 159, 185, 228;

causation (*cont.*)
and immersion, 31, 42–43; as manipulation, 26, 28, 30, 31; and narrative realism, 30–31, 42–43; as necessary and sufficient conditions, 26–28; as progeneration, 25–26, 27–30, 31, 35, 52, 107, 115, 149, 160–61, 165–65, 191, 192, 220; and randomness, 30, 31; subversion of in postmodernist narrative, 35–36, 108, 168, 220, 229–31. *See also* kinship; plotting principle

chance, 29, 103–4; as absence of causation, 29; as synonym for coincidence, 90

character. *See* double identity in coincidental relationships; kinship; multiple character identities in the coincidence plot; multiple character versions in counterfactuals; transworld identity

character trajectories, 1–2

Churchill, Winston, "If Lee Had Not Won the Battle of Gettysburg," 202–3

closure. *See* plot

cognitive approaches to narrative, 11–12, 14

cognitive desire, 13, 92–93, 114, 127

cognitive metaphor: *decisions are junctions in the road*, 71, 196, 212; *life is a journey*, 67, 71, 197, 212; *reading is a journey*, 21, 67; *time is a path*, 65–67, 67–73. *See also* image schemata in the representation of space; time, spatialization of

cognitive plotting, 19–43, 228–31. *See also* cognitive metaphor; plotting principle; suspense

cognitive stratification, 40, 99–100, 101–2, 143–44, 146–47, 151, 162–63, 173, 249. *See also* suspense

coincidence, 2–3, 12, 14–16, 89–108, 141–80, 225–31, 250; analogical, 92–93, 104, 105–8, 164, 167, 168–69, 170–72, 175, 176–77, 241n21, 249; and chance, 90, 164–55; explanation of, 3, 14, 28–30, 90, 92–93, 102–3, 104–5, 152, 147, 157, 159, 161, 165, 167, 177, 178–79, 228–29, 241n17, 241n29; general definition of, 93; metanarrative commentaries on, 171, 173; role of links and connections in, 89–90, 93, 97, 107–8, 161; research into literary forms of, 89–91, 239nn1–2, 239n5, 240n7; research into real-life forms of, 91–93, 240nn9–10; of dates, 104–5; as parody, 173–74; and Romanticism, 150, 152–54, 160–61, 172–73; as serial repetition, 92; as synchronicity, 92, 154; as Victorian excess, 91. *See also* coincidence, modernist; coincidence, postmodernist; coincidence plot, traditional; coincidental encounter; coincidental relationships; convergence and divergence; negative coincidence; recognition

coincidence, modernist, 3, 105–6, 108, 164–66, 251

coincidence, postmodernist, 3, 34–35, 91, 105–8, 168–72, 252; transtemporal encounters in, 169–70, 245n26

coincidence plot, traditional, 2–3, 27–29, 31–32, 33–34, 35, 77–84, 90, 93–102, 105, 108, 141–63, 166–67, 172–80, 253; basic features of, 94, 108; as cognitive plot of links, 97–98, 108, 153; cultural shifts in narrative explanation of, 27–29, 90–91, 102–3, 104–5, 147, 152, 154, 157, 159, 161, 178–79, 228–29, 243n8, 244–45n22; influence of Darwinian theory on, 153; euphoric and dysphoric forms of, 95; focalization in, 142–43; and the love plot, 96, 145–46, 150; in modernist fiction, 96; Oedipus story as fundamental pattern of, 51–53, 95; and the picaresque tradition, 95–96, 100, 147–48; in postmodernist fiction, 97, 172–80; previous relationship within, 94–97; and recognition scene, 31–33, 76–84, 145–46, 146–47, 148–49, 149, 153–54, 174–75, 176, 177–78; temporal orchestration of character identities in, 51–53, 148–49; temporal vs. spatial forms of, 100

coincidental encounter, 28, 77–80, 82, 94, 95–96, 99–100, 101–2, 156, 158–59, 160–61, 166, 173, 176, 250; ad hoc form of, 99, 156; structure of, 68

coincidental relationships, 97–98, 143, 151, 152, 156–57, 166, 168, 174–75, 175–77, 244nn11–12, 244n16, 250. *See also* double identity in coincidental relationships; multiple character identities in the coincidence plot

comparator, 115

Congreve, William, *Incognita*, 145, 184

container. *See* image schemata in the representation of space

Conrad, Joseph, *Chance*, 72, 106, 164–66

convergence and divergence, 1–2, 16, 67, 137–38, 194, 195–96, 198–99, 215, 226–28

Coover, Robert, "The Babysitter," 36, 61, 131, 216, 248n28

counterfactual emotions, 112–13, 120, 250; regret, 110, 112–13, 115, 120, 123, 125, 161, 188, 197, 214–15; satisfaction, 112, 161

INDEX

counterfactuals, 3–5, 12, 14–16, 29–31, 35–36, 53–62, 68–73, 109–32, 181–224, 225–31, 250; actual and virtual worlds in, 68–70; as alternate version of a novel's story, 68–69, 187, 189, 191–93, 198–99; basic structure of, 111, 119; behavioral vs. characterological forms of, 112, 120, 122; binary relationships in, 120; and causation, 29–31, 113–14, 122, 127, 129, 182, 185, 192, 201, 206; and the challenge to romantic convergence, 193–99; as characterization, 182, 183–84, 187; cognitive and psychological research into, 110–14, 118–19; in contrast to multiple futures, 63, 70–71, 120, 121, 131, 238n13, 242n11; counter-counterfactuals, 120, 197, 208–10; and the counterfactualizing agent, 119; and decision making, 70–72, 196–97; definitions of, 110, 111–12, 119; distinguished from other alternate worlds, 63, 119; downward form of, 112, 119, 123–24, 161, 185, 189, 246n7, 251; as fantasy, 200–202, 212–15; in film, 109, 113, 222–23; and heterodiegetic narration, 123–24, 183, 184, 190–93; and intertextuality, 61; as natural narrative, 110; and negative coincidence 104, 125–26, 165, 198–99; and ontological pluralization in fiction, 183, 186, 193, 197, 202–5, 223–24, 229–30; plausibility of, 114; and the point of divergence, 36, 70–73, 111, 205–6; and postmodernist alternate worlds, 61–62, 119, 121, 129–30; in realist narrative, 68, 69, 122–24; reality effect of, 31–32, 54–55, 114, 123–24, 184, 190, 192–93; research into in narrative studies, 115–16; research into in political and historical sciences, 111, 113–15; as rhetorical device, 181–83; in science fiction, 203–11; upward form of, 112, 119, 123–24, 161, 186, 188, 198–99, 247n11, 253. *See also* alternate history; alternate story plotting; convergence and divergence; multiple character versions in counterfactuals; multiple futures; ontological hierarchy; transworld identity

counterfactuals, autobiographical, 54, 118–19, 122–23, 120, 161, 184–90, 197, 246n7, 249; as life review, 112–13, 189–90

counterfactuals, biographical, 119, 126, 206–7, 211, 212–15, 218–20, 249

counterfactuals, historical, 53–54, 70, 73, 114, 117, 118, 119, 121, 126–30, 199–211, 200–211, 218–20, 220–22, 223, 229, 251; and the counterfactual historical essay, 115, 202–3.

See also alternate history; historiographic metafiction

Darwin, Charles, *The Origin of Species*, 137, 153, 200

De Camp, L. Sprague, 223; *Lest Darkness Fall*, 204–5; "The Wheels of If," 4, 70, 205

Defoe, Daniel, 5, 13; *Moll Flanders*, 4, 40–41, 100, 102, 123, 146–48, 185–86; *Robinson Crusoe*, 29–30, 57, 62, 104–5, 184–85

DeLillo, Don, *Libra*, 130, 175–77

Deloney, Thomas, *Jack of Newbury*, 141, 246n1

Dent, Guy, *Emperor of the If*, 247n18

diachronic analysis: of coincidence, 90–91, 135–39, 225–31; of counterfactuality, 135–39, 225–31; of fictional space, 74–75, 77, 84; of plot, 10, 13–14

Dick, Philip K., 5, 223–24, 247n19; *The Man in the High Castle*, 127, 208–10, 220–21, 248n20, 248n22

Dickens, Charles, 74–75, 96, 102–3; *Bleak House*, 74–75, 244n21; *Great Expectations*, 45, 138, 157–59, 244n17; *Martin Chuzzlewit*, 79–80, 84, 101, 155–57

disnarrated concept, 46, 48, 115–6

divergence. *See* convergence and divergence

Doctor Who series, "Inferno," 223

Donnie Darko, 223

double identity in coincidental relationships, 97–98, 156–57, 174–75

Drabble, Margaret, *The Realms of Gold*, 172–73

Eliot, George, 13, 223; *Daniel Deronda*, 2, 4, 16, 45, 51, 63, 72, 138, 160–61, 195–98, 215, 244–45n22, 247nn9–11; *Middlemarch*, 131, 159, 194–95, 244n18, 247n9

expulsion, 14, 22–25, 27, 251. *See also* immersion

The Family Man, 223

fantasy, 24, 179–80, 200–202, 212–15

feminist narratives. *See* plots of female development

Fielding, Henry: *Joseph Andrews*, 51, 62; *Tom Jones*, 31, 148–49, 190–91, 243nn7–8

film. *See* counterfactuals, in film

Flaubert, Gustave, *Madame Bovary*, 74

Ford, Ford Madox, *The Good Soldier*, 82, 84, 105, 166, 167

fork. *See* counterfactuals, and the point of divergence; image schemata in the representation of space

Forster, E. M., *A Room with a View*, 28–29, 167
Fowles, John, *The French Lieutenant's Woman*, 4, 216–17
Frost, Robert, "The Road Not Taken," 71
Frye, Stephen, *Making History*, 206

genre. *See* alternate history; fantasy; historiographic metafiction; ontological hierarchy; plotting principle; realism; the romance; science fiction
Gibson, William, and Bruce Sterling, *The Difference Engine*, 61, 63, 211
Greene, Robert, *Pandosto*, 29, 40
Groundhog Day, 223

Hale, Edward Everett, "Hands Off," 200–201, 247n14
Hardy, Thomas, 4, 161; *The Mayor of Casterbridge*, 90; *The Return of the Native*, 138, 162–63; *Tess of the d'Urbervilles*, 16, 54, 90, 104, 125, 138, 198–99, 245n23
Hawthorne, Nathaniel, "P.'s Correspondence," 126, 200
Henry, O., "Roads of Destiny," 212
historical counterfactual. *See* counterfactual, historical
historiographic metafiction, 4–5, 16, 91, 106–8, 118, 121, 129–30, 168–72, 174–77, 218–21, 230–31, 245nn32–33; alternate history as conceptual precursor of, 204, 207, 210, 218, 220–21, 229; role of analogical coincidence in, 169, 170–71, 177, 230
Homer, *The Odyssey*, 99
hypothetical focalization, 116

identity. *See* double identity in coincidental relationships; kinship; multiple character identities in the coincidence plot; multiple character versions in counterfactuals; transworld identity
image schemata in the representation of space, 75–76, 122; center-periphery, 76, 79, 81, 83; the container, 75–76, 77, 78–82, 84, 162–63, 178; the fork, 70–73, 111, 218; horizontality, 76, 78, 83–84; the link, 66–68, 76, 78, 83, 97; the path, 66–73, 76, 79, 197, 247n9; the portal or window, 76, 77, 78–82, 162–63, 175, 176, 178, 238–309n6; verticality, 76, 78, 83–84. *See also* time, spatialization of; space; cognitive metaphor

immersion, 5, 8, 20–24, *24*, 26, 27, 36, 136, 209, 251; as the cognitive simulation of ontological liberation, 21, 24; and coincidence in fiction, 93, 175; and genre, 42; and reading as a journey, 22, *24*, 67; and the plotting principles, 42–43; role of spatial representation in, 75, 84–85; and suspense, 38–41; temporal vs. spatial, 74. *See also* cognitive desire
It Happened Here, 222
It's a Wonderful Life, 113, 222

James, Henry, "The Jolly Corner," 212–13
Johnson, B. S., "Broad Thoughts from a Home," 61–62, 63
Joyce, James: *A Portrait of the Artist as a Young Man*, 74–75; *Ulysses*, 106, 167

kinship, 25–26, 31–36, 251; in the coincidence plot, 32–33, 83, 95, 98, 100, 153–54, 172–73; in counterfactuals, 35–36; and the discovery of identity, 31–34, 98; and genetic similarity, 31; influence of Darwinian theory on plots of, 153; as lineage, 25–26, 31, 32–33, 35; role of in immersion, 34, 98. *See also* analogy; causation; plotting principle

Lawrence, Edmund, *It May Happen Yet*, 56, 202
Le Guin, Ursula K., 223; *The Lathe of Heaven*, 210
Leinster, Murray, "Sidewise in Time," 203–4
Lennox, Charlotte, *The Female Quixote*, 243n9
Lewis, Matthew, *The Monk*, 149
liminal plotting, 38–42, 251. *See also* suspense
link. *See* image schemata in the representation of space; time, spatialization of
Lodge, David, *Small World: An Academic Romance*, 173–74
Lodge, Thomas, *Rosalynde*, 143–44, 243n2

many-worlds interpretation of quantum theory, 73, 129, 247n17
modernist coincidence. *See* coincidence, modernist
multiple character identities in the coincidence plot, 51–53, 142–44, 146–50, 156–57, 178. *See also* recognition; temporal orchestration

multiple character versions in counterfactuals, 56–61, 116, 119–20, 121–22, 186, 197, 203, 206–7, 210–11, 212–15, 217. *See also* transworld identity
multiple futures, 51, 129, 130–31, 183, 194–95, 196; and decision-making, 71–72, 183, 196, 246n5; relationship to counterfactuals, 63, 70–71, 120, 121, 131, 238n13, 242n11; and suspense, 39–40

narrative as liberation, 19, 110. *See also* immersion
narrative communication models, 22–24
narrative explanation, 26. *See also* causation; coincidence, explanation of; kinship; plotting principle; similarity
narrativeness, 6, 13
narrative progression, 9
narrativity, 5, 6, 13, 225
Nashe, Thomas, *The Unfortunate Traveller*, 141
negative coincidence, 90, 103–4, 148, 161–63, 251

ontological hierarchy, 120–21, 252; and genre, 47, 62–64, 72–73, 120–21, 127–29, 130, 199–202, 229; and historical relativity, 121; narratorial juggling of, 49–50, 217; static vs. dynamic, 121; and suspense, 40
ontological plotting, 45–64. *See also* counterfactuals; multiple futures; ontological hierarchy; ontological pluralization; temporal orchestration; transworld identity
ontological pluralization: overall historical development in fiction, 119, 137, 223–24, 229–30; evolution in realist fiction, 183, 186, 193, 193–94, 196–97, 199–202; influence of Darwinian theory on, 137, 200; in science fiction and postmodernism, 70, 202–11, 213–14, 215–21, 247n15

path. *See* cognitive metaphor; image schemata in the representation of space; time, spatialization of
perspectivism, 74–75; and the three-dimensionalization of space, 81. *See also* space
The Philadelphia Experiment, 2, 223
plot, 6–14, 25, 45–49, 63–64, 108; and closure, 2, 9–10, 13, 193–94, 215, 217, 227–28; definitions of, 6–9, 12–13, 235n5, 238n2; and the historical development of narrative fiction, 225–26

plots of female development, 7–8, 10, 138, 154–55, 172–73, 190, 193–94, 195–98, 199, 210–11, 214–15, 217, 226–28, 245n23
plots of mystery genealogy, 95, 146, 148–49, 160–61. *See also* kinship
plotting principle, 25–36, 66, 103, 147, 252; connections in, 25–26, 66; and cultural history, 36, 154; and genre, 36. *See also* causation; kinship; similarity
portal. *See* image schemata in the representation of space
possible vs. impossible worlds, 41–43
possible-worlds theory, 10, 47–48, 55–56
postmodernist coincidence. *See* coincidence, postmodernist
Prawer Jhabvala, Ruth, *Heat and Dust*, 34, 106, 107
principle of diversification, 46; and virtual character worlds, 48, 116

Radcliffe, Ann, *The Romance of the Forest*, 149–50, 244n20
the reader, 19–246, 236n6
realism: and coincidence, 90–91, 135–37, 141, 150; combined with fantasy in postrealism, 179–80; contrasted with metafiction, 22–24, 42–43; and immersion, 21–22, 24; and ontological hierarchy, 47, 62–64, 72–73, 120–21, 200, 202; and the plotting principle, 42–43, 228–29; role of counterfactuals in, 30–31, 54–55, 114, 123–24, 184, 190, 192–93; and the romance, 3, 135–36, 141; and Romanticism, 152–53; and semirealism, 36, 42–43; and the three-dimensionalization of space, 77–82, 84
recognition, 2–3, 31–34, 90, 98–102, 252; *anagnorisis*, 98–99, 241n16; delayed, 40–41, 99–102, 142, 143–44, 146–47, 155, 177–78; as denouemental insight, 99; as discovery in the coincidence plot, 51–53, 97, 157–58; as discovery of identity in the traditional coincidence plot, 31–33, 51–53, 76–84, 142, 143–44 145–46, 148–50, 153–54, 160–61, 177–78; within an estranged kinship plot, 3, 31–34, 51–53, 90, 94, 95, 98, 142, 144, 146–47, 149–50, 151, 153–54, 160–61, 177–78; between estranged lovers, 145–46; facial recognition in the coincidence plot, 31–32, 33–34, 82–84, 151, 155, 158, 160, 244nn19–20; between foes, 79–80, 174–75; in modernist and postmodernist forms of

recognition (*cont.*)
  the coincidence plot, 105–8, 168; noncoincidental recognition plots, 99; between parent and child, 31–32, 142, 144, 147, 160, 177–78, 244n21; between siblings and cousins, 146–47, 149, 151, 160, 240n13; staggered (unilateral), 40–40, 79–80, 99, 143–44, 146–47, 151, 158–59, 176, 245n23
replotting, 116, 126
Richardson, Samuel: *Pamela*, 123, 186–87, 246n5; *Clarissa*, 187–90
Roberts, Keith, *Pavane*, 53–54, 55, 62, 127, 238n12
the romance, 3, 136; coincidence in, 141–44, 173–74; counterfactuals in, 181–83; and/vs. the novel, 3, 91, 135–36, 141
Roth, Philip: *The Counterlife*, 213–14; *The Plot Against America*, 221–22
Rushdie, Salman: *Shame*, 105; *Midnight's Children*, 91
Russ, Joanna, *The Female Man*, 129, 210–11, 215

Sachar, Louis, *Holes*, 97, 179–80
science fiction, 4, 24, 31, 42–43, 70, 72–73, 116–17, 126–29, 203–11, 215, 229–30; and ontological hierarchy, 121, 203–6; and postmodernist agendas, 207–11; as precursor of postmodernist ontological pluralization, 203–5, 229, 247n15; real-world cognitive patterns in, 36–37. *See also* alternate history; counterfactuals, historical; fantasy
Scott, Sir Walter, *The Bride of Lammermoor*, 71–72
semirealism. *See* fantasy; realism; science fiction
Shakespeare, William, *Romeo and Juliet*, 125–26
Sidney, Sir Philip: *The Old Arcadia*, 3, 4, 141–42, 181–83; *The New Arcadia*, 77–79, 84, 142–43, 183, 243n1, 246n3
similarity, 33–36, 252; analogous form without kinship, 34, 164–65; in the coincidence plot, 33–35; in counterfactuals, 35–36. *See also* analogy; plotting principle
Sliding Doors, 223
Smollett, Tobias, *Roderick Random*, 27, 100, 148, 243n5
Sophocles, *Oedipus the King*, 51–52
space: backgrounding of spatial environment in fiction, 77, 79, 84; bodily negotiation of, 65–66, 74–76; fictional representation of, 74–85, 162–63, 175, 245n23; physiognomical spatialization, 77, 82–84; spatial innovation in the history of fiction, 74–75, 77, 84, 162–63; three-dimensionalization, 77, 78–82, 84, 162–63. *See also* cognitive metaphor; image schemata in the representation of space; time, spatialization of
spatialization. *See* space; time, spatialization of
spatial metaphor. *See* cognitive metaphor; image schemata in the representation of space; time, spatialization of
spatial plotting, 65–85. *See also* image schemata in the representation of space; space; time, spatialization of
Star Trek, "Mirror Mirror," 222
story, 6–7, 45–46, 63–64, 235n4
story-discourse distinction, 8, 51–52, 63–64
suspense, 36–42, 43, 253; and the character-cognitive level, 39–40, 162–63; and coincidence, 36, 156, 163; and double immersion, 38–39; and Hitchcock's "bomb under the table" scenario, 37–38; *how* and *what* forms of, 37–38; and liminal plotting, 39–42; and recognition in the traditional coincidence plot, 29–41, 98, 99, 101–2; resiliency of, 38–39; vs. curiosity, 37–38. *See also* cognitive stratification; recognition

tellability, 5
temporal orchestration, 41, 45–46, 49–53, 253; in the coincidence plot, 51–53, 98, 148–49, 149–50; role of focalization in, 49–50; role of narrator in, 48–49; and ontological hierarchy, 62, 121
The Terminator, 223
Thackeray, William Makepeace, *Vanity Fair*, 124
time: and conceptualization of historical time, 199–200; spatialization of, 65–73, 122, 129, 197–98, 203–5, 215, 238n1. *See also* causation; cognitive metaphor; ontological plotting; plot; temporal orchestration
time travel. *See* alternate history
traditional coincidence plot. *See* coincidence plot, traditional
transworld identity, 14, 55–62, 119, 121–22, 253; transworld identification vs. differentiation, 57–61, 122, 127–28, 206–7, 208–9, 211, 216

Trollope, Anthony, *Barchester Towers*, 124
Twain, Mark, *A Connecticut Yankee at King Arthur's Court*, 201–2, 247n16

the unreal, 47

Wells, H. G., "The Man Who Could Work Miracles," 247n15

Williamson, Jack, *The Legion of Time*, 73, 204
window. *See* image schemata in the representation of space
Winterson, Jeanette, *The Passion*, 2, 83–84, 96–97, 174–75, 214–15, 245n32
Woolf, Virginia, *Mrs. Dalloway*, 166–67
Wyndham, John: "Random Quest," 31, 35, 58–61, 62–63; "Opposite Number," 129

In the Frontiers of Narrative series:

Coincidence and Counterfactuality
Plotting Time and Space in Narrative Fiction
by Hilary P. Dannenberg

Story Logic
Problems and Possibilities of Narrative
by David Herman

Handbook of Narrative Analysis
by Luc Herman and Bart Vervaeck

Spaces of the Mind
Narrative and Community in the American West
by Elaine A. Jahner

Talk Fiction
Literature and the Talk Explosion
by Irene Kacandes

Storying Domestic Violence
Constructions and Stereotypes of Abuse in the
Discourse of General Practitioners
by Jarmila Mildorf

Fictional Minds
by Alan Palmer

Narrative across Media
The Languages of Storytelling
edited by Marie-Laure Ryan